English Poetry of the Victorian Period

Longman Literature in English Series

General Editors: David Carroll and Michael Wheeler
Lancaster University

For a complete list of titles see pages viii and ix

English Poetry
of the
Victorian Period
1830–1890

Bernard Richards

Longman

London and New York

Longman Group UK Limited
Longman House, Burnt Mill, Harlow,
Essex CM20 2JE, England
and Associated Companies throughout the world

*Published in the United States of America
by Longman Inc., New York*

First published 1988
Third impression 1992

BRITISH LIBRARY CATALOGUING IN PUBLICATION DATA
Richards, B. A.
   English poetry of the Victorian period,
   1830–1890.—(Longman literature in
   English series)
   1. English poetry — 19th century —
   History and criticism
   I. Title
   821'.8'09   PR591

ISBN 0-582-49344-7 CSD
ISBN 0-582-49345-5 PPR

LIBRARY OF CONGRESS CATALOGING IN PUBLICATION DATA
Richards, Bernard Arthur.
   English poetry of the Victorian period, 1830–1890.

   (Longman literature in English series)
   Bibliography: p.
   Includes index.
   1. English poetry — 19th century — History and
criticism.   I. Title.   II. Series.
PR591.R5   1988   821'.8'09   87–4187
ISBN 0-582-49344-7
ISBN 0-582-49345-5 (pbk.)

Set in Linotron 202 9½/11 pt Bembo
Produced by Longman Singapore Publishers (Pte) Ltd.
Printed in Singapore

Contents

Editors' Preface

The multi-volume Longman Literature in English Series provides students of literature with a critical introduction to the major genres in their historical and cultural context. Each volume gives a coherent account of a clearly defined area, and the series, when complete, will offer a practical and comprehensive guide to literature written in English from Anglo-Saxon times to the present. The aim of the series as a whole is to show that the most valuable and stimulating approach to literature is that based upon an awareness of the relations between literary forms and their historical context. Thus the areas covered by most of the separate volumes are defined by period and genre. Each volume offers new and informed ways of reading literary works, and provides guidance to further reading in an extensive reference section.

As well as studies on all periods of English and American literature, the series includes books on criticism and literary theory, and on the intellectual and cultural context. A comprehensive series of this kind must of course include other literatures written in English, and therefore a group of volumes deals with Irish and Scottish literature, and the literatures of India, Africa, the Caribbean, Australia and Canada. The forty-seven volumes of the series cover the following areas: Pre-Renaissance English Literature, English Poetry, English Drama, English Fiction, English Prose, Criticism and Literary Theory, Intellectual and Cultural Context, American Literature, Other Literatures in English.

David Carroll
Michael Wheeler

Longman Literature in English Series

General Editors: David Carroll and Michael Wheeler
Lancaster University

Pre-Renaissance English Literature

* ★ English Literature before Chaucer   *Michael Swanton*
* English Literature in the Age of Chaucer
* ★ English Medieval Romance   *W. R. J. Barron*

English Poetry

* ★ English Poetry of the Sixteenth Century   *Gary Whaller*
* ★ English Poetry of the Seventeenth Century   *George Parfitt*
* English Poetry of the Eighteenth Century, 1700–1789
* ★ English Poetry of the Romantic Period, 1789–1830   *J. R. Watson*
* ★ English Poetry of the Victorian Period, 1830–1890   *Bernard Richards*
* English Poetry of the Early Modern Period, 1890–1940
* English Poetry since 1940

English Drama

* English Drama before Shakespeare
* ★ English Drama: Shakespeare to the Restoration, 1590–1660
  Alexander Leggatt
* ★ English Drama: Restoration and Eighteenth Century, 1660–1789
  Richard W. Bevis
* English Drama: Romantic and Victorian, 1789–1890
* English Drama of the Early Modern Period, 1890–1940
* English Drama since 1940

English Fiction

* ★ English Fiction of the Eighteenth Century, 1700–1789   *Clive T. Probyn*
* ★ English Fiction of the Romantic Period, 1789–1830   *Gary Kelly*
* ★ English Fiction of the Victorian Period, 1830–1890   *Michael Wheeler*
* ★ English Fiction of the Early Modern Period, 1890–1940   *Douglas Hewitt*
* English Fiction since 1940

English Prose

* English Prose of the Renaissance, 1550–1700
* English Prose of the Eighteenth Century
* English Prose of the Nineteenth Century

Criticism and Literary Theory

Criticism and Literary Theory from Sidney to Johnson
Criticism and Literary Theory from Wordsworth to Arnold
Criticism and Literary Theory from 1890 to the Present

The Intellectual and Cultural Context

The Sixteenth Century
* The Seventeenth Century 1603–1700 *Graham Parry*
* The Eighteenth Century, 1700–1789 *James Sambrook*
The Romantic Period, 1789–1830
The Victorian Period, 1830–1890
The Twentieth Century, 1890 to the Present

American Literature

American Literature before 1880
* American Poetry of the Twentieth Century   *Richard Gray*
American Drama of the Twentieth Century
* American Fiction, 1865–1940   *Brian Lee*
American Fiction since 1940
* Twentieth-Century America   *Douglas Tallack*

Other Literatures

Irish Literature since 1800
Scottish Literature since 1700

Australian Literature
* Indian Literature in English   *William Walsh*
Southern African Literature in English
African Literature in English: East and West
Caribbean Literature in English
* Canadian Literature in English   *W. J. Keith*

* *Already published*

Author's Preface

Astonishingly, as the bibliography on pp. 279–80 shows, there has not been a general history of Victorian Poetry since J. Drinkwater's of 1923 and B. I. Evans's of 1933. Perhaps no one has been sufficiently courageous or foolhardy to tackle it. This volume, it is hoped, fills a gap. Of course there have been many specialised studies on aspects of Victorian poetry and on individual authors, and during the past two or three decades it has been increasingly studied in schools and universities. The rich and fruitful body of history and criticism may be seen in its daunting scope on pp. 278–83 of the bibliographies. Perhaps, in view of the accumulated mass of critical material which it is difficult for the student to master, the time is particularly ripe for a short and manageable general study by way of introduction.

It will be at once obvious that my survey does not proceed like many literary histories, since there are no chapters on single authors: everything has been arranged thematically. It might seem that a further blow has been struck on behalf of the now fashionable concept of the 'death of the author', but this is not my intention, and once immersed in the chapters, readers will soon perceive that I think that the concept of the author as a valuable and distinct individual is still very much alive. It would have been perfectly possible to proceed in the traditional way of writing literary history that is concentrated on the notion of a sequence of authors. However, the thematic method has been chosen, largely in an attempt to make Victorian poetry seem more homogeneous than it often is. The authors were all distinct, and some were highly individualised, but they also have a good deal of common ground, and their Victorian qualities emerge much more clearly when they are dealt with in this way, even with poets as apparently aberrant as Barnes and Hopkins. The chosen themes are, in many cases, interesting to us still, and some of them are highly relevant, but the method of concentration pursued here enables us to recognise the particularly Victorian aspect of the treatment they receive in the poetry. It makes a good deal of sense to study the technical features of versification and diction as a unit. The function of the approach adopted here is not to glean interesting facts and opinions from the poems in order to build up a picture of the Victorian age, but to characterize a body of poetry in the light of its historical context. That context is better understood if one does not treat the poets as isolated and entirely discrete units, but as individuals contributing to and drawing on the resources of a culture. The richness of this culture can be seen at a glance in the chronological tables (pp. 252–72).

Thematic considerations are not the only ones operating in this study; in addition there are aesthetic principles of choice, and the poems singled out for treatment are, for the most part, of the kind easily assimilable to modern taste. The principal feature of this taste is its appreciation of challenging verse written in colloquial and forceful language; audiences of the 1980s do not readily appreciate dreamy, decorative, escapist, mellifluous and anodyne material. What I demonstrate is that in the enormously varied and productive Victorian period there was a good deal of the latter kind of poetry, but there were also vast quantities of the poetry that meets with our immediate approval. So that this survey, like my companion volume *English Verse 1830–1890* (in the *Longman Annotated Anthologies of English Verse* series, 1980), is very partial in its tastes, and could not claim to be the last word: on the whole it belongs to that species of criticism in which attention is more lively when the products of a previous culture resemble our own rather than differ from it. It is not that current taste is in the process of over-throwing the canonical authors, but increased consideration is being given to parts of the canonical authors that might have received slightly less attention in their own time. I dredge up a few minor and half-forgotten writers, but the major figures are not deposed and banished.

I should like to thank the Governing Body of Brasenose College, Oxford for giving me a term's leave of absence to finish the book. Especial thanks to the secretarial staff of the College for cheerful and invaluable help: Pauline Shepheard, Susan Cotterill, Wendy Williams and Lorna Fullard. I am grateful to the general editors, Michael Wheeler and David Carroll, for asking me to contribute this volume to the series and for making so many useful suggestions, and I should also very much like to thank the staff at Longman for numerous contributions of both a general and a particular nature; their generously tendered help has been prevented this work from being the inferior production it was in its earlier stages. Finally I am deeply indebted to my wife Sandra for help and encouragement at every stage; without her unstinting assistance and encouragement it would still be an inchoate mass, haunting me, the general editors and the publishers.

B. A. Richards
May 1987

In loving memory
of my mother
Jessie Richards
June 1913–May 1987

Chapter 1
Introduction

If the following study needed to be summarised by an emblem it would be Turner's *Dudley Castle*.[1] It has strong personal associations for me, since I passed near the spot, or rather spots, from which it was painted every Sunday up until about twenty-five years ago on my way to the Victorian Wesleyan church (now demolished) where Victorian England lingered on. And each time I marvelled that Turner had got it spectacularly right; his topographical caricature of the actual industrial landscape of the Black Country was so powerful that it continually erased, as it were, the scene before me. Ruskin recognized the prophetic importance of the painting, with the old England 'of the baron and the monk', represented by the castle of the Earls of Dudley, passing away in a sort of spectral pallidity[2] (even as the ghostly old *Téméraire* was dragged away to oblivion by the smoking tugboat) and the new England of heavy industry advancing in its power and destructiveness. Using a poetic image, Ruskin associated this invasive force with 'the cloud and flame of the dragon'.[3] Turner and Ruskin were alarmed, and not a little excited, by the new waste-land, a waste-land where natural and organic activity was replaced by mechanical production, and the poets and novelists were often similarly alarmed and excited. In our time, of course, yet another form of waste-land is visible in the Black Country – in which little or no human activity takes place, since the whole area is in the grip of a pervasive industrial recession. This painting, like *The Fighting Téméraire* (1839) and *Rain, Steam, and Speed – The Great Western Railway* (1844), might stand as an emblem for Victorian poetry, that on the one hand glances back wistfully at fading beauty and romance, and on the other hand confronts the new industry and the new and exciting conditions of life with a measure of alertness and enthusiasm. In all three paintings an older, leisured England confronts a dynamic and progressive one. Certainly there were some poets in the century who were enamoured of the romantic past, and there were others who attempted literary versions of the industrial sublime; and there were some (one thinks of Tennyson and Browning) who projected images of both. Tennyson's brother, Charles Tennyson

Turner, cultivated the characteristically elegiac mode, regretting, in 'Old Ruralities', the disappearance of the traditional country scene: 'Ah! sweet old world! thou speedest fast away!' But even he could see that in the new age there were aspects that posed a challenge that should be met rather than shirked. So that he did not entirely turn his back on the new forces of mechanization in agriculture:

> I thought of mind and matter, will and law,
> And then of him, who set his stately seal
> Of Roman words on all the forms he saw
> Of old-world husbandry. *I* could but feel
> With what a rich precision *he* would draw
> The endless ladder, and the booming wheel!

('The Steam Threshing Machine', ll. 9–14)

Kipling was to respond to machinery with more excitement than this in 'McAndrew's Hymn' (1896), but Victorian poets before him were making some efforts! If this study has a running theme it is the ubiquitous contrast in the poetry of the period between versions of escapism and attempts at forms of realism.

The search to find a responsible attitude to actual modern conditions may in part have been a defensive reaction in the interest of self-preservation, since even before Victoria came to the throne in 1837 poetry had been under attack, as an outmoded and merely entertaining genre, from writers such as Bentham, Peacock, and Macaulay. Later Matthew Arnold was so depressed by the discouraging circumstances of his time and the unsympathetic reading public that he called it a 'deeply unpoetical' age.[4] Many of his contemporaries would have agreed with him, and the further one looks the more one comes to the conclusion that there were many forces militating against poetry. But at the same time one can think of twenty major, important, and very good poets in the period from 1830 to 1890, whereas from 1930 to 1980 only about fifteen names spring rapidly to mind. In addition to the well-known Victorian poets, the *New Cambridge Bibliography* (1969) lists 193 poets from 1833 to 1900 and Arthur Miles's *Poets of the Century* (1891–97, 1905–07) has about 190 poets, 42 of them women. The recent *Dictionary of Literary Biography* (vols 32 and 35; 1984, 1985) surveys 82 poets; it researches poets that other scholars do not even reach. Many of these poeticules, as Swinburne would have called them, should be allowed to remain in undisturbed obscurity, but some of them wrote worthy and striking poetry.

This study is mainly historical in its approach; it aims to consider the poets and their works in historical contexts. Sometimes this critical method can lead one to suspend judgement, but it must be said at the outset that many Victorian poems are superb by any standard, and make a vivid impact on the reader even when detached from their surroundings. I proceed thematically, rather than by authors, hoping in this way to give a general sense of Victorian poetry. Even though the different practitioners are often highly individual it does have a distinct character that sets it apart from poetry of the Romantic Movement on the one hand and of the Modernist Movement on the other. In the last resort it is desirable to have a sense both of the particularity of a certain author and of the way in which he shows the signs of his age and its creative traditions, but this study does place more emphasis on the search for the poetic character of the age than the isolation of discrete units. No book on Victorian poetry has proceeded in quite this way; indeed there have not been very many general surveys of the poetry, as the bibliography shows (see below, pp. 279–80). Viewed as a whole, Victorian poetry is not as impressive an achievement as Romantic poetry or seventeenth-century poetry; for one thing its belatedness and derivativeness work against it (as they work against twentieth-century poetry); poets haunted by 'belatedness' worry that the themes, the attitudes, and the techniques they use have been used before, and are now drained of life and originality. As T. S. Eliot put it, 'Not only every great poet, but every genuine, though lesser poet, fulfills once for all some possibility of the language, and so leaves one possibility less for his successors.'[5]

It is probably only the exceptional and slightly unusual Victorian poems that *really* catch the attention of the modern reader, but at the same time the poetry is a considerable achievement worthy of study. I have suggested that previous eras might make prior claims on one's attention, but in the period itself there is a rival genre that might also make such a claim: the novel. This was the dominant literary genre at the time (in the sense that it appealed to a wider readership) and from our perpsective it is tremendously impressive simply because it embodies so coherently the combination of a new rhetoric and a new vision of life. Most Victorian novelists did not need to spend anxious hours worrying about belatedness, since they could rest assured that the material they were dealing with and the techniques they were using were new to their century. And in addition most of them caught the ready ear of an appreciative public. In its totality the Victorian novel is almost certainly a better reflection of the age than the poetry (it is certainly a less oblique reflection) and it is probably a more impressive literary achievement. It was able to provide its readership with most of what they needed by way of distraction, consolation, challenge, and instruction. Given its flexible and variable form almost anything could be expressed, often with virtually no aesthetic transformation. It pushed on inexorably towards acceptability and respectability, over-coming finally the opposition of forces as varied as the élitism of the quarterlies (for whom poetry was the worthiest literature) and the moralism of the Evangelicals (for whom the novel was a time-waster and an incitement to laxity and vice). As I shall be showing, the prestige of the novel, and the novel-reading habits of both the public and the poets themselves, had an inevitable effect on the poetry. One should not, however, forget that poetic habits of mind were also lively and potent enough to have an impact on the novel, very much to its advantage, and some of the most distinguished novelists – such as Emily Brontë, George Meredith, and Thomas Hardy – were also (perhaps pre-eminently so) poets.

I have spoken of Victorian poetry as if it were a coherent entity. To some degree it is, and even the most divergent poems maintain *some* family resemblance to each other; but its richness and variety should be emphasized. Of course in previous periods there was richness and divergence, but there has been a tendency for literary historians to isolate single strains as constituting the principal achievements. So that in the Romantic Movement poets such as Wolcot, Moore, and Campbell were at work, and were popular, but we think of the significant works as those of Wordsworth, Coleridge, Blake, Keats, Shelley, and Byron, and although these manifest some considerable differences from each other there is nevertheless a coherent pattern running through them. In the Victorian period a different state of affairs occurs. We find side by side major poets as diverse as Tennyson and Browning, Arnold and Clough, Swinburne and Hopkins. In Victorian poetry one finds Parnassianism and anti-Parnassianism (see below, pp. 26–37), escapism and realism, frivolity and utility, activity and lethargy, religiosity and secularity, solidarity and alienation, élitism and populism, ruralism and urbanism, obscurity and clarity, euphony and cacophony; the list goes on, and sometimes indeed the disconcerting variety is found even within the *oeuvre* of single poets. This rich diversity arose in the wake of the decline of both classical and romantic visions; there was no basis for orderly progression and coherent development. Even in the Romantic Movement it had been necessary to think in terms of literary 'publics' rather than of a single, monolithic public, but in the Victorian period the proliferation of publics went on apace. The classic account of this is Richard Altick's *The English Common Reader* (1957), which studies the rapid increases in literacy and the tremendous efforts made by the steam press to satisfy the demands. In economic and social thinking a *laissez-faire* attitude encouraged individuals and small groups to produce a workable way of life, and it could be said that the poetic scene produced a similar pattern. There were fresh opportunities for individual initiative, but all operating in a cultural setting that increasingly came to lack homogeneity.

Any historical approach to literature has to take account of the historical setting. Historians are fond of referring to all ages as transitional, but the Victorian age merits this label more than most. It witnessed the last gasp of the sacramental, spiritually homogeneous view of the universe and of society, followed by the emergence of mechanistic and ruthlessly rational principles. Many of the transitional features have a direct bearing on the literature, and indeed on the language itself. In the seventeenth century a sceptic like Donne had been able to maintain that 'all coherence' was gone, but it remained for a majority of people. One hundred years later Pope was able to have recourse to the ancient idea of the Great Chain of Being, not merely as a convenient poetic fancy but as an intellectual idea that made sense of the universe and was still widely accepted, despite the growing scepticism engendered by the new sciences.[6] Serious doubts concerning the existence of God started to grow among advanced thinkers in the eighteenth century, but left vast areas of the population untouched, and even in the early nineteenth century there survives an underlying faith in the sanctity of nature and the ability of man to make a significant imaginative relationship to it. When Wordsworth writes in the Prospectus to *The Excursion*,

> How exquisitely the individual Mind
> (And the progressive powers perhaps no less
> Of the whole species) to the external World
> Is fitted: – and how exquisitely, too –
> Theme this but little heard of among men –
> The external World is fitted to the Mind;
>
> (ll. 63–68)

he is not indulging a poetic fancy; he is expressing what he believes, and would also believe even if he were writing prose. One might say that in the seventeenth century the world-picture, with all its systems of correspondences, analogies, allegories, coherencies, hierarchies, and sacraments was in itself poetic. This is why a good deal of poetry from this time scarcely separates itself from the rest of life and was not necessarily even placed in a separate category known as 'literature'; it might also explain why there is so little good argumentative prose in the English Renaissance that one can trust to come to a logical and argued conclusion. This world-picture was gradually eroded, and by the end of the Romantic Movement there was very little of it left as an account on which poets and their audiences could draw. As it disappeared a residual faith in the efficacy and magic of language disappeared too. The world-picture that came to replace it, and which the Victorian poets had to live with, even though some of them had a nostalgic hankering after the earlier conditions, was urban rather than rural, rational rather than intuitional, divisive rather than communal, self-seeking rather than self-abnegating, sceptical rather than fideist, democratic rather than aristocratic, prosaic rather than poetic, scientific rather than mystic.

The single word that might sum up the nature of the changes is 'utilitarianism'. Led by Bentham, generations of men looked at society and man's activity in it in quite a new way, trying to measure out a system of just deserts – a 'rationale of reward' as Bentham called it.[7] The immediate and oft-quoted effect this thinking had on poetry is summed up in the remark: 'Prejudice apart, the game of push-pin is of equal value with the arts and sciences of music and poetry.[8] Poetry is relegated to the status of amusement and distraction, whereas in Sidney's time, and before, it had been, alongside history and philosophy, an instrument of knowledge. But utilitarianism's impact was much wider than a simple loss of status for poetry; the habits of thought it propagated, and the fabric of society it helped to construct, cut off the life-stream of poetry at its very source. In an important sense poetry has remained peripheral ever since, not because the Utilitarians argued the case that it should be but because the way of life they instituted has made it impossible to take poetry with complete seriousness. If we now take poetry seriously it is with a segment of our consciousnesses which recognizes that, valuable or not in the practical realms, poetry can continue to say things which the everyday language is incapable of conveying. Of course it is possible to attribute too much importance to the utilitarians, since to some extent they rode on the crest of a wave not entirely of their making, the wave, that is, of technological and industrial expansion which had its own irresistible and inexorable force. Utilitarianism helped to produce individualism (which is the benign word for the capacity and opportunity for the private citizen to develop and fulfil himself), but it also helped to produce alienation (which is the malign word for a society constituted of separate, atomized, competing, selfish individual members).[9] The strengths and weaknesses of Victorian poetry are directly derived from this rampant form of individualism, whose fruition had only been dimly glimpsed as a possibility (and quickly condemned) in the seventeenth century.[10]

This dominant world-picture was absolutely inescapable for those living through the period. It remains the central determining factor of Victorian poetry, both for people who tried to accommodate themselves to the surrounding conditions, and exploit their poetic possibilities (some of which were novel) and those who tried to turn their backs on them, or face up to them only in the most indirect and oblique way. As I have already suggested, the dominant theme of this volume is that in the poetry one witnesses a variety of strategies adopted by the poets faced with the challenging and alarming modern world, ranging from acceptance and acquiescence on the one hand to hostility, protest, and evasion on the other. The chapters on love poetry, on nature, on the elegy, and on the past are particularly dominated by these strategies. Viewed against the modern conditions, the vast array of the machinery of the age in particular (in the various senses of that word, ranging from the industrial hardware to the elaborate legislation and bureaucracy), the poetry has a kind of heroism, a kind of pathos, often a kind of desperation. In this sense it is not difficult for it to strike easy echoes with twentieth century readers. Some poets were very excited by the modern age and tried to do justice to the novel experiences of rapid train travel, for instance, and the new man-made sublimity of the cities (see below pp. 230–46) and it would be an exaggeration to say that the poets turned their backs completely on the progressive aspects of the age.

I have defined 1830 to 1890 as a period. All attempts at periodization are open to question, and even the most apparently solid of them remain provisional. These dates have a degree of sense, however. They correspond, roughly, to the optimistic and progressive years of Victoria's reign, even though closer inspection reveals whole decades of crisis, such as the 1840s and the 1870s, and they also correspond, roughly, to the careers of poets. By 1833 Keats, Shelley, Blake, Byron, and Scott were dead; Wordsworth and Coleridge (in the opinion of the younger poets) were in a state of living death. Tennyson and Browning were beginning their careers, Tennyson with *Poems, Chiefly Lyrical* (1830) and Browning with *Pauline* (1833). The theoretical basis of poetry was shifting too, with Sir Henry Taylor, in the preface to *Philip Van Artevelde* (1834), criticizing the Romantic Movement and the poetry produced under the influence of 'impassioned sentiment'; he wanted something more sensible, that was 'Reason's self sublimed'.[11] In effect he was calling for a new classicism, and although his prescriptions were not adopted by the majority of poets, a classical, non-expressive aesthetic played a more significant part in Victorian poetry than it had done in the previous era.[12] This new classicism was supposed to draw sustenance from general wisdom, and rescue poetry from the waywardness of subjectivity, and it relates to the theme of an alternative bid for the status and respect accorded to the poet. The full story of this is told in the next chapter.

The terminal date 1890 is a little more open to question, since the consensus of opinion has always been that the big watershed in poetry occurred in 1917 with T. S. Eliot's 'Prufrock'. As Eliot, Pound, and the young iconoclasts of *Blast* (1914) saw it, the sins of Victorian poetry continued even when Victoria was in her grave. Yet many of the foundations of modern poetry were being laid in the 1890s: new rhythms, new diction, new themes were being tentatively sought then, especially by poets such as Hardy, Davidson, Dowson, and Housman. Victorian poetic voices continued into the 1890s, but with an increasing lack of conviction and inventiveness. Certainly some of the major figures died at about this time – one thinks of Rossetti (1882), Browning (1889), and Tennyson (1892). Of the old guard, Meredith and Swinburne went on living and even writing, but their really significant poetic creation was over. To complicate the picture a shade, there is an alternative view that 1890 is too late, and Victorian poetry as a relatively homogeneous whole comes to an end some time in the 1870s. It is especially tempting to take this view if one accords great importance to Hopkins (as most critics do these days), whose 'Wreck of the Deutschland' (1875–6) is a revolutionary poem, but of course it was known at the time to only a handful of readers. Even so, observers in that decade thought they could detect a radical change, E. C. Stedman clearer than most.[13]

Inevitably the following chapters give only a partial view of the riotously rich and prolific period. Completeness is impossible, and the avoidance of treating authors as entirely discrete entities makes the map more difficult to draw. It is hoped that the particular merits of authors will emerge, however, since isolating the unrepeatable and unique features of authors is one of the principal requisites of criticism; but the main drift of this survey is to demonstrate the ways in which the authors fit together to create a productive and fascinating chapter in the history of English poetry.

This is a very personal, but I hope not eccentric, survey of the period. A sense of my priorities may be gauged from what is, to some degree, the companion volume to this: my anthology English Verse, 1830–1890 (1980). Inevitably, both the anthology and this book diverge from the kind of history the Victorians themselves might have produced, or the generations at the beginning of this century conservative enough to remain relatively unaffected by the challenge of Modernism. Even those of us who have not swallowed whole the recommendations of Eliot, Richards, Leavis, and others that poetry should have a line of wit and should avoid self-indulgence nevertheless find that these features of poetry do still constitute the central core of what is admired – at least in Great Britain. The poetry that catches our ear is stark, energetic, exuberant, self-conscious, and not too unintelligible. Philip Larkin has become, to a large extent, the touchstone of the 1970s and 1980s – although, paradoxically, he disapproved of some tendencies of Modernism (principally the pretentiousness, the obscurity, and the disdain of the common reader). The Victorians produced plenty of poetry that seems to be an adumbration of the poetry we like, but it was not always regarded as main-line then. So that in our time the map has been redrawn, and whereas the Victorians themselves often thought that lyric poetry occupied the centre of the stage, we find ourselves drawn towards more dramatic and striking genres, such as the dramatic monologue. A Victorian history would almost certainly have given more prominence to legend and mythology, but I share Hopkins's distaste for this area of experience, and fully endorse what he said in a letter to Bridges: 'Believe me, the Greek gods are a totally unworkable material; the merest frigidity, which must chill and kill every living work of art they are brought into.'[14] A very similar objection has been made in our time by Philip Larkin, when he says that classical and biblical mythology 'not only fills poems full of dead spots but dodges the writer's duty to be original' [15] So to a large extent I have avoided what is actually a fairly prominent area in the poetry of the period. The picture of Victorian poetry offered here corresponds very closely to J. R. Watson's *Everyman's Book of Victorian Verse* (1982), which at once recognizes some of the very characteristic features of the poetry (as I do in Chapters 6 and 9, 'The Past' and 'The Elegiac') and promotes the slightly more unusual ones: unusual, that is, if one only views the century through the glass that has been darkened by the intervening myth of its tiresome irrelevance propagated by the Modernists.

Notes

1 Turner's *Dudley Castle* exhibited 1833; now in the Lady Lever Collection, Port Sunlight Cheshire. It was once owned by Ruskin.

2. J. Ruskin, *Notes on Mr. Ruskin's Drawings by Turner*, in *Works*, XIII, 435.

3. Ruskin, *Lectures on Landscape*, in *Works*, XXII, 64.

4. *The Letters of Matthew Arnold to Arthur Hugh Clough*, edited by H. E. Lowry (1932), p. 99.

5. Cited in W. J. Bate *The Burden of Past and the English Poet* (Cambridge, Mass., 1970), p. 4.

6. For the survival of the concept of The Great Chain of Being see A. O. Lovejoy, *The Great Chain of Being* (Cambridge, Mass., 1936).

7. See J. Bentham, *The Rationale of Reward* (1825), reprinted in *Victorian Poetry and Poetics*, edited by W. E. Houghton and G. R. Stange, second edition (Boston 1968), pp. 833–44.

8. For the conflicting attitudes to individualism see K. W. Swart,

'"Individualism" in the Mid-Nineteenth Century (1826–1860)', *JHI*, 23 (1962), 77–90.

9. For the seventeenth-century attitude to individualism see M. F. Bottrall, *Every Man a Phoenix: Studies in Seventeenth-Century Autobiography* (1958).

10. See R. G. Cox, 'Victorian Criticisms of Poetry: The Minority Tradition', *Scrutiny*, 18 (1951), 2–17. Other essays concentrating on the 'classical' tendency in certain Victorian poets to respect the audience and write carefully formed, objective and impersonal poetry are J. K. Robinson, 'A Neglected Phase of the Aesthetic Movement: English Parnassianism', *PMLA*, 88 (1953), 733–54; and K. Amis, 'Communication and the Victorian Poet', *Essays in Criticism*, 4 (1954), 386–99.

11. Sir Henry Taylor's Preface is reprinted in *Victorian Poetry and Poetics*, pp. 861–65.

12. See note 11 above.

13. E. C. Stedman, *Victorian Poets* (1887), p. 31.

14. *The Letters of Gerard Manley Hopkins to Robert Bridges*, edited by C. C. Abbott (1955), p. 217.

15. Quoted in Ian Hamilton, 'Four Conversations', *London Magazine*, 4 (1964), 72.

Chapter 2

The Image of the Poet and the Function of Poetry

The Introduction gives the impression that poetry in the Victorian period was somehow in retreat, somehow marginal, addressing itself only to a fragment of a person's being, making only a minor contribution to life. This was indeed the case to a large extent, yet the situation goes hand in hand, paradoxically, with a kind of rearguard action to prevent the poet from being shorn of all his power and with a fresh campaign to give the poet almost more power and purpose than he had ever had before.

First the rearguard action. The Romantic Movement poets had promulgated an expressive aesthetic, teaching that the first duty of the poet is to disseminate his private, individual vision, however unusual and even anti-social it might be. The Romantics could never quite decide whether or not a poet was born different from other men, but they were in no doubt that sustained development of habits of vision and modes of expression led to highly specialized states of being. An extreme Romantic poet, like Blake, continued to believe in the ancient notion that the greatest poetry was divinely inspired, and had access to mystical sources and to highest truth; but even those with their sights set lower thought that feelings and emotions, especially those generated by the secondary imagination, gave access to a special order of knowledge necessary to man. Typical of the strong claims made for these special faculties is Wordsworth's, when he states that imagination is 'Reason in her most exalted mood'.[1] Shelley made ambitious claims for the visionary power of the poet: 'For [the poet] not only beholds intensely the present as it is, and discovers those laws according to which present things ought to be ordered, but he beholds the future in the present, and his thoughts are the germs of the flower and the fruit of latest time.'[2] A good deal of criticism made strenuous distinctions between the kinds of knowledge and experience poetry dealt with and the experience of the scientific and rational mind, and a lot of criticism, in reaction against the excessively didactic principles of previous eras, stressed the pleasure rather than the utility of poetry. (Although pleasure, as Coleridge understood it, experienced in response to literature, would have been more subtle and rarefied than any concept of pleasure Bentham was capable of understanding.) Wordsworth did not like this compartmentalization and specialization, and recommended something much more over-arching and comprehensive: 'Poetry is the breath and finer spirit of all knowledge; it is the impassioned expression which is the countenance of all Science.'[3]

Victorian poets and critics continued to maintain opinions of this kind, but it became increasingly hard to do so, since the power of science and objectivity grew by leaps and bounds and the forces needed to organize an increasingly dynamic society became more and more logically arranged and earnestly recommended. Rossetti especially diagnosed the condition a modern poet would have to endure as one of diminishment and retrenchment:

> Of [the highest] order of poetic action – the omnipotent
> freewill of the artist's mind, – our curbed and slackening
> world may seem to have seen the last. It has been
> succeeded by another kind of 'finish', devoted and ardent,
> but less building on ensured foundations than self-
> questioning in the very moment of action or even later.[4]

The Victorians tended to call the expressive poet relying on his emotions and private experiences 'subjective'. This is Browning's description of the subjective poet in 'An Eassy on Percy Bysshe Shelley' (1852):

> He is rather a seer . . . than a fashioner, and what he
> produces will be less a work than an effluence. That
> effluence cannot be easily considered in abstraction from
> his personality, – being indeed the very radiance and
> aroma of his personality, projected from it but not
> separated.

With the objective poet we consider the work projected from himself and distinct:

> We are ignorant what the inventor of *Othello* conceived of
> the fact as he beheld it in completeness, how he accounted
> for it, under what law he traced its coincidence. We learn
> only what he intended we should learn by that particular
> exercise of his power, – the fact itself . . . .[5]

Browning concedes that greatness is possible for either type of poet, but he thinks that the subjective poet has the best chance of achieving the kind of success that was always the prerogative of the prophetic or vatic poet:

> He . . . is impelled to embody the thing he perceives, not so much with reference to the many below as to the One above him, the supreme intelligence which apprehends all things in their absolute truth, – an ultimate view ever aspired to, if but partially attained, by the poet's own soul. Not what man sees, but what God sees – the *Ideas* of Plato, seeds of creation lying burningly on the Divine Hand – it is toward these that he struggles.[6]

In grandiose diction, Browning claims that the subjective poet's soul is 'the nearest reflex of that absolute Mind'. Browning had neither the personality, the intellect, nor the cultural environment to follow Shelley, the 'sun-treader', but he retained great admiration for him, and the image of his predecessor gave him the moral support to ignore and despise his public. In *The Ring and the Book* he refers scornfully to its members:

> Well, British Public, ye who like me not,
> (God love you!) and will have your proper laugh
> At the dark question, laugh it! I laugh first.
> (I. 410–412)

This antipathy had been building up for years, not only with Browning but other poets, and it is a sad and involved story. It results from a distortion and exaggeration of the myth of the poet. This myth was propagated and extended both by the poets themselves, and by essayists such as Carlyle, Mill, and Arthur Hallam. It was in part a response to the hostility marshalled against poetry which had started to become prominent in the 1820s. The whole process of counter-attack was something like James I's extreme emphasis on the Divine Right of Kings – at its most extravagant when the forces of opposition were gathering strength.

Thomas Love Peacock playfully thought, in *The Four Ages of Poetry* (1820), that since mankind had grown up it was time to put away childish things and speak as a man – in prose rather than in verse. This occasioned Shelley's famous riposte *The Defense of Poetry* (1821), although since this was not published until 1840 it did not make any immediate public contribution to the debate. Bentham and the Utilitarians placed no value on poetry, other than as a species of effective rhetoric and pleasant entertainment. Macaulay, in his essay on Milton (1825), thought that poetry was being superseded:

> Generalization is necessary to the advancement of
> knowledge; but particularity is indispensable to the
> creations of the imagination. In proportion as men know
> more and think more, they look less at individuals and
> more at classes. They therefore make better theories and
> worse poems.[7]

He goes on to say that 'perhaps no person can be a poet, or can even enjoy poetry, without a certain unsoundness of mind'. This did not prevent him, however, from writing poetry, and it was admired by impressionable schoolboys who went on to become civil servants and governors of the Empire. Macaulay, like Peacock, thought the time had come for man to stop looking through the glass darkly, and start looking at truths face to face in a clear light:

> And as the magic lantern acts best in a dark room, poetry
> effects its purpose most completely in a dark age. As the
> light of knowledge breaks upon its exhibitions, as the
> outlines of certainty become more and more definite and
> the shades of probability more and more distinct, the hues
> and lineaments of the phantoms which the poet calls up
> grow fainter and fainter.[8]

During the rest of the century there was a great body of people who would have agreed with Macaulay that one could not 'unite the incompatible advantages of reality and deception, the clear discernment of truth and the exquisite enjoyment of fiction'.[9]

The response of the poetic establishment to all of this was not defensive but aggressive. Perhaps what the poets should have done was to identify the particular contribution (albeit limited) that poetry could unquestionably make and emphasize its uniqueness and indispensability. Instead the poets and their defenders started to make grandiose and ambitious claims. They were not content to be 'unacknowledged legislators of mankind' as Shelley had envisaged them; they wanted to be acknowledged legislators. Their arguments proceeded with a certain kind of logic.

As the age became more and more analytical, more and more concerned with accurate knowledge and hard fact, so the poet's statements became more and more alien and remote. It had been part of the Romantics' image of the poet, although not necessarily a major one, that poetry was inspirational. The post-Romantics emphasized this almost as a defence mechanism. They felt alien, so they would make a virtue out of necessity: their separation would either derive from genius or it would *suggest* it. Typical of this bid for the poet's special place is Tennyson's 'Armageddon' (January 1828), which was worked up into 'Timbuctoo' for the Chancellor's Gold Medal poem in Cambridge (1829):

> I felt my soul grow mighty, and my Spirit
> With supernatural excitation bound
> Within me, and my mental eye grew large
> With such a vast circumference of thought,
> That in my vanity I seemed to stand
> Upon the outward verge and bound alone
> Of full beatitude. Each failing sense
> As with a momentary flash of light
> Grew thrillingly distinct and keen. (ll. 88–96)

There is a similarity to 'the flash that has revealed the invisible world' of Wordsworth's *The Prelude* (1850) (VI. 601–02). Other passages like this are found in Tennyson. In 'The Mystic' (published in 1830, but never reprinted by Tennyson) the poet has access to experience denied the common man:

> . . . he in the centre fixed
> Saw far on each side through the grated gates
> Most pale and clear and lovely distances.
> He often lying broad awake, and yet
> Remaining from the body, and apart
> In intellect and power and will, hath heard
> Time flowing in the middle of the night,
> And all things creeping to a day of doom.
> How could ye know him? Ye were yet within
> The narrower circle.
> (ll. 33–42)

Tennyson deals with similar kinds of experience in the late poem 'The Ancient Sage' (1885), and he described it as 'no nebulous ecstasy, but a state of transcendent wonder, associated with absolute clearness of mind'.[10] These states may have had a physiological basis, and may have been close to the 'weird seizures' of *The Princess*: they were the benignant aspect of the Tennysonian melancholy and madness. They emphasized his separation from ordinary men.[11] Whatever the source, Tennyson could always believe, as Shelley does in *Alastor*, in the divine nature of inspiration. In *The Alien Vision of Victorian Poetry* (1952), E. D. H. Johnson explores the mysterious and even anti-social origins of poetry in madness dream and reverie. Tennyson is a prime example, but one finds the phenomenon in his contemporaries, both in theory and practice. Somewhat surprisingly, since he came from the hard-headed mercantile class, Ruskin was sympathetic to the strange sources of great art:

> I believe . . . that the noblest forms of imaginative power
> are also in some sort ungovernable, and have in them
> something of the character of dreams; so that the vision,
> of whatever kind, comes uncalled, and will not submit
> itself to the seer, but conquers him, and forces him to
> speak as a prophet, having no power over his words or
> thoughts.[12]

Curiously, the visionary poets were not content to remain outsiders; indeed, rather than beat the Utilitarians they decided to join them, and recommend the usefulness of their poetry and its centrality to life. This may have been because in the sceptical age they could not *quite* believe that their inspirational sources validated their prophetic stature, so that they ensured they would be prophetic by consciously attempting to take on this role. As I shall show, there were plenty of exceptions to this development but most of the principal poets were involved in it to a greater or a lesser degree. Browning's friend W. J. Fox wrote: 'Poetry is no longer a plaything, or a mere drawing-room ornament', but 'a weapon of strife in the social conflict.'[13] Arthur Hallam, reviewing *Poems, Chiefly Lyrical* in August 1831, regretted the hiving off of poetry into separate categories, 'hence the melancholy which so evidently characterises the spirit of modern poetry; hence that return of the mind upon itself and the habit of seeking relief in idiosyncrasies rather than community of interest'.[14] The implication was that some kind of recovery was needed, and four years later John Stuart Mill started to push Tennyson in the direction of purposive expression, when he advised him to 'cultivate, and with no half devotion, philosophy as well as poetry'.[15] The problem in Tennyson's particular case was that he had little or nothing to say of public interest; in this respect he was completely unlike the revolutionary Shelley, so that when he self-consciously tried to assume the stance of vates or prophet the best he could often manage was to versify the common political and social philosophy of his age, the received ideas. Tennyson partly wanted this useful role for himself; he was partly driven to it by his public. Typical of the prompting was the *Christian Remembrancer's* regret that he had separated 'the world and the actings of the imagination from the real world', coupled with the request that he should cultivate more responsibility.[16] But a position of this kind is not something one can consciously aspire to; it is given. And the genuine prophet often conveys to his listeners surprising and even shocking messages. Tennyson was unable to do that; for the most part he suffered the poetic misfortune of being accepted and understood in his own country. Unlike some of the French poets of the nineteenth century, the English poets, though concerned with alienation, dreams, and madness, tended not to propagate the image of the *poète maudit*. Our culture provides nothing as alarming and exciting as Baudelaire and Rimbaud.

One concomitant of the line of thought we have just been considering was that discussion of poetry often tended to neglect analysis of metrics and diction, since so much attention was devoted to content. Indeed some writers thought that the poet was defined not by his ability to write well-crafted verse but a certain kind of identity, and a propensity to deal with certain topics. Carlyle wrote of Tennyson that 'he wants a *task*; and, alas, that of spinning rhymes, and naming it "Art" and "high Art", in a time like ours, will never furnish him'.[17] As it happened this did not cause Tennyson to neglect the technical features of his art, but one can see what advice of this kind could lead to with a weaker poet. Fortunately there were few critics around to remind practitioners of essentials; G. H. Lewes wrote that 'verse is the form of poetry: not the form as a thing *arbitrary*, but as a thing vital and essential; it is the incarnation of poetry. To call it the *dress*, and to consider it apart as a thing distinct, is folly . . .'.[18] The terms he uses here of incarnation as opposed to dress owe something to Wordsworth of course, and to Blake, who wrote that 'ideas cannot be given but in their minutely appropriate words'.[19]

The high claims made by poets and critics continue throughout the century, and became more urgent as orthodox religious faith continued to wane. Poetry, it was felt, could fill the vacuum caused by the disappearance of the view of higher states that religion used to afford. There was a continuation and a re-emphasis of the claims made for the imagination by the Romantic poets. These claims were not only on behalf of the aesthetic function of the imagination, but the ideological and the pedagogic. To modern ears they often seem like so much hot air. The most famous, perhaps one should say the most notorious, of these functional recommendations was made by Matthew Arnold, when he said that poetry should be a '*magister vitae*' (a guide for life).[20] This aspect of Arnold's theory has tended to receive a bad press in our century, since we set our faces firmly against the didactic impulse in art, and are instinctively suspicious when art attempts to take on functional purposes so useful and so clearly directed. But the good feature of Arnold's theory was that he did not regard poetry as hermetically sealed from the thoughtful and intelligent operations of culture in its wider sense: it partook liberally of the 'best self' and derived inspiration not only from mysterious and prophetic sources but from intellectual and critical activities. There are quarters nowadays in which Arnold's aesthetic is severely castigated, since he is regarded as the apostle of a high culture which is illiberal (and hence fraught with contradictions, since Arnold is supposed to be a liberal) and socially divisive, but the valuable contribution he has made to poetry has been the emphasis he has placed on its connection with day-by-day life; there was a danger, in some of the extreme neo-Romantic theories, that poetry would be hived off from life and from other forms of discourse, but Arnold attempted to guard against that tendency.

Many poets since Arnold have concurred with him in recognizing that the critical faculty may have an invaluable part to play in creativity. He did, however, see the potential dangers lying in wait for the self-conscious didactic poet with a purpose, and he could be sceptical about the willed desire to write significant poetry. He criticized poets attempting to pull themselves up by their own bootstraps, pointing, by contrast, to true poets free of these vanities: 'They do not talk of their mission, nor of interpreting their age, nor of the coming poet; all this, they know, is the mere delirium of vanity; their business is not to praise their age, but to afford to the men who live in it the highest pleasure which they are capable of feeling'.[21] He tended to think of this 'pleasure' as positive, and he was aware that modern society provided comparatively few opportunities for men to experience such optimism; indeed, even classical Roman society, to which the English Augustans looked back with such approval, did not satisfy Arnold's high standards; he saw Lucretius withdrawing from contemplation of society 'with gloomy despair . . . to rivet his eyes on the elementary reality'.[22] Even Virgil is somehow inadequate because he is involved in the reconstruction of a long-dead past rather than immediate representation, and he is ineffably melancholy rather than completely fulfilled.[23] Some of Arnold's own poetry, such as *The Scholar Gipsy* and *Empedocles*, is elegiac, even despairing, and the latter poem was suppressed in the 1853 edition of his *Poems* as an unprofitable example of 'the dialogue of the mind with itself.'[24]

It was inevitable, since the image of the poet and the function of poetry were such diurnal concerns of the poets, that these themes should find expression in their *œuvres*, and it would be possible to glean a whole history of poetic theory from the works themselves. I refer to works in which this is an explicit theme; it is easy to multiply the prevalence of the theme by considering implicit statements (a favourite fad of modern criticism). If one wishes to go slightly further afield one finds no lack of material, so that John Goode, for instance, regards Clough's *Amours de Voyage* as growing from an 'urgent need for an ironic verbal discrimination and of its impossibility'.[25] However, concentrating on the works in which the craft of poetry is a self-consciously articulated theme rather than an implicit one brings a sufficiently large catch into the net.

The first work, crouching like a dragon at the gate at the beginning of the period, is Browning's *Sordello* (1840). It haunts this study like some wicked fairy that one cannot quite ignore. It remains unreadable, unperformable, unassimilable. At least one contemporary locked away in a hospital with it thought he had lost his mind, and one can be sure that there is undoubtedly not a word of exaggeration in the anecdote.[26] Even Ezra Pound, whose allusive method owes a lot to *Sordello*, found it 'unreadable'.[27] I regard the work as an insufferable impertinence, and the contrast between it and the delightful *Amours de Voyage* is extreme. Clough's poem is everything that *Sordello* is not – readable, cultivated, subtle, instantly appealing, inexhaustibly worth rereading. However, *Sordello* cannot be quite avoided, not least because a number of stubborn and earnest critics make such extravagant claims for it. What most critics do with it is to hack out some of the bits that come occasionally into focus and try to speak intelligbly about them, and that is what I shall be doing every so often.

Browning had already considered the poet's role in *Pauline* (1833) and *Paracelsus* (1835). Paracelsus is an early scientist, but in Browning's mind the pursuit of knowledge is not unlike the pursuit of poetry. In *Sordello* the role and nature of the poet is the central theme. Sordello was a shadowy predecessor of Dante; he is encountered in *Il Purgatorio*. He lived in violent times, since he finds himself in the midst of the war between the Guelfs and Ghibbelines. For modern readers this may seem a shade recherché, but intelligent readers in the 1840s were often quite well informed about medieval Italian history; many of them would have read the standard work by Sismondi for instance.[28] Browning told his friend Milsand that the setting was merely background, yet the drama and bloodthirstiness of the time throws into high relief the dilemmas facing Sordello as he agonizes over what kind of poet to be. Eglamour is a rival poet, but he is unsatisfactory because he regards poetry as a private gift, confined to poets, 'and men, the whole of them, must shift Without it' (II. 224–25). Sordello goes to the other extreme by wishing to entertain men, 'perform their bidding and no more,/At their own satiating-point give o'er' (II. 437–38). But he soon becomes more ambitious, and recognizes that the key to greatness lies in his ability to create a fit language, 'welding words into the crude/Mass from the new speech round him, till a rude/Armour was hammered out' (II. 575–77). It is not long before he comes to grief – 'Sundered in twain; each spectral part at strife/With each; one jarred against another life' (II. 657–58). He withdraws from public life, still dreaming of becoming a complete man. In this alienated state he seems to be drawing close to the position previously occupied by Eglamour. He is tempted to involve himself in the world of action, where individual influence is more certain. The man of action who achieves so much is Salinguerra, and in Book IV Sordello tries to follow his example, and yet his plans for Italy are so dream-like that they are like poems, and he seems to suffer an ener-vation of will which Browning cannot quite diagnose. Browning seems to have thought that Sordello should have been both a poetic dreamer and a man of action, and yet except for the decisive step of snatching away Elizabeth Barrett, Browning was never a man of action. One feels in *Sordello* that problems are being grappled with, rather than solved. This produces great richness, but not ultimately satisfaction. Still, these are not the principal difficulties of the poem; the real stumbling-block is that Browning has the events clearly in his mind (one presumes that at least), but feels no need to let the readers into the secret, so all is veiled and allusive. The poem should be read as some sort of comment on the 1830s and 1840s, but before one tries to understand that one wants to know what comment it is making on the thirteenth century, and that is far from clear.

A much more accessible poem is *In Memoriam*, which presents the image of a mourning man and a mourning poet. As with many previous elegies this one draws a wide range of themes into its ambit, the function and value of the poet being one of them. Early on Tennyson expresses at once the guilt one experiences in exploiting feel-ings for poetic purposes and the therapeutic use of regular metre and the ultimate inadequacy of language – all seventeenth-century themes:

> I sometimes hold it half a sin
>> To put in words the grief I feel;
>> For words, like Nature, half reveal
> And half conceal the Soul within.
>
> But, for the unquiet heart and brain,
>> A use in measured language lies;
>> The sad mechanic exercise,
> Like dull narcotics, numbing pain.
>
> In words, like weeds, I'll wrap me o'er,
>> Like coarsest clothes against the cold:
>> But that large grief which these enfold
> Is given in outline and no more.
>>>>   (v. 1–12)

In Memoriam was in a sense a public poem, since many readers found it spoke not exactly *to* them but *for* them: it put into words more effectively than they could have devised experiences they were familiar with. And there were prophetic and philosophical sections fully in accord with the speculative aims of the young ambitious poets at the outset of the period. And yet one's main impression of it is that most of the experiences are very private, and so inevitable that questions of their worth and validity hardly occur: they are there; they provide ready material for poetry. Like many elegies *In Memoriam* does not provide a vivid portrait of the one mourned; it is more a record of grief:

> I leave thy praises unexpressed
> In verse that brings myself relief,
> And by the measure of my grief
> I leave thy greatness to be guessed.
>
> (LXXV. 1–4)

The poet is not in quest of fame or personal immortality, as section LXXVII indicates: 'To breathe my loss is more than fame,/To utter love more sweet than praise.' In the final section he reflects that much of the poetry is 'idle brawling rhymes,/The sport of random sun and shade', but it remains nevertheless valuable as immediate record.

As in Browning's 'One Word More', the poet of *In Memoriam* is virtually *propria persona*, but more common in the period is the projected image of a poet. A good example is found in Arnold's *Empedocles*, where the lyric poet Callicles is given a subsidiary role alongside the philosopher. Empedocles is tortured, something has 'impaired [his] spirit's strength,/And dried its self-sufficing fount of joy' (II. 21–22). He muses along on the edge of Etna's crater before jumping in. He puts aside his purple robe and his laurel bough. In a world he does not love he can only 'subsist in ceaseless opposition' (II. 277–78), and feel 'joy and the outward world . . . die to him'. The death of joy and the loss of creative and imaginative power are symptomatic of the impotent state Coleridge so movingly evoked in his important poem *Ode to Dejection*. Now he is 'nothing but a devouring flame of thought – /But a naked, eternally restless mind!' (II. 329–30). Like Coleridge, who is tormented by 'viper thoughts', Empedocles is lost in the 'fantastic maze/Forged by the imperious lonely thinking-power' (II. 375–76). He finds, as Arnold often found, how difficult it is to be faithful to his own 'true, deep-buried self'. The leap into the crater is at once an act of self-assertion and a bid to be at one with nature. Further down the slope the lyric poet Callicles sings of the Olympians and Apollonian mastery, of the flaying of Marsyas and Typho buried under Etna, and Cadmus and Harmonia. Callicles is ineffectual, so far as saving Empedocles from suicide, and his poetry remains decoratively Parnassian.

The Scholar Gipsy and *Thyrsis* are two other poems concerned with the poet's role. The scholar gipsy of the *donnée*, described in Glanville's

The Vanity of Dogmatizing (1661), was concerned with seeking after occult quasi-scientific lore (especially mesmerism), but as presented by Arnold is closer to a figure of alien, brooding imagination, wandering just out of reach of modern man, who is beset with the 'strange disease of modern life' and 'its sick hurry, its divided aims,/Its head o'ertaxed, its palsied hearts' (ll. 203–05). All that this figure can do, if he is to survive, is to 'fly our paths, our feverish contact fly'. (ll. 221) *Thyrsis* celebrates Arnold's friend Clough, who died in 1861. Arnold, not entirely accurately, sums up Clough's career, which involved a loss of the 'happy, country tone' (l. 222) of his early poetry, and the adoption of 'a stormy note/Of men contention-tossed, of men who groan,/Which tasked thy pipe too sore, and tired thy throat' (ll. 222–25). But the better Clough, the Clough who retains the immortality of the scholar gipsy, remains associated with pastoral lyricism, youth, the Cumnor countryside, and the curiously elusive 'lone, sky-pointing tree' (l. 174) which symbolized the pursuit of the 'fugitive and gracious light' (l. 201) so remote from 'the world's market'. (l. 205) These images of the poet that Arnold projects are disconcertingly remote from the improving and useful functions he envisaged for poetry when he came to sum them up in prose, but they continue to have a certain force.

The figure of David in Browning's *Saul* (1855) produces a very different kind of poetry from that recommended by Arnold – thoughtful and challenging – since the poetry David produces relaxes and cures the taut and traumatized Saul and asserts its power over creation. Arnold was capable of producing anodyne poetry, but he always felt guilty and uneasy when he did.

Saul and *Empedocles* speak of times long past, and perhaps refer to the Victorian age by a kind of remote analogy. But there are plenty of poems in the century which speak of the stance of the modern poet and the nature of up-to-date poetry. One of the most famous recommendations of the modern subject is in Elizabeth Barrett Browning's *Aurora Leigh* (1856):

> Nay, if there's room for poets in this world
> A little overgrown (I think there is),
> Their sole work is to represent the age,
> Their age, not Charlemagne's, – this live, throbbing
>   age.
>   (v. 200–03)

This plea for the modern subject obsessed the Pre-Raphaelite painters too: Holman Hunt did not 'flinch from modern varnish' when he painted that expensive rosewood piano in *The Awakening Conscience*.

Elizabeth Barrett Browning wanted to do justice to the heroines of *her* age, not a past one. Her plea is the poetic equivalent of the observation made by John Sterling when he reviewed Tennyson's *Poems* in 1842:

> These seventy millions of pounds have been subscribed by private persons at their own choice in one small country, and have created nearly fifteen hundred miles of railroads – structures that surpass all pyramids and Cyclopean walls, and machines that would puzzle Archimedes, by which myriads of men are perpetually travelling like the heroes of fairy tales . . . In the state of society that has produced such results there may be, we know there is, enough torpor, even rottenness. But it cannot be, on the whole, an insignificant stage of human existence, one barren for imaginative eyes.[29]

At the opposite end of the spectrum is the equally famous urging from William Morris in the introduction to *The Earthly Paradise* to 'Forget six counties overhung with smoke.'

The Victorian poets expressed a great deal of self-confidence in their role as guides and prophets, but every so often the heart-wringing cry of frustrated creativity breaks out; the note struck by Coleridge in *Dejection* sounds again, as when Hopkins cries 'birds build but not I build'. In his last letter to Robert Bridges[30] Hopkins included a poem which expressed his frustration at being unable to produce effortlessly and vibrantly:

> The fine delight that fathers thought; the strong
> Spur, live and lancing like the blowpipe
> flame,
> Breathes once and, quenched faster than it
> came,
> Leaves yet the mind a mother of immortal song.
> Nine months she then, nay years, nine years she
> long
> Within her wears, bears, cares and combs the
> same:
> The widow of an insight lost she lives, with
> aim
> Not known and hand at work now never wrong.
> Sweet fire, the sire of muse, my souls needs this;
> I want the one rapture of an inspiration.
> O then if in my lagging lines you miss
> The roll, the rise, the carol, the creation,

My winter world, that scarcely breathes that bliss
   Now, yields you, with some sighs, our
               explanation.

There is something very moving about this. It is the cry of the outcast poet, but not *so* outcast as to be picturesque, heroic, and romantically alienated; it is more the *cri de cœur* of someone who has faced loneliness and exile, believing in poetry, but finding it has given him little consolation and satisfaction. It is the attitude one finds often in twentieth-century poets. All the Victorian poets took their work seriously, and they were sufficiently romantic at heart to value the integrity and privacy of the poetic experience. None of the major poets regarded himself as a lightweight entertainer, complacently giving the audience a familiar reflection of itself. A pervasive artistic conscientiousness existed, and one searches in vain for the relaxed middle-brow philistinism, evinced as an artistic principle, of the kind one finds in Trollope's *Autobiography* (1883). The absence of this complacency in the poetic theory and practice is one of the elements that established the difference between the tradition of the Victorian novel and that of the poetry.

Notes

1. W. Wordsworth, *The Prelude* (1850), 192.

2. P. B. Shelley, *The Defence of Poetry*, in *The Works of Percy Bysshe Shelley*, edited by R. Ingpen and W. E. Peck (1930), VII, 112.

3. W. Wordsworth, *Lyrical Ballads*, edited by R. L. Brett and A. R. Jones (1963), p. 253.

4. D. G. Rossetti, 'Hake's Parables and Tales', in *The Works of Dante Gabriel Rossetti*, edited by W. M. Rossetti (1911), p. 630.

5. R. Browning, 'Eassy on Shelley', in *Victorian Poetry and Poetics*, edited by W. E. Houghton and G. R. Stange (Boston, 1968), second edition, pp. 336–37.

6. Ibid., p. 336.

7. T. Macaulay, *The Works of Lord Macaulay* (1898), VII, 6–7.

8. Ibid., VII, 9.

9. Ibid., VII, 9.

10. *Alfred Lord Tennyson, Memoir*, edited by Hallam Tennyson (1897), II, 473–4.

11. Several critics, beginning with H. Nicolson in *Tennyson: Aspects of His Life, Character and Poetry* (1923, repr. 1962), have stressed the importance of madness in Tennyson; see also R. B. Martin, *Tennyson: the Unquiet Heart* (Oxford, 1983), *passim*, and A. C. Colley, *Tennyson and Madness* (Athens, Georgia, 1983).

12. J. Ruskin, *The Stones of Venice* (1851–53), in *Works*, XI, 178.

13. W. J. Fox, *The Monthly Repository* (August 1832).

14. A. Hallam, reprinted in *Tennyson; The Critical Heritage*, edited by J. Jump (1967), p. 41.

15. J. S. Mill, in *Tennyson: The Critical Heritage*, p. 96.

16. 'Poetry of the Year 1842', *Christian Remembrancer*, 4 (1842), 49.

17. Quoted by Martin, *Tennyson: the Unquiet Heart*, p. 303

18. G. H. Lewes, *Principles of Success in Literature* (1898), p. 193.

19. Quoted by W. B. Yeats in *Essays and Introductions* (1961), pp. 127–28.

20. Arnold to Clough, 28 October 1852, in *The Letters of Matthew Arnold to Arthur Hugh Clough*, edited by H. F. Lowry (1932), p. 124.

21. M. Arnold, Preface to *Poems* (1853), in *The Complete Works of Matthew Arnold*, edited by R. H. Super, 11 vols (Ann Arbor, 1960–77), I, 13.

22. M. Arnold, 'On the Modern Element in Literature' (1857), *Works* I, 33.

23. Ibid., I, 35.

24. Ibid., I, 1.

25. J. Goode, '*Amours de Voyage*: the Aqueous Poem', in *The Major Victorian Poets: Reconsiderations*, edited by I. Armstrong (1969), p. 292

26. J. Sutherland in *The Oxford Book of Literary Anecdotes* (1975), includes the story of Douglas Jerrold trying to read *Sordello* in hospital, but concluding that he was 'an idiot', until visited by his wife, who reassured him by asserting that the work was 'gibberish', pp. 310–11

27. E. Pound, 'Chinese Poetry II', *Today*, 3 (May 1918), 93.

28. J. C. L. Sismondi's *History of the Italian Republics in the Middle Ages*, 16 vols (1809–18).

29. J. Sterling, in *Tennyson: The Critical Heritage*, pp. 104–5.

30. *The Letters of Gerard Manley Hopkins to Robert Bridges*, edited by C. C. Abbott (1955), pp. 303–6.

Chapter 3
The Diction of Victorian Poetry

The Parnassian and Delphic tradition

When Hopkins was an undergraduate at Balliol 'a horrible thing' happened to him: he began 'to *doubt* Tennyson'.[1] So far as Hopkins was concerned the doubt proved salutary, since it gave rise to his own revolutionary view of poetry; so far as Tennyson was concerned it did no immediate harm, since it was expressed in a private letter that remained unpublished until 1938. However, for modern readers the criticism in the letter to A. W. M. Baillie is a classic statement of the objections that may be levied against Parnassian poetry; it is a forceful critique of a long tradition of poetic diction – of which Tennyson was the latest exemplar.

In descending order Hopkins identified five kinds of poetry: Inspirational, Castalian, Parnassian, Olympian and Delphic. It is doubtful whether Hopkins himself could always have made precise discriminations and his discussion is more useful as a series of suggestions than hermetically sealed definitions. Inspirational poetry is written in 'a mood of great, abnormal in fact, mental acuteness, either energetic or receptive'.[2] Its processes are mysterious and Hopkins does not investigate them. Castalian is 'the lowest kind' of inspirational poetry, bearing the hallmark of the particular personality of a poet and with a tendency towards mannerism. If one were to slot Hopkins's own poetry into one of his categories it would be this one. It shades into the Parnassian, and this is the kind that receives most attention from him. Parnassian poetry is more extreme than Castalian in its use of personal mannerisms, and once the language has been learnt the Poet can go on producing it with little or no inspiration. Hopkins cites these lines from *Enoch Arden* as an example:

> The mountain wooded to the peak, the lawns
> And winding glades high up like ways to Heaven,
> The slender coco's drooping crown of plumes,

> The lightning flash of insect and of bird,
> The lustre of the long convolvuluses
> That coiled around the stately stems, and ran
> Even to the limit of the land, the glows
> And glories of the broad belt of the world,
> All these he saw.
>
> (ll. 568–76)

Hopkins identifies the penultimate line as especially Parnassian and especially characteristic of Tennyson. The leisurely pace and the alliteration are part of Tennyson's 'secret' which makes the poet pall on us when we have found it out.

Tantalizingly Hopkins does not discuss the interesting point at which Parnassian becomes Delphic. This is 'merely the language of verse as distinct from that of prose' and is available to any poetaster who wants to use it.[3] When employed it produces something that is obviously not prose, but is not necessarily poetry in the highest sense. It is a poetic lexicon, a prosodic treasure-house, a cultural·set of assumptions, easily exploited but ultimately the foundation on which Parnassian poetry will be built. It was coming to the end of its life in Hopkins's time, yet it continued to flourish, and Rupert Brooke and the young Wilfred Owen wrote in it. In remote corners of the poetic world it is not dead yet! Coleridge, Shelley, Tennyson, Arnold, Swinburne, and Rossetti all wrote in it, and even Wordsworth relapsed into it in the days of his apostasy. The full story of poetic diction as a separate order of language is told in Bernard Groom's *The Diction of Poetry from Spenser to Bridges* (1955) which shows that a separatist tradition evolved, which had classical precedents. Some poets, such as Shakespeare and Donne, wrote as if the barrier were not there, or at least should not constrain them, and Wordsworth did his best to argue the case that poetic vision is best presented in the language of ordinary men. Browning, Hopkins, and Hardy wrote as if the barrier were not there, but most Victorian poets found the supporting systems of traditional poetry indispensable.

A typical example, from Tennyson's *Morte d'Arthur* (1842) will show how densely the features are present, even in a relatively short extract:

> Dry clashed his harness in the icy caves
> And barren chasms, and all to left and right
> The bare black cliff clanged round him, as he based
> His feet on juts of slippery crag that rang
> 190   Sharp-smitten with the dint of armèd heels –
> And on a sudden, lo! the level lake,

And the long glories of the winter moon.
   Then saw they how there hove a dusky barge,
Dark as a funeral scarf from stem to stern,
195 Beneath them; and descending they were ware
That all the decks were dense with stately forms
Black-stoled, black-hooded, like a dream – by these
Three Queens with crowns of gold – and from them
            rose
A cry that shivered to the tingling stars,
200 And, as it were one voice, an agony
Of lamentation, like a wind, that shrills
All night in a waste land, where no one comes,
Or hath come, since the making of the world.

There are a number of features that one could point to as poetic. 'Dry' in line 186 is an adverb without the -ly ending; 'based' in line 188 is a poetic form of 'placed'; 'armed' in line 190 is both an archaism and a metrical make-weight; 'hove' is a poetic archaism, 'ware' in line 195 is an archaic form of 'aware'; and 'hath' in line 203 is an archaic form. In almost every line of the long poem there is some uncommon or poetic usage that reminds us that we are in touch with non-prosaic, non-familiar language. The archaic words in this poem help to transport us back in time, but there are some occasions in Victorian poetry where the diction might seem to be archaic, but is actually closer to the poetic, since the intention is not especially to take us back in time, rather to take us into some alien poetic world. Words such as *teen, dole, ween, sooth, doom* (for judgement) and odd formations such as *foughten, holp, glode,* etc. are often used by Rossetti, and yet he does not always wish to remove us from the present time; it is rather that he wants to latch on to a strange diction that will withdraw us from this world, and take us into an imagined rather than a specific world of the past. The Blessed Damozel enters what looks like a medieval heaven, but *so* stylized and consciously archaic as to be almost a fake to be enjoyed on Victorian terms. It is as if Rossetti intended it to be viewed that way. Hopkins was impatient with archaism, even, it would appear, when it was used in appropriate contexts, such as Bridges's 'Ulysses':

I must add there was another fault I had to find with
Ulysses and it was to the same effect and defect, of
unreality; I mean the archaism of the language, which was
to my mind overdone. I hold that by archaism a thing is
sicklied o'er as by blight. Some little flavours, but much
spoils, and always for the same reason – it destroys
earnest: we do not speak that way . . . .[4]

It is obviously not the 'pale cast of thought' that is bothering Hopkins here but unnatural poetic diction. Hopkins did not like all the contractions (such as *e'er* and *ne'er*) which had been the stock-in-trade of poets for centuries – mainly because their employment facilitated scansion. Neither did he like the poetic formulae – such as the 'say nots' and 'what times'. Sometimes these phrases have an archaic flavour; sometimes they transport us from the present, but not necessarily into the past – rather into some curiously timeless world of poetry.

It is an unfortunate fact that the language poets use was largely derived from Spenser; he of course forged a language for specific archaizing purposes, but his imitators usually forgot that, so that often their diction inadvertently has an other-worldly flavour. Another great seminal figure was Milton, and his language was also created for specific purposes, which his imitators likewise frequently forgot. One of the most essential features of poetic diction is periphrasis, and examples are readily found in the Victorian Parnassians. It is a device that by definition turns its back on common usage, and it tends to be used by poets who sense a very clear demarcation between words available for poetry and those beyond the pale. Tennyson felt that he could not introduce 'champagne' into *In Memoriam*, so he has 'the foaming grape of eastern France' instead (Epilogue, l. 80). A notorious example is 'the knightly growth that fringed his lips' in the *Morte d'Arthur*, which is not so far removed from the intentionally amusing 'bristled grunters' of *The Princess*. But some examples of this device are beautiful, as when icebergs are called 'moving isles of winter' in the *Morte d'Arthur*. The kingfisher is 'the sea-blue bird of March' in *In Memoriam*, and the dandelion is 'the flower,/That blows a globe of after arrowlets' in *Gareth and Lynette*. Modern readers usually disapprove of periphrasis, perhaps because they see it as a branch of euphemism, perhaps because they instinctively resist notions of demarcation within a *parole*, but for poets writing in a high poetic style this awareness of demarcation amounts to a kind of poetic tact, and not to have it leads to disaster. The central cause of William McGonnigal's sublime ineptitude (and he has rightly been identified as one of the greatest bad poets of all time) is that he utterly lacked any sense of this tact. Periphrasis leads ·to emblem and conceit, in which abstracts are given the power to act – as in a line such as 'And all the pavement streamed with massacre' in 'The Last Tournament'. In this sense it is close to the central energizing sources of poetry. Often in Tennyson it is employed when he feels the need to interpose a mysterious veil between himself and what is seen. Tennyson's activating imagination is also on display when he employs functional change – when he makes a noun perform as a verb (although he is not always original of course): he is fond of 'orb', 'round', and 'gloom' as verbs, and likes to emphasize the process of becoming by adding the preposition 'into' – as is 'orb into the perfect star' in *In Memoriam*, XXIV.

Another device for cramming density into words and making language operate in a way far removed from prose is the compound epithet. Bernard Groom has listed the various combinations.[5] Some of them, such as the adjectival, were common in Spenser. Prose writing does not eschew compounds altogether, but it can be claimed that when it employs them it is moving towards the syntactical character of poetry and dissolving some of the formal and logical relations normally determined by such things as particles.

This discussion of compounds demonstrates one of the problems that arises when one tries to overemphasize the divisions between poetry and what has been called 'ordinary language'. The following section deals with points at which poetry draws very close to the practices of 'ordinary language', and certainly the principles on which poetic discourse operates are different from those of everyday discourse, even though at the local level they may look very similar. Compound epithets, for instance, do after all exist in ordinary speech. Hopkins hoped that he was drawing on the energies of colloquial speech, and no doubt as he composed he was; but many readers who first encounter him may be forgiven for thinking that they have stumbled on a high poetic aesthete. So that although compounds are familiar in everyday speech lines like

           curls
Wag or crossbridle, in a wind lifted,
   windlaced –
See his wind- lilylocks -laced;

('Harry Ploughman', ll. 12–13)

hardly sound familiar, and not merely because the noun 'lilylocks' is parenthetically inserted into the compound 'wind-laced'. Although it is probably the case that poetic diction will never appear in everyday speech (except in the conversational equivalent of quotation marks) many of the other features we are considering in this chapter – such as alliteration, assonance, inversion, functional change, and compounding – do come into its ambit. This should be borne in mind as the following examples are considered. It may be that many of the features of the Parnassian and Delphic tradition are different from ordinary speech in degree rather than kind, and that we should be thinking about these differences along the lines proposed by Stanley Fish.[6]

In word coining the relationship between 'ordinary language' and poetic language is highly problematic. Poets are more inventive than the average man or woman, and put more pressure on the language.

Sometimes their inventiveness makes a considerable contribution to the ordinary language. It is often said that Shakespeare played an important part in the formation of the language we use. More usually though the innovations remain within the pale of poetic language. Milton and Spenser are supposed to have contributed very little, but we owe 'pandemonium' and 'blatant' to them. The ordinary language has grown by the use of prefixes and suffixes; so too has the poetic language, but it is often the case that poetic coinings do not enter the common domain. Tennyson has a penchant for the prefix *dis-*, which produces the rare coinings *dislink, dishelm, discage, disprince, disedge*, and *disroot*. Browning and Hardy, on the other hand, favoured the prefix *un-*, the former producing the very strange 'unbutted at, unbickered with' (*Bishop Blougram's Apology*, l. 894), the latter *unbe, undreaming, unadornment*, and *unrueing*. Hopkins's use of the prefix produces some powerful and unusual words – *unchancelling, unchilding* and *unfathering*, the last two in the same line in *The Wreck of the Deutschland*. *In-* and *en-* prefixes often create poetic-sounding words: in Tennyson one finds *inswathe, immantle, encarnalize, empanolpy*, and *ensepulchre*; in Browning *enarm, enchase, encircle, enhaloed, enisled*, and *enwreathe*. Of course the *en-* prefix exists in ordinary language, but from Spenser onwards it has been utilized by poets wishing to withdraw from the commonalty. Another prefix common to both ordinary speech and high poetry is *a-*. In a sense its continuing possibilities for ordinary speech are dead, since ordinary speech is not now utilizing it for innovation, so that there is a clear demarcation between ordinary words such as *astride, astraddle*, and *aflutter* and *abloom, adown, anear, agrin, anight, ablush, abubble, achuckle, a clatter, acrackle, acrumble, aflare, aflaunt, aglimmer, aseethe, asimmer, asmoke, atangle, awhirl*, and *awing*. These poetic words are found in Tennyson and Browning.

Suffixes too have been a great resource in the expansion of English vocabulary. Poets have contributed to this growth, and many a word ending in *-y* is not normally regarded as poetic, even though it was a favoured poetic suffix in the Renaissance. Similarly the suffixes *-ness, -ful, -ity, -ize, -ify, -ery*, and *-some* have all made new words possible in the language we use, even though many of the words thus coined have never entered into common use, and have remained strictly poetic. Many of these suffixes make functional change possible – so that, for instance, a noun may become a verb. These have contributed energy and strangeness to poetry. The poetic lexicon is rich in these words, but to add prefixes and suffixes does not necessarily guarantee Parnassian beauty. It might only guarantee oddity. Tennyson and Browning have been lumped together for the purpose of this discussion, yet ultimately their linguistic purposes are different. When Tennyson cultivates ugly and harsh sounds, as he does sometimes, there remains an impression that they are suspended in the thick amber-like medium of poetry. These lines in *Maud* are hysterical and strained, and every feature (the compound, the assonance, the alliteration, the metaphors) contributes to the uncanny effect, yet we remain aware that it is a poetry directly in line with the Parnassian tradition:

> I remember the time, for the roots of my hair were
> stirred
> By a shuffled step, by a dead weight trailed, by a
> whispered fright,
> And my pulses closed their gates with a shock on
> my heart as I heard
> The shrill-edged shriek of a mother divide the
> shuddering night.
> (I. 13–16)

But with Browning, and to large degree with Hardy, the case is different. They seem to wish to stand aside from the tradition, and produce something less coated in amber gum. This is not to say that their work is exactly colloquial; it would be better to describe it as 'quasi-colloquial'. Certainly it is strange.

Browning was one of those rare birds who reads dictionaries. He is supposed to have read Johnson's *Dictionary* as other people read novels. To encounter words in this way is to see them free from association and context – as rich and isolated phenomena, full of suggestive possibilities. His vocabulary is from widely scattered spheres – science, religion, philosophy, art – and unlike Tennyson he was not enamoured of sound for its own sake; it had to connect with a thinking mind, or a 'soul' as he would have called it. A glance at some of his odd suffixes and prefixes suggests the nature of his strangeness: *cousinry, gossipry, varletry, playsome, pranksome, beseemingness, darlingness, griefful, blinkard, plenitudinous, morbidy, dissheathe, celestiality.* Indeed, if one were to engage on a full-length study of Browning's language it might be more profitable to consider him alongside imaginative prose writers such as Carlyle, Ruskin, and Meredith. These stretch and bend the language to do their bidding, and produce something strange and distinctive. It may be that the label one should use to describe the works of Browning and these prose writers is Hopkins's term 'Olympian' – which he defines as 'the language of strange masculine genius which suddenly, as it were, forces its way into the domain of poetry without naturally having a right there'.[7] Much of the character of Browning's language arose from his scepticism about words – the kind of thing one sees no trace of in Tennyson:

> Because perceptions whole, like that he sought
> To clothe, reject so pure a work of thought
> As language: thought may take perception's place
> But hardly co-exist in any case,
> Being its mere presentment.
>
> (*Sordello*, II. 589–93)

Perhaps the difference between Tennyson and Browning may be seen most typically in their contrasting attitudes to allusion. There is a well-known story of Churton Collins recognizing various allusions in Tennyson's work of which the poet was not himself conscious.[8] However, Collins was not so very wide of the mark, since Tennyson wished to pursue the same trail as his forebears, and it was inevitable that there should be echoes, both conscious and unconscious, and that his works should be in contact with the vast web of previous literature. Christopher Rick's splendid edition of Tennyson (1969; Second Edition 1987) indicates hundreds of allusions, and even in the cases where they are probably not conscious one is aware that the lines are making contact with the complicated poetic fabric woven in previous centuries. Allusion fits into the general atmosphere of cultural reminiscence which is so prevalent in Tennyson. There is a strongly classical vein in his poetry, and poetry of this kind tends to thrive more on remembered phrases and *topoi* than poetry straining to be original. *In Memoriam* is a richly allusive poem, and it is right that it should be, since it makes contact with previous elegies both on the large-scale formal level and in details of phrasing.

In *Richard III* Clarence speaks of the pain of drowning:

> but still the envious flood
> Kept in my soul, and would not let it forth
> To seek the empty, vast and wandering air.
>
> (I. 4 37–39)

In *In Memoriam* the phrasing is subtly modified to describe a mother praying for her son at sea:

> while thy head is bowed,
> His heavy-shotted hammock-shroud
> Drops in his vast and wandering grave
>
> (VI. 16)

In *Hamlet* the ghost at morning 'started like a guilty thing' (I. 1. 148); in Wordsworth's *Immortality Ode* the 'blank misgivings' of man are described, 'moving about in worlds not realised,/High instincts before which our mortal Nature/Did tremble like a guilty Thing surprised'. In *In Memoriam*, either in reality or nightmare, the poet creeps to Hallam's door 'like a guilty thing' (VII. 7). The literary reminiscence helps him to become a ghost almost like Hallam, and the poem derives from the play, by a process of association, something of the mystery of obscure guilt. These lines are followed by 'He is not here', which immediately summons up 'He is not here, but is risen' of Luke 24. 6. The lines "Tis better to have loved and lost/Than never to have loved at all' echo Lovelace's cavalier love poetry, but in a manner that suggests debate with the predecessor. Tennyson's 'loss' is probably greater than that evinced by the light love lyric, in which 'loss' *may* be connected with betrayal, and the love has the intensity of traditional erotic love, but not its precise character. Tennyson's love is more like the religious love of George Herbert, and the Prologue does, as Churton Collins observed, look like 'a transfusion' from the seventeenth-century Divine – although Tennyson was not conscious of this and commented, 'No, close as it seems.'[9] Such closeness is inevitable for a poet working in a great humanist tradition. In these examples the allusive method is at its most active, since direct reference is being made to previous works, either to support or modify their gist. There are hundreds more examples where Tennyson is catching the note or the voice of other poets, not so as to engage with specific lines or definite sentiments, but to share in their poetic spirit. The cloud in *In Memoriam* that 'onward drags a labouring breast' (XV. 18) is very like (though not precisely like) *L'Allegro*'s 'Mountains on whose barren breast/The labouring clouds do often rest' (ll. 73 – 74), but Tennyson did not intend that we should make any specific connection between these lines at this point. We are into the world here of reminiscence or half-reminiscence rather than pointed and functional allusion.

With Arnold the allusive method is similar: reference to classical and English poetry sometimes establishes definite contact with predecessors and at other times is sharing in the pervasive sense of the poetic language. Browning is different. He did not see himself writing classical poetry with a lifeline to the past. Some of his characters might make the occasional literary allusion, but when Browning writes as narrator or in *Propria Persona* he almost never wishes to remind readers of other authors or other poetic traditions. As Bernard Groom pointed out[10] he borrows from Shakespeare, but from out-of-the-way places, and the plants he pulls up tend not to have soil clinging to the roots; 'chop-fallen', 'let me the canakin clink', 'lily-livered', and 'clapper-clawing' come from *Hamlet, Othello, Macbeth*, and *Merry Wives* respectively, but the average reader would be hard put to remember the original context. The plays, in effect, are just another quarry from which to mine recondite and startling words. From Milton he gets not fine-sounding phrases (as Tennyson might), but 'scrannel' ' (*The Ring and the Book*, VI. 1000). There are exceptions to this rule however. In *The Ring and the Book* the word 'relume' is used twice, both times in connection with the Promethean power of art and the representation of events (I. 738; VI. 148). 'Relume', like 'incarnadine', is one of those rare Shakespearean words that invariably reminds us of its original context; in other words, the soil is always clinging to the roots, and we are always reminded of the Promethean power of which Othello speaks in his final scene.

Clough uses allusion interestingly – and so far as Arnold was concerned it was a further indication that he was veering away from the poetical. He seems to adumbrate certain Modernist poets, such as Eliot and Pound, in citing poets from the past, but mainly with a view to suggesting that the present has progressed an ironical distance. So when he borrows from *Macbeth* it is the famous word 'incarnadine':

> Should I incarnadine ever this inky pacifical
> > finger,
> Sooner far should it be for this vapour of Italy's
> > freedom
> > > (*Amours*, II. 74–75)

But unlike Macbeth the word in his mouth puts him further from the experience. Religious and poetical phrases are common in Clough, but always held at arm's length with tweezers. In *The Bothie* the Homeric Phrase 'cloud-compelling' appears, but associated with tobacco rather than Zeus. James Thomson also uses this mock-heroic epithet in 'Polycrates on Waterloo Bridge'.

We saw earlier that the classical vision inevitably found its expression in the Parnassian tradition, but Clough presents an interesting paradoxical case, since his classicism is perhaps like Pope's – easily aware of the mock-heroic and of the limitations when a highly poetic style is applied to modern life. He values poetry, but unlike Tennyson does not find it an all-engulfing force in life: there are things more immediate and urgent, perhaps even more important and more truthful. He does not wish to offer the victim 'to the mere possible shadow of Deity' (*Amours*, II. 94), especially if that victim happens to be himself. Clough's friend Arnold, however, although he tried at times to catch the conversational tone (see below, pp. 43–44) did not have strong inclinations to leave the Parnassian tradition. His stiff pieces of classicism – such as *Sohrab and Rustum* and *Balder Dead* – are famous, notorious even.

One has the very strong impression that the classical tradition is much less effective when it is applied to modern subjects. *Thyrsis* could be open to criticism if one were unsympathetic, but as a swan-song of pastoralism it occupies a special place in readers' affections – especially Oxonian readers. We get a sense of the tiredness of the tradition in considering two less well-known poems, 'Stanzas from Carnac' and 'A Southern Night.' These grow from personal experience, of the death of his brother William at Gibraltar in April 1859. But put alongside Wordsworth's 'Elegiac Stanzas' (also mourning the death of a brother) they are weak. In 'Carnac' there is one powerful image

> But, on the horizon's verge descried,
> Hangs, touched with light, one snowy sail!
>
> (ll. 31–32)

It is very like the evocative sail image associated with the bringing of friends in 'Tears, Idle Tears'. But the poem makes excessive use of exclamation, apostrophe, and rhetorical questioning, and somehow it seems not to have the kind of emotional or linguistic energy that would make one tolerant towards the inversions, the elision of 'o'er', the poetic 'lave' that provides a handy rhyme for 'wave', and the poetic 'strand' that performs likewise for 'land'. 'A Southern Night' has similar faults. It too seems to grow from emotions experienced in a real place at a specified time (in this case Cette on the Mediterranean, so he is only a few yards from Valéry's *Cimitière Marin*), but it does not really spring to life. 'Of yore' is a poetic archaism. 'O'er frowns' is a poetic compound. He likes nouns propped on either side by adjectives – 'glistening houses white' and 'bodily anguish keen' (this was one of Milton's favourite combinations). The second person singular is used (a poeticism, since this form had more or less disappeared from common speech). 'The limbs their wonted tasks refuse' (l. 41) is a very eighteenth-century-sounding line. There is an image of a girl 'with furtive step and cheek of flame' coming from a 'castle bower' (ll. 101–02), and Kenneth Allott has observed that 'the Byronic romanticism of this vignette was outmoded even in 1859.'[11] 'Plaint' is a poeticism – forced on Arnold for reasons of scansion, and 'lucid sheen' is perhaps necessary as a rhyme for 'serene'. This poem only comes to life when the poeticisms are forgotten for a while, and Arnold writes about one of his persistent themes: the buried life:

> And glance, and nod, and bustle by,
> And never once possess our soul
> Before we die.
>
> (ll. 70–72)

He fails to grip on to experience by over-using the word 'some'. Considering how much strain had been placed on this word by Parnassian poets it was a wonder it had any poetic life left in it at all when Yeats took it up as one of his favourite words!

Parnassianism did not altogether die out with the Victorians; as I have said it survived in minor poets at the beginning of this century – Bridges, Brooke, Noyes, the young Wilfred Owen, and countless more. It was a helpful crutch to young poets, since almost without effort, without vision, without original experience even, one could produce something not so very far removed from the work of giants. Modernism destroyed it, left poets out in the cold, and forced them to draw on contemporary resources and lived experiences as the subject of the poetry. One should not condemn the Parnassian tradition utterly though, since to do so would be to deprive oneself of some beautiful and even strange poetry, which can offer pleasures characteristically Victorian and not to be found in the harsher tones of Modernism.

The colloquial tradition

We have just been considering Victorian poetry in its most artificial guise. That tradition produced some very beautiful and striking poetry, but much of it is not to the liking of modern readers brought up on the harsher fare of Eliot, Pound, late Yeats, Auden, and MacNeice. They like their poetry to have the immediacy of familiar speech, to stay close to the contours of the familiar world, in the words of Eliot assiduously to obey 'the law that poetry must not stray too far from the ordinary everyday language which we use and hear'.[12] The desire for colloquial immediacy is not however new, and not the special prerogative of our century. It goes right back to the Middle Ages, to the time when Chaucer and Langland sought to inject into their work the kind of power that derives from simple and direct speech. The extreme forms of visionary and lyrical and bardic poetry had existed in an environment separate from the familiar and diurnal, but there has also been a good deal of poetry through the centuries that has not espoused such separatism, and has exploited the sense of urgency and commitment to be derived from the belief that its statements are close to those of the real world. Previous centuries did not necessarily make so strong a separation between literature and other forms of discourse as we do, and rhetorical practice recognized the category of low or familiar style.[13] To adopt a low style in the Middle Ages or the Renaissance did not mean that one abandoned *all* the metrical and rhetorical resources available, and whereas in our century it would be possible to find some poems totally indistinguishable from everyday speech, this state of affairs would not have existed then. Readers would have recognized a poem as a poem, but unlike us they would not necessarily have thought that it was thereby disqualified from making a true statement or, to allude to Auden, from making something happen.

The colloquial tradition was very strong in sixteenth- and seventeenth-century poetry, and one factor in this situation was the dominant influence of Shakespeare, who was at once a poet and a dramatist. Even before Shakespeare wrote, the strain was very vigorous in Wyatt and Sidney, and it continued in Donne. Pope and Dryden carry on the tradition; one nearly always has the sense that they are speaking to us, not singing to us. For readers whose knowledge of literature goes back no further than the Romantic Movement it might seem that Wordsworth was making a revolutionary statement when he said that he wanted to utilize the language of common men, but it only seems revolutionary in the context of his immediate predecessors, who had indeed come to regard poetry as a separate dialect, operating in a thoroughly alien register. Perhaps without even quite knowing it himself Wordsworth was recalling poetry to a former healthy condition. John Drinkwater made observations similar to these more than sixty years ago: 'Good minds make good speech, and cumulatively they give the common diction of an age a character which cannot escape the poets when poetry has any health in it, which, to do it justice in looking back over five hundred years of achievement, is nearly always.'[14] When Wordsworth recommended the language of ordinary men it was not merely that he wanted to drop the gaudy phraseology of the eighteenth century into the deepest part of Windermere with a stone round its neck; he wanted to get at truth in the kind of way that we have access to it in conversation when we know that there is a close relationship between our words and what is being discussed. He wanted to avoid the anaesthetizing effect that sometimes comes with poetry, even great poetry, and to present truth in as unvarnished a guise as possible. Coleridge picked many holes in Wordsworth's theory, but I am not sure that he ever properly understood this central point about it. Following in the footsteps of Wordsworth, Arnold thought that 'the language, style and general proceedings of a poetry which has such an immense task to perform [the task, that is, of replacing orthodox religion as a *magister vitae*], must be very plain direct and severe', and he wrote to Clough in October 1852:

> More and more I feel the difference between a
> mature and a youthful age of the world compels the

poetry of the former to use great plainness of speech as compared with that of the latter, and that Keats and Shelley were on a false track when they set themselves to reproduce the exuberance of expression, the charm, the richness of images, and the felicity of the Elizabethan poets.[15]

The colloquial impetus in poetry can take one in two directions. On the one hand it can go towards grand and stark effects, almost along the lines of what Archibald Macleish would call 'public speech'. Most of Wordsworth's *Prelude* is in this vein. It is grand, stark and plain. As Wordsworth phrased it, the language is 'purified of its defects'. But the other direction is towards the informal, chatty, low-key, anti-poetic (or at least anti high-poetic). The Romantic poet who took this direction is Byron, but he often gets left out of surveys of the influence of Romantic poetry on subsequent poetry, since critics are obsessed with following the visionary and psychologically serious tradition. The influence of the serious and melodramatic Byron, the Byron of *The Guiaour* and *Childe Harold*, did untold harm (fortunately most of it outside the English-speaking world), but the influence of the sceptical and humorous Byron, though less strong, was largely beneficial. Arnold took a dim view of the sceptical Byron, but his friend Clough derived great help and inspiration from him. The mastery of an easy-flowing, inquiring, relaxed English in *Don Juan* is one of the unmitigated delights of English poetry, and at his best Clough achieves something reminiscent of Byron:

Some of Clough's poems are as prosaic as it is possible for poetry to be, in terms of syntax and diction – although perhaps 'prosaic' is not quite the right word, since they actually partake of the liveliness and dramatic emphasis of good audible speech rather than written prose. 'The Music of the World and of the Soul' is a good example:

> Why should I say I see the things I see not,
>> Why be and be not?
> Show love for that I love not, and fear for what I
>> fear not?
> And dance about to music that I hear not?
>> Who standeth still i' the street
>> Shall be hustled and justled about;
> And he that stops i' the dance shall be spurned
>> by the dancers' feet, –
> Shall be shoved and be twisted by all he shall meet,
>> And shall raise up an outcry and rout;

> And the partner, too, – What's the partner to
> do?
> (ll. 1–11)

The poem goes on to describe a secret music that addresses the inner
man. Clough was a painfully honest and questioning man; with his
scrupulosity, his scepticism, and his originality it was inevitable that
he should find it difficult to work within a given system – whether
the system was an Oxford college or the traditional schemes of poetry.
His favourite resource was a poetic form in which it was possible to
hide the technical features so completely that the inattentive reader
might be excused for thinking certain works formless. In our time
Philip Larkin has adopted a similar approach. Two passages from
Clough will suffice:

> Philip shall write us a book, a Treatise upon *The laws of*
> *Architectural Beauty in Application to Women*;
> Illustrations, of course, and a Parker's Glossary
>   pendent,
> Where shall in specimen seen be the sculliony
>   stumpy-columnar,
> (Which to a reverent taste is perhaps the most
>   moving of any,)
> Rising to grace of true woman in English the
>   Early and Later,
> Charming us still in fulfilling the Richer and
>   Loftier stages,
> Lost, ere we end, in the Lady-Debased and the Lady
>   Flamboyant.
>   (*The Bothie of Tober-na-Vuolich*, ii. 144–51)

(John Henry Parker (1806–84) was a scholar of Gothic architecture, and
produced a 'Glossary of Terms' in 1836).

The following extract is from Canto iv of *Amours de Voyage*:

> What shall I do? Go on through the Tyrol,
>   Switzerland, Deutschland,
> Seeking, an inverse Saul, a kingdom, to find only
>   asses?
> There is a tide, at least, in the *love* affairs of
>   mortals,
> Which, when taken at flood, leads on to the
>   happiest fortune, –

Leads to the marriage-morn and the orange-flowers
                                    and the altar,
And the long lawful line of crowned joys to
                            crowned joys succeeding. –
Ah, it has ebbed with me! Ye gods, and when it
                            was flowing,
Pitiful fool that I was, to stand fiddle-faddling
                    in that way!
                                    (ll. 31–38)

It is fairly typical of the texture of the poem; there is a nice alternation from the fine-sounding and the familiarly poetic (ll. 35 and 36 for instance) to the bathetic and slangily idiomatic at line 38. Lines 33 and 38 *could* be scanned and read aloud as regular hexameters, but working against the standard pattern there is a freer and more informal movement, and of course in line 33 there is an arch-extension and qualification of the serious lines in *Julius Caesar* (IV. 3. 217–20). Likewise in line 32 there is an ironic inversion of I Samuel 9–10. The whole poem could sustain detailed analysis of this kind, but most of its telling effects arise from the subtle interplay of the colloquial and the traditionally poetic. There are a number of italicized sections which are like the italicized sections in Virginia Woolf's *The Waves* in that they operate in another more serious dimension – perhaps like the other-worldly dimension of 'the music of the soul' discussed earlier, of lyrical plangency.

A Clough poem in which the poetic is played off against the colloquial is the long semi-dramatic *Dipsychus* (alas, unfinished; how many reams of Browning's dross one would gladly sacrifice to have *Dipsychus* complete). In this poem a serious and earnest figure is taunted by a Spirit who is a combination of Mephistopheles and extreme eighteenth-century sceptics. One should not forget, incidentally, that the inquiring traditions of the free-thinking thought of the previous century were much more alive in Clough than in most of his contemporaries. The visit to the Lido in Venice accentuates very strongly the contrast between the colloquial tradition (which does not have to be sceptical, but often is) and something more high-flown:

DIPSYCHUS
Vineyards and maize, that's pleasant for sore eyes.
                    SPIRIT
And on the island's other side,
The place where Murray's faithful Guide
Informs us Byron used to ride.

DIPSYCHUS

These trellised vines! enchanting! Sandhills, ho!
The sea, at last the sea – the real broad sea –
Beautiful! and a glorious breeze upon it.

SPIRIT

Look back; one catches at this station
Lagoon and sea in combination.

DIPSYCHUS

On her still lake the city sits,
Where bark and boat about her flits,
No dreams, her soft siesta taking,
Of Adriatic billows breaking.
I do; and see and hear them. Come! to the sea!

SPIRIT

The wind I think is the *sirocco*.
Yonder, I take it, is Malmocco.
Thank you! it never was my passion
To skip o'er sand-hills in that fashion.

DIPSYCHUS

Oh, a grand surge! we'll bathe; quick, quick!

undress!

Quick, quick! in, in!
We'll take the crested billows by their backs
And shake them. Quick! in, in!
And I will taste again the old joy
I gloried in so when a boy.

SPIRIT

Well; but it's not so pleasant for the feet;
We should have brought some towels and a sheet.

DIPSYCHUS

In, in! I go. Ye great winds blow,
And break, thou curly waves, upon my breast.

SPIRIT

Hm! I'm undressing. Doubtless all is well –
I only wish these thistles were at hell.
By heaven, I'll stop before that bad yet worse is,
And take care of our watches – and our purses.

DIPSYCHUS

Aha! come, come – great waters, roll!
Accept me, take me, body and soul! –
        Aha!

SPIRIT

Come, no more of that stuff,
I'm sure you've stayed in long enough.

(Scene 6, 188–223)

At the Lido they are on sacred ground, since this is where Shelley and Byron used to come riding. Shelley's 'Julian and Maddalo' describes 'the bare strand of hillocks' and the contact with a romanticized nature made by swimming echoes the serious Byron of *Childe Harold*, IV:

> And I have loved thee, Ocean! and my joy
>   Of youthful sports was on thy breast to be
> Borne, like thy bubbles, onward: from a boy
>   I wantoned with thy breakers – they to me
>   Were a delight; and if the freshening sea
> Made them a terror – 'twas a pleasing fear,
>   For I was as it were a child of thee,
> And trusted to thy billows far and near,
> And laid my hand upon thy mane – as I do
>   here.
>   (IV. 174)

Dipsychus is partly colloquial, but he adopts poetic phrases that he takes seriously. The Spirit undercuts, and the emphatic feminine rhymes introduce humorous touches rather as they did in the comic Byron. There is a sense in which Clough, like Byron, perpetrates 'the spoiler's art', but not exactly in a Philistine fashion – it is more that he wants to investigate the terms on which serious and traditional poetry operates, so as to suggest that in questioning and revising it there may be ways of being less deceived. For readers accustomed only to modern poetry there will not be much of a sense of surprise that words such as 'towels', 'purses', and 'watches' should appear in poetry, but in most eighteenth-century serious poetry and a good deal of Romantic poetry, even assuming the objects were allowed in (as Touchstone finds, a watch is very hostile to a pastoral environment), they would have to be doctored by periphrasis.

The adoption of this colloquialism did not take place without a protest. Coleridge had severe misgivings concerning the unmusicality of Wordsworth, and a few decades later we find more dissension between old friends. Arnold complained, in a letter of 24 February 1848, of 'a growing sense of the deficiency of the *beautiful*' in Clough's poems.[16] There was a marked difference between the two poets: in *The Scholar Gipsy*, for instance, Arnold was able to take the pastoral seriously in a way that would have been impossible for Clough, even though the Cumnor countryside had cast a magical spell over him too; the comic or the speculative would keep breaking in. Nevertheless, Clough did have an influence on his young friend, and one often traces in Arnold's poetry the attempt to capture the natural movement of

speech and the silent speech of brooding introspection. A classic case
is *Rugby Chapel*:

> Coldly, sadly descends
> The autumn-evening. The field
> Strewn with its dank yellow drifts
> Of withered leaves, and the elms,
> Fade into dimness apace,
> Silent; – hardly a shout
> From a few boys late at their play!
> The lights come out in the street,
> In the school-room windows; – but cold,
> Solemn, unlighted, austere,
> Through the gathering darkness, arise
> The chapel-walls, in whose bound
> Thou, my father! art laid.
>
> (ll. 1–13)

The inversion of subject and verb at lines 11 and 12 is typical of poetry,
and the sequence of four adjectives in lines 9 and 10 is hardly conversational, but a great deal of the passage progresses with conversational
relaxation. The three stress lines only just hold it all together. The
second person singular, incidentally, was not exclusively poetic in the
nineteenth century; it was still used in actual serious and earnest
circumstances. Arnold's most famous poem, 'Dover Beach', it is true,
has some of the marks of high poetry on it. The adjectives surrounding
a noun in 'tremulous cadence slow' and 'vast edges drear' are a
Miltonic device, and the compound 'moon-blanched land' is hardly
idiomatic; but there are points where the poem could be written out
as prose, or reported conversation, and more or less accepted as such:

> The sea is calm to-night.
> The tide is full, the moon lies fair
> Upon the straits; – on the French coast the light
> Gleams and is gone; the cliffs of England stand,
> Glimmering and vast, out in the tranquil bay.
> Come to the window, sweet is the night-air!
>
> (ll. 1–6)

There is a poetic inversion in the last line, but without the rhythm
would be too jauntily dactylic. The last stanza has no inversions, and
other than the word 'darkling' no words from the poetic lexicon; it
is, in effect, ordinary language heightened. But of course the created
image and its implications, of a nightmare landscape 'where ignorant
armies clash by night', is not ordinary and familiar.

The quintessential bardic poet in the Victorian age is Tennyson: he even looked like one – when he was not looking like a dirty monk that is. A good deal of his poetry is heightened and poetic, but even he can make use of effective colloquialisms sometimes, and draw closer to familiar speech that prophetic utterance. The colloquial tendency in Tennyson was actually noticed in his own lifetime, as we discover in Pater's 'Essay on Style:' 'How illustrative of monosyllabic effect, of sonorous Latin, of the phraseology of science, of metaphysic, of colloquialism even, are the writings of Tennyson. . . .'[17] Colloquialism will obviously occur when direct speech is inserted into a poem, as it is in 'Mariana' for instance; and there are other occasions where the speech of a persona dominates a whole poem, as in 'Locksley Hall', 'Ulysses', 'Tithonus', and large parts of *Maud*. These lines from *Maud* do not precisely resemble cool prose, but they are not far from the ravings of a paranoiac:

> And the vitriol madness flushes up in the ruffian's
> head,
> Till the filthy by-lane rings to the yell of the
> trampled wife,
> And chalk and alum and plaster are sold to the
> poor for bread,
> And the spirit of murder works in the very means
> of life,
> And Sleep must lie down armed, for the villainous
> centre-bits
> Grind on the wakeful ear in the hush of the
> moonless nights,
> While another is cheating the sick of a few
> last gasps, as he sits
> To pestle a poisoned poison behind his crimson
> lights.
>   (i. 37–44)

'Sleep' is allegorical, and the alliteration in line 44 is planned (although we should remember that strong feeling in real situations is likely to produce alliteration), but there are no inversions in this passage, and it proceeds with emphasis and energy and urgency. A quite different atmosphere pervades Tennyson's 'Tears Idle Tears'. It has a powerful lyrical feeling, so powerful that many readers forget, or never notice, that it has no rhymes. There is some inversion ('by hopeless fancy feigned' for instance), but most of the poem sounds like relaxed reverie, and there are no exclusively poetic words, unless one wants to count 'casement' – which for many Victorians was a perfectly ordinary word. The opening stanza is as natural as could be:

> Tears, idle tears, I know not what they mean,
> Tears from the depth of some divine despair
> Rise in the heart, and gather to the eyes,
> In looking on the happy autumn-fields,
> And thinking of the days that are no more.
>
> (ll. 1–5)

In Tennyson's *œuvre* there is more of this kind of naturalness than one might think.

In any study of colloquialism and poetry Browning must be a prime exhibit. He is of crucial importance. But an immediate caveat has to be made. The examples we have been considering so far are all taken from poems that attempted to sound approximately colloquial; like Wordsworth the poets wanted to have it both ways – they wanted a poetry that had the power, the economy, and the effective sound of poetry proper, but they also wanted the kind of attention and involvement that one experiences when listening to good speech in the real world. But Browning was not after these kinds of effects; he wanted something completely different, even though at first glance his poetry seems to be based on an endeavour to reproduce the world of colloquial speech. Browning is not usually compared to Milton, but his ambitious aims are not dissimilar. He wanted to create a poetry that would operate on his own terms, and the whole range of language was his quarry, but he did not wish to be dominated by provenance and association. Browning goes to colloquialism for inspiration, as it were, not for patterns and models. This is why his poetry is often analogous to colloquialism rather than imitative of it. It partly explains why his poetry has such a prevalent sense of strain – as J. A. Boulton has noticed.[18] Browning's erratic education, psychological make-up, and years of residence in Italy may partly explain his linguistic oddity, and one critic has suggested that Browning's semantic stuttering may have neurotic origins.[19]

Perhaps so, but he was reinforced in his practice by a number of beliefs about poetry and language. One of them was directly derived from the Romantic Movement cult of sincerity and spontaneity. This placed great value on expression, but since expression could be revised and tampered with if committed to paper, then authenticity and sincerity could only be guaranteed if first and immediate thoughts were given special privileges. Browning was so obsessed with this principle that he hated revising, and even when his letters ran into syntactical mud-banks he did not retreat but cherished the accidents as felicitous and significantly inevitable. He was undoubtedly hoping for a kind of clarity and immediacy, and he thought that latching on to colloquial speech was a way of achieving it. In general terms he was on the right track, and in our time William E. Baker has suggested that colloquial syntax 'imitates the assimilation of sense data, the spontaneous formation of thoughts to be uttered, and the coalescing forces underlying consciousness'.[20] But the forces in Browning were too curious and unusual to make for easy understanding! Like many moderns he thought that process was as significant as finish, so he liked to leave the steps to a discovery in view. To follow this procedure is quickly to diverge from traditional standards, since gropings towards sense are in their nature provisional and deviant, even though an auditor might be able to guess the direction a thought is going to take and make sense of the discontinuities. The final stanza of 'Count Gismond' mimics the interrupted flow of a real conversation:

> Our elder boy has got the clear
> > Great brow; tho' when his brother's black
> Full eye shows scorn, it . . . Gismond here?
> > And have you brought my tercel back?
> I was just telling Adela
> How many birds it struck since May.
>
> > > > (ll. 121–26)

But disconcertingly the phrase 'black full eye' is not idiomatic – that is part of the language Browing has fabricated. Most of the poetry has the alarming combination of the over-determined cohabiting with the seemingly under-determined. This is one of the things that on occasion makes him so tiresome.

'Soliloquy of the Spanish Cloister' has the raggedly colloquial 'Gr-r-r – you swine!' but 'fire-new spoon' does not come from any idiomatic world. These effects have some justification when Browning is evoking characters in dramatic situations, but he also makes use of them for his own narrative and poetic voice. One finds examples in Book I of *The Ring and the Book*:

> But human promise, oh how, short of shine!
> How topple down the files of hope we rear!
> > How history proves! . . . nay, read Herodotus
> > > > (ll. 295–97)

The interruption suggests immediacy, but 'short of shine' is a nonce phrase. Over and over again in Browning, passages are encountered that sound as if they might be colloquial (the opening of *Fra Lippo Lippi* for instance), but on further investigation they turn out to be like nothing anyone has ever heard. This suggests that Browning was to a large degree inventing language, spinning it out from his own head, turning his own anxious and insecure relationship to the Queen's English into a poetic virtue. The Italian years seem to have the same impact as Meredith's deafness, Clare's madness, and Rossetti's paranoia: they put him out of touch with natural and urbane speech. But at the same time an accurate reproduction of this speech would have been inappropriate for the poems dealing with previous centuries and foreign countries, and often Browning achieves startling and memorable effects beyond anything that one finds in Tennyson, Clough, and Arnold.

There were various influences on Browning, but one of them was the poetry of Donne, largely neglected since the seventeenth century – a response continued by Palgrave, who omitted him from *The Golden Treasury*.[21] Browning read him avidly, and Donne influenced both his style and his tendency to regard any matter as suitable for poetry – provided it had been fully processed by the mind. Donne's habits of qualification and parenthesis mimic the mind in motion, and Browning follows him; but Browning was much more high-handed with the language than Donne had been, and finally he seems much more outlandish. The strange paradox about Browning is that much of his poetry is very difficult to perform and hear; one would have thought that someone creating in a colloquial tradition would be accessible, but as I suggested earlier, that tradition is a base rather than a complete superstructure. Strangely, one can adopt all the principles of colloquial speech – inversion, functional change, ellipsis, discontinuity, allusion, parenthesis, qualification, and elision – and yet produce something totally unlike it! This is what Browning did. The opening of *Fra Lippo Lippi* is fairly typical:

> Who am I ?
> Why, one, sir, who is lodging with a friend
> Three streets off – he's a certain . . . how d'ye
>   call?
> Master – a . . . Cosimo of the Medici,
> I' the house that caps the corner. Boh! you were
>   best!
> Remember and tell me, the day you're hanged,
> How you affected such a gullet's-gripe!
> But you, sir, it concerns you that your knaves
> Pick up a manner nor discredit you:
> Zooks, are we pilchards, that they sweep the
>   streets
> And count fair prize what comes into their net?

(ll. 14–24)

This is supposedly direct speech, but the main thing it conveys, as does the rest of the poem, is the impression of a strange and quirky idiolect. In general terms that might be right for the particular artist, but it is not always easy to follow.

To a great extent Hopkins also produced an original speech founded on colloquial English, but modern audiences have been more charitable to him than to Browning. One thinks of Hopkins primarily as a musical poet whose works need performance and a range of modulation, variation in pitch, stress, and rhythmic emphasis that is close to music; indeed, he seems to have been searching for a way of producing the verbal equivalent of a musical score. When one first hears Hopkins's poetry one's immediate impression is of extreme unfamiliarity; it certainly does not sound like colloquial speech. And yet it is based on such speech, and the central thesis of W. H. Gardner's and James Milroy's excellent studies of Hopkins's language is that he went much further than Wordsworth, who claimed to be rooting his poetry in the language of men, but in fact is more influenced by 'written prose language' than actual speech.[22] The key statement made by Hopkins about the relationship of his poetry to speech is in a letter to Bridges of 14 August 1879:

> I do avoid [inversions], because they weaken and
> because they destroy the earnestness or inearnestness of the
> utterance . . . . So also I cut myself off from the use of
> *ere, o'er, wellnigh, what time, say not* (for *do not say*),
> because though dignified, they neither belong to nor ever
> could arise from, or be the elevation of ordinary modern
> speech. For it seems to me that the poetical language of an
> age should be the current language heightened, to any
> degree heightened and unlike itself, but (I mean normally,
> passing freaks and graces are another thing) an obsolete
> one.[23]

We can see how much further he has gone than Clough, whose best-known poem begins 'Say not the struggle nought availeth'.

In Hopkins there are instances of where he is close to the staccato and improvisational character of Browning. In *The Wreck of the Deutschland* he is casting around for the right word in a state of excitement and impatience:

> But how shall I . . . me room there:
> Reach me a . . . Fancy, come faster –
> Strike you the sight of it? look at it loom there,
> Thing that she . . . There then! the Master,
> *Ipse* the only one, Christ, King, Head:

(ll. 217–21)

He does not write like this very often, however, and most of his poetry
has the *feel* of colloquial speech – with its emphasis, urgency,
commitment, and vividness – without closely resembling it or aiming
to be any kind of literal transcript. For instance, inversion is often
thought of as primarily a poetic device, but it is also used in conversation, so that if we shout at someone in anger we might add, 'Heard
that did you!' There is also ellipsis here, since a fuller version would
be, 'You heard that did you!' Hopkins reproduces something like this
in the *Wreck*:

> Ah, touched in your bower of bone,
> Are you! turned for an exquisite smart,
> Have you! make words break from me here all
>   alone,
>   Do you!
>   (ll. 137–40)

Sometimes when Hopkins explains a line he makes an appeal to a
colloquial expression, and his gloss helps us both with the meaning and
our performance of the line should we wish to read it aloud. The final
stanza of 'Morning, Midday, and Evening Sacrifice' reads:

> The vault and scope and schooling
>   And mastery in the mind,
> In silk-ash kept from cooling,
>   And ripest under rind –
> What death half lifts the latch of,
> What hell hopes soon the snatch of,
> Your offering, with despatch, of!
>   (ll. 15–21)

In a letter to Bridges of 22 October 1879 Hopkins explains the last line
by way of an appeal to common language: '"Your offer, with
despatch, of" is said like "Your ticket", "Your reasons", "Your
money or your life", "Your name and college"; it is "Come, your
offer of all this (the matured mind), and without delay either!"'[24] There
are many points in Hopkins where the sense becomes clearer if one
listens to the words and thinks of some of the conventions of the
spoken language. Speech often has things missing – relative pronouns
and the like. 'My own heart let me more have pity on' contains ellipsis:

> I cast for comfort I can no more get
> By groping round my comfortless, than
>   blind
> Eyes in their dark can day . . .
>   (ll. 5–7)

In more formal speech we should say, 'I can no more get comfort than blind eyes in their dark can get day'. There is a missing word after 'comfortless' – 'world' perhaps. 'I do advise/You, jaded' in expanded and more formal guise would be, 'I do advise you, since you find yourself in a jaded state'. In 'To seem the stranger' there are lines obviously built on colloquial principles, but without reminding us precisely of actual idioms:

> I am in Ireland now; now I am at a third
> Remove. Not but in all removes I can
> Kind love both give and get.
>   (ll. 9–11)

In common speech we should be more likely to say, 'Not that I cannot both give and get kind love in all removes'. The importance of bearing in mind common speech as the basic matrix behind Hopkins's poetry should always be kept in mind.

The story of colloquial English in poetry continues with Hardy and Yeats and their successors, but that is outside the scope of this book. Hardy did not know Hopkins's work, but he made independent discoveries along the same lines, both in diction and rhythm. In the formative years Yeats did not know Hopkins's work, although he actually met him in Dublin; but as he developed he came to value the direct and uncluttered impact of colloquial speech and moved away from Parnassianism. Likewise Edward Thomas sought a relaxed and casual-seeming movement for his verse, owing a good deal to non-poetic speech, and the terms in which he praised his friend Robert Frost announce a line of development which twentieth-century poets have increasingly followed, and which, as we have seen, was a feature of some nineteenth-century poetry, the poetry which many readers find the most palatable:

> These poems are revolutionary because they lack the
> exaggeration of rhetoric, and even at first sight appear to
> lack the poetic intensity of which rhetoric is an imitation.
> Their language is free from the poetical words and forms
> that are the chief material of secondary poets. The metre
> avoids not only the old-fashioned pomp and sweetness [he
> is probably thinking of Tennyson here], but the later
> fashion also of discord and fuss [he is probably thinking of
> Browning and Meredith here]. In fact, the medium is
> common speech and common decasyllables. . . . Yet
> almost all these poems are beautiful.[25]

This section has considered standard speech, recognizing that this is not a monolithic concept, and that it will shade off into substandard speech and various accents, regional and class. However, a large proportion of the population speaks dialect or non-standard speech, if not all the time at least some of the time, and although observers have been bewailing the disappearance of dialect for generations it is a resilient force in the language and has made a significant impact on the poetry, as has non-standard speech. This impact is the subject of the next section.

Dialect poetry

The colloquial tradition, in what may be termed its main-line stream, owed quite a lot to previous practice, and tended not to produce actual transcripts of direct speech but modifications: ordinary speech 'purged of its defects' as Wordsworth would have put it, or 'ordinary speech heightened' in Hopkins's phrase. This is not to say that a certain amount of poetry was not written which could almost be called 'transcript'; I say almost because many writers experience difficulty in producing exact copies and find, whether they like it or not, that their own habits of speech are carried over even into invented characters. This applies to Browning, whose marked tendency to produce discontinuities and staccato effects in his letters (and one assumes this is very close to the way he talked) also crops up in his characters. Similarly, many of Clough's characters speak like him (again, using the evidence of his letters), but then, unlike Browning's, they are meant to be like him, so that this achieves a kind of immediate realism. So long as the poetry is in standard English, or near-standard, the grey area in between straight transcript and invention is going to be very difficult to map out, but dialect poetry presents us with a slightly different case, where it is possible to see a more emphatic gap between the poet's own voice and his invention. Dialect poetry is a neglected area; in N. F. Blake's *Non-Standard Language in English Literature* (1981), Tennyson and Kipling are the only Victorian poets to earn a mention.

Before the Victorian period there is little or no dialect poetry in English, especially in the sense in which I am using the term here: poetry written in dialect by poets whose normal speech is standard. The leading dialect poet was Robert Burns, who was perfectly capable of writing a standard English, but whose adoption of dialect for the purposes of life and colour was an inspiration to subsequent poets. The two principal exponents of this genre in our period are Barnes and Tennyson. Clare is not quite in this category, since he tends to write in standard English with standard grammar, but with a scattering of dialect words to give rural flavour (rather as Spenser did in the *Shepherdes Calendar*). Sometimes, though, he tried to produce the syntax and the inconsequential flow of rural speech and writing. A good example is the charming 'Country Letter':

> This leaves us well in health, thank God for
> > that!
> For old acquaintance Sue has kept your hat
> Which mother brushes ere she lays it by
> And every Sunday goes upstairs to cry.
> > (ll. 7–10)

Later in the poem the dialect word 'noises' (complains) is used. Like many countrymen Clare was possibly bilingual (the condition Hardy describes in Chapter 2 of *Tess of the d'Urbervilles* where 'the dialect was on [Tess's] tongue to some extent, despite the village school'), and when trying to impress the metropolitan audience the basic matrix of his language was the received standard, but interestingly in the poems of his madness he lapses or reverts (if those are the right words) into dialect. 'Song – Molly Magee' (after 1845) is an example:

> Her back war so white and her leg war so round,
> The sight o't war worth half the coin in a pound,
> But bother the sight it has stolen my e'e,
> I'm blind wi' the beauty o' Molly Magee.
> > (ll. 21–24)

Perhaps he no longer feels the need to ingratiate himself with an educated audience and he is relaxing in a register that he regards as close to his authentic rural self. Certainly many of the poems of the asylum years exhibit this characteristic. This is not to claim that they are not well crafted. In these latter years he is writing something that is more truly dialect poetry, where the whole movement of the speech is unlike that of standard English, and the dialect is not merely a matter of surface decoration and random diction: it is lettered all through. There seems to be a basic authenticity.

Barnes and Tennyson are somewhat different. They both grew up in remote areas where dialect was dominant, but to some degree they were aliens in this environment, and destined as they were from an early age to be members of the establishment they could not afford to be immersed in the local languages of the tribe. At the same time they heard this language every day, and perhaps assumed it, more or less effortlessly, in certain social circumstances. Judging by the wax recordings Tennyson had a trace of a Lincolnshire accent,[26] but accent is not quite the same thing as dialect: a man with a strong local accent would betray his origins in speech, but not necessarily in his writing. A man who could only speak dialect (and in its extreme forms dialect almost amounts to a separate language) would betray himself in both speech and writing.

Barnes's output in dialect poetry is considerable; in Bernard Jones's *The Poems of William Barnes* (Carbondale, Illinois, 1962), there are 579 pages of poems in the Dorset dialect, and 6 pages of glossary. It is a marvellous body of poetry, that deserves to be much better known, and it gives an indication that the scholarly and learned Barnes, like Browning, was strongly gifted with 'negative capability', since many of the poems are in the direct speech of characters, and hence are dramatic monologues. There is a considerable range here, elegiac poetry mourning loss, poetry celebrating love of place and the sense of the past, love poetry, poetry of social comment, and conversational poetry. On the one hand the poems seem to be immediate and naive, but on the other one senses a wide range of classical background and literary tradition behind them. There are eclogues on political themes which clearly relate to parts of *The Shepherd's Calendar* and classical eclogues. Some have Latin titles, but thoroughly vernacular content – such as and 'Rusticus Emigrans' and 'Rusticus Res Politicas Animadvertens'. 'Eclogue: The Common A-Took In' deals with an important topic in the nineteenth century – that common land was being increasingly enclosed by the lord of the manor, thus depriving country folk of the opportunity to collect firewood and graze animals (quite apart from the distressing upheaval of dramatically changed surroundings). This may have been in the early years an issue very remote from the interests of townspeople, but when in 1865 the Commons Preservation Society was founded a part of its policy was the preservation of common land that might give breathing-space to claustrophobic city-dwellers.[27] These political poems of Barnes have a way of going straight to the heart of the matter' as if the voice of the country people is given direct and unmediated articulation:

> 'Tis handy to live near a common;
> But I've a-zeed, an' I've a-zaid,
> That if a poor man got a bit o' bread,
> They'll try to teake it vrom en.
>
> (ll. 59–62)

Another poem called 'The Common A-Took In' celebrates not only the utilitarian advantages of the common land, but the depressed feelings of psychic enclosure once it had gone:

> Oh! no, Poll, no! Since they've a-took
> The common in, our lew wold nook
> Don't seem a bit as used to look
> When we had runnen room.
>
> (ll. 1–4)

Clare also lamented the displacement caused by new developments in agriculture. 'The Flitting' paints a melancholy picture of uprootedness, and it has been described, by John Lucas, with some justification, as 'one of the greatest poems to have been written in the nineteenth century'. He states: 'To the agony of dispossession Clare adds anger, a radiant love for what lives on in memory at least, and finally a wonderful, exuberantly radical sense of triumphing over his enemies.'[28]

In other Barnes poems there are few if any political messages, but the country life is brought before us with sparkling intensity. 'The Waggon A-Stooded' is a vivid piece of dialogue as two carters extricate a vehicle from the mud; 'A Bit O'Sly Coorten' is a charming depiction of country life. The gipsy in 'Haven Woone's Fortune a-Twold' is able to tell girls everything – except that the gipsy's dog is 'a lappen milk vrom ouer pails' at that very moment. There is a whole gallery of crusted characters. It is no wonder that Hardy admired Barnes so much, and produced a selection of his work in 1908. His work is not a curio or a bypath, since he was, as a linguist and a scholar, interested in identifying the native vigour still resident in alternative modes of English, in the hope that 'National English', as he called it, might be revived. He had a strong antipathy to the Latin element in the English language, and a strong love of the Anglo-Saxon element. His interests and attitudes are not so very far removed from those of Hopkins, who took an alert interest in dialect and sometimes incorporates dialect words into his poetry (although he does not write complete poems in dialect).

With the help of the glossary Barnes's dialect poems are not difficult to read – at least not for native English speakers. They are to be strongly recommended, and one can but endorse the words of E. M. Forster: 'He should have been a popular poet, for he writes of matters which move everyone and in a way which everyone can understand.'[29] Barnes was not alone in writing poetry in the dialect of the West Country. At exactly the same time one G. Pulman was publishing charming poems about fishing in the *Sherborne Journal* and other local papers. These were collected as *Rustic Sketches* in 1842. Considerable local piety is on display:

> I've draw'd th'vly in lots of streams
> Ver trout; an'trolld in zummer jacks, But nivver itt ev I
> zeed one
> Za good by half as es th'Axe.

There are parallels with Barnes, since this poet was an educated man, conscious of his predecessors Cotton and Thomson and expecting his readers to recognize and appreciate the highly literary tradition. He was interested in the very particular dialect round Axminster, and regretted that the schoolmaster is 'rapidly and effectually' obliterating it. So the process of enforced linguistic uniformity was well under way even in the decade when Hardy was born! The secretary of the Society of Antiquaries, John Yonge Akerman (whose *Wiltshire Tales* (1853) preserves local dialect), also regretted the disappearance of dialect, in the way that the cultured anthropologist does: 'But the schoolmaster has been active, and material changes have taken place, even in our English dialects, during the last forty years. Time, and the facility of intercommunication, are daily wearing away the traces of an older form of speech . . . and those now amongst us may live long enough to witness still further innovation!'[30] Hardy was later to regret the disappearance of 'varieties of English which are intrinsically as genuine, grammatical, and worthy of the royal-title as is the all-prevailing competitor which bears it', but recognized that, in Darwinian fashion, they were 'worsted in the struggle for existence'.[31] Pulman's poetry is not always easy to make out, but it has great charm, and much of it stands direct comparison with Barnes. The line 'An'zum zes edden' 'xac'ly saff' might take a little deciphering, but it resolves itself into 'And some says it isn't exactly safe' (referring to some newfangled bridge over the Axe).

It was not only in the West Country that educated people were undertaking the record of dialect in poetic form. In Essex Charles Clarke was doing something similar, in Lancashire one finds Edwin Waugh (died 1891), Ben Brierley (died 1896) and Samuel Laycock, and in Lincolnshire John Brown, 'the Horncastle Laureate' (died 1890) and Mabel Peacock. Their work is often accompanied by elaborate footnotes and glossaries, and the kind of local pride in dialect that is found in Barnes; one might almost call it 'county chauvinism'. Most of this poetry is nurtured on agricultural traditions, but in *The Industrial Muse* (1974) Martha Vicinus has demonstrated that it also flourishes in the industrial centres of the North.

Possibly the best-known writer of dialect poems is Tennyson, but it is obvious, when one considers the figures just mentioned, that he is functioning in the midst of a thriving and recognized literary tradition. It is a pity that among many readers of Victorian poetry

Tennyson's dialect poems are completely unknown; certainly in the accepted sense of the word they are completely un-Tennysonian, since they are so full of character and incident and so fully in touch with a hard-headed view of the world. There is a splendid pair of Northern Farmer poems, one depicting an 'old style' of farmer and another a 'new style', the latter, as might be expected very canny and property-mad: he hears the word 'property' obsessively beaten out by the rhythm of the horse's hooves as he canters round the countryside. One recognizes at least that the alertness to a dominant sound and rhythm is truly Tennysonian! He is hostile to the notion of his son marrying for love; he would rather he married for money, and he deals with his son with a mixture of bullying and cajoling. This is a poem that has survived in the recorded archive, and although Tennyson was a great age when he performed it he has forgotten none of the Lincolnshire accent. The 'old style' farmer is an equally strong-minded and vivid character, who asks 'Do godamoighty knaw what a's doing a'taakin' o'mea?' (rather as the original farm bailiff in real life asked). He has a vision of his beloved fields being ploughed by someone 'wi'' is kittle o'steam' and is glad that he will not live to see it: 'But sin' I mun doy I mun doy, for I couldn abear to see it.' There is a vigorous appreciation of character and situation in these two poems that equals and possibly surpasses anything that Browning produced.

The Northern Cobbler (1880) is a temperance tract, about a cobbler who ruined himself with drinking: 'But sin' I wur hallus i' liquor an' hallus as droonk as a king,/Foalks' soostom flitted awaay like a kite wi' a brokken string.' The 'hennemy' is in the bottle, so the cobbler puts it in the window where he can see it and fight it day by day; it is a big bottle, quart size: 'Wouldn't a pint a' sarved as well as a quart? Naw doubt:/But I liked a bigger feller to fight wi' an' fowt it out.' There is a lot of whimsical humour in this poem, it is a minor masterpiece. 'The Spinster's Sweet-Arts' (1885) is an interesting exploration of the psychology of an old maid who queens it over her cats, and has no regrets at not having had children, with 'their bottles o' pap, an' their mucky bibs, an' their clats an' the clouts'. This has the impression of being closely observed, but if Tennyson himself is to be believed the only dialect poem that is actually 'drawn from life' is 'The Village Wife or, The Entail' (1880). *Owd Roa* is a poem about a heroic black retriever; its great strength is that it has a lot of incidental humour deriving from the narrative figure who is using dialect. The Corn Law issue has nothing much to do with a poem about a dog, but it contributes towards lifting it above the usual sentimental animal poem:

> Saw I turned in agean, an' I thowt o' the
> good owd times 'at was goan

> An' the munney they maade by the war, an'
>   the times 'at was coomin' on;
> Fur I thowt if the Staate was a gawin' to
>   let in furriners' wheat,
> Howiver was British farmers to stan'agean
>   o'their feeat?
>   (ll. 43–46)

'Tomorrow' (1885) is an interesting poem, since it is not in the Lincolnshire dialect but the Irish. Tennyson had help with the language from the Irish poet William Allingham. Quite apart from the vividness of the story and the characterization of the heroine Molly Magee, the poem derives strength from the well-evoked narrative character. It tells of the disappearance of Molly's sweetheart Danny O'Roon; for years Molly will not allow anyone else to court her, since she is sure he will show up, and indeed he does, perfectly preserved in a peat bog. By then she is an old crone, but her love is perfectly preserved, and she dies from the shock, so that they can be buried 'like husban' an' wife'. It has all the makings of the worst kind of sentimental Victorian ballad, but it is rescued from this by the seriousness and the flippancy of the narrative figure. Like the Irish bards Yeats celebrated, who immortalized beauties such as Mary Hines, this poet preserves, as in a peat bog, the youthful beauty of Molly, even though the actual woman is 'lamed iv a knee':

> Achora, yer laste little whishper was
>   sweet as the lilt of a bird!
> Achushla, ye set me heart batin' to music
>   wid ivery word!
> An' sorra the Queen wid her sceptre in sich
>   an illigant han',
> An' the fall of yer foot in the dance
>   was as light as snow an the lan'
> An' the sun kem out of a cloud whiniver
>   ye walkt in the shtreet,
> An' Shamus O'Shea was yer shadda, an'
>   laid himself undher yer feet.
>   (ll. 33–38).

Hopkins admired the dialect poems of Barnes and Tennyson, and said that the 'lawful charm' of the genre guaranteed 'the spontaneousness of the thought'.[32] Charles Wilson has an appreciation of the dialect poems, saying, with some justification, that 'save for Chaucer, no one has portrayed bucolic life with technique so consummate or knowledge so intimate',[33] and Sir Charles Tennyson has warmly recommended this part of the *oeuvre*,[34] but generally they have not received the praise they deserve. Tennyson was perhaps influenced in the Irish poem by Thackeray, but Tennyson is superior, since there is not much depth or suggestiveness in Thackeray; he is more or less content to create a comic friction between subject-matter and language, as in 'The Pimlico Pavilion' (*Punch*, August, 1845), 'Mr. Molony's Account of the Ball' (*Punch*, August 1850), and 'The Crystal Palace' (*Punch*, April 1851).

Barnes and Tennyson were educated and cultivated men; it is interesting that they should have written dialect poems, and it is probably to be explained by the fact that standard English did not provide them with the scope for all that they wished to express. They had a catholic interest in the broad range of English, and were continuing a tradition begun in the eighteenth century when poets began to collect and to imitate poems in a wide variety of dialects, past and present. A poet who consciously uses dialect opens a door that provides an exit from the narrowing effects of standard English. Even Swinburne, whose poetry might seem to operate on a rather narrow spectrum, experimented with dialect. There are examples in *Poems and Ballads* (third series). 'The Witch-Mother' is in ballad form:

> And a sair grief sitting at my foot,
> And a sair grief at my head;
> And dule to lay me my laigh pillows
> And teen till I be dead.
>
> (ll. 5–8)

Work of this kind is slightly more familiar than the Tennyson and Barnes examples, since it is attached to the traditions of the true and the fake archaism. Spenser's *Shepherdes Calendar* has already been mentioned, and it will be recalled that in this poem the dialect word and the archaism met, since the non-standard dialect speech often preserved archaic forms. Other Swinburne poems, such as 'A Reiver's Neck-Verse' and 'The Bride's Tragedy' are in this pastiche tradition. 'The Tyneside Widow' is a keening lament, but seemingly distant in time as well as place, and it does not seem to spring from the kind of expertise and affectionate knowledge that informed Tennyson and Barnes, beautiful as it is. One would not go to it to find out how real Geordies spoke; still, one would not do much better going to Joseph Skipsey, who spent his childhood as a 'trapper' in Percy Main Colliery near North Shields. Later in life he was hob-nobbing with the Pre-Raphaelites, and although his poetry grew very directly from working experience, and makes use of common speech, like so many poets brought up in the working class he seizes on the traditional aristocratic and bourgeois language of poetry when he comes to create, and consciously avoids anything like transcript. His work has recently been promoted by Basil Bunting.

A sad but inevitable fact is that poets with every opportunity to hear dialect every day were not able to use it in poetry. There is the case of two Northamptonshire poets, John Plummer and William Askham. Their conditions were not exactly like Clare's (another Northamptonshire man), since they were urban: Plummer was a stay-maker of Kettering and Askham was a 'truant' in the countryside. Their problem was that they took their cue from Parnassian writers such as Gerald Massey, and tended to write in a faded and jaded poetic diction. Plummer's 'The Dying Workman' is a dramatic monologue, but it is in standard speech. Still, Askham has some of the artless and direct descriptive capacity of Clare, and Plummer writes interestingly about trade unions and 'scabs' in *Songs of Labour* (1860), but without reaching into sources of folk speech to any great extent.

Interestingly, Hardy did not write very much dialect poetry, but an early published work was 'The Bride Night Fire' (1875). In revision this was made closer to actual rural speech, so that simple words such as 'crabbed', 'seasons', 'frightened', 'stumbled', and 'bridle-path' were replaced in 1898 by 'thirtover', 'tidetimes', 'gallied', 'lumpered', and 'halter-path', and in the revised edition Hardy provided a glossary. The poem has the stuff of the regional novels, including a skimmity ride, and as so often in his life, Hardy sailed close to the opposing winds of propriety in the story.

The dialect tradition continued in poetry after our period, some of the most successful written by Kipling, in poems such as 'McAndrew's Hymn' and 'The Ladies'. Like Barnes he is fascinated by men at work; he thinks, rightly perhaps, that men are most themselves and at their most admirable when they are pursuing their familiar tasks and talking about them, and so he writes many poems showing men at work. They convey a very strong sense of Britishness, almost certainly sharpened and brought into focus by the years of exile. Another later poet who has employed dialect is D. H. Lawrence, in fine poems like 'The Drained Cup'. 'Whether or Not', 'Violets' and 'The Collier's Wife'. These utilize the North Midlands accent that give such vividness and life to some of the plays and novels.

As N. F. Blake suggests it is the novel which primarily uses dialect, but in that medium it is fraught with difficulties, since the narrative voices in received standard English have the effect of making the dialect speech seem grotesque, inadequate, and substandard. We thereby become alienated from characters using it. Hardy admitted that 'if a writer attempts to exhibit on paper the precise accents of a rustic speaker, he disturbs the proper balance of a true representation by unduly insisting upon the grotesque element'.[35] But in poetry this can be less of a problem, since usually there is not the presence of implied criticism in the shape of standard English, and the dialect speech can make its direct, isolated appeal. It has to be admitted that some readers find dialect poetry difficult and even incomprehensible, and the attempts at phonetic spelling often create a formidable initial obstacle. However, once these difficulties have been overcome there are some rewarding experiences in this body of literature.

Dialect poetry is worth paying attention to because it takes us very rapidly to questions of the persona, characterization, the dramatic monologue and objectivity, as well as questions of 'alternative speech' in poetry, and archaizing poetic diction. Perhaps it does not always have the suggestive beauty of main-line poetry, but its freshness and apparent originality ('apparent' from the metropolitan poet's point of view, that is) can often give literature a shot in the arm – as Synge discovered when he brought the exotic speech of the Aran Islands into the comparatively sophisticated urban theatre. There is always the danger that the educated speaker of standard English will get danger-ously close to facetiousness and condescension when giving phonetic representations of alternative dialects. Tennyson and Barnes seem to avoid it on the whole, but I am not sure that Kipling does not stand accused of a slightly unpleasant jocularity and knowingness. This is hardly the place to debate whether dialect poetry and even dialect novels continue to be possible in an era when education, of a kind, is available to the masses, and much of the speech of the common man is moulded for him by newspapers, radio, and television. Henry James thought it was not; he did not wish to imitate the naturalists, and he could only find charm in dialect that *precedes* the invasion of schools and the sophistication they offer. Otherwise one merely has 'the thick breath' and 'the ugly snarl', 'the bastard vernacular of communities disinherited of the felt difference between the speech of the soil and the speech of the newspaper, and capable thereby, accordingly, of taking slang for simplicity, the composite for the quaint and the vulgar for the natural'.[36] And he had no wish to plumb these 'unutterable depths'.

There remains the problem of where one should put varieties of slang in this study. It is non-standard speech, and exists in all walks of society, from thieves to lawyers, from tradesfolk to university dons. One hears of 'class dialects', and of the special jargon of all kinds of activities, from manufacturing industries to the professions. Very often in these cases the specialized usage is a matter of diction rather than anything more pervasive. Poets have a special alertness to any speech that is out of the ordinary, and they have had an interest in slang and jargon over the ages – one thinks of Ben Jonson and alchemical terms and the splendid reproduction of low-life slang in Canto XI of Byron's *Don Juan*. There is nothing in Victorian poetry quite as splendid as this latter piece, but there is plenty of slang. Clough is excellent at reproducing university slang, especially in *The Bothie*: Browning gives us the special terminology of artists, grammarians, lawyers, theologians, philosophers, and the like; in 'Harry Ploughman' Hopkins's fascination with all the words to do with harnesses leaves its impress on the poem, in words like 'cross-bridle', and when he met countrymen he quizzed them avidly on the special vocabulary of their tackle and trades, and regarded dialect as one of the sources for the renewal of language.[37] The main thing these words of dialect origin have to contribute to poetry is their strangeness; there is not a lot that can be done with them once they are incorporated into the poems, since they have a kind of unassimilable quality about them, by which I mean that they do not dissolve into the surrounding medium, but remain discrete and detached. Still, the momentary effect of oddity and strangeness can make a brief, valuable contribution.

Notes

1. *Further Letters of Gerard Manley Hopkins*, edited by C. C. Abbott, second edition (1956), p. 215.

2. Ibid., p. 216.

3. Ibid., p. 220.

4. *The Letters of Gerard Manley Hopkins to Robert Bridges*, edited by C. C. Abbott (1955), p. 218.

5. B. Groom, 'The Formation and Use of the Compound Epithet in English Poetry from 1579', *SPE Tract*, 49 (Oxford, 1937).

6. For an article narrowing the gap between poetic language and ordinary language see S. Fish, 'How Ordinary is Ordinary Language?' reprinted in *Is There a Text in This Class?* (Cambridge, Mass., 1970), pp. 97–111.

7. *Further Letters*. p. 220.

8. See J. C. Collins, 'A New Study of Tennyson', *Cornhill Magazine*, 41–42 (1880), 17–35, 36–50. Tennyson's marginal comments on the article are on the copy in the Research Centre, Lincoln.

9. Cited in *The Poems of Tennyson*, edited by C. Ricks (1969), p. 862. In the Second Edition (1987), it appears in Volume II, p. 315.

10. B. Groom, 'On the Diction of Tennyson, Browning and Arnold', *S.P.E. Tract*, 53 (Oxford, 1939), p. 123.

11. *The Poems of Matthew Arnold*, edited by K. Allott (1967), p. 461.

12. T. S. Eliot, *On Poetry and Poets* (1957), p. 29.

13. For an account of the different levels of poetic style see A. J. Gilbert, *Literary Language from Chaucer to Johnson* (1979).

14. J. Drinkwater, *Victorian Poetry* (1923), pp. 33–34.

15. *The Letters of Matthew Arnold to Arthur Hugh Clough*, edited by H. F. Lowry (1932), p. 124.

16. Ibid., p. 66.

17. W. Pater, 'Essay on Style', in *Works*, v, 17.

18. J. A. Boulton, 'Browning – A Potential Revolutionary', *Essays in Criticism*, 3 (1953), 165–76.

19. S. W. Holmes, 'Browning: Semantic Stutterer,' *PMLA*, 60 (1945), 231–55.

20. W. E. Baker, *Syntax in English Poetry 1870–1930* (Berkeley and Los Angeles, 1967), p. 129.

21. For a study of Donne's reputation in the period see K. Tillotson, 'Donne's Poetry in the Nineteenth Century', in *Elizabethan and Jacobean Studies Presented to Frank Percy Wilson*, edited by H. Davis and H. Gardner (Oxford, 1959), pp. 307–26. See also J. E. Duncan, 'The Intellectual Kinship of Browning and Donne', *SP*, 50 (1953), 81–100.

22. See J. Milroy, *The Language of Gerard Manley Hopkins* (1977), p. 20.

23. *Letters to Bridges*, p. 89.

24. Ibid., p. 98.

25. Extract from Edward Thomas's review in the *Daily News* reprinted in E. Farjeon, *Edward Thomas: the Last Four Years* (1958, reprinted 1979), pp. 77–78.

26. Recordings of Tennyson's voice, made in 1890, available on the disc *Alfred Lord Tennyson Reads from his Own Poems*, produced by the Tennyson Society.

27. For an account of the society's activities see Lord Eversley, *English Commons, Forests and Footpaths* (1894) and my article 'Ruskin and Conservation', *Texas Quarterly*, 21 (1978), 65–83. For detailed studies of the impact of enclosure on John Clare see J. Barrell, *The Idea of Landscape and the Sense of Place, 1730–1840* (Cambridge, 1972), and T. Brownlow, *John Clare and Picturesque Landscape* (1983).

28. J. Lucas, *VS*, 28 (1985), p. 539.

29. E. M. Forster, *Two Cheers for Democracy* (1951), p. 209. See also R. A. Forsyth, 'The Conserving Myth of William Barnes', in *Romantic Mythologies*, edited by I. Fletcher, (1967), pp. 137–67.

30. J. Y. Akerman, *Wiltshire Tales* (1853), p. vi.

31. T. Hardy, *The Spectator* (15 October 1881), p. 1308, reprinted in *Thomas Hardy's Personal Writing*, edited by H. Orel, (1967), p. 93. Hereafter cited as *Hardy's Personal Writing*.

32. *Letters to Bridges*, pp. 87–88.

33. C. Wilson, 'Mirror of a Shire: Tennyson's Dialect Poems', *Durham University Journal*, 52 (1959), p. 28.

34. C. Tennyson, 'Tennyson as a Humorist', in *Six Tennyson Essays* (1954), pp. 1–38.

35. T. Hardy, 'Dialect in Novels', *The Athenaeum* (30 November 1878), p. 688; reprinted in *Hardy's Personal Writing*, p. 91.

36. H. James, *The Art of the Novel*, edited R. P. Blackmur (1947), pp. 279–80.

37. For examples of Hopkins's discussions with countrymen on the specialized language of their trades see *The Journals and Papers of Gerard Manley Hopkins*, edited by H. House and G. Storey (1959), pp. 191, 225–27.

Chapter 4
Victorian Versification

If this chapter were to have an epigraph it might be Congreve's aphorism: 'For soul is form and doth the body make.' What a poem accomplishes is to a large extent dependent on its technical features, and in many cases, although it could never be proved on internal evidence, the very exercise of employing verse forms has been entirely responsible for the generation of poetic meaning. Studying versification opens new dimensions in the study of poetry and brings different poets together in ways often completely impossible for ideologically based criticism. Who would ever think of comparing Dryden and Blake from the thematic point of view, but very direct similarities are noticeable in their treatment of lyric modes in 'The Secular Masque' and 'Night'. The study of versification completely realigns one's sense of poetic tradition and makes for interesting and challenging juxtapositions. Ultimately all the effects and devices have to be related to content. If there is a criticism to be made of Saintsbury's masterly study of English prosody it is that thematic concerns do not loom very large, and appreciation of the craftsman's skill leads to an overvaluation of certain poets – of Swinburne for instance. He is marvellously skilful with words, but that should not deafen one to the fact that very often they are not saying very much. However, the opposite tends not to be true, that one can think highly of a poet who seems to be saying something that matters but is technically inept: witness the case of Elizabeth Barrett. Usually the revelations of bungling in this department are one more nail in the coffin.

As we shall see there is a great deal of exciting innovation and experimentation in the period, although some of the main advances had been made in the Romantic Movement. It was then that eighteenth-century standards of regularity were relaxed and a great range of subtle technical variation introduced. Some of this was, strictly speaking, rediscovery of older conventions from the medieval and Elizabethan period, but it had a liberating effect, from which the Victorians continued to enjoy the benefits. Most of the poets were interested in the craft of poetry, and this interest is perhaps analogous to the architects' fascination with a wide variety of styles and the painters' interest in formal and technical experimentation: it was all part of the pervasive delight in work and achieving a job well done. For the most part Victorian poetic techniques are an adaptation and development of what had gone before. There are often precedents for forms; the *In Memoriam* stanza was actually used, whether Tennyson remembered it or not, by Lord Herbert of Cherbury in the seventeenth century. With the exception of Hopkins there was very little that was really revolutionary in the techniques of Victorian poetry, and certainly nothing as startling as the American poet Whitman, whose practice is completely without reference to established tradition.

Scansion

When theorists talked about prosody they sometimes used the terminology of classical scansion, but attempts to write classical measures do not play a major part in the history of Victorian poetry, any more than they did in the sixteenth century.

The names for the different kinds of poetic feet, listed below, are taken from classical scansion, with lightly accented syllables marked thus × and heavily accented syllables thus / (although as many theorists have pointed out there is a wide range of accentuation possible from light to heavy). Working in conjunction with accent is stress, marked thus \ , which corresponds with our instinctive sense of performance, and although it is often possible to stress a syllable that does not take a metrical accent, and to fail to stress a syllable that does take a metrical accent, it is usually impossible to stress an unaccented syllable in a foot if the metrically accented syllable is not also stressed. Often in prosody not much distinction is made between the use of the terms 'stress' and 'beat', but it is probably best to confine the use of the latter term to those occasions when the regularity of the stress pattern is such that a distinct rhythmic structure is perceived. These are the main types of poetic feet:

iamb × /	
trochee / ×	disyllabic
spondee / /	
anapaest × × /	
amphibrach × / ×	trisyllabic
dactyl / × ×	
paeonic / × × ×	quadrisyllabic

It is possible to substitute varying kinds of feet in otherwise regular lines, but the sense of a trochaic norm is more easily disturbed by substitution than is the case with iambic norms. As we shall see it is also possible to alter the metrical form within a short poem or stanza. Divergence from norms keeps the poetry alive and interesting, but it has always been found that the illusion of freedom is easier to maintain if there is some metrical framework present. No Victorian poet, not even Clough, wished to obliterate the boundaries between verse and conversation, and although Victorian verse is usually much freer than poetry of the previous century it still sounds like poetry when read aloud; there are natural-sounding forms of poetry which have their own conventions. Take these lines of Christina Rossetti's in 'Last Night': these are the stresses a modern reader might put on the words, especially if he did not know he was reading poetry (the stresses are marked thus: \ ):

Where were you | last night? | I watched | at the gate;

I went | down early, | I stayed | down late.

Were you snug | at home, | I should like | to know,

Or were you | in the copp|ice wheedl|ing Kate?

Also marked in the line below are the feet and the metrical accents. Some of the stresses do indeed correspond to the accents, but it is probably best to read these lines following accent rather than stress, since there is such a thing as the 'natural movement of verse' – which does not always correspond exactly to the natural movement of speech. Still, there are problems with these lines, since the stress patterns derived from natural speech make one wonder whether the scansion is right, since it is not clear whether anapaests or amphibrachs should predominate. It would be difficult to justify stressing 'I' in line 3, since to do that would require the substitution of a dactylic foot – which would be highly irregular.

English poetry has different traditions behind its versification, of stressed poetry on the one hand, and syllabic poetry on the other. It was in the nineteenth century that the nature of the dual inheritance was explored, by poets and writers on prosody. An important experimental work is Coleridge's *Christabel*, which pays strict attention to stress, but is cavalier about the syllable count. Most of the lines have eight syllables, but some have seven, and some have nine: 'She shrunk and shuddered, and saw again' (l. 454) has no possibility for elision (that is, regarding two syllables as one), but like all the other lines it does have four stresses. It seems that the normal foot might be iambic, but there are sufficient variations for one to wonder even about that, and sometimes if one reads lines as regular iambs they sound very archaic – which was doubtless part of the intention: 'With trump and solemn heraldry' (l. 435). Rossetti's 'The Blue Closet' and Arnold's

Tristram and Iseult are written in something like the *Christabel* metre. Like Old English this poetry is conceived in terms of stress rather than syllable, and in the 1830s a theorist came on to the scene called Edwin Guest. His *History of English Rhythms* (1836–38) emphasized the primacy of the Old English inheritance, and called the whole notion of poetic feet into doubt. His theories antedate some of Hopkins's, except that unlike Guest, Hopkins believed that it was possible to have two adjoining syllables taking heavy stresses even though there was no pause between them. When Saintsbury wrote his extended survey of prosody Hopkins was not in print (except for a few minor examples) and his theories were known to him only by way of Bridges, but Saintsbury knew enough about him to recognize that he was a member of the 'anti-foot and pro-stress division', and hence a peripheral experimenter of no very great interest.

This is a convenient point at which to consider Hopkins's theories of versification, since he explored the differences between the various systems. His views on prosody are laid out in the Preface to his poems and in his letters. For the conventional approaches to scansion Hopkins employed the labels 'common English rhythm', 'running rhythm', and 'standard rhythm', although he tends to use the word 'stress' where many metrists would prefer the word 'accent'. He realized that most lines of traditional poetry adhered to a standard rhythm which was sufficiently marked for violations to be registered by the reader, and when these non-standard feet occurred in lines and contradicted the norms of 'by rights what we should be hearing' (what we should call 'substitutions') he recognized 'counterpoint rhythm'. However, he was worried by poems such as Milton's *Samson Agonistes* in which the normal 'ground-rhythm' was so frequently opposed that a new term seemed to be required to identify it, so he coined the label 'sprung rhythm'. Where this system differs from others is that feet may contain any number of syllables. In the last line of stanza 31 of *The Wreck of the Deutschland* there are six stresses, as in other corresponding lines, but there are twenty-three syllables! One might scan it thus:

Startle the poor sheep back! is the shipwrack

then a harvest, does tempest carry the grain

for thee.

Here I take it that the placing of the stresses corresponds exactly to the placing of the metrical accents.

By admitting that 'strict sprung rhythm cannot be counterpointed' Hopkins lets the cat out of the bag: his lines have no basic tune, and the stresses fall as they might fall in conversation. He explained to

Bridges that he employed it 'because it is the nearest to the rhythm of prose, that is the native and natural rhythm of speech, the least forced, the most rhetorical and emphatic of all possible rhythms'.[1] In a note to *The Wreck* he writes that 'which syllables however are strong and which light is better told by the ear than by any instruction that could be in short space given'.[2] But at this a yawning chasm opens, since Hopkins was appealing to a common-sense notion of how a sequence of English words should sound, and as each year goes by there is less and less agreement about this. Even he knew that he was heading for trouble, since he wanted to develop an elaborate system of notation that would make the performance of his poems as regulated as a piece of music. He realized, as many modern theorists realize, that there are gradations of strength in the stresses placed on syllables, both in conversation and in the reading of poetry. His theories are a step or two away from free verse, and they have held a delusive charm for poets and readers of poetry since they seem to offer the attractive prospect of being able to dispense with the fascination of what is difficult in the composition of poetry, while at the same time offering the equally attractive prospect to experts who wish to deduce some method in the apparent madness. Significantly, one hardly ever hears a performance of Hopkins's poetry that bears out his theories, and when one does it sounds distinctly odd. These are harsh words, aimed in part at those who have made 'sprung rhythm' into a kind of shibboleth. It is perhaps the case that Hopkins's laboured theory is *post hoc facto* in relation to the poetry, and hence of only limited value as a guide to imitators and disciples.

By a process that could be simultaneous discovery, Hardy evolved a system of versification very like Hopkins's – witness these lines from 'Afterwards':

× × / × × / × / × × / ×
When the Present has latched its postern behind my

/ × × /
tremulous stay,

× × × / × / × / × × ×
And the May month flaps its glad green leaves like

/
wings,

× × / × / × / × ×
Delicate-filmed as new-spun silk, will the

/ × /
neighbours say,

/ × × / × / × / × × /
'He was a man who used to notice such things?

(ll. 1–4)

It seems that six beat lines alternate with five beat lines here, but the syllable count varies from eleven to sixteen. It is true that this poem was not published until 1917, but Hardy was evolving the concepts of a poetry that should be based on the rhythms of conversational speech during our period. The practice of Hopkins and Hardy has been followed by many twentieth-century poets, which is why their poetry seems so modern and acceptable.

Hopkins has received a good deal of praise and admiration for his 'sprung rhythm', but neither in theory nor in practice is it spectacularly original, and the substituted feet in earlier poetry were perhaps introduced by poets following their instincts rather than adopting deliberate prosodic theories. Tennyson's *The Princess* is basically iambic, but this line has dactylic and anapaestic substitution: 'Myriads of rivulets hurrying through the lawn'(VII. 205). Swinburne, on the other hand, introduces into *Atalanta in Calydon* (which has predominantly trisyllabic feet) a certain number of iambic feet:

> When the hounds of Spring are on winter's traces
>
> The mother of months in meadow or plain
>
> Fills the shadows and windy places
>
> With lisp of leaves and ripple of rain.
>
> (ll. 65–68)

All of these lines have four stresses, but the syllable count varies from nine to eleven. Perhaps those readers who lavish such extravagant praise on Hopkins's versification should glance at Swinburne? Hopkins was not alone in searching for ways of utilizing metrical freedom without indulging in total lawlessnes. The subtle effects of Christina Rossetti's *Goblin Market* deserve to be better known. Saintsbury called the form 'dedoggerelised Skeltonic'. There are trochaic, iambic, dactylic, and anapaestic feet, although the basic form is iambic. The sister who buys forbidden fruit described them thus:

> What melons icy-cold
>
> Piled on a dish of gold
>
> Too huge for me to hold,
>
> What peaches with a velvet nap,

    × / ×   / × / × /
Pellucid grapes without one seed;

    / × × × / × / ×
Odorous indeed must be the mead

    × / ×   / ×   / × × /
Whereon they grow, and pure the wave they drink

    × / × / × /
With lilies at the brink,

    ×   / ×   / × /
And sugar-sweet their sap.
                 (ll. 175–84)

In this passage the number of syllables per line ranges from six to ten, and some lines have as few as three stresses. This then is an extreme version of the variety possible in choice of poetic feet and stress patterns.

The line

The concept of the line is important to poetry, and without it poets and critics could never find their bearings. The line is particularly emphasized when it is end-stopped, but even with enjambment a slight pause is created, which is like a secondary mode of punctuation, in many instances introducing pauses where they would never occur in prose, and helping to distinguish between prose and poetry. Lines very greatly in length, and some Victorian poets experimented with long lines, some even risking the dreaded fourteen-syllable line which had spelt doom to much sixteenth-century poetry. William Morris tried it, with success, in *Sigurd the Volsung* and *The House of the Wolfings*; Tennyson was less successful with the form in 'The May Queen'. One remembers the famous trochaic fifteeners of 'Locksley Hall'. Alexandrines are hazardous things to employ in English poetry, but Browning tried them, to good effect, in the long poem *Fifine at the Fair*. Lyric forms and short regular lines are inappropriate for the long poem, and the Victorians continued to recognise what generations of poets had always known, that iambic pentameter (unrhymed) was the most natural medium for the long poem. Tennyson and Browning were masters of the form, and it is a tribute to them that they managed to avoid offering unintentional reminiscences of Shakespeare, Milton, Wordsworth, and Shelley. Arnold in *Sohrab and Rustum* falls into the

Miltonic trap more easily. These lines sound as if they came from the seventeenth century, not the nineteenth:

> It was that griffin, which of old reared Zal,
> Rustum's great father, whom they left to die,
> A helpless babe, among the mountain-rocks;
> Him that kind creature found, and reared, and
>   loved –
>   (ll. 679–82)

But Milton would never have written a line like this:

> And his knees tottered, and he smote his hand.
>   (l. 662)

This seems to have only four feet, only one of which is iambic.

Saintsbury thought that the greatest blank verse in the period was to be found in 'Ulysses', 'Morte d'Arthur', *The Princess*, 'St. Simeon Stylites', and 'Love and Duty'. Of 'Tithonus' he said that it was so beautiful it was hard to believe it did not rhyme. Tennyson adopts a Miltonic trick in 'Tithonus' of having a two-syllabled word follow an enjambment, yet it does not sound Miltonic (probably because of the scansion of the preceding line):

> Me only cruel immortality
> Consumes.
>   (ll. 5–6)

Browning's blank verse can be very efficient and engaging, but it possibly gave him a licence that was not always beneficial. It could make a sort of relaxed rambling possible.

There is a poetic line that cannot be avoided in any discussion of the period since it is so prominent (Saintsbury devoted a whole chapter to it): the hexameter. This was the medium employed by poems that have received considerable praise in this study: Clough's *Bothie* and *Amours de Voyage*.

Unlike classical hexameters, which are quantitative (that is, based on the number of syllables), Clough's lines are accentual and based on the stresses of everyday speech. Each of the six feet in his lines may contain two or three syllables, except the last foot, which normally contains two, so that a line may contain between twelve and seventeen syllables. A reader unused to the mysteries of poetry might be able to read the lines as if they were perfectly ordinary prose, but once one has learnt something of the basic tune it is certainly best to read the poetry so as to bring out the stresses: identifying the feet and indicating the pauses at mid-line that might not necessarily correspond to the pauses one would make in everyday speech. It would be as undesirable to read the lines aloud in such a way as to overemphasize the metre as to underemphasize it. Clough realized that there was a problem when he produced a metaphrase of a passage from the *Odyssey*, 'constructed as nearly as may be upon the ancient principle; quantity, so far as, in our forward-rushing, consonant-crushing, Anglo-savage enunciation – long and short can in any kind be detected, quantity attended to in the first place, and care also bestowed, in the second, to have the natural accents very frequently laid upon syllables which the metrical reading depresses.'[3]

> × / × × / × × / × × / ×
> But I, with my ships in a body, the whole that
> × / ×
> obeyed me,
> / × × × /. × × / × × / ×
> Fled, well perceiving that wrath was rising
> × / ×
> against us,
> / × × / × / × × / × × / ×
> Tydides also fled with me, his company calling;
> / × × / × / × / × × × / ×
> Later, upon our track followed the yellow
> × × / ×
> Menelaus.
> (ll. 1–4)

The accentual markings here correspond to what they would be if one were reading it as a Greek line. Clough realized that modern hexameters in English (always excepting a regular piece like Longfellow's *Evangeline*) tended to be 'lengthy, straggling irregular' and 'sprawling bits of rhythmical prose'.[4] Still, there is a kind of tune to the lines, which gives them a tautness that would not have been available in free verse. The following four lines are examples of the variety possible in Cloughean hexameters:

> / × × / × × / × × / × ×
> 1. Weary of wondering, watching and guessing and
> / × × / ×
> gossiping idly
> / × × / × × / × / × / ×
> 2. Drawn by moon and sun from Labrador and Greenland

/ ×   × /   ×   /   × × /× /×× /×
3. Over the low sea banks of the fatal Ilian city

× ×   /   × × / × / ×   ×   / ×
4. In the next, if I had, I shouldn't know how I

×   / ×
should use it.

In (1) every foot but the last has three syllables, in (2) every foot has two syllables, and (3) and (4) are mixed, as the scansion shows. Clough increases the sense of variation by requiring that in many feet there should be secondary stresses (indeed in much English poetry there are several intermediate stages between heavily and lightly stressed syllables). He allows himself further irregularities by sometimes having four syllables to the foot, as in the line

/ ×   × ×   /   ×   / ×   ×   / ×
Hampered as they haste, those running, these others

/   ×× / ×
maidenly tripping.

Rhythmically speaking, Clough seems to anticipate Hopkins, but of course he does not sound like him because he keeps to standard idiom: he does not heighten colloquial speech as much as Hopkins did. It is the case that one may probably trace the influence on both of these poets back to their undergraduate studies in classical scansion.

In this chapter the term 'poetic feet' has been employed, but it should be mentioned that many theorists wish completely to abandon the concept of feet in English verse in the interest of a critical responsiveness to some of the more complex patterns of stress.[5] They have a plausible case, but since most Victorian poets composed with feet in mind there is some validity in continuing to use the term, even though it is more appropriate for classical poetry than English.

Before going on to consider stanzaic form it is necessary to consider two rhymed forms used as alternatives to blank verse in long poems. These are the couplet (usually in four or five beat lines) and English adaptations of Dante's *terza rima*. The octosyllabic couplet (which does not, of course, always have eight syllables) is a traditional form, very effectively used in Milton's *L'Allegro* and *Il Pensoroso*, but it is potentially tedious in very long poems, and Byron referred to 'the fatal facility of the octosyllabic verse'.[6] As Samuel Butler discovered in *Hudibras* clever rhymes and jogging rhythm could easily lead to bathos. Possibly the most accomplished exponent of this form in our period is William Morris; like Keats, who in *The Eve of St. Mark* captured something of the spirit of the Middle Ages, Morris found that the medium could make a significant contribution to the creation of an archaic flavour. In these lines from 'The Haystack in the Floods' there are subtle variations that keep the poetry alive:

> By fits and starts they rode apace,
> And very often was his place
> Far off from her; he had to ride
> Ahead, to see what might betide
> When the roads crossed; and sometimes, when
> There rose a murmuring from his men,
> Had to turn back with promises;
>
> (ll. 15–21)

Other Morris poems in this form described by Saintsbury as 'unfaltering in craftsmanship' are 'The Watching of the Falcon', 'The Land East of the Sun and West of the Moon', and 'The Ring Given to Venus'. The great strength of Morris is that he manages to infuse an archaic flavour into his works without seeming precious or Chattertonian.

Decasyllabic couplets are also a well-tried medium, going back to Chaucer, and perfected as 'the heroic couplet' (usually a self-enclosed unit) by Dryden. The medium makes both strictness and extreme freedom possible, but none of the major Victorians was much interested in using the balanced and disciplined forms of the Augustans. They were more ready to follow the flexibility of the couplet as it was used, say, in Keats's *Endymion*. It is always difficult to remember that Browning's 'My Last Duchess' is in couplet form; there are twenty-three couplets in the poem, but not a single one is self-enclosed and thirty-six of the lines enjamb. Two sentences sprawl over eleven lines each. The opening sets the style:

> That's my last Duchess painted on the wall,
> Looking as if she were alive. I call
> That piece a wonder, now: Fra Pandolf's hands
> Worked busily a day, and there she stands.
>
> (ll. 1–4)

Saintsbury thought that the 'Nymphs' "Song to Hylas"' in Morris's *Life and Death of Jason* was one of the best examples of the enjambed couplet in existence, and avoided 'some of the mawkish extravagances of *Endymion*'.

Terza rima was invented by Dante for *La Divina Commedia*, and is composed of iambic tercets rhyming aba bcb cdc, etc. It was first used in English by Chaucer in 'Complaint to his Lady', then by Byron in 'The Prophecy of Dante' and Shelley in *The Triumph of Life* and 'Ode to the West Wind'. The most successful use of the form in our period was Morris's *The Defence of Guenevere*. Here are some characteristic lines:

> But shortly listen – in that garden fair
> Came Launcelot walking; this is true, the kiss
> Wherewith we kissed in meeting that spring day,
> I scarce dare talk of the remembered bliss,
> When both our mouths went wandering in one way,
> And aching sorely, met among the leaves;
> Our hands being left behind strained far away.
>
> (ll. 132–38)

The other significant example of *terza rima* in the century is Richard Watson Dixon's *Mano*.

Stanzaic form

The Victorian poets, especially those with an interest in the past, borrowed the stanzaic forms of their predecessors with zest, and often the forms give as much of an archaizing flavour to the poems as the ideas and the diction. During the period one finds ballads, carols, Spenserian stanzas, sestinas, and sonnets in abundance. Rhyme royal was used by Morris in *Earthly Paradise*. Christina Rossetti came quite close to the spirit of the Shakespearian and Petrarchan sonnet, and Dante Gabriel Rossetti even produced a sonnet cycle: *The House of Life*. Meredith produced a sonnet cycle too (*Modern Love*), but his sonnets were sixteen lines long.

However, I should like to concentrate on the stanzaic form produced by the Victorians themselves. There is quite a crop of them, and many are very beautiful and inventive. Perhaps the most famous is the *In Memoriam* stanza, which seems to be a case of independent invention, although Tennyson may have remembered that Lord Herbert of Cherbury had used it in the seventeenth century. Tennyson actually first used the form in 'Hail Briton!' The stanza consists of four tetrameter lines, rhyming abba. The second 'a' rhyme seems to turn the stanza back on itself, just as one thought it about to progress, and this makes it ideal for the expression of elegiac feeling. But there are many variations possible with the form, depending on where the lines enjamb. And there is always the possibility for lines to enjamb in adjacent stanzas. Tennyson often begins a new sentence in mid-line, but not as often as Browning might have done had he used the form, and the reflective equanimity of the whole poem is to some degree dependent on the integrity of the line. The second of the 'b' rhymes often enjambs, but with just sufficient emphasis in the rhyme to produce a slight pause and indicate the unit of the line. The poem is not quoted here; the reader is urged to dip into it and savour its subtle and ingenious effects, many of which are achieved by the masterly use of line division and enjambment. Variation and controlled irregularity are central features of Tennyson's poetic skill. After the opening Spenserian stanzas of *The Lotos-Eaters* Tennyson produces great variety in the 'Choric Song'. There is no set pattern, but considerable differences between the effects made by short and long lines. Some of the four beat lines have as many as twelve syllables, and in both mood and technique he is close to Section II of T. S. Eliot's *The Dry Salvages*. It is not far from

> Let us alone. Time driveth onward fast,
> And in a little while our lips are dumb.
>
> (ll. 88–89)

to

> Where is there an end of it, the soundless
> wailing,
> The silent withering of autumn flowers
> Dropping their petals and remaining motionless;
>
> (ll. 51–53)

Maud is rich in stanzaic forms which follow the moods of the hero and his experiences, from the lilting 'Come into the garden Maud' (which is supposed to be rhythmically like a polka) to the tortured and undisciplined movement of v section 1: 239–309 'Dead, long dead.'

Browning, too, has some interesting and varied stanza forms. He is famous for having invented the ingenious form of *Love Among the Ruins*, a twelve-line stanza of six beat lines alternating with two beat lines in couplets. (At the first publication the typography was such that there were only six lines per stanza.) Each stanza has a break at midpoint, to move the perspective from past to present or present to past. The *Childe Roland* stanza (abbaba) is unusual; it begins as an *In Memoriam* stanza with a pentameter line, but two lines are tagged on, matching the 'a' and 'b' rhymes. The end of each stanza produces a curious effect, whereby one seems impelled to turn back and then to advance. The strange hesitancy this produces is very much in accord with the meaning of the poem. Most of the stanzas are self-enclosed, but three of them run into the following ones. 'James Lee's Wife' is a strange and beautiful poem, and like *Maud* it uses a wide range of stanzaic forms. In Section III there is an inventive form:

> The swallow has set her six young on the rail,
>   And looks sea-ward:
> The water's in stripes like a snake, olive-pale
>   To the leeward, –
> On the weather-side, black, spotted white with the
>   wind,
> 'Good fortune departs, and disaster's behind,' –
> Hark, the wind with its wants and its infinite wail!
>
> (ll. 54–60)

The long lines are tetrameters, with pretty regular anapaests. The short lines have more iambic and trochaic variation and are separated also by having their own rhymes. The 'a' rhyme runs through the poem like a persistent motif. Line 60, for instance, recalls us to an earlier point in the stanza after the temporarily distracting aphorism. Stark, short lines interspersed with longer ones are almost a hallmark of Browning. We have seen this combination used effectively in 'Love Among the Ruins'; in 'James Lee's Wife' three of the nine sections adopt this device. 'In a Gondola' has a rich variety of forms, causing one to reflect that, in some respects Browning is very like his contemporaries Tennyson and Swinburne, who were also interested in exploring different forms. However, it was no part of his aim to produce poetry as effortlessly musical as theirs. Finally, it should be noted that 'Rabbi Ben Ezra' has a rare stanzaic form, invented by Browning:

> Grow old along with me!
>   The best is yet to be,
> The last of life, for which the first was made:
>   Our times are in His hand
>   Who saith 'A whole I planned,
> Youth show but half; trust God: see all nor be
>   afraid!
>
> (ll. 1–6)

Critics are so concerned with the merits or demerits of the message that they pay no attention to the odd form, a couple of rhyming trimeters, followed by a pentameter, then another couple of rhyming trimeters, then an alexandrine, rhyming with the pentameter. How this relates to the sense I should not like to say – the ingenious reader will probably be able to work something out to his own satisfaction.

Arnold uses a wide variety of stanzaic forms, but his most interesting invention is *The Scholar Gipsy* stanza, as skilled and beautiful an achievement as Keats's *Odes*. The form is also used in *Thyrsis*. It is a ten-line stanza and consists of a sestet followed by the first half of the octet of a Petrarchan sonnet, with line 6 as a trimeter. There is very little enjambment. In this stanza Arnold manages to catch something of the lyric intensity of Keats:

> Still nursing the unconquerable hope,
>   Still clutching the inviolable shade,
>   With a free, onward impulse brushing
>   through,
>   By night, the silvered branches of the glade –
>   Far on the forest skirts, where none
>   pursue,
> On some mild pastoral slope
> Emerge, and resting on the moonlit pales
>   Freshen thy flowers as in former years
>   With dew, or listen with enchanted ears,
> From the dark dingles, to the nightingales!
>
> (ll. 211–20)

This is a long way from the prosaic and slightly ungainly movement of a poem like *Rugby Chapel*. When Arnold writes his own poem to the nightingale it is not like Keats; 'Philomela' goes back to classical myth, and the nourishing of 'wild, unquenched, deep-sunken, old-world pain'. Its form is interesting, with lines varying between two and five beats. Another ten-line stanza invented by Milton is employed by Arnold in 'Westminster Abbey', celebrating the death of his father's biographer, Arthur Penrhyn Stanley. Stanza 2 reads:

> – Rough was the winter eve;
>   Their craft the fishers leave,
> And down over the Thames the darkness drew.
>   One still lags last, and turns, and eyes the
>   Pile
>   Huge in the gloom, across in Thorney Isle,
> King Sebert's work, the wondrous Minster new.
>   – 'Tis Lambeth now, where then
> They moor their boats among the bulrush stems;
>   And that new Minster in the matted
>   fen
> The world famed Abbey by the westering Thames.
>
> (ll. 111–20)

As Saintsbury acutely observed, this form is reminiscent of Milton's hymn in *On the Morning of Christ's Nativity*. It is not identical, since Milton's stanza is of seven lines, but both poets open with a trimeter couplet followed by a pentameter which rhymes with a trimeter couplet followed by a pentameter which rhymes with line 6. However, whereas lines 4 and 5 in Milton are trimeter couplets Arnold has pentameters. The form seems to throw an aura of faith over a poem written in a sceptical age by a sceptical poet.

Possibly the most famous stanza invented in the period was Edward FitzGerald's *The Rubáiyát of Omar Khayyám*. The form is so married to the content that it is impossible to imagine the poet saying what he says in any other form:

> Wake! For the Sun, who scattered into flight
> The Stars before him from the Field of Night
> Drives Night along with them from
>   Heaven, and strikes
> The Sultan's Turret with a Shaft of Light.
>   (ll. 1–4)

Like the *In Memoriam* stanza there are many ways of dividing it up by the varied use of end-stopped lines and enjambment. The unrhymed third line has the effect of making many of the opening couplets seem like an aphoristic couplet and the remaining two lines like some leisurely comment, with the use of the rhyme in line 4 recalling one to the opening. It is a brilliant poem, and in its jewelled impersonality unlike anything else in the rest of Victorian poetry. Swinburne's *Laus Veneris* also utilizes the stanza (except that l. 3 rhymes with the following stanza in pairs), but it does not really sound the same when in Swinburne's hands since he goes for more melodramatic expriences:

> Ah, not as they, but as the souls that were
> Slain in the old time, having found her fair;
>   Who, sleeping with her lips upon their eyes,
> Heard sudden serpents hiss across her hair.
>
> Their blood runs round the roots of time like
>   rain:
> She casts them forth and gathers them again;
>   With nerve and bone she weaves and multiplies
> Exceeding pleasure out of extreme pain.
>   (ll. 112–20)

When the form is used for narrative, as it is in *Laus Veneris,* it changes somehow, and Swinburne enjambs between stanzas, which FitzGerald

only does twice. The non-rhyming line in a rhyming stanza has challenging possibilities. A famous instance of the device is Rossetti's *The
Blessed Damozel* stanza, in which lines 1, 3, and 5 fail to rhyme;

> 'And I myself will teach to him
>> I myself, lying so,
> The songs I sing here; which his voice
>> Shall pause in, hushed and slow,
> And find some knowledge at each pause,
>> Or some new thing to know.'
>>>>>>> (ll. 91–96)

This is a more regular stanza than most in the poem, where there are
inverted and substituted feet and so on. One could imagine the poem
typographically reduced to three-line rhyming stanzas, in which case
we should have the dreaded fourteeners! A lot would be lost though
if the sense of non-rhyming line endings was obliterated.

   Swinburne was a master of his craft and invented other effective
stanza forms. 'Itylus' is in the form of six-line stanzas of tetrameters,
rhyming abcabc. The lines with feminine endings have ten syllables;
the lines with masculine endings have nine or ten syllables:

> Swallow, my sister, O sister swallow,
>> How can thine heart be full of the spring?
>> What hast thou found in thine heart to sing?
>> What wilt thou do when the summer is shed?
>>>>>>> (ll. 1–6)

The Triumph of Time has a highly unusual form, a stanza of eight lines
with tetrameters, with a varied syllable count, some lines as few as
eight ('Clasped and clothed in the cloven clay', l. 115) others as many
as twelve ('Will you lift up your eyes between sadness and bliss',
l. 165). The rhyme-scheme is strange:

> Before our lives divide for ever,
>> While time is with us and hands are free,
> (Time, swift to fasten and swift to sever
>> Hand from hand, as we stand by the sea)
> I will say no word that a man might say
> Whose whole life's love goes down in a day;
> For this could never have been; and never,
>> Though the gods and the years relent,
>>>>>>> shall be.
>>>>>>> (ll. 1–8)

It is ababccab. The third set of ab lines is separated from the others
by the cc couplet, so we catch a faintly distant echo with the first half
of the stanza. The form seems to suggest a love experience in which
there is little progression, but claustrophobic reflection circling back
on itself. Because it is fairly regular, and not broken up as much as
it would have been in Browning's hands, the form is able to contribute
to the meaning; indeed, it is generally true that if elaborately wrought
forms are to affect the meaning they have to be fairly strictly
articulated.

It could be that Swinburne is too regular for modern tastes, too
close to music. 'Stage Love' is completely regular, with trochaic feet
(the final foot in the first two lines of each stanza being catalectic –
meaning that the unaccented syllable is dropped and it is not a
monosyllabic foot in metrical terms).

> When the game began between them for a jest,
> He played king and she played queen to match
> > the best;
> Laughter soft as tears, and tears that turned
> > to laughter,
> These were things she sought for years and
> > sorrowed after.
> > (ll. 1–4)

There are three more stanzas exactly like that. 'Before the Mirror' is
an exotic poem recording an aesthetic response to Whistler's *White
Girl*, reminding us how easily Whistler (who revered Rossetti as 'the
king') fits into the aesthetic movement:

> White rose in red rose-garden
> > Is not so white;
> Snowdrops that plead for pardon
> > And pine for fright
> Because the hard East blows
> Over their maiden rows
> > Grow not as this face grows from pale to
> > bright.
> > (ll. 1–7)

In this regular poetry we often find parts of speech at the same points
in lines, so that line 15 is 'Soft snows that hard winds harden', and line
57 is 'Face fallen and white throat lifted'. Line 13 is 'White rose of
weary leaf' and line 61 is 'Old loves and faded fears'.

And finally Swinburne's 'Dolores'. It is a key exhibit in Mario

Praz's gallery of perverse erotica, and its very tune is memorable and notorious:

> Cold eyelids that hide like a jewel
>> Hard eyes that grow soft for an hour;
> The heavy white limbs, and the cruel
>> Red mouth like a venomous flower;
> When these are gone by with their glories,
>> What shall rest of thee then, what remain,
> O mystic and sombre Dolores,
>> Our Lady of Pain?
>>> (ll. 1–8)

All the lines are trimeters except the last, which is a dimeter. The poetry gains its lilt from the frequent anapaests, and yet this suavity is oddly separate from the decadent content. It is altogether powerfully perverse. But where did Swinburne get this form from? Curiously, from the eighteenth century, where it was used by Shenstone and Cowper. It was then perfected by Praed, who, like his predecessors, kept the last line as a trimeter. For Praed the form was employed not for perverse passion but for *vers de société*! This is the typical note in 'A Letter of Advice':

> You tell me you're promised a lover,
>> My own Araminta, next week;
> Why cannot my fancy discover
>> The hue of his coat and his cheek?
> Alas! if he look like another,
>> A vicar, a banker, a beau,
> Be deaf to your father and mother,
>> My own Araminta, say 'No!'
>>> (ll. 1–8)

Swinburne in 1891 referred to 'these charming little pieces whose genuine and high-bred elegance is most evidently inimitable'[7] so that it is a *tour de force* to use this polite and lightweight form for something as morbidly horrible as *Dolores*. It is true of course that the two beat final line does halt the movement of the poem, as if in reflective pain, but the other lines too are curiously transformed by Swinburne, suggesting, despite what I have often said and implied in this chapter, that perhaps the forms on their own do not have *inherent* tendencies towards certain meanings and moods. That is not to say that in the hands of a skilled practitioner they do not seem to possess special character.

Rhyme

Emphasis has been placed on the manner in which rhyme binds poetry together and helps to define the limits of lines and the shapes of stanzas. Most of the poetry we have been considering is fairly straightforward and the rhymes, on the whole, are not too emphatic. Masculine rhymes, in which the rhyming syllable receives a final stress, are usually unexceptionable. However, feminine rhymes, in which the stress of the rhyming word or words does not fall on the last syllable, introduce problems and dangers for the poet. This is not unconnected with problems of prosody, since there is always a danger that the emphatic rhythms of trochaic and dactylic verse will produce comic effect, often when not required. There is a reason for this: one of the mainsprings of the comic is to be found in mechanical predictability; the fat man slipping on the banana skin walks with unerring regularity and fails to take avoiding action. The comic and absurd universe is made up of relentless regularity with no room for manœuvre.[8] The inevitability of the polysyllabic rhyme seems to share in the grotesque over-determinacy of the comic and absurd universe. Even the sun-treader Shelley moves dangerously close to bathos with his over-frequent feminine rhymes, such as 'ocean' and 'motion'. Some poets succeed in being serious despite feminine rhymes; we have seen examples in Swinburne. However, emphasized rhymes are always in danger of coming close to doggerel. Some of the grotesque effects that Browning achieves in *The Pied Piper of Hamelin* and *Christmas-Eve and Easter-Day* are achieved by bold rhymes:

> I very soon had enough of it.
>   The hot smell and the human noises,
> And my neighbour's coat, the greasy cuff of
>   it,
>   Were a pebble-stone that a child's hand
>   poises,
> Compared with the pig-of-lead pressure
>   Of the preaching man's immense stupidity,
> As he poured his doctrine forth, full measure,
>   To meet his audience's avidity.
>
>   (l. 139–46)

Oddity is always compounded if a group of words rhymes – either with another group or with a single word, as in the case of 'struck him/duck him', 'untied it/inside it', 'leave him/grieve him', 'beneath it/seethe it' and 'office, I/prophecy', 'equipt yours/Scriptures', 'face on/mason'. The oddity of rhyme is always increased when unusual words (which one might expect to be totally unrelated to any other) find rhymes. *Baldachin, succinctly, vestiment, pattens, tallyho, scimitar, symmetrical, cavils, preludious* all find rhymes in 'Christmas-Eve', to mention just a few. Oddity is further accentuated when proper names (names of persons and places) find rhymes. One thinks of these names being so distinct and so apart from the rest of the language that it is always a minor miracle if connection can be established via rhyme. Even with masculine rhymes oddity is possible, but with disyllabic and trisyllabic rhymes it is more or less impossible to avoid it. This was the stock-in-trade of Byron's *Don Juan*, with his *Cadwallader/swallowed her* and the like. There are some intentionally dreadful rhymes like this in Browning, all helping to bolster the impression that he is uncouth (though functionally so in 'Christmas-Eve'). We find 'knows if/Joseph', 'eye on/Mount Zion', 'gem/Jerusalem', 'Pilate/Smile at', 'Pascal/task call', 'thus/Aeschylus', 'Lucumons/pros and cons', and 'Queen Mab/stab' in *Christmas-Eve and Easter-Day*. And in this poem one of the most strained rhymes in the century – Manchester/haunches stir.

There some pretty odd rhymes in 'Sibrandus Schafnaburgensis' (a poem alluded elsewhere as testimony to Browning's weird strangeness) (see below p. 189). He has *laurustine/line, Stonehenge/revenge, crevice/pont-levis, Chablis/Rabelais, in limbo/akimbo, deposit/closet, John Knox/front-row box* and *Munich/tunic*. There are two examples of the kind of rhymes Byron always found amusing – where an English word (which one might imagine is separated from all other languages by a *cordon sanitaire*) rhymes with a foreign word. In this poem he has and *laetis* and *treatise* and *is it* and *sufficit*. This somehow undermines the dignity of *both* languages. The device continues in a good deal of scept-ical and racy modern poetry. Browning's use of rhyme exasperated Wilde rather as it has exasperated modern readers; it was just one of the various means whereby 'he turned language into ignoble clay': 'rhyme, the one chord we have added to the Greek lyre, became in Robert Browning's hands a grotesque misshapen thing, which at times made him masquerade in poetry as a low comedian, and ride Pegasus too often with his tongue in his cheek'.[9]

English of course is not a language well endowed with rhyming words (which makes some of the crazy collocations just catalogued all the more astonishing), but with various forms of cheating one can enlarge the number. One way is to break words at line-endings. In his *The Rules of Rhyme: A Guide to English Versification* (1869) the son of the comic poet Thomas Hood indicated the 'extremely absurd effect' which could be produced by lopping words. His example is

> Here doomed to starve on water gru-
> -el, never shall I see the U-
> > > -niversity of Gottingen.

Devices of this kind can cause the kind of pained groans one makes in the presence of a bad pun. All the more remarkable that Hopkins flirts with the art of sinking in *The Wreck of the Deutschland*:

> She drove in the dark to leeward,
> She struck – not a reef or a rock
> But the combs of a smother of sand: night drew her
> > Dead to the Kentish Knock;
> > > > (ll. 105–8)

There is also an example in 'No worst, there is none':

> on an age-old anvil wince and sing –
> Then lull, then leave off. Fury had
> > shrieked 'No ling-
> > > ering!'
> > > > (ll. 6–8)

The typographical layout here emphasizes the fact that he is employing the device, but if one were to listen to the lines it might be difficult to identify the rhyming syllable – unless the reader made some strange emphases. Elsewhere in *The Wreck* Hopkins is close to the kind of absurdity I have been identifying of feminine rhymes, with some of the single words rhyming with pairs of words (and for unsympathetic readers he is actually guilty of it). He has *Francis/lance, his, Master/cast her, Bremen/women, Galilee/maiden's knee*. Many readers will find no objection to these examples, but I find them very disconcerting and unfortunate.

If Hopkins is possibly close to bathos here, Swinburne certainly achieves it in 'Dolores'. Its rhythmical regularity brings him danger- ously close to the comic, but some of the rhymes are surely a mistake – if he wished to be taken seriously: *Virgin/purge in, stories/Dolores, bedrape us/Priapus* (a touch of the Irish here?), *floor is/Dolores, adore us/Dolores, core is/Dolores, passion/Thallassian, kiss be/Arisbe, shady/Our Lady, escape us/Priapus*. The notorious opening of a comic poem runs:

> 'Twas on the good ship Venus
> By God, you should have seen us.

How then can one possibly take seriously the '*Venus/between us*' and

'*Venus/seen us*' rhymes in this poem? In 'By the North Sea' there are rhymes for *ruin/blew in*, *witch is/riches*, *rejoices/choices* (twice), *passion/lash on*, *thousand/bows and*, *call so/also*, *waft her/after*, *speech is/beaches*, *ruin/grew in* and *rejoices/choice is*. In my view there is simply no place in serious poetry for rhymes of this kind, and somewhere in Swinburne's poetic make-up there is a defective component. Another distasteful element in Swinburne is the virtuoso energy with which he finds rhymes in a language where they are a rarity. He finds many rhymes for 'Our Lady of Pain' in 'Dolores', and, incredibly, forty-one rhymes for Faustine in 'Faustine'. Some of them are only half-rhymes, but their ubiquity merely increases the sense of claustrophobia and grotesqueness. In 'Itylus' there are rhymes for 'swallow' in all ten stanzas, and the sense of the presence of rhyme is heightened by internal rhyme: 'Sister, my sister, O fleet sweet swallow'.

Rhyme for the Victorians was an important constituent of the soul of poetry, but its treacheries, as exemplified in Butler's *Hudibras* (1662–78) and Barham's *Ingoldsby Legends* (1840–47), were never far from their minds. In extreme cases strange and difficult rhymes invite the suspicion that the search for them has generated the meaning and nothing is more damaging to the spirit of poetry than that.

Notes

1. *The Letters of Gerard Manley Hopkins to Robert Bridges*, edited by C. C. Abbott (1955), p. 46.

2. *The Poems of Gerard Manley Hopkins*, edited by W. H. Gardner and N. H. Mackenzie (1970), p. 256.

3. *The Poems of Arthur Hugh Clough*, edited by F. L. Mulhauser (Oxford, 1974), p. 557.

4. Ibid., p. 556.

5. See D. Attridge, *The Rhythms of English Poetry* (1982), for discussion of the outmodedness of the concept of poetic feet, especially pp. 4–18.

6. Byron, letter to Thomas Moure, 2 January 1814, in *Byron's Letters and Journals*, edited by L. A. Marchand (1973–82), VI, 13.

7. A. C. Swinburne, 'Social Verse', in *The Complete Works of Algernon Charles Swinburne* (1926), XV, 26–88.

8. For an analysis of the mechanical and the predictable as a mainspring of comedy see H. Bergson, *Laughter*, edited by W. Sypher (New York, 1956).

9. O. Wilde, *The Critic as Artist*, in *Complete Works of Oscar Wilde*, introduction by V. Holland (1966), p. 1012.

Chapter 5
Genres

In European literature since the Renaissance there has been a tendency for genres to be fluid, to merge with each other, to metamorphose, to decay. Writers have been increasingly reluctant to write in pre-determined genres, especially major artists. The quest for originality has almost demanded that readers' expectations should not be readily gratified, but rather challenged and surprised. Dissatisfaction with the predetermined genre has intensified since the Romantic Movement, since the notion of a pre-existent form into which one could pour one's original experience was abhorrent. The aesthetic of incarnation demanded the creation at once of body and spirit; it would not do to infuse novel spirit into inherited body. The whole resistance to the circumscription of genre is encapsulated in these lines of *Aurora Leigh*:

> What form is best for poems? Let me think
> Of forms less, and the external. Trust the spirit,
> As sovran nature does, to make the form;
> For otherwise we only imprison spirit
> And not embody.
>
> (VI. 223–27)

In so far as Elizabeth Barrett thought positively of forms, it was of innovatory forms: 'I am inclined to think that we want new *forms* . . . as well as thoughts. The old gods are dethroned. Why should we go back to the antique moulds? . . . Let us all aspire rather to *Life* – and let the dead bury their dead.'[1]

There has been a continuing tendency for modern thought to promote the anti-hierarchical, and genres were traditionally indicative of hierarchical societies, merely by the precedence accorded to some of them. This hierarchy is studied by Alastair Fowler in a comprehensive review of literary genres.[2] Epic and tragedy are accorded pride of place, with georgic, pastoral, elegy, and lyric following, and satire and epigram at the bottom of the list. Even in classical times there were, inevitably, attempts to compromise or reverse the dignity of the respected genres, and burlesque and travesty flourished (one thinks of Homer's *Margites* and Aristophanic comedy). And yet mock-heroic *needs* the heroic as a parasitic plant needs its host. Questions of genre are complicated because genres are not merely forms; they also embrace some concept of attitude to experience, and shade into modes. At one point Alastair Fowler describes the sonnet as a 'genre'. One's first reaction is that this is stretching the term too far, since a sonnet is basically a poetic form and the label has no significance beyond the technical identification, but on reflection the main-line sonnet did include the notion of a certain stance and frame of mind, and a predictable range of subject-matter, to such an extent that modifications made by Milton and others are registered as challenges to and extensions of the original concept. If Harold Bloom's literary map of 'anxiety' is reliable, then genres will play their part, since the inherited genre is just one more way in which one feels perturbed in the presence of ancestors.[3] And the strategies for dealing with this 'anxiety' can be traced through the centuries. Burlesque and inversion is one, arising from a tendency to pull down the pretentious and the intimidating. Incremental addition is another – to add to a previous tradition in such a way that one's own contribution and originality is visible. Wordsworth's *Prelude* will fit into some such scheme; he wanted to write epic, since that almost seemed to be demanded of a career-poet, yet he could repose faith in neither classical secular epic nor Miltonic religious epic, so had to find a way of making intimate experience epic. In one sense this procedure is close to burlesque and travesty, but on the other hand it could be said to glorify the genre, by demonstrating that the form and the attitudes promoted by epic were capable of hitherto undreamt-of extension into private realms.

An interesting recent study of the modification and transmutation of genres has been undertaken by Peter Conrad, who claims that 'the formal originality of English literature declares itself in the reordering of relations between the classical genres'.[4] The principal motive force in this 'reordering' is more than a blind drive for originality; it would be better to attribute it to some continuing quest for reality, as if each generation of writers wished to get closer and closer to reality as they saw it, but were impeded by the machinery at their disposal, the expressive machinery of literary and other artistic types. This accounts, for instance, for the brusque manner in which Ruskin and George Eliot dismissed pastoral operetta.[5]

But nineteenth-century writers did not wish to ditch concepts of genre altogether, since these types did in some ways give birth to actual experience, so that the struggle to win through to an accurate diagnosis of life had to take place in the territory mapped out by the genres, not in some alien region. This explains why Victorian novelists found it necessary to rewrite the Gothic novel over and over again. Contemporary writers are still concerned with questions of genre, but some of them have hoped, misguidedly I think, that it might be best to bypass concepts of genre altogether, and write a literature that eludes taxonomy. True to the spirit of spontaneity and avoidance of genre, D. H. Lawrence even became worried that a concept such as *vers libre* might become set in a mould, and wrote of its practitioners: 'They do not know that free verse has its own *nature*, that it is neither star nor pearl, but instantaneous like plasm. . . . For such utterance any externally applied law would be mere shackles and death. The law must come each time from within.'[6] This sums up a widespread twentieth-century attitude among writers suspicious of the predeterminations of genre and literary forms. Throughout this study I emphasize the quest for realism and closeness to lived experiences; it was very earnest and intense in the nineteenth century, and it must be the underlying reason for the century having been, in Fowler's words, possibly 'the most prolific of all literary periods in experimentation with genre'.[7] The novel certainly underwent fascinating and complicated changes, moving, on the one hand, towards a completer realism and documentary reliability, and on the other (although this need not invariably be regarded as a contradictory movement), towards lyricism.[8]

It is possible to isolate some large-scale tendencies in the poetry. The major poets did not find the epic inviting, partly because they were not interested in the consensus attitudes which its creation and reception demands, partly because, as Mario Praz has shown, there was a modification of concepts of heroism in the century.[9] Hence, as Peter Conrad has noticed, at the end of Arnold's *Sohrab and Rustum* 'epic conflict dies into pastoral.'[10] If epic did exist it was in some curiously mutated form, as G. K. Chesterton recognized when he called *The Ring and the Book* an 'epic of free speech'.[11] Certainly the poem is very long, and the story-line does not surprise us very much, especially after we have heard it half a dozen times or so in the early books; in this sense it comes to resemble those epics that deal with familiar material. It is very dense in specification and introduces us to a wide swathe of social practices after the manner of epic. It includes a number of epic features. There is, for instance, something resembling an invocation:

> O lyric Love, half angel and half bird
> And all a wonder and a wild desire, –
> Boldest of hearts that ever braved the sun,
> Took sanctuary within the holier blue,
> And sang a kindred soul out to his face, –
> Yet human at the red-ripe of the heart –

When the first summons from the darkling earth
Reached thee amid thy chambers, blanched their
        blue,
And bared them of the glory – to drop down,
To toil for man, to suffer or to die, –
This is the same voice: can thy soul know change?
Hail then, and hearken from the realms of help!
                                        (I. 1390–1402)

It continues for another fourteen lines. The appeal for help is to his
dead wife Elizabeth – ironical when one recalls that while living she
discouraged him from writing the poem that we now recognize as his
supreme masterpiece. There is also the paradox that although he is
writing a poem on a massive scale he seeks inspiration from a 'lyric'
source. In this passage, with its protracted and complicated syntax,
there is something that reminds us of the Miltonic invocations. The
poem also ends with an invocation to 'lyric Love'.

Other epic features in *The Ring and the Book* are the long metaphors
and comparisons, and even when they are not in exactly the formula
of the epic simile they have a similar effect. There is also a good deal
of epic mythological machinery; not that the gods appear in their own
persons, but are present as analogues to the action: the principal myths
are of the fall of Satan, Perseus, and Andromeda, St George and the
Dragon, and Mars, Vulcan, and Venus. Sometimes the references are
nothing other than mock-epic, as when 'the Other Half-Rome' thinks
of Guido 'playing Vulcan's Part' (III. 1450), and Pietro is amazed to
think of Guido as Hercules. But when Guido recognizes mythological
parallels it is with a savagely sardonic tone, as in these lines when he
confronts Caponsacchi in flight:

'Vulcan pursuing Mars, as poets sing, – Still at the last
    here pant I, but arrive,
Vulcan – and not without my Cyclops too.'
                                        (VI. 1459–61)

Despite these epic features however, it would be wrong to think that
Browning was trying to write an epic. One's constant awareness,
reading the work, is that Browning is trying to evade genre altogether,
both in the kinds of technical limitations it can impose, and the specific
modes and moods it requires. Indeed, although at the beginning and
end of the poem Browning, as creator, recognizes that he is engaging
in artistic activity, during the poem he tries to induce the sense that
one can get closer to life by evading genres and perhaps art itself.

Throughout the poem there are references to the way in which various genres could deal with the material. The participants are haunted by the possibilities of calumniating versions of their ordeals – rather as Shakespeare's Cleopatra is haunted by the image of the 'squeaking Cleopatra' who will impersonate her. Guido imagines satirical treatment:

> Has the priest, with nobody to court beside,
> Courted the Muse in exile, hitched my hap
> Into a rattling ballad-rhyme which, bawled
> At tavern-doors, wakes rapture everywhere?
>
> (v. 1450–53)

And Caponsacchi feels that he has strayed not into tragic or epic events, but farcical:

> Would Molière's self wish more than hear such man
> Call, claim such woman for his own, his wife,
> Even though, in due amazement at the boast,
> He had stammered, she moreover was divine?
>
> (vi. 1487–90)

Caponsacchi, who knows a great deal about literary forms, is urged by friends to write a travesty of events, 'De Raptu Helenae' (vi. 1747) in scazons (iambic verse, with a spondee in the final foot). The Pope imagines that in the future the events will be forgotten, and 'No bard describe in verse how Christ prevailed/And Satan fell like lightning!' (x. 617–72). To some degree he is right, since Browning does not accord Guido Miltonic treatment, and even though he is Satanic his fall is more like a series of slithers; this, at least, is the image Caponsacchi uses:

> As the snake, hatched on hill-top by mischance,
> Despite his wriggling, slips, slides, slidders
>   down
> Hill-side, lies low and prostrate on the smooth
> Level of the outer place, lapsed in the vale:
> So I lose Guido in the loneliness,
> Silence and dusk.
>
> (vi. 1924–29)

The tendency of these references is twofold: to make us believe that there is truth and experience anterior to artistic treatment of it; and to make us believe that even as we live our lives we recognize a diversity of parallels between our experience and the matter of literature, but literature not of one genre, not in one mode, but a multiplicity. The sheer range of reference to a large number of genres and modes in *The Ring and the Book* ultimately has the effect of making us believe that the poem itself does not readily belong to any of them, and is close to the unmediated fabric of life itself. One can think of other works of literature, especially novels and dramas, that have made this bid to elude the aesthetic categories of genre, and writers wishing to do this always have before them the encouraging precedent of Shakespeare.

In Tennyson's *Idylls* we see a rather different procedure: the attempt not so much to elude genre categories, but to modify them. It might have seemed that when Tennyson seized on Arthurian material the epic form was called for; Milton casting about for epic subject-matter thought that there were possibilities there. But as I show later (see below p. 113) Tennyson approached it in a more allusive manner, sketching in scenes rather than going in for full development, and thinking in idyllic terms. The tragic mode remained a possibility for the Victorians (although good tragic drama was not possible), emphasized, to some degree, by the erosion of religious faith and the emergence of theories of scientific determinism. These theories corresponded to certain tragic attitudes, but the Victorian writers were interested in the operations of chance, in the accumulation of particular details, and in the presence of unrepeatable conditions – all elements encouraged by the dominance of the novel. This world view militates against tragedy, so that potential tragedy in *The Ring and the Book* is averted – though perhaps not by any conscious artistic decision.

The lyric is found in the period, and there are some very fine ones, although Swinburne complained that in 'in the huge bulk of [Browning's] lyrical baggage there is not one good song'.[12] Likewise Henry James said that Browning was 'a poet without a lyre', who 'had the scroll, but not often the sounding strings'.[13] There is a tendency in twentieth-century criticism to undervalue the lyric, so that these days that part of the canon is not considered very much. It is connected with the suspicion that loomed large in T. S. Eliot's criticism that mellifluous sound axiomatically compromised sense and significance. And yet because of the Victorian poets' continued sentimental attachment to the idea of the vatic they were reluctant completely to forgo the idea of the lyric (as a mode, perhaps, rather than as a genre) and they sought to retain it, but incorporating some modifications of their own. This explains Browning's espousal of the notion of the 'dramatic lyric' – although this does not perform a radical dislocation of the traditional lyric; it is more that a tendency which had existed even in the Elizabethan lyrics is now underlined and made explicit. Peter Conrad is pretty close to the mark when he says: 'A lyric can exist only if it is not felt: that is why Browning's love-poems . . . refuse, in their tortuous argumentation and interrogative barrages, to be mellifluous.'[14] The lyrical impulse survives in a less heavily modified form in Tennyson. It survives in Rossetti, and his sonnet cycle *The House of Life* possibly has greater lyrical intensity and concentration even than his Elizabethan models, unlike Meredith's cycle *Modern Love*, which is more speculative and analytical than them, and unlike Elizabeth Barrett Browning's *Sonnets from the Portuguese*, which is more personal and confessional. In Tennyson and Rossetti the elegiac mode is dominant, and this keeps the poetry musical and mellifluous; and the impulse is so strong in them, and in other poets, that a whole chapter is devoted to it later. But it is worth mentioning here that *In Memoriam* is far from straightforward in generic terms, since it is longer than most elegies, more anecdotal, more discursive. It does not overthrow the tradition, but strains its boundaries.

The ode continues to exist; the ballad is still written – Meredith's 'Jumping Jenny' being a particularly striking example. Descriptive poetry exists, under the heading of what Wordsworth called in the 1815 Preface 'The Idyllium' – 'descriptive chiefly either of the processes and appearances of external nature, or of characters, manners, and sentiments'.[15] But as I suggest in Chapter 11 (see below pp. 192–93) purely descriptive poetry is not that common (unless one reads a slightly old-fashioned poet like Clare), and description has a tendency to be incidental to theme or characterization.

Undoubtedly the most significant generic innovation in the poetry of the century was the dramatic monologue.[16] This drew into poetry the interest in character and incident, set in specific times and specific places, which had been cultivated by the dominance, in the immediately preceding centuries, of the novel and drama. Most of the poems we find interesting and arresting from the period are either dramatic monologues or forms not too far distant from them. *Maud* does not have an implied listener in the poem of the kind found in *Bishop Blougram*, for instance, but the poem's stark effects result from the projection of a strong personality. *Dipsychus* is not dramatic monologue, it is more like dramatic dialogue, but it too derives its power from vivid scene and personality. *Amours de Voyage* is an especially lively presentation of self in letter form, and not so remote from Browning's dramatic monologues, and is an example of the kind of poetry Wordsworth had seen coming into dominance in the 1815 Preface to his collection of poems when he listed the 'impassioned Epistle' as 'a species of monodrama'.[17] Browning is thought to be the principal exponent of the dramatic monologue, but Tennyson's 'St. Simeon Stylites' is a fine example of the genre, likewise the two Northern Farmer poems. (see above pp. 56–57). Rossetti's 'Jenny' is a vivid interior monologue poem, and there are few preceding examples.

The greatest achievement in the field of the dramatic monologue is Browning's *The Ring and the Book* (1868); indeed, it is one of the very greatest achievements of Victorian poetry, partly because its method, the accumulation of a series of monologues, amounts to the creation of what is virtually a new genre from a technical point of view, even though, as I suggested earlier, there is a tendency for the poem to try and evade the limitations of the easily identifiable genre. It is written in twelve books, and the same story is approached by a sequence of different monologists, one of them being the poet himself. Its length and its tendency to repetitiveness might at first seem very off-putting, but once the reader is immersed in the poem it is hard to put down – and there are very few long poems in the English language of which that could honestly be said! That one should be so enthralled by the poem, even though knowing the main lines of the story ahead of time, is a great tribute to its power.

To conclude: the period is very rich in exploration of genres, and a great deal of energy was expended, especially by a restless and innovatory poet like Browning, in the modification and development of them. A reader always needs to know when such developments take place, since inevitably they constitute an important part of the total meaning; they are not merely part of the operation of the technical devices.

Notes

1. *The Letters of Robert Browning and Elizabeth Barrett Browning 1845–1846*, edited by E. Kintner (Cambridge, Mass., 1969), I, 43.

2. A. Fowler, *Kinds of Literature: An Introduction to the Theory of Genres and Modes* (Oxford, 1982). This is the only comprehensive study of genre theory ever undertaken. See also W. D. Shaw, 'Victorian Poetics: An Approach Through Genre', *Victorian Newsletter*, 39 (1971), 1–4 and 'Philosophy and Genre in Victorian Poetics: the Idealist Legacy', *ELH*, 52 (1985), 471–501.

3. For a study of the *Angst* of belatedness see H. Bloom, *The Anxiety of Influence: A Theory of Poetry* (New York, 1973).

4. P. Conrad, *The Everyman History of English Literature* (1985), p. 145.

5. For objections to the absurdities of operetta see J. Ruskin, *Modern Painters*, IV, Ch. 19, *Works*, VI, 390–92, and G. Eliot, 'The Natural History of German Life', in *Essays of George Eliot*, edited by T. Pinney (1963), pp. 266–99.

6. D. H. Lawrence, Introduction to *New Poems* (New York, 1918), in *The Complete Poems of D. H. Lawrence*, edited by V. De Sola Pinto, 2 vols (1964, reprinted 1967, 1972), p. 185.

7. Fowler, p. 206.

8. Ibid., p. 211.

9. See Mario Praz, *The Hero in Eclipse* (1956).

10. Conrad, p. 494.

11. G. K. Chesterton, *Robert Browning* (1903), p. 73.

12. A. C. Swinburne, 'The Chaotic School', c. 1863–64 (a posthumously published essay), in *Browning: The Critical Heritage*, edited by B. Litzinger and D. Smalley (1970), p. 217.

13. H. James, *English Hours* (1905), p. 47.

14. Conrad, p. 522.

15. W. Wordsworth, 'Preface to *Poems*' (1815) in *The Prose Works of William Wordsworth*, edited by W. J. Bowen and J. W. Smyser, 3 vols (Oxford, 1974), III, 28.

16. The main studies on dramatic monologue are: A. Sinfield, *Dramatic Monologue* (1977); R. Rader, 'Dramatic Monologue', *Critical Inquiry*, 3 (1976), 131–51; and A. D. Culler, 'Monodrama and the Dramatic Monologue', *PMLA*, 90 (1975), 366–85. The Summer 1984 edition of *Victorian Poetry* was entirely devoted to articles on the dramatic monologue.

17. Wordsworth, p. 27.

Chapter 6
The Past

Tennyson's Ancient Sage reflects on the appeal of the past:

> for oft
> On me, when boy, there came what then I
>   called,
> Who knew no books and no philosophies,
> In my boy-phrase 'The Passion of the Past'.
> The first gray streak of earliest summer-
>   dawn,
> The last long stripe of waning crimson gloom,
> As if the late and early were but one –
> A height, a broken grange, a grove, a flower
> Had murmurs 'Lost and gone and lost and
>   gone!'
> A breath, a whisper – some divine farewell –
> Desolate sweetness – far and far away –
>   (*The Ancient Sage* (1885), ll. 216–26)

These lines are characteristic of Tennyson and emanate from a central
motive in his art. 'Tears, idle tears' of forty years before expresses the
'divine despair' that arises

> In looking on the happy Autumn-fields,
> And thinking of the days that are no more,
>   (ll. 24–5)

and compares the sadness and strangeness of 'the days that are no
more' with 'dark summer dawns'. The lyric was written at Tintern
Abbey, not far from where Hallam was buried, and Tennyson said that
it expressed 'the yearning that young people occasionally experience
for that which seems to have passed away from them for ever'.[1] One
questions the word 'occasionally' in the context of Tennyson, since

yearning and regret for the past were so dominant in his life. He told James Knowles that this poem was

> in a way like St. Paul's 'groanings which cannot be uttered'. . . . It is what I have always felt even from a boy, and what as a boy I called the 'passion of the past'. And it is so always with me now; it is the distance that charms me in the landscape, the picture and the past, and not the immediate to-day in which I move.[2]

Tennyson's friend James Spedding observed in 1835 that Tennyson was 'always discontented with the Present till it has become the Past, and then he yearns toward it, and worships it, and not only worships it, but is discontented because it is past'.[3] Since the principal event in Tennyson's real and poetic life occurred so early – the death of Hallam – it was inevitable that his poetry should be retrospective, but Tennyson's backward-looking was not confined to the events of his own life; it extended to include whole eras previous to his own. Even without the death of Hallam the fact that so much of the influence on Tennyson was by way of literature which either dealt with the past or *came* from the past would inevitably have meant that his poetry would give every appearance of being haunted. Time and time again one finds this characteristic state of mind:

> The Present is the vassal of the Past:
> So that, in that I *have* lived, so I live
> And cannot die, and am, in having been –
> A portion of the pleasant yesterday,
> Thrust forward on today and out of place;
> A body journeying onward, sick with toil,
> The weight as if of age upon my limbs.
>
> (*The Lover's Tale* ll. 115–21).

Tennyson is an extreme case, and his poetry is dominated by reverie, nostalgia, longing, and melancholy. His main rival is Hardy, who was similarly obsessed by the past – especially his own past. But Hardy was able to review past and present with a much more sceptical and inquiring eye. Most other poets of the period, to a greater or lesser degree, had this dominant orientation to their own pasts and the pasts of their own and other societies. One thinks of Browning, Arnold, Swinburne, Rossetti, and Morris. Arnold's Empedocles feels the magnetic pull:

> And we shall struggle awhile, gasp and rebel –
> And we shall fly for refuge to past times,

> Their soul of unworn youth, their breath of
>   greatness;
>   (*Empedocles*, ii. 382–84)

It seems especially impossible to forget, in the Victorian era, that Mnemosyne is the mother of the Muses. As a number of critics have pointed out the past is a dominant interest for Victorian writers.[4]

One's dominant impression is that the passion for the past among these Victorian poets is directly related to their sense of alienation and their desire for some kind of escape. Even the sceptical Claude in Clough's *Amours de Voyage* wishes to escape from the 'clamour of arts' in the present, so that he may be hidden '*in the past and the Arts*' (ii. 343). In his series of twenty sonnets *Thoughts While Reading History* (1845) Frederick Faber oscillates from valuing the restrospective view (which was in fact his natural and dominant tendency) to castigating it:

> There is no bent of mind so vile, so weak,
> As that which on the glorious Past doth set
> In currents of inordinate regret;
> And with a sphere of dreams content, doth wreak
> Itself upon the love of beauty.
>   ('Use of the Past', ll. 1–5)

He is half-hearted in his condemnation though, since the past is allowed to figure as 'the glorious Past'. The two poems 'Chivalrous Times' demonstrate diametrically opposed views of the past, of approval and disapproval.

It will be seen, and particularly in the interest taken in previous cultures rather than the private world of the individual poets, that the pursuit of the past was not necessarily escapist and satisfying a taste for fantasy. In many cases it was part of an exercise in self-definition and self-knowledge: one chose moments in the past as landmarks from which to measure one's own position – often, as it happened, a very superior position, since there was a certain amount of historical Pharisaism in the Victorian era. Macaulay proposes ideas with Philistine complacency when he opines that 'nothing is so interesting and delightful as to contemplate the steps by which . . . the England of crusaders, monks, schoolmen . . . became . . . the classic ground of liberty and philosophy, the school of all knowledge, the mart of all trade'.[5] Macaulay's *Lays of Ancient Rome* was a best-seller; it was healthy and athletic and suitable for every schoolboy in Britain who would grow up and take part in the expansion of the Empire. His

History of England from the Accession of James II celebrated Whig progressivism, and it too was staggeringly popular, selling 22,000 copies in
1849, which puts his sales on a level with Dickens. Many men were
grateful that they had been born in the nineteenth century rather than
some previous one; the classic utterance is by J. A. Froude when he
writes, in 'On Progress' (1870): 'Our lights are before us, and all
behind is shadow. In every department of life, in its business and in
its pleasures . . . in its material developments and in its spiritual
convictions – we thank God that we are not like our fathers'.[6] When
Browning's corrupt Renaissance Bishop orders his tomb the poet can
afford to take a connoisseur's delight in him because he knows that in
that precise form such humanistic cynicism cannot return to blight his
society, even though a diluted form of the phenomenon could pose a
minor threat if one were not vigilant.

The Victorian age was very eclectic in its interests. In previous
centuries a rather narrow range of pasts had been available for inspection, but suddenly in the nineteenth century the scope became extraor-
dinarily wide. Undoubtedly there were some favourite areas of interest
– such as Periclean Athens and the Christian Middle Ages – but if one
were interested in venturing into untrodden ways, such as Moorish
Spain, Assyria, or Byzantium, there were plenty of aids for doing so,
and every opportunity for turning them into poetry. William Morris
may, in an over-arching sense, have been fairly single-minded, but his
interests were typically eclectic – Iceland, Norse mythology, medieval
Gascony, classical times to name but a few. Browning is extremely
eclectic. Arnold's poetry may have the habit of sounding homogeneous, but his sources at least are very varied. The wide availability
of the past has been well studied by Peter Conrad in *The Victorian
Treasure House* (1973). The eclecticism was beginning in the Romantic
Movement, but was much expanded in the era we are considering.

As I shall go on to show, there was a utilitarian element in the study
of the past has been well studied by Peter Conrad in *The Victorian*
definition and self-knowledge. The past was also a theatre in which
problems could be acted out, but in an environment free from modern
associations, so that one almost produced 'scientific conditions' to
study the operations of psychology or social struggle. This had the
immediate benefit of making the interest seem relevant to modern
concerns, yet there is a curious sense in which this very pragmatism
and functionalism brought the wheel full circle, to produce a history
which we should be inclined to call fantasy. Atmospherically the Utilitarian historians may not have produced other-worldly Keatsian and
Tennysonian images (which have clearly been generated in the drugged
and dream-haunted mind), but the images they did produce were none
the less unreal, since their very relevance and applicability meant that

they were constructed in the terms of the present. It could fairly be said, both of most historians proper and of historical novelists and poets choosing the past for their subject, that in the Victorian era they were not whole-heartedly interested in the pastness of the past, or in those ways in which the past resembled nothing at all in the present. They were more interested in those moments in the past when there is an uncanny resemblance to the present, and if the resemblance did not naturally present itself they were all too ready to fabricate it. They did not regard the past as dead. But it is only when the past is regarded as dead that we are able to see it plain and listen for *its* note, not the one we think should have been sounding. Only then can it breathe its own life and not ours. The strength and the weakness of Victorian poetry of the past is that it breathes nothing other than Victorian life. Perhaps this could not be perceived at the time; it is not unlike the axiom well known to painting connoisseurs: the art fakes stand a good chance of deceiving the generation they were meant to deceive, but will never deceive (stylistically at least) subsequent ones. The energies and motives producing the Victorian images of the past were then very varied, and atmospherically there is a great variety too (as there was in the thousands upon thousands of paintings of historical scenes), but there remains, nevertheless, a kind of family likeness about them.

There were of course other Victorian appropriations of the past in which little or no pretence was made that the past was in any way being reproduced. This can be understood by considering Victorian neo-Gothic architecture. Some of it (G. E. Street's work for instance) does make the attempt to reproduce buildings in authentic styles. Many are, in effect, fakes, although they usually betray themselves to *us* as Victorian. Other work, and William Butterfield's could be cited as an example, uses Gothic motifs and principles, but is to be regarded as modern, and more like a continuation of the Middle Ages than a reproduction of them. This could lead to a kind of inappropriateness. Ruskin lived long enough to regret that fine Venetian Gothic was pressed into the service of the sale of gin,[7] and Hardy regretted, at the Crawford–Dilke trial in July 1866, that the implicit freedom of Gothic decoration was now associated with the repression of the Law Courts: 'As to the architecture of the courts, there are everywhere religious art-forces, masquerading as law symbols! The leaf, flower, fret, suggested by spiritual emotion, are pressed into the service of social strife'.[8]

Victorian Gothic architecture is a hybrid, amalgamating the old and the new, and although hybrids may be not unsuccessful in buildings they often do not work particularly well in literature. One of the most notorious literary hybrids of this kind is *The Princess*, which is unable to commit itself whole-heartedly to the Middle Ages (even though a degree of commitment to the past is needed to create the implausible

Love's Labour's Lost type of situation). A sense of possible failure is even built into the work:

> And I, betwixt them both, to please them
> both,
> And yet to give the story as it rose,
> I moved as in a strange diagonal,
> And maybe neither pleased myself or them.
>
> (Conclusion, ll. 25–28)

To some degree the *Idylls* are hybrid too, but since less self-consciously so than *The Princess* they are much more open to criticism; it often seems that they were meant to engage in some sort of evocation of the Middle Ages, but actually they are about as authentic as Lerner and Loewe's musical *Camelot*. The vigour, the earthiness, the extreme religiosity, the sexuality of the Middle Ages are simply not there, but Tennyson thought he could stint his attention to those aspects because what he wanted to say about the present was so important. This was grossly misplaced confidence, however, and explains why virtually no one now gives either *The Princess* or the *Idylls* unqualified praise. Without wishing to seem too Philistine, isn't there something entirely refreshing in Elizabeth Barrett's comment to Robert Browning, apropos of *The Princess*: 'Now isn't the world too old and fond of steam, for blank verse poems, in ever so many books, to be written on the fairies?'[9] The fact that the *Idylls* are idylls represents a profound loss of confidence in the capacity to produce epic, which requires an ability to grasp a historical and a transcendental world in entirety. All that Tennyson could manage were allusive glimpses into relatively brief and often isolated episodes, though he was sufficiently intelligent to be aware of his deficiency. In the end perhaps there was not much hope for Tennyson, since other writers have managed to make their pasts vivid by building on their lively sense of the present. This resource was not fully available to him, as he explains in a letter to Emily Sellwood: 'To me the far-off world seems nearer than the present, for in the present is always something unreal and undistinct.'[10]

The most famous plea for modernity in poetry, which, naturally, involved turning one's back on the past, was made by Elizabeth Barrett Browning at the opening of Book v of *Aurora Leigh*:

> I do distrust the poet who discerns
> No character or glory in his times,
> And trundles back his soul five hundred years,
> Past moat and drawbridge, into a castle
> court . . .
>
> (ll. 189–92)

She continues that the 'sole work' of modern poets

> is to represent the age,
> Their age, not Charlemagne's, – this live,
> > throbbing age,
> That brawls, cheats, maddens, calculates, aspires,
> And spends more passion, more heroic heat,
> Betwixt the mirrors of its drawing-rooms,
> Than Roland with his knights at Roncesvalles.
> To flinch from modern varnish, coat or flounce,
> Cry out for togas and the picturesque,
> Is fatal, – foolish too. King Arthur's self
> Was commonplace to Lady Guenever;
> And Camelot to minstrels seemed as flat
> As Fleet Street to our poets.
> > > (ll. 202–13)

One sees her point – that sometimes the descriptions of bric-à-brac in Camelot have the breathless excitement of a travel-writer newly set down in Disneyland (the description of the gateway in *Gareth and Lynette* would be an example). Still, she should not have it all her own way, since good Victorian city poets did not regard London streets as flat, but actually rather exciting.

There is often a strongly escapist vein in Victorian poetry with historical settings. Many works are in *The Eve of St. Agnes* tradition – remote, decorative, only impinging on a recognizable life at a psychological level. Some even have strongly archaized diction – especially Morris's 'Tune of the Seven Towers' (modelled not on actual life but a Rossetti painting) and Rossetti's 'The Ballad of Dead Ladies' (a translation of Villon). 'Dule and teen', 'yester-year', 'with pearls arow', 'my coif and my kirtle' are not phrases that will appeal to readers expecting sterner and more immediately relevant stuff. One could write a lengthy monograph on such works. There are other poems that are less dream-like and less precious, which do in fact try to enter the past on its own terms – unpalatable though it might be. Morris's poems about late medieval France – the kind of France Froissart chronicled – would be good examples (poems such as 'The Haystack in the Floods' and 'Shameful Death'). These are stark and unsentimental presentations of the violent and unromanticized late Middle Ages – but in a sense they are irrelevant to the present except very obliquely, as all history pursued in a dispassionate spirit of enquiry must be. No doubt psychologically they helped to release the anger and turbulence that plagued Morris's private life, but this is not to say that they are readily relevant to his period. Even Tennyson realized that the Middle Ages might not always provide models for good modern behaviour. In *Geraint and Enid* we have a picture of a 'realm of lawless turbulence' where violence is done to unprotected women, and a brawny spearman with deficient table manners lets 'his cheek/Bulge with the unswallowed piece' (ll. 629–30).

The Victorian poets had a catholic interest in history, but finally the pasts that spoke most clearly to them were the Middle Ages and the Renaissance, and their appropriation of these periods for their own uses, while, very often, retaining a fair awareness of what they were actually like, is much more impressive than anything of a similar kind *we* have managed to produce in our century. It would be hard to think of a piece of writing since 1900 that has promoted as many excellent buildings and as much enlightened social and progressive thought as Ruskin's essay 'The Nature of Gothic'.[11] We have an inclination in our time to borrow the outward rhetoric of vanished styles with alarming rapidity, but the Victorians, in many cases, often made strenuous efforts to borrow both form and inner substance. Our century seems to have cut the umbilical cord connecting us to the past; for the Victorians it was frayed but not severed.

It has been stressed that the Victorians had a tendency to reshape the past to make it resemble their own times, but when they were prepared to register its difference from themselves it became apparent that its great utility was that it offered challenging contrasts with the present (in many cases to their discomfiture). The classic example of the method of direct comparison is Pugin's *Contrasts* (1836). Likewise Carlyle's *Past and Present* (1843) contrasted the Bury St Edmunds of the Middle Ages with impious and commercial modern times, and the habit of juxtaposition continued until the end of the century: awestruck by a dynamo at the Paris Exposition, Henry Adams contrasted its machine-like force (which was actually promoting multiplicity) with the singleness of purpose that had produced Mont-Saint-Michel and Chartres.[12] It was not just the colour and trappings of the Middle Ages that appealed to the Victorians (although the appeal of those things is very physically exemplified in the Eglinton Tournament[13]); it was the homogeneity, the devoutness, and the certainty of purpose. Appropriately, Alice Chandler's study of the spell of medievalism is titled *A Dream of Order* (1971). Even among those whose very existence depended on wilful individualism, such as Ruskin and Rossetti, the appeal of a close-knit society and a single-minded life was very potent, and in *News from Nowhere* (1890) William Morris tried to imagine the impossible combination of a static society and untrammelled individuals; he invents a vague simulacrum of medieval life, but without its piety, its militarism, its feudalism, and its progressivism. (It might seem odd to attribute the latter feature to the Middle Ages, but

Maurice Beresford's work *The New Towns of the Middle Ages: Town Plantation in England, Wales and Gascony* (1967) concentrates on the emergence of developing forces opposed to feudalism and reaction.) The 'contrast' habit appealed to Morris, as in the familiar lines which juxtapose a modern London with a fourteenth-century one:

> Forget six counties overhung with smoke,
> Forget the snorting steam and piston smoke,
> Forget the spreading of the hideous town;
> Think rather of the pack-horse on the down,
> And dream of London, small and white and clean,
> The clear Thames bordered by its gardens green;
>
> (*The Earthly Paradise* Introduction, ll. 1–6).

Sometimes direct comparisons between past and present seemed possible. In Browning's 'Love Among the Ruins' the young man can almost reach out and touch 'the monarch and his minions and dames' and 'all the causeys, bridges, aqueducts' as he waits for his mistress, whose love will eclipse the residual memory of that world. In 'Stanzas from the Grande Chartreuse' Arnold has an even closer encounter with a vanished world:

> The silent courts, where night and day
> Into their stone-carved basins cold
> The splashing icy fountains play –
> The humid corridors behold!
> Where, ghostlike in the deepening night,
> Cowled forms brush by in gleaming white.
>
> (ll. 31–36)

Rossetti's 'The Burden of Nineveh' also depicts a direct encounter between an old civilization and modern England, as one of Layard's excavated statues is brought into the British Museum.[14] The prevailing attitude is that once exhibited in a museum an ancient idol is anaesthetized, and may be viewed as nothing more than a curio, but Rossetti wonders if potency may not still reside in the statue. Certainly it has looked on a more vivid and sunlit past:

> Within thy shadow, haply, once
> Sennacherib has knelt, whose sons
> Smote him between the altar-stones:
> Or pale Semiramis her zones
>   Of gold, her incense brought to thee,
> In love for grace, in war for aid:
>
> (ll. 61–66)

The statue continues to cast its shadow:

> From their dead Past thou liv'st alone;
> And still thy shadow is thine own.
>
> (ll. 48–49)

More characteristically, however, Victorian poets try to create complete imagined worlds in the past for their characters to move about in. Morris was very adept at such creation, and since he was involved in making objects which followed the spirit of the Middle Ages he had a better than average sense of the physical and tactile quality of the period. In the short story 'A Dream' he imagines a medieval knight walking down an avenue, so that the 'moonlight lit up the waves of his mail coat'; here he is writing as if he had actually seen this strange phenomenon – and perhaps he had. As I have already suggested he had a good psychological sense of those past ages too.

But the most sustained creativity was probably exercised by Browning, who possessed an uncanny sense of the past. Henry James referred to 'the all-touching, all-trying spirit of his work, permeated with accumulations and playing with knowledge',[15] and much of that knowledge was historical. Perhaps the supposed deadness of the past was a challenge to Browning's virtuoso creativity so that by performing an act of resurrection he could seem to defeat the powers of life and death:

> Bring good antique stuff.
> Was it alight once? Still lives spark enough
> For breath to quicken, run the smouldering ash
> Red right-through.
>
> (*Parleyings with Certain People*: 'With Charles Avison',
> ll. 293–6)

Into his dragnet came all kinds of things. His knowledge of the past seems inexhaustible. In *The Ring and the Book* it is by the incidental accumulations of information that one is particularly impressed. The seemingly effortless way in which he brings forth a bishop who has a pet scholar writing against Fénelon, and would like a pet musician writing erotic religious madrigals (vi. 321–335) is a good example of this power. Likewise the thick-textured passage on the social climbing of a lackey known to Guido, that is the equivalent of the dense and impressive knowledge that Thackeray has at his fingertips (v. 298–335). Then just a few lines later there are some throw-away observations on

the tribulations of the artmarket, in reference to Pietro of Cortona and
Ciro Ferri (v. 485–492). At every point the prodigious genius is on
display. Browning liked the palpability of the past, and there are parts
of Sordello which fill it out for us as vividly as some of the scene-
painting in Tennyson's *Idylls*. These descriptions are often cited,
presumably because they are rare points in the work where the average
reader actually understands what is going on. This is the description
of the font in Goito:

> A dullish grey-streaked cumbrous font, a group
> Round it, – each side of it, where'er one sees, –
> Upholds it; shrinking Caryatides
> Of just-tinged marble like Eve's lilied flesh
> Beneath her maker's finger when the fresh
> First pulse of life shot brightening the snow.
> The font's edge burthens every shoulder, so
> They muse upon the ground, eyelids half closed;
> Some, with meek arms behind their backs disposed,
> Some, crossed above their bosoms, some, to veil
> Their eyes, some, propping chin and cheek so pale,
> Some, hanging slack an utter helpless length
> Dead as a buried vestal whose whole strength
> Goes when the grate above shuts heavily.
> So dwell these noiseless girls, patient to see,
> Like priestesses because of sin impure
> Penanced for ever, who resigned endure,
> Having that once drunk sweetness to the dregs.
>
> (*Sordello*, I. 410–27)

But even more than to the settings, he was drawn to the rich and
varied identities of the men and women who inhabited the past. He
liked their definiteness, their self-knowledge, their extrovert attitudes,
their sense of purpose, their vigour. These qualities even seemed to go
some way towards extenuating villainy. Years later Yeats was to
express what Browning had undoubtedly felt when he entered the
minds of the long dead: 'I have felt . . . that by assuming a self of past
years, as remote from that of today as some dramatic creation, I
touched a stronger passion, a greater confidence than I possess, or ever
did possess'.[16]

Browning was much disappointed in his own son Pen, but cherished the vain hope that Oxford would make something positive and
distinct out of him. Browning did not have a romantically optimistic
dream of what the past was like; he realized that wickedness was there,

but he found the prospect of the living, breathing people exciting. His major achievement in reanimating the past is *The Ring and the Book*, in which he has the rare courage to take us into the poetic laboratory and exhibit the processes of creation. The main features are psychic power reanimating old documents. Historians often say that history starts to live at the point when one starts to hear the figures speak – and by this definition Browning's figures manifestly live. Count Guido exhibits an overpowering sense of life, at any point in his hundreds of lines. A random quotation will indicate his vitality:

> Life!
> How I could spill this overplus of mine
> Among those hoar-haired, shrunk-shanked odds and
> ends
> Of body and soul old age is chewing dry!
> Those windle-straws that stare while purblind
> death
> Mows here, mows there, makes hay of juicy me,
> And misses just the bunch of withered weed
> Would brighten hell and streak its smoke with
> flame!
> How the life I could shed yet never shrink,
> Would drench their stalks with sap like grass in
> May!
> Is it not terrible, I entreat you, Sirs?
> With manifold and plenitudinous life,
> Prompt at death's menace to give blow for threat,
> Answer his 'Be thou not!' by 'Thus I am!' –
> Terrible so to be alive yet die?
>
> (XI. 143–57)

These lines were strong stuff, and offered the original readers something vivid and startling, perhaps not so very far removed from the theatrical melodramas and gruesome poetry recitals the Victorians found so entertaining. It is surely significant that Guido has more lines to speak than any other character, and Browning found him a fascinating human being. He is an extended version of the Duke in 'My Last Duchess', but he also has affinities with Caliban, in that although he is very nearly a monster, he remains sufficiently human to engage not only our interest but our sympathy, as he himself realizes:

> Let me turn wolf, be whole, and sate, for once, –
> Wallow in what is now a wolfishness

Coerced too much by the humanity
That's half of me as well!

(XI. 2056–59).

At every point he is antipathetic to the listener, whether he is asserting a form of Utilitarianism (as he does at XI. 529: 'For, pleasure being the sole good in the world') or a form of aestheticism, in considering murder as one of the fine arts (XI. 1553–63) and in dismissing Pompilia as the wrong artistic type:

Titian's the man, not Monk Angelico
Who traces you some timid chalky ghost
That turns the church into a charnel: ay,
Just a pencil might depict my wife!

(XI. 2121–24)

He also loses sympathy when he asserts that unbelief may be moving man like a machine (XI. 612–13). But perhaps he loses sympathy most of all not merely because he murders Pompilia, but because he has never valued her, and although he speaks a good deal about ownership, has never earned the right to be married to her. It is a significant and moving fact about this long poem that we first begin to hear Pompilia's direct speech at length through Caponsacchi's report of her, and we have a strong sense that he has watched her and listened to her 'That voice immortal (oh, that voice of hers!)' VI. 1601). Guido's dominant images are of the wife conforming to his 'not disadvantageous mould'.

One of Browning's consistently brilliant achievements, which partly gives the lie to my earlier statement that the Victorians were not really capable of understanding the past, is to present former modes of thought. When the Pope thinks of Pompilia's 'purity of soul/That will not take pollution, ermine-like' (X. 678–79) he is in fact employing the emblematic habit of mind, prevalent throughout the Renaissance and slightly beyond. When Guido follows an elaborate line of thought about his family coat of arms the whole cast of his mind at this point is entirely appropriate for an age obsessed by heraldry, *impreses*, hieroglyphs, and emblems.

Faced with the stupendous achievement of *The Ring and the Book* we are compelled to ask what it is about. Usually at this point, when critics have to say what a literary work is about, they come up with some perverse statement that the work is about language or writing or imagination: they prefer to make the attempt to be original than to state the obvious. *The Ring and the Book* is about a group of people brought into association by a brutal series of events. They lived a long time ago, and their story would have been forgotten were it not for the survival of certain documents and their reanimation at the hands of a creative artist. The actors in the drama are a mixture of the idealistic and the cynically pragmatic; some are obsessed by the search for truth, but others merely wish to survive and prosper. Their lives are complicated and involved, and, as George Eliot might have said, their existence partly explains ours. The pathos is that they are dead and forgotten. Always reading this poem I find lines from Hopkins's 'Heraclitean Fire' running through my head:

> Man, how fast his firedint, his mark on mind, is gone!
> Both are in an unfathomable, all is in an enormous dark
> Drowned. O pity and indignation!
>
> (ll. 11–13)

The poem is about the complicated motifs of life, and it gains in richness and immediacy for the reader because the creative acts that Browning is employing in writing and the reader is employing in reading are directly analogous to the activity of mind so continually on display in the poem from a wide range of characters. But this is not to say that the poem is 'about writing', or even about the difficulty in searching for the truth, since that would narrow and diminish it. It is not a narrowly epistemological puzzle in the sense that Henry James's *The Sacred Fount* is. The poem ranks with Proust's *A la Recherche du Temps Perdu* as a noble endeavour to redeem time past. And yet . . . There is a point at which one resists this vast and impressive work. Browning says that 'Art remains the one way possible/Of speaking truth, to mouths like mine at least' (xii. 843–44). He has made high claims all along for the penetrative imagination, but many times as one has been reading one has realized that the speeches, and even the deeds, are nothing more than suppositions of one man, even as some of the characters within the poem itself invent suppositious speeches and actions. *The Ring and the Book* is as full of fabulists as a Faulkner novel. One finds it very hard to believe that Caponsacchi and Pompilia in the real world were not lovers; Carlyle certainly found it hard to believe, and this nagging doubt is not going to be dislodged even by vast monologues, each of which is about as long as a Shakespeare play. And documents have since come to light which suggest that Pompilia and Caponsacchi were indeed lovers. In the last resort that kind of truth is going to be of much more value than the alternative truth of imaginative supposition, which may turn out not to be truth at all.

Browning, like the best of his contemporaries, seemed to hold in his hands a life-creating potency that was almost magical. In an age when belief in immortality was beginning to wane, the power of men with this measure of creative control must have seemed very impressive. Browning is the salient example of the phenomenon that Yeats identified when he wrote, 'every passionate man . . . is, as it were, linked with another age, historical or imaginary, where alone he finds images that rouse his energy'. Elsewhere Browning's fascination with artists from the past is considered (see below pp. 210–16); and the poems dealing with them are among the most compelling he wrote. The poem that most intrigues modern critics is *Sordello*, which dramatizes the struggle of the poet to grasp and imagine the past and make sense of it. It is a death-defying art:

> Confess now, poets know the dragnet's trick,
> Catching the dead, if fate denies the quick,
> And shaming her;
>   (I. 35–37)

Sordello deals with medieval Italian history, which modern English and American readers are likely to find obscure and irrelevant, but cultivated Victorians were readier to take an interest in it, either independently or in groups. In America a Sordello society was founded, so that a number of heads could be put together to try and make sense of it; a prose paraphrase was concocted to guide them through the labyrinth.[17] *Sordello* has had its admirers, but the average reader is likely to find himself in the state that Henry James experienced when he tried to read Meredith's cryptic *Lord Ormont and his Aminta*: 'A critical rage, an artistic fury, utterly blighting . . . the indispensable principle of respect'.[18] It is, I believe, much less engaging and successful than *The Ring and the Book*.

Finally Tennyson's *Idylls* must be faced, since they loom so large and seem to command so much attention. They do not require as much painful explication as *Sordello*, but it is a challenge to make out a case for their purpose and significance. The Arthurian subject had appealed to Tennyson for a long time, and there were 'trial runs' in 1832 with 'The Lady of Shalott' and in 1842 with *Morte d'Arthur, Sir Launcelot and Queen Guinevere*, and *Sir Galahad*. These early works, characteristically, show Tennyson focusing on points of interest and relatively brief episodes rather than trying to hold a complete epic form in his mind. In the early *Morte d'Arthur* he protects himself with a 'frame': the piece is read by Everard Hall on Christmas Eve, and his dismissive kick at the log which sends 'a blast of sparkles up the flue' suggests momentary illumination and not much more. 'Some modern touches here and there' redeem it, for the listeners, 'from the charge of nothingness'. The *Morte d'Arthur* is at least a conventional blank verse narrative, but 'The Lady of Shalott' is more lyrical than narrative, as if the lives were already caught in the deadly grip of artistic stasis:

> And moving through a mirror clear
> That hangs before her all the year,
> Shadows of the world appear.
> There she sees the highway near
>   Winding down to Camelot:
> There the river eddy whirls,
> And there the surly village-churls,
> And the red cloaks of market girls,
>   Pass onward from Shalott.
>
>   (ll. 46–54)

The sequence of four rhymes, followed by three, has the effect of producing incantatory stasis. This poem is in the dreamy, escapist tradition of Keats's *La Belle Dame Sans Menci*.

From early childhood Tennyson had been fascinated by Arthurian themes, and his sources were not only Malory but Thomas Croker's *Fairy Legends* . . . (1825–28) and Thomas Keightley's *The Fairy Mythology* (1833). The interpretative possibilities were opened up by works such as G. S. Faber's *Horae Mosaicae* (1818) and *The Difficulties of Infidelity* (1833). In 'The Lady of Shalott' he did not feel the need to go far beyond its obviously decorative appeal (although later, as we shall see in the *Idylls*, he was capable of expanding the material into the narrative which became *Lancelot and Elaine* (1859)). However, nine months after 'The Lady of Shalott' was published Arthur Hallam died, and the shock of this had an impact on Tennyson's output: suddenly poems with ostensibly historical subjects were aligned with his personal concerns. The *Morte d'Arthur*, for instance, was composed immediately after Hallam's death and it expresses belief in an after-life 'where falls not hail, or rain, or any snow, nor ever wind blows loudly' (ll. 260–61), in nobility of spirit and in some form of continuity for its influence: 'and all the people cried, "Arthur is come again: he cannot die"' (ll. 295–96). Interests of this kind lie alongside those that are purely antiquarian.

The Idylls were published over a period of twenty-eight years, beginning with the privately printed *Enid and Nimue* of 1857 and extending to *Balin and Balan* of 1885. The 1842 *Morte d'Arthur* was incorporated into *The Passing of Arthur* (1869). It represented a tremendous investment in time and creative energy, even though serious objections had been made decades before when John Sterling said that 'the miraculous legend of "Excalibur" does not come very near to us, and as reproduced by any modern writer must be a mere ingenious exercise of fancy'.[19] Clearly, in a Homeric and Virgilian sense, it had epic possibilities, since the fate of a group of heroes is bound up with the fate of a civilization, but even Malory had not produced an epic (his *Morte d'Arthur* is too episodic and unfocused to be so regarded; it is really a romance), and Milton, though tempted to adopt Arthurian legend as a suitable epic subject, in the end could not feel confident in its value. Tennyson has a sketch in prose dating from the early 1830s of what the opening might be like, and he claims to have had a twelve-book epic 'all in his mind',[20] but was discouraged by Sterling's review. There was also a memorandum for a plan, and the draft of a scenario for a musical masque. In the memorandum it is clear that Tennyson was trying to think allegorically as to how the work might be relevant – with King Arthur as 'Religious Faith' and the two Guineveres as 'primitive Christianity and Roman Catholicism'.[21] Composition took place piecemeal, partly because Tennyson liked to wait for inspiration, and there was no epic plan.

Tennyson simply did not have the confidence to produce a true epic, and he was getting no moral support from his age. Allusive sketches, episodes, vignettes are what the work is finally made up of, and it depends upon a readership that already has some idea of the main story and the main characters. The vigorous sense of life of Malory and *The Mabinogion* is largely absent in the *Idylls*, inevitable when one remembers that Tennyson was not really concerned to reproduce the past. He is creating a separate time that operates by its own laws, and the drift of the work is not antiquarian but parabolic. He said himself: 'Of course Camelot for instance, a city of shadowy palaces, is every-where symbolic of the gradual growth of human beliefs and insti-tutions, and of the spiritual development of man'.[22] But he was also anxious to castigate those critics who 'have taken my hobby, and ridden it too hard, and have explained some things too allegorically'.[23] Tennyson attacked the work with stabs and jabs; he did not compose to a strict programme, and at one point he even thought of side-stepping the Grail legend: 'I doubt whether such a subject as the San Graal could be handled in these days without incurring a charge of irreverence. It would be too much like playing with sacred things'.[24] That was in 1862, but seven years later *The Holy Grail* was published.

One is driven to make allegorical interpretations of the material since the story and its settings are so elusive, rather as the waywardness and impalpability of *The Faerie Queene* compels us in that direction. It is hard to know where Camelot is (though Malory placed it near Winchester), and Tennyson makes Arthur's lineage inscrutable and obscure. He is not specific about the size of the Round Table. His imagination of the whole thing occupying space in a particular historical world is quite vague, and quite unlike the clarity and specificity of Malory. The gateway to Camelot depicts

> 'Arthur's wars in weird devices done,
> New things and old co-twisted, as if Time Were
>   nothing'
>   (*Gareth and Lynette*, ll. 221–23),

and this intermingling might almost be an analogue for the poem. Tennyson was not greatly interested in the historical conditions that might have made courtly love possible, and this means he has to play down the intensity of Lancelot and Guinevere's relationship somewhat, while not absolving them from blame, and play up the unsatisfactoriness of Arthur's position. Characters take on curiously Victorian characteristics: Enid has 'bashful delicacy' – which does not sound medieval, and Arthur expects his subjects to reverence him 'as if he were/Their conscience', which sounds more like something from Matthew Arnold than Thomas Malory. An episode in *Lancelot and Elaine* shows the distance Tennyson has come from the Middle Ages. In Malory Elaine makes a direct and plain proposition to Launcelot:

> 'Have mercy upon me, and suffer me not to die for
> your love' – 'What would you that I did' said Sir
> Launcelot.
>   'I would have you unto my husband,' said the maid
> Elaine. 'Fair damsel, I thank you,' said Sir Launcelot, 'but
> certainly,' said he, 'I cast me never to be married.' –
> 'Then, fair knight,' said she, 'will ye be my paramour?'
>   'Jesu defend me!' said Sir Launcelot,' for then should
> I reward your father and your brother full evil for their
> great goodness.' 'Alas!' said she, 'then must I needs die for
> your love. . . . For but if ye will wed me, or else be my
> paramour at the least, wit ye well, Sir Launcelot, my good
> days are done.'

The parallel passage in Tennyson is quite different, suggesting an enormous change in sensibility. Elaine begins: 'I have gone mad. I love you: let me die.' There is a sort of neurotic extremism here; the medieval woman does not want to die, she wants to go on living, and she does not have an extreme romantic death-wish but a regret that without love she may not be able to sustain life. Tennyson continues

> 'Ah, sister,' answered Lancelot, 'what is this?'
> And innocently extending her white arms

'Your love,' she said, 'your love – to be your
>wife.'
And Lancelot answered, 'Had I chosen to wed,
I had been wedded earlier, sweet Elaine:
But now there never will be wife of mine.'
'No, no,' she cried, 'I care not to be wife,
But to be with you still, to see your face,
To serve you, and to follow you through the
>world.'
>(ll. 926–34)

One cannot quite imagine a medieval woman offering to serve her lover, and is far from specific about what 'to be with you' might involve. Certainly she uses no word as direct as 'paramour'. Lancelot is angry that if they set up an illicit relationship the world will 'blare its own interpretation', yet surely the interpretation will be justified, and will come closer to calling things by their proper names than Lancelot is able to manage. He wants to retain a kind of indefiniteness – as does his creator. Similarly in *The Defence of Guenevere* William Morris cannot quite face up to the sinfulness and ugliness of Lancelot's adultery. When he is found in Guinevere's room they are talking 'like children once again'; no mention of sex and they are in a state Malory would have found it difficult to swallow, 'free from all wrongs'.

In the *Idylls* a kind of indefiniteness permeates a good deal of the description. This often creates splendid effects, but it also diminishes the sense of palpability. The last view of Arthur from Guinevere's point of view is typical:

>and more and more
The moony vapour rolling round the King,
Who seemed the phantom of a Giant in it,
Enwound him fold by fold, and made him gray
And grayer, till himself became as mist
Before her, moving ghostlike to his doom.
>(*Guinevere*, ll. 596–601)

It is a powerful scene, with Arthur presented as a *maior humano* figure, but there is a suggestion that his huge presence may be an optical illusion.

The *Idylls* is a very rich and lovingly wrought work, and although composed over a long period of time it has a unity – perhaps, finally, more of a unity than 'the elegies', which were also composed over a number of years and became *In Memoriam*. The sense of that unity has to be found in the ways that Tennyson thought the content related to his age, and from the beginning it was assumed that there was such a relation. In 1860 the Prince Consort complimented Tennyson by writing that the *Idylls* 'quite rekindle the feeling with which the legends of King Arthur must have inspired the chivalry of old, whilst the graceful form in which they are presented blends those feelings with the softer tone of our present age'.[25] But in the form that the compliment takes, twentieth-century readers will see the central causes of their nagging discontent with this poem and many other Victorian poems trying to appropriate the past on nineteenth-century terms.

This chapter has emphasized the growth of an ever-sharpening awareness of the particularity and uniqueness of past eras as the Victorians saw them. There was always a tendency to make certain of these eras resemble the nineteenth century, and it is easy to condemn the irresponsible acts of appropriation, but given this limitation it was often remarkable how sensitive the Victorians were to the precise character of periods in the past. At a picturesque level they often had an impressive range of detailed knowledge. But when it came to re-creating and imagining the psyches of figures in distant history, many of the Victorians were the victims of an underlying assumption that has been increasingly questioned in our time: the assumption that the human heart is unchanging. If one believes that underlying human traits do not vary from one age to another it solves at a stroke the difficulty of psychological re-creation. On the whole the Victorian poets and historical novelists did believe in this perenniality, and it had a way of making representations of the past seem more relevant than they often do to us. The classic Victorian statement on the subject is Matthew Arnold's preface to *Poems* (1853). He thought the poet's main responsibility was to 'appeal to the great primary human affections: to those elementary feelings which subsist permanently in the race, and which are independent of time'.[26] And he continues:

> The externals of a past action . . . he cannot know
> with the precision of a contemporary; but his business is
> with its essentials. The outward man of Oedipus or of
> Macbeth, the houses in which they lived, the ceremonies
> of their courts, he cannot accurately figure to himself;
> but neither do they essentially concern him. His business
> is with their inward man; with their feelings and
> behaviour in certain tragic situations, which engage their
> passions as men; these have in them nothing local and
> casual; they are as accessible to the modern Poet as to a
> contemporary.[27]

There is a great deal here to which many of us would refuse to give unqualified assent, and even among Arnold's contemporaries those labouring with pedantic conscientiousness in the realist tradition would have had considerable reservations. But for poets like Arnold who were able to maintain this attitude it provided a ready alibi for the value and authenticity of representations of the past – at least in the area of human experience. And we should not mock Arnold and his colleagues too loudly, since many writers and film producers in our time still find the delusive belief in the consistency of human emotion both an inspiration and a convenience.

Notes

1. *Alfred Lord Tennyson: A Memoir*, edited by H. Tennyson, (1897), ii. 73. See J. Kissane, 'Tennyson: The Passion of the Past and the Curse of Time', *ELH*, 32 (1965), 85–109.

2. *Nineteenth Century*, 33 (1893), 170.

3. Quoted in R. B. Martin, *Tennyson: The Unquiet Heart* (Oxford, 1983), p. 203.

4. See J. H. Buckley, *The Triumph of Time: A Study of the Victorian Concepts of Time, History, Progress and Decadence* (Cambridge, Mass., 1966); M. Gent, '"To Flinch from Modern Varnish"', *Stratford-upon-Avon Studies*, 15 (1972), 11–35; J. D. Hunt, 'The Poetry of Distance: Tennyson's *Idylls of the King*', ibid., 89–121; P. A. Dale, *The Victorian Critic and the Idea of History* (1977); J. W. Burrow, 'The Sense of the Past', in *The Contexts of English Literature: The Victorians*, edited by L. Lerner (1978), pp. 120–138; J. Burrow, *A Liberal Descent: Victorian Historians and the English Past* (1982); S. Bann, *The Clothing of Clio* (1984); A. D. Culler, *The Victorian Mirror of History* (1986); and R. Chapman, *The Sense of the Past in Victorian Literature* (1986). On medievalism in particular see H. E. Roberts, 'Victorian Medievalism: Revival or Masquerade?', *BIS*, 8 (1980), 11–44; R. Jann, 'Democratic Myths in Victorian Medievalism', *BIS*, 8 (1980), 129–49; A, Chandler, *A Dream of Order: The Medieval Idea in Nineteenth-Century English Literature* (1970); and K. L. Morris, *The Image of the Middle Ages in Romantic and Victorian Literature* (1984).

5. T. Macaulay, 'Review of Mackintosh's *History of the Revolution* (1835)', in *Works*.

6. J. A. Froude, *Short Studies on Great Subjects*, 3 vols (1877), ii, 352.

7. J. Ruskin, Preface to 1874 edition of *The Stones of Venice*, in *Works*, ix, 11–12.

8. *The Life of Thomas Hardy 1840–1928*, edited by F. E. Hardy (1962), p. 183.

9. *The Letters of Robert Browning and Elizabeth Barrett Browning 1845–1846*, edited by E. Kintner (Cambridge Mass., 1969), i, 427.

10. *Tennyson: A Memoir*, ii, 172.

11. 'The Nature of Gothic' is Chapter 6 of Volume II of *The Stones of Venice* (1853), in *Works*, x, 180–269.

12. Chapter 25 of *The Education of Henry Adams* (1907) records his awareness of a new kind of power, experienced at the Paris Exposition of 1900.

13. For the Eglinton Tournament (August 1839) see I. Anstruther, *The Knight and the Umbrella* (1963), and M. Girouard, *The Return to Camelot* (1981), pp. 88–110.

14. For a full account of Henry Layard, explorer of Assyria, see his *Nineveh and Its Remains* (1849).

15. H. James, 'Browning in Westminster Abbey' (1890), *English Hours* (1905), p. 47.

16. Quoted in R. Ellmann, *The Identity of Yeats* (1964, reprinted 1968, 1975), pp. 239–40.

17. Annie Wall produced for the club *Sordello's Story Told in Prose* (1886).

18. *Henry James Letters*, edited by L. Edel, 4 vols (1974–84), III, 485.

19. J. Sterling, 'Review of *Poems* (1842)', in *Tennyson: The Critical Heritage*, edited by J. Jump (1967), p. 119.

20. The prose sketch is printed in *The Poems of Tennyson*, edited by C. Ricks (1969), pp. 1460–61. In the Second Edition (1987), it appears in Volume III, pp. 255–56.

21. Ibid., p. 1461.

22. Ibid., p. 1463.

23. Ibid., p. 1463.

24. Ibid., p. 1463.

25. *Tennyson: A Memoir*, I, 455.

26. *The Complete Works of Matthew Arnold*, edited by R. H. Super, 11 vols (Ann Arbor, 1960–77), I, 4.

27. Ibid., p. 5.

Chapter 7
Love Poetry

Ah, love let us be true
To one another! for the world which seems
To lie before us like a land of dreams,
So various, so beautiful, so new,
Hath really neither joy, nor love, nor light,
Nor certitude, nor peace, nor help for pain.

(ll. 29–34)

cries Arnold in 'Dover Beach', and in the face of the massed force of 'ignorant armies' the cry might seem desperate and poignantly ineffectual, but for Arnold and his contemporaries this *egoism à deux*, as it has been called, was a force in which one could repose faith. Victorian love poetry, on the whole, attests to the strength and resilience of the love relationship, and takes it as a major theme. This chapter will give undue emphasis to the problematic and questioning treatments of the subject, since modern readers are likely to find them more interesting, but the majority view among writers and their audience was that love was a powerful, life-enhancing force that inspired belief, even when religious faith was called into question. The novels of the period provide a parallel view: only the odd ones out cast a sceptical eye on Eros, though many regard the Pale Galilean askance.

First, the positive picture. Many Victorian poets continue the tradition that love ennobles and leads men and women into the highest and most praiseworthy states. It is somehow an antidote to the seven deadly sins – including lust. Strong traces of the sacrifice and humility that had been recommended in medieval courtly-love traditions survived into the nineteenth century, and curiously were grafted on to women's psychology too (in the former centuries it was the man's duty to be subservient – at least before marriage). In the Middle Ages a quasi-religious vocabulary permeated the love relationship; this continued in the nineteenth century, if anything intensified by the decline in actual religious faith.

But there are differences between Victorian love poetry and that of previous centuries. Patricia Ball suggests what the principal ones are:

> But if the Romantic poet refuses emotional journeying
> with another person as his theme, the Victorians not
> only welcome, they specialise in it. They are fascinated
> by the challenge of recording the psychological
> repercussions when two lives are brought into intimate
> conjunction. . . . The poetic centre remains the
> individual, but his or her world now expands to contain
> two people, caught willingly or unwillingly in each
> other's emotional web.[1]

Mutuality was not of course unknown in previous love poetry. Donne often uses the pronoun 'we' and depicts shared activity: he found the egotistic activity of the self-regarding lover far too lonely, and he had a relatively enlightened view of the shared relationship. It is possible that the development of the novel disseminated pictures of relationships and prompted interest in love as a mutual rather than an isolated state.

We have our images of Victorian sexuality. The myth until recently was that Victorians were frightened of sex and ignorant about it. Certainly there was a good deal of reticence and timidity then, and ignorance too. But a number of recent works, such as Steven Marcus's *The Other Victorians* (1964), Ronald Pearsall's *The Worm in the Bud: the World of Victorian Sexuality* (1969), R. M. Goldfarb's *Sexual Repression in Victorian Literature* (Lewisburg, 1975), and Wendell Stacy Johnson's *Sex and Marriage in Victorian Poetry* (Ithaca, New York 1975) have shown that there was an interest in sexuality, which we might be in danger of missing because it often takes disguised or covert forms. Generally speaking, however, sexuality is seen as a component of a complete psychological relationship rather than an independent force. Another possible distinction between Victorian love poetry and that of previous centuries is that there is more love poetry set within marriage. The facile response would be to say that there was not much in marriage previously, but the truth is perhaps that for inscrutable reasons earlier literary and cultural fashions had not developed an interest in this area of experience. The central work in this genre of matrimonial poetry is Patmore's *Angel in the House*, whose prologue to the first edition provides the title for Patricia Ball's study:

> The Song should have no incidents,
> They are so dull, and pall, twice read;
> Its scope should be the heart's events.

(ll. 78–80)

Patmore, like many of his contemporaries, places his love in a domestic environment, and although there are exceptions in the Romantic Movement, one thinks of love at that time needing heightened settings – Don Juan and Haidée's remote cave for instance. As we shall see, Victorian love poetry reuses many of the *topoi* of earlier works, but finally, so long as it had any contact with reality, it would never resemble them exactly since the status of women, from the legal and cultural point of view, was undergoing a change. Mary Wollstonecraft's *Vindication of the Rights of Women* (1792) was the first trumpet blast in the struggle, but there were other revolutionary treatises, such as William Thompson's *Appeal of One Half the Human Race, Women, Against the Pretensions of the other half, Men . . .* (1825), Robert Owen's *Lectures on the Marriage of the Priesthood of the Old Immoral World* (1835) and John Stuart Mill's *The Subjection of Women* (1869). These works contributed to a long debate on the nature of love and marriage: was it 'secular', that is, open to social, political, and psychological influences, or was it 'sacramental', that is, open to transcendental influences and interpretation? The 'sacramental' aspects have a wide spectrum, orthodox at one end (and hence limiting the power of sexuality), and romantic at the other (either glorifying sexuality, or replacing it with a kind of mystical sexuality).

The best way to make sense of the vast field is to treat the serious and positive relationships first, progressing through courtship and marriage and loss, then to look at these stages in the problematical relationships.

Perhaps the most exciting and fresh poem of courtship in the whole century is Meredith's *Love in the Valley* (first published in 1851 in a ten-stanza version, then revised in 1878, enlarging it to twenty-six stanzas). The girl's presence in the landscape animates the whole of surrounding nature, and all the natural elements fill and complement the girl's existence. It is a traditional picture of first love, but with more impetuous and vibrant life than virtually anything of its kind in the whole English language. The strong emphatic rhythm is just one of the features that gives it zest and energy; unlike much of Hopkins's poetry it has a 'sprung rhythm' that one can actually hear, and Wimsatt and Beardsley are sadly misguided in describing it as a 'pleasant little monstrosity'.[2] The life is so complete in Meredith's beautiful poem that one cannot imagine it changing, and one would not wish it to change, and it is exactly this feeling that strikes the lover:

> Boldly she sings, to the merry tune she marches,
>   Brave in her shape, and sweeter unpossessed.
> Sweeter, for she is what my heart first awaking
>   Whispered the world was; morning light is she.

Love that so desires would fain keep her changeless;
Fain would fling the net, and fain have her free

(ll. 43–48)

Meredith's poem is an extreme example of what is generally true of Victorian love poetry – that the relationship in its positive states finds its most appropriate setting in the country. Nature endorsed the rightness and inevitability of the experience and prompted it to develop harmoniously. As 'Dover Beach' suggests, love is a refuge from a hostile and unpleasant world, and it is appropriate that it should flower in natural settings – which increasingly became sources of recuperation and consolation as the century went on. And even if the love-affairs do not progress deep in rural settings, natural imagery is imported. Arnold wooed the mysterious Marguerite in Thun, a pleasant and respectable little Swiss town, but the recording of it is flooded with more natural imagery:

But on the stairs what voice is this I hear,
Buoyant as morning, and as morning clear?
Say, has some wet bird-haunted English lawn
Lent it the music of its trees at dawn?
Or was if from some sun-flecked mountain-brook
That the sweet voice its upland clearness took?

('Parting', ll. 17–22)

When Arnold dreams of Marguerite the town is replaced by Alpine scenery for the visionary setting:

Behind the pines
The mountain-skirts, with all their sylvan change
Of bright-leafed chestnuts and mossed walnut trees,
And the frail scarlet-berried ash, began.

('A Dream', ll. 6–9)

He is snatched away from this scene and from Marguerite and carried to where 'burning plains,/Bristled with cities'. The Marguerite sequence of poems, which may well be based on experience Arnold had in 1848 and 1849[3], shows the intensity of love, but in this case it does not lead anywhere, and is doomed:

A God, a God their severance ruled;
And bade betwixt their shores to be
The unplumbed, salt, estranging sea.

('To Marguerite', ll. 22–24)

There is in the phrasing an echo of two passages in Horace,[4] but Horace's God had a measure of independent palpability; Arnold's is a combination of his own conscience and a penumbra of social duties and parental disapproval: the Father is present, but not God the Father as the orthodox might understand him. He reflects in Berne, after a gap of ten years (by which time he is satisfactorily married):

> For wherefore try,
> To things by mortal course that live,
> A shadowy durability,
> For which they were not meant, to give?
>
> ('The Terrace at Berne', ll. 41–44)

The fact that many of Hardy's characters do not grasp this truth, or grasp it too late, is a central cause of their tragedies.

Tennyson's Maud is closely associated with the flowers and trees of her garden, so much so that she and her setting and the state of mind of her hero make a kind of seamless web. The 'Come into the garden, Maud' is the most famous section, but one finds the intense interrelation everywhere in the poem: in Section i. xvii the cedars of Lebanon sigh for their own country, but are also haunted by Maud, as is the hero. He remembers that trees like this must have overspread Eden. Like *Love in the Valley* Tennyson captures the elusive aspects of desire, that it is *only* longing for attainment in the future, but an equally impossible longing that the past might be recaptured and the present infinitely maintained. And desire in its most romantic manifestations will certainly wish to involve the natural world.

Swinburne's *Triumph of Time* is a poem of frustrated desire, but the lover has a strong theoretical impression of the contribution the environment *should* make:

> I shall never be friends again with roses;
>   I shall loathe sweet tunes, where a note grown strong
> Relents and recoils, and climbs and closes,
>   As a wave of the sea turned back by song.
> There are sounds where the soul's delight takes fire,
>   Face to face with its own desire;
> A delight that rebels, a desire that reposes;
>   I shall hate sweet music my whole life long.
>
> (ll. 353–60)

In his thwarted and frustrated passion the landscape that speaks to him is grimly appropriate: this is the other side of the coin; benign love enhances the sense of beauty just as malign love emphasizes the sense of ugliness:

The low downs lean to the sea; the stream,
    One loose thin pulseless tremulous vein,
Rapid and vivid and dumb as a dream,
    Works downward, sick of the sun and the rain;

(ll. 57–60)

Swinburne is notorious for exploring some out-of-the-way paths in love; he is a central exhibit in Mario Praz's *Romantic Agony* in a gallery of perverts and deviants haunted by the shadow of 'the divine Marquis'. But he was also a strange kind of idealist, who thought that in its most extreme manifestations sexuality could transport man and woman to mystical realms, transcending individualism, time, and natural processes. In the total merging that Swinburne envisages the discrete person is annihilated and self-consumed.

Absolutely antipodal to Swinburne is Clough's *Bothie* and *Amours de Voyage*. The latter could be compared with *The Triumph of Time* since it also deals with a failed courtship, but that is about all it has in common, since Claude, in Clough's poem, is sceptical, urbane, self-regarding, and timid. This makes him at once less capable of commitment but more appreciative of the special qualities of the girl he drifts into love with – Mary Trevellyn. The setting is Rome during the French invasion. Here is the chance for public and private heroics, but a strongly developed sense of self-preservation holds Claude back. Unlike many lovers he seems capable of observing the object of his love through clear glass rather than coloured haze:

> I am in love, meantime, you think; no doubt you
>   would think so.
> I am in love, you say; with those letters, of course
>   you would say so.
> I am in love, you declare. I think not so; yet I
>   grant you
> It is pleasure indeed to converse with this girl.
>   Oh, rare gift,
> Rare felicity, this! She can talk in a rational way,
>   can
> Speak upon subjects that really are matters of mind
>   and of thinking
> Yet in perfection retain her simplicity; never,
>   one moment,
> Never, however you urge it, however you tempt her,
>   consents to
> Step from ideas and fancies and loving sensations to
>   those vain

Conscious understandings that vex the minds of mankind.
No though she talk, it is music; her fingers desert
    not the keys; 'tis
Song, though you hear in the song the articulate
    vocables sounded
Syllabled single and sweetly the words of melodious
    meaning.
I am in love, you say: I do not think so, exactly.

(II. 252–65)

He goes on to explain that he does not wish the kinesis of desire, but the stasis of some other state, which perhaps does not have a name. Something prevents him from self-surrender and self-revelation, and he is under the impression that Mary does not like him. As we see from her letters this is with some justification, but she also has a perceptive awareness of him: she has called him 'repulsive' but was it in the normal sense of the word?

Yes, repulsive; observe, it is but when he talks of
    ideas
That he is quite unaffected, and free, and expansive
    and easy;

(III. 32–33)

All this looks like novelistic cliché – that the couple do not know their own minds, and that the initial hate will merely increase the piquancy of the final revelation of love. But in this story the barriers and masks remain to place, and they are classic actors in an Arnoldian situation:

Yes: in the sea of life enisled,
    With echoing straits between us thrown,
Dotting the shoreless watery wild,
    We mortal millions live *alone*.

('To Marguerite', ll. 1–4)

The Bothie is a happier work, since the young couple come together, and in a style that does not strike one as typically Victorian; the poem is a 'long vacation pastoral', chronicling the summer spent by Oxford undergraduates on a reading-party in the Scottish highlands. They are fully armed with all the wit and prejudice of typical undergraduates of their time, but one of their number, Philip Hewson, falls in love with and marries a crofter's daughter, Elspie Mackaye. Love enables them to cross barriers, since without it Philip's extreme radicalism might not have made him so tolerant that he could entertain marrying a social inferior. His friends mock his curious mixture of sexuality, sentimentality, and condescension, and he is far from immune from Cloughean irony. The relationship is nicely studied, and Clough sensitively registers the social and sexual differences. Elspie has a dream, which we should now glibly call 'Freudian'; in it she fears her identity being invaded. The metaphor is taken from her familiar surroundings:

> You are too strong, you see, Mr. Philip! just
> like the sea there,
> Which *will* come, through the straits and all
> between the mountains,
> Forcing its great strong tide into every nook and
> inlet,
> Getting far in, up the quiet stream of sweet inland
> water,
> Sucking it up, and stopping it, turning it, driving
> it backward,
> Quite preventing its own quiet running: and then,
> soon after,
> Back it goes off, leaving weeds on the shore, and
> wrack and uncleanness:
> And the poor burn in the glen tries again its peaceful
> running,
> But it is brackish and tainted, and all its banks in
> disorder.
> That was what I dreamt all last night. I was the
> burnie,
> Trying to get along through the tyrannous brine, and
> could not;
> I was confined and squeezed in the coils of the great
> salt tide, that
> Would mix-in itself with me, and change me, I felt
> myself changing;
> And I struggled, and screamed, I believe, in my
> dream. It was dreadful.
>
> (VII. 120–33)

In one sense Elspie is distanced from Philip; after all, she is still calling him 'Mr. Philip'. But in another sense she is making revelations more intimate (albeit by way of a metaphor) than one finds in most Victorian literature. Elspie comes to make a positive, conscious modification of the dream image, so that the stream seeks 'with a delicious forefeeling, the great still sea before it' and she surrenders to 'sweet multitudinous vague emotion'. The readiest comparison to make with this passage is the scene of mutual surrender between Charlotte Verver and the Prince in James's *The Golden Bowl*.[5]

In addition to the fluid imagery of a stream flowing into an estuary, Elspie uses another metaphor (which modern readers will also wish reductively to call 'Freudian'). In thinking of the establishment of a firm relationship she reaches for a figure from the building of arches. (One has some indication of the reverence of the Victorians for the arch in reading Ruskin for instance[6]):

> But oh, we must wait, Mr. Philip!
> We mustn't pull ourselves at the great key-stone
>   of the centre;
> Some one else up above must hold it, fit it and fix
>   it;
> If we try ourselves, we shall only damage the archway,
> Damage all our own work that we wrought, our painful
>   up-building.
>   (VII. 104–8)

Elspie, though a social inferior, knows her own mind, and with her quiet firmness continues to educate Philip, and to transform his outlook on the world. Often in love one's eyes are opened to a regenerated or enhanced nature, but in Canto 9 he becomes aware of a beautiful and benign city. Philip wins his bride, they marry in 'gorgeous bright October' and emigrate to New Zealand (as did Matthew Arnold's brother Thomas), where the 'democratic fervour' may have a better chance of flourishing than in the Old World.

The Bothie must have challenged some conventional Victorian readers, and many would have been notably alarmed if they had understood what the Gaelic of the original title meant: Clough discovered that *Toper-Na-Fuosich* could be translated as 'what Horace calls [by way of euphemistically referring to Helen of Troy's sexual attractions] *tetirrima belli causa*', and changed it to *Tober-Na-Vuolich*.[7]

However, they would have been much more alarmed had they been able to read *Dipsychus* in its unexpurgated version (not published in full until 1974). This presents an idealized and idealizing young man, tempted and challenged in Venice by a Mephistophelean spirit, who is like a survival from the rational, sceptical, and libertine eighteenth century. Dipsychus is prone to romantic clichés (not merely about women – see below p. 181) and is constantly presented with an alternative view by the Spirit:

> Ho, Virtue quotha! trust who knows;
>   There's not a girl that by us goes
> But mightn't have you if she chose:
>   No doubt but you would give her trouble;
> But then you'd pay her for it double;
>
> (III. 197–201)

The reluctance of Dipsychus to accept such views is sometimes so emphatic that one feels he more than half realizes the truth of them and at some subconscious level is generating them himself, so that the Spirit is a kind of *alter ego*. Clough was alarmed at the thought that his fiancée Blanche Smith might read the manuscript, and wrote begging her not to.[8] Another controversial poem of Clough's, which his widow wished to suppress in preparing the posthumous edition, was 'Natura Naturans' (it was in fact omitted from the first three editions of 1862, 1893, and 1895). Blanche may have thought it referred to some previous liaison, and objected to it on those grounds, but in addition she may not have approved of its deterministic philosophy.

In this poem sexual attraction seems not so much a matter of minds as of blind natural forces – a materialist version, perhaps, of Goethe's mystical 'elective affinities'. We are not very far from the spirit of Huxley's notorious pamphlet 'On the Physical Basis of Life' (1862):

> Yet owned we, fused in one,
>   The Power which e'en in stones and earths
> By blind elections felt, in forms
>   Organic breeds to myriad births;
> By lichen small on granite wall
>   Approved, its faintest feeblest stir
> Slow-spreading, strengthening long, at last
>   Vibrated full in me and her.
>
> (ll. 41–48)

Yet the poem is in a sense idealistic, since the naturalness and inevitability of the processes lead to a kind of innocence. The love may be remote from soul, but as Marvell realizes, soul tends to use its wit to create a sense of sin, so that the sexual potency of 'Natura Naturans' leads the lovers to something 'unconscious, unashamed', reminiscent of 'Eden's sinless place'. It is a remarkable poem – in some ways an anticipation of Dylan Thomas's 'The Force that Through the Green Fuse', but without the vatic enthusiasm. One would look a long time in the work of Clough's contemporaries for anything quite like it.

For comprehensiveness and open-mindedness in the treatment of love Clough's natural compeer is Browning. He is generally known as a positive and optimistic thinker, but he was perceptive enough to register timidity, inadequacy, and other failings in love relationships. Love was a great central value for him – perhaps that was why he took shortcomings in its pursuit so seriously. 'The Statue and the Bust' is a key document in the study of courtship. It is the story of the Duke of Florence's illicit love for a bride of Riccardi. They meet and exchange knowledge of love in a split second. The husband, suspecting his wife, locks her up. The lovers delay elopement, and when the woman is aware of ageing she orders Della Robbia to make a statue of her, to place in the window where she was wont to look out for the Duke. Since she has not been animated by divine commitment the 'lady of clay' is an adequate substitute. The Duke likewise is aware that his youth is going and his 'dream escapes'; he commissions John of Douai to fashion a bronze statue to capture the love of life he once had but has now lost. Both lovers are content with external images of themselves, which arrest their love at a certain point. Strictly speaking the images do not tell the whole truth either, since they do not capture the timidity and idleness. They failed the test of life, and the speaker says that a crime is just as effective a judge 'as virtue golden through and through'. The sin he imputes 'to each frustrate ghost/Is – the unlit lamp and the ungirt loin'. The speaker here need not be Browning – for one thing he seems rather more definite than Browning – but he expresses views not far from views that Browning entertained at one time or another. (One could say something like this about virtually all of Browning's personae.)

A much more macabre arresting of a moment of love at a certain point is 'Porphyria's Lover'. At the instant when Porphyria surrenders herself to her lover he kills her, perhaps so that he can arrest the relationship at this stage. Also the dead mistress (who still shows sufficient colour in her cheeks to present an appearance of lifelikeness, and rests her head on his shoulder in a simulacrum of loving submission) is less disconcertingly independent than when she came to see him at her own choice. An extreme and unusual situation, but time and time again Browning shows he is capable of imagining and expressing such extreme and unusual situations. His inventive capacities seem to be inexhaustible. He is also capable of course of doing justice to the normal! The 'normal', as Browning sees it, would involve change and acceptance of change:

> Rejoice that man is hurled
> From change to change unceasingly,
> His soul's wings never furled!
>
> ('James Lee's Wife', ll. 219–21)

That is not to say that in the appalling process of time's destruction
man should not attempt to rescue something, make his mark:

> Only, for man, how bitter not to grave
>   On his soul's hands' palms one fair good wise
>   thing
> Just as he grasped it! For himself, death's wave;
>   While time first washes – ah, the sting! –
> O'er all he'd sink to save.
>
>   ('James Lee's Wife' ll. 227–231)

A similar awareness of the pathos of flux and the fragility of the 'good
minute' is in the famous poem 'Two in Campagna':

> Already how am I so far
>   Out of that minute? Must I go
> Still like the thistle-ball, no bar,
>   Onward, whenever light winds blow,
> Fixed by no friendly star?
>
> Just when I seemed about to learn!
>   Where is the thread now? Off again!
> The old trick! Only I discern –
>   Infinite passion, and the pain
> Of finite hearts that yearn.
>
>   (ll. 51–60)

Victorian poets were living in a time when political and philosophical emphasis was increasingly being placed on individualism. The
individual 'taste' of a human being – as Hopkins would have called it
– was to be cherished and revered. Individual liberties were to flourish
– so long as they did not grossly interfere with the lives of others. The
impact of this on the love relationship was to emphasize the precious-
ness of single identities. The rhetoric of complete fusion and merging
survives, but the style of loving we find most amenable respects
distinctness and even opposition. We are used to thinking of Lawrence
as having made a big stride forward in speaking of polar opposites,
and the purity of distinct halves in the sexual relationship, but actually
one can find any number of predecessors – even the apparently unlikely
figure of Coventry Patmore, who is regarded, especially by people
who have never read a line of his work, as purveying the worst kind
of Victorian sentimentality. In *The Angel in the House*, Felix, watching
Honoria dance, realizes the importance of distance as a component of
desire:

He who would seek to make her his
    Will comprehend that soul of grace
Own sweet repulsion, and that 'tis
    The quality of their embrace
To be like the majestic reach
    Of coupled suns, that, from afar,
Mingle their mutual spheres, while each
    Circles the twin obsequious star;
And reverently understand
    How the two spirits shine remote.

                    (I, II. 97–106)

Patmore, then, is appreciative of 'the space which makes attraction felt'. In a sense Patmore is returning to older styles of love, in vogue before Romantic extremism set in, and his poetry has a curious mixture of intellectual finesse, lightness of touch, relish of paradox, and conceit with Victorian sentimentality and religiosity. At times it might almost be mistaken for the love poetry of the sixteenth and seventeenth centuries, but finally it is tamer and more domesticated than that.

In any review of the poetry of happy marriage Patmore will be a central figure; he brings to the institutions of wedlock the emotional intensity and mystical connoisseurship which had been reserved in previous centuries (with a few exceptions like Spenser and Donne) for courtship. Of course some of it involves the lovers in pretence and artifice – as when the wife 'assumed the maiden coy'. Bathos lurks constantly in ambush for Patmore, as it must for any poet of the domestic, but he avoids it, on the whole, by being aware of it:

I, while the shop-girl fitted on
    The sand shoes, looked where, down the bay,
The sea glowed with a shrouded sun.
    'I'm ready, Felix; will you pay?'
That was my first expense for this
    Sweet Stranger, now my three days' Wife.
How light the touches are that kiss
    The music from the chords of life!

                    (II. 12. 49–56)

Patmore's ease and facility, the absence of strain on the language or on the intellect of the reader make it easy to see why he was popular *then* and reviled now. At his best, however, he has some of the poise and archness one associates with seventeenth-century poetry:

Because she's constant, he will change,
  And kindest glances coldly meet,
And, all the time he seems so strange,
  His soul is fawning at her feet;
Of smiles and simple heaven grown tired,
  He wickedly provokes her tears,
And when she weeps, as he desired,
  Falls slain with ecstasies of fears;
He blames her, though she has no fault,
  Except the folly to be his;
He worships her, the more to exalt
  The profanation of a kiss.

(II. 637–48)

A central question that will intrigue modern readers is: what do Victorian poets do with sexuality in marriage? In Patmore it tends to be muted by spirituality, yet some of the most striking poems of the period manage a powerful fusion of spirituality and sexuality in which we do not feel that one or the other is compromised. Buchanan made a notorious attack on Rossetti for being too sexual in a fleshly manner,[9] but his aim was not quite on target. One of Rossetti's most compelling poems was dropped from the *House of Life* sonnet sequence; it was titled 'Nuptial Sleep', and depicts post-coital trance:

At length their long kiss severed, with sweet smart:
  And as the last slow sudden drops are shed
  From sparkling eaves when all the storm has fled,
So singly flagged the pulses of each heart.
Their bosoms sundered, with the opening start
  Of married flowers to either side outspread
  From the knit stem; yet still their mouths
                                        burnt red,
Fawned on each other where they lay apart.

(ll. 1–8)

Buchanan was surely wrong to call poetry of this kind 'mere animal sensations'. Browning too, on occasions, conveys a strong impression of the power of sexuality. Ottima's reminiscences in *Pippa Passes* are surprisingly sensual for the period:

While I stretched myself upon you, hands
To hands, my mouth to your hot mouth, and shook
All my locks loose, and covered you with them –
You, Sebald, the same you!

(ll. 219–22)

Another poem in which one finds an intense eroticism is Christina Rossetti's *Goblin Market* (1859). It is a highly enigmatic and much explicated work. Two sisters, Lizzie and Laura, encounter little goblin men, who are close to the animal world (one of them, who prowls 'obtuse and furry', resembles D. G. Rossetti's ill-fated pet wombat). They offer luscious fruit, but there is obviously something wrong with the merchandise since cherries and apples, blackberries and strawberries, damsons and gooseberries, and peaches and greengages do not appear in the same season, and the kernel of one of the fruits produces no plant. There is a consensus that nothing in the poem is quite as it seems, and it all has to be decoded, but no critics have ever agreed quite what the fruit is meant to represent: the pleasures of sexuality, the fantasies of the imaginative world, sterile artefacts, these have all been suggested. Certainly the poem is heavily impregnated with sexual suggestiveness, as in the image of the beleaguered Lizzie 'like a royal virgin town'. Laura pays for her enjoyment with a lock of her golden hair, suggesting some form of rape. But having tasted the fruit, like the unfortunate Jeanie who 'pined and pined away', 'her hair grew thin and grey' and she goes into a decline. Lizzie restores her to life by going to visit the goblin men, but she will not eat the fruit. In their anger they crush it against her, so that when she returns Laura is able to taste the fruit:

> 'Never mind my bruises,
> Hug me, kiss me, suck my juices
> Squeezed from goblin fruits for you,
> Goblin pulp and goblin dew.
> Eat me, drink me, love;
> Laura, make much of me.
>   (ll. 467–72)

Laura thinks that Lizzie may have tasted 'the fruit forbidden'. Some of the phrasing here seems to invite Christian allegorical interpretation, with Lizzie as a Christ-figure who has made the supreme sacrifice for her sister, but it would be difficult to sustain a full-blown religious reading of this kind. When Laura tastes the fruit on Lizzie's body, 'that juice is wormwood to her tongue', and she falls into a death-in-life state, from which she recovers. The events then become a story that can be told to their children, with an apparently trite object-lesson:

> 'For there is no friend like a sister
> In calm or stormy weather;
> To cheer one on the tedious way,
> To fetch one if one goes astray.'
>   (ll. 562–65)

But this conclusion does no justice to the mystery, the impenetrability and the chaotic sense of grotesque life (mainly conveyed by the rough verse form, which has the wayward vigour of Skelton). It is difficult to resist the impression that the poem is about lawless eroticism, but much harder to assess how much of it is under the complete control of Christina Rossetti. The goblin men emerge from some obscure depth in her consciousness, even as they might emerge from some similar origin in the consciousness of the two sisters. At an impressionistic level the poem is a powerful portrayal of the strange forces of sexuality, which inevitably closely resemble the forces of artistic creation and the search for imagined desire. It is when one begins to attempt detailed decoding that one runs into trouble, and the poem finally proves baffling and elusive, which may be its strength: there is something attractive about a work of art that at one level is perfectly clear, but at another defeats the critics. It is difficult to make any sense of Laura's drinking the crushed juices that have lodged in Lizzie's dimples: why, in this circumstance, have they become bitter, and an antidote? It does not seem possible to make a coherent allegorical interpretation of that, or any other form of interpretation. It is a poem that emerges from a very Victorian consciousness, characterized by the schizophrenic struggle between renunciation and gratification, between repression and surrender. More perhaps than in any other Victorian poem erotic love is experienced as an irresistible force rather than as a state of mind that keeps the beloved object in view, and even the *agape* the sisters experience is forcefully tinged with eroticism.

Much Victorian love poetry dealt with the positive aspects of relationships, but some of the most powerful work treated relationships blighted by loss and disillusion. Browning looms large as the celebrant of damaging and harrowing love experiences; this is somewhat surprising, since he has the reputation of being an optimist. Through some of the marriages he depicts runs a torrent of devastation and destruction, culminating in extended works such as *The Ring and the Book* and *The Inn Album*. In the early work *Pippa Passes* Jules and Phene seem to be an ill-matched couple, and Ottima and Sebald have conspired to kill Ottima's husband to promote their relationship. Browning seems to have a measure of sympathy for the Pygmalion myth – that the lover creates the mistress in his own image and loves her, worships her even, on his own terms – but he was aware that extreme versions of this lead to life-denying possessiveness and arid aestheticism. The classic case is the connoisseur Duke in 'My Last Duchess', who, like Porphyria's lover, has conferred a stasis on his image of the wife by having her murdered. Even in the picture she shows a recalcitrance – as she must, since it was painted by a sharp-eyed painter – but there is no capacity for further change and further betrayal. In miniature we have the situation expanded some years later in *The Ring and the Book*, but in the latter poem the intractable wife makes a decisive escape and is pursued to her death. In this long poem Browning is extremely adept at showing a wide range of feelings and emotions present in love relationships. Caponsacchi is an interesting case-study of the kind of love that comes within a hair's breadth of sexual fulfilment, but in missing it turns out to have certain advantages, since he knows and appreciates Pompilia in a manner that might be superior to those caught in blind, erotic obsession: he knows her with the clear-eyed perception that an author might know his character, as Henry James knows Isabel Archer, as Hardy knows Tess, as Browning knows Pompilia. Browning is equally effective at presenting the obsessive and proprietary attitude Guido is dominated by, even though he seems to place a low valuation on his wife Pompilia. As a picture of the obverse side of human relationships there is very little to equal *The Ring and the Book* in Victorian literature. The heroine of 'The Flight of the Duchess' also flees from a possessive husband who regards her as one of his 'trophies'. The hero of 'The Last Ride Together' realizes that the relationship has come apart, but wants, for one last time, to enter a timeless world in which there is brief harmony. The language has caught Browning out here, since 'ride' has a long history of sexual innuendo, but he seems to have been unaware of it, despite his browsing in old books.[10]

In many of the poems of failed love or love mixed with other moral and ethical questions, Browning avoids making black and white judgements, since it is the quality and nature of experience that interests him. *In a Balcony* is a chapter of deceit and misunderstanding, but Browning does not go for easy condemnation of the lovers. He seems to have entertained the idea that love bypasses or reduces to irrelevance simple questions of good and bad. A wide variety of experiences in love intrigued him, and unlike Patmore he is prepared to treat the imperious and dominant woman not as a monster but as someone who might be capable of fulfilling a need in a man of a certain temperament – witness 'The Glove' for instance. 'Life in a Love' presents a picture of hunter and quarry in marriage:

> So long as the world contains us both,
> Me the loving and you the loth,
> While the one eludes, must the other pursue.
>
> (ll. 5–7)

Browning allows a sceptical spirit to enter into considerations of marriage – as in 'Any Wife to Any Husband' and 'One Way of Love'

and 'Another Way of Love'. One of his most famous presentations of
a flawed marriage is 'Andrea del Sarto' (which is treated in Chapter
12). Unlike the assertive Duke this weary artist maintains a sort of
resigned self-composure. There is less resignation in 'James Lee's Wife'
as a lonely woman goes through the melancholy reflections that her
husband is growing estranged from her. She is trapped, as it were, in
constancy, but her husband is roving; yet she longs to give and receive
love again.

Tennyson too finds a fascination in love, lost love, illicit love,
unhappy love, unrequited love, and in its various guises it dominates
the *Idylls*. The exotic and remote setting of Arthurian Britain allowed
Tennyson's taste for unorthodox and unusual relationships to flourish,
and gave him the opportunity for exploration that might have been
difficult in contemporary settings; one recalls how much he reviled
Zola and his school in *Locksley Hall Sixty Years After*, and yet stripped
of their medieval trappings some of the episodes and some of the states
of mind in the *Idylls* would have the shock of works in the realist and
sensationalist school. The relationship between Merlin and Vivien is
very unwholesome for instance.

But undoubtedly the classic treatment of the failed marriage and its
attendant disturbances is the sonnet-cycle *Modern Love* which grows
out of Meredith's failed marriage – although that is not to assume that
it is poetic autobiography in every sense. Meredith's wife Mary ran
off with the Pre-Raphaelite painter Henry Wallis in 1858, after nine
years of marriage. This new liaison failed, and she died in a broken
and miserable state in 1861. *Modern Love* shows a couple pursuing
happiness with other partners, yet each is unable to forget the other
or make a clean separation. Ancient forces of passion live in them, but
they are equally tortured by the modern malaise of introspection and
analysis. A Byronic flippancy and cynicism haunts the poem, but there
is not much Byronic ardour. It shocked its original readers, some of
whom felt it was 'a grave moral mistake', but modern readers, accustomed to Strindberg and Ibsen, are more likely to find it vivid and
engaging. *Modern Love* is an easier poem to find one's way through
than many a Browning poem, since there is a narrative figure with a
personality (often cynical) as well as the two principal protagonists.

The cycle begins with an emblem that on the face of it seems
medieval:

> Like sculptured effigies they might be seen
> Upon their marriage-tomb, the sword between.
>
> (I. 14–15)

There is a reminiscence of Tristan and Isolde, except that this sword is not to preserve chastity but to keep married partners apart and to symbolize their wish for death. Interestingly, Meredith, who once shared a house in Chelsea with Rossetti, has a penchant for updating and realigning traditional images in Pre-Raphaelite fashion. What is 'modern' about the cycle is the capacity of the pair relentlessly to strip away sentimental illusions and dispassionately study love alongside other forces and principles. And the narrator has this same capacity to interject the cynical, deflationary remark:

> She issues radiant from her dressing-room,
> Like one prepared to scape an upper sphere:
> By stirring up a lower, much I fear!
>
> (VII. 1–3)

As in Meredith's novels there are forces operating in the poem which have almost palpable and deterministic existence, so that the relationship suffers from the influence of a 'discord loving clown', and the capitalized Delusion, Philosophy, and Passion almost have existence as personified allegorical figures. Nature in *Love in the Valley* offered nothing but prospects encouraging love, and in this cycle such scenes still exist, as in the lark song showered on the pair in Sonnet XI, but in Sonnet XIII, where laughing Nature actually speaks, a starker picture is presented:

> Upon her dying rose
> She drops a look of fondness, and goes by,
> Scarce any retrospection in her eye;
> For she the laws of growth most deeply knows,
> Whose hands bear, hear, a seed-bag – there, an urn.
>
> (XIII. 5–9)

Comparison has been made with Rossetti, but another comparison to be made is with Hardy, who learnt much from Meredith. Both of them had moods in which they held to a grim view of life, and both of them allowed their novelistic sense to influence their poetry (counterbalanced in both cases by their giving due recognition to the power which the poetic spirit is able to contribute to the novel). *Modern Love* is a satisfying poem to read because it etches scenes and characters so strongly. Sonnet XVI, illuminated by 'the red chasm . . . among the clicking coals', has the same kind of intensity as Tess's confession to Angel in *Tess of the D'Urbervilles* (Ch. 34). The scene in the country-house attic (Sonnet XXII) has the vividness of a novel, with the wife in the bed and the husband 'couched upon the floor' – startlingly specific for Victorian literature. The husband takes a mistress and the wife a lover, and, shockingly, many emotions not connected with love enter into the relationships. In Sonnet XXXIX the husband, even as he dallies with his mistress in the moonlight, can be jealous of his wife and her lover, and the moon seems to dance like a spectre. The death of love is symbolized by a seascape, more melodramatic than 'the pond edged with greyish leaves' in Hardy's 'Neutral Tones' (dated '1867' in *Wessex Poems*, which may indicate the date of original composition), but operating in a similar way, and we should not forget that this poem was published about forty years before Hardy's:

> Mark where the pressing wind shoots javelin-like
>   Its skeleton shadow on the broad-backed wave!
>   Here is a fitting spot to dig Love's grave;
> Here where the ponderous breakers plunge and strike,
> And dart their hissing tongues high up the sand:
>   In hearing of the ocean, and in sight
>   Of those ribbed wind-streaks running into white.
>
> (XLIII. 1–7)

There is a truce and parley between the two in a wood where their courtship first began, but 'the swallows gathering in the sky' announce winter, and the sunset, which on a previous occasion had figured 'an amber cradle' with 'a dead infant' (Sonnet XI) is now the colour of 'pale blood' (Sonnet XLVII). Finally there is a kind of reunion by the sea, but by now the wife is 'shadow-like and dry' and near death. It is only at the moment of death that she softens to her husband with the words 'Now kiss me, dear! it may be now!' The last scene provides the emblem for the final summing up of this and many other relationships, that all the energy expended in relationships produces a turbulence like the sea's, but ends up in merely throwing a 'faint thin line upon the shore!' In this century, as Arnold saw it, the mind's dialogue with itself could provoke unhappiness and lack of fulfilment; in the Meredith cycle we have evidence that the mind's dialogue with the loved being could lead to a similar malaise. Perhaps in the end 'the May-fly pleasures of a mind at ease' (XVIII. 9) are to be preferred.

Notes

1. P. Ball, *The Heart's Events: The Victorian Poetry of Relationships* (1967), pp. 1–2.

2. W. K. Wimsatt and M. C. Beardsley, *Hateful Contraries* (Lexington, 1965), p. 137.

3. Park Honan discusses the possibility that Marguerite was invented or imagined, and based on Arnold's love for Mary Sophia Claude; see *Matthew Arnold: a Life* (1981), pp. 151–67. In 1848 he had been hoping to meet her in Thun, but just missed her.

4. Horace, *Epodes*, XIV. 6 and *Odes*, I, III. 21–23.

5. Henry James, *The Golden Bowl* (1923), I, 279.

6. J. Ruskin, *The Stones of Venice* and *Lectures on Architecture and Painting*, in *Works*, XI, 153–81; XII, 24.

7. *The Correspondence of Arthur Hugh Clough*, edited by F. L. Mulhauser (Oxford, 1957), I, 224.

8. Ibid., II, 350.

9. R. Buchanan, 'The Fleshly School of Poetry: D. G. Rossetti', *Contemporary Review*, 18 (October 1871), 334–50 (signed 'Thomas Maitland'), expanded in pamphlet form in 1872; reprinted in *Victorian Poetry and Poetics*, edited by W. E. Houghton and G. Stange, second edition (Boston, 1968), pp. 888–98.

10. See R. M. Goldfarb, *Sexual Repression and Victorian Literature* (Lewisburg, 1970), pp. 66–81.

Chapter 8

Domesticity

In our rough-and-ready myths of history we attribute the invention of both Christmas and home life to the Victorians. Of course they both existed previously, but they certainly received increased emphasis during our period. In earlier centuries the extended family was a dominant unit in society, particularly among the middle and upper classes. A classic study of this phenomenon is Lawrence Stone's *The Family, Sex and Marriage in England, 1500–1800*; by selecting some texts and ignoring others he reaches the overstated conclusion that whatever bonds held these extended families together in the early modern period, love and affection were not predominantly among them.[1] There is undoubtedly some truth in what he says, but most of the reviewers rightly castigated him for proposing crude and insensitive theories.[2]

In the Victorian period there was a tendency for families to be more inward looking and for the domestic virtues to be celebrated. It was part of the movement to recommend individualism (astonishingly a word not recorded before 1833), privacy and anti-heroism. If the individual was to gain respect and recognition it was felt that this could most effectively begin in the nuclear family, where concentration and intimacy were possible. The broad sweep of this movement has been most suggestively charted by Mario Praz in *The Hero in Eclipse in Victorian Fiction* (1956); certainly, as he shows, it had a considerable effect on art and literature, which turned away from the grandiose and the public to the small-scale and the private. So far as literature is concerned this tendency, which had begun in the eighteenth century, had been particularly encouraged by the development of the novel, and the key statement recommending the domestic and the 'heroism of daily life' as compelling subjects for art is found in Chapter 17 of *Adam Bede*. Novel after novel has fond evocations of cosy domestic interiors where happiness may flourish; there is a whole sequence of them in Mrs Gaskell's *Ruth* (1853), for instance. The cult of domesticity was finally so prevalent that it even affected the Royal Family; the embourgeoisification of the monarchy began, and the phrase 'the home life of

our dear Queen' enjoyed a currency which would have been unthink-
able in the reign of Queen Anne. Depending on one's ideology the
most famous (or the most notorious) tribute to the domestic ideal is
Ruskin's *Sesame and Lilies* (1862):

> The man, in his rough work in the open world,
> must encounter all peril and trial: – to him, therefore,
> must be failure, the offence, the inevitable error: often he
> must be wounded or subdued, often misled; and *always*
> hardened. But he guards the woman from all this; within
> his house, as ruled by her, unless she herself has sought it,
> need enter no danger, no temptation, no cause of error or
> offence. This is the true nature of home – it is the place of
> Peace; the shelter, not only from all injury, but from all
> terror, doubt, and division. In so far as it is not this, it is
> not home; so far as the anxieties of the outer life penetrate
> into it, and the inconsistently-minded, unknown, unloved,
> or hostile society of the outer world is allowed by either
> husband or wife to cross the threshold, it ceases to be
> home; it is then only a part of that outer world which you
> have roofed over, and lighted fire in. But so far as it is a
> sacred place, a vestal temple, a temple of the hearth
> watched over by House-hold Gods, before whose faces
> none may come but those whom they can receive with
> love, – so far as it is this, and roof and fire are types only
> of a nobler shade and light, – shade as of the rock in a
> weary land, and light as of the Pharos in the stormy sea; –
> so far as it vindicates the name, and fulfils the praise, of
> Home.[3]

This was written by a man whose home life as a child had indeed been
a kind of paradise (except that in the garden *all* the fruits were
forbidden),[4] but the home life that he and his wife had created was
shattered in 1854 when she sought an annulment on the grounds that
the marriage had not been consummated. So that the classic passage
in *Sesame and Lilies* is in part the poignant expression of an ideal he
himself achieved only for a very short time.

On the whole the family was thought to be a genial and beneficent
institution, and often in Dickens, for instance, the family and its nook-
like home is a secular refuge from a threatening and chaotic outer
society; in extreme cases, as with Wemmick's miniature castle in *Great
Expectations*, it is an armed refuge as well as a hermitage: fortress
Walworth. In these constricted environments some of the characteristic
Victorian activities could be pursued; for instance, the cult of close

attention to detail could be very readily practised in the familiar and intimate setting, and it was no accident that many Pre-Raphaelite genre paintings deal with the small room and its familiar and much-loved bric-à-brac. Likewise Pre-Raphaelite poems, such as Rossetti's 'My Sister's Sleep', dwell on the known and the treasured items in the small interior. The apotheosis of this trend is perhaps Pater's *The Child in the House* (1887), which suggests that some of the highest levels of aesthetic intensity are achieved when the surroundings are intimately known and are the repositories of valued associations: by familiarity 'the early habitation thus gradually becomes a sort of material shrine or sanctuary of sentiment'.[5] And whereas for Goethe and Arnold[6] custom and habit is binding in an adverse sense, Pater presents a view of the bonds as more like links in the Great Chain of Being than the fetters of a prison. I refer to English literature, but the fullest exploration of the high aesthetic possibilities of the domestic is to be found in Proust's *A la recherche du temps perdu*. The well-known contours of both the inanimate and the human furniture are the material for the well-developed aesthetic sensibility. This intimacy and familiarity was largely genial and therapeutically beneficial, and to this day the satisfaction and sense of well-being engendered by the domestic setting is recognized: the fostering of this family life, where it was achieved, was a positive and valuable feature of Victorian life, but it should not be forgotten that many homes exhibited nothing remotely like comfort and familial well-being. The grim obverse side of the coin is presented in Tennyson's *Locksley Hall Sixty Years After* (1886):

> There a single sordid attic holds the living and
>   the dead
> There the smouldering fire of fever creeps across
>   the rotted floor,
> And the crowded couch of incest in the warrens of
>   the poor.
>   (ll. 221–24)

And it was also very often the case that many of those in prosperous and comfortable situations found the home the claustrophobic theatre in which all the negative aspects of their lives were acted out. The married couple in Tennyson's 'Walking to the Mail' (1842) end up at war: 'they that loved/At first like dove and dove were cat and dog.' Most emphatically the phrase 'hearth and home' had its negative side.

But first, the positive side to the picture. The Victorians did not invent domestic poetry; one finds it in earlier centuries, but it starts to become noticeable with Shenstone and Cowper, and in the Romantic Movement with Wordsworth and Coleridge, especially in parts of *The Prelude* and some of the 'conversation poems'. In our period Tennyson is the main exponent of happy domestic poetry. Adverse views have been expressed of this part of his work: J. Buckley does not like all the 'straining after a determined modernity',[7] and Clyde Ryals thinks they are dross.[8] But Philip Drew regards them as an essential part of the *oeuvre*,[9] and William E. Fredeman has made out a case for their worth.[10] Many of the poems we are concerned with come under the heading of 'English Idyls', but there are noticeable domestic elements in poems such as *Enoch Arden* and *Maud*.

What the modern reader will find interesting in these poems is the tendency for them to go right up to the boundary of where poetry leaves off and prose begins, and in some cases actually to cross it. Bathos and inconsequentiality seem to be ever present dangers; but then, so are they in much twentieth-century poetry. The other problem that arises with domestic poetry of a genial home life is that violent and sudden action is not possible, and the poetry settles into the static and the picturesque. 'The Miller's Daughter' speaks of 'the settled bliss' of the married state, and both at the time of original experience and in retrospect it is the picture that comes most naturally into the mind, often frozen and held. In 'The Miller's Daughter' this is the caught image of Alice as the narrator is staring at the mill-pool:

> And there a vision caught my eye;
> The reflex of a beauteous form,
>   A glowing arm, a gleaming neck,
> As when a sunbeam wavers warm
>   Within the dark and dimpled beck.
>
> (ll. 76–80)

Then the lover looks up, to confront the real person. It is like a low-life version of the reflected images in 'The Lady of Shalott'. It is worth remembering that the alternative title of 'The Gardener's Daughter' is 'The Pictures', since the poet is depicting the girl he loved before she knew his heart:

> But this whole hour your eyes have been intent
> On that veiled picture – veiled, for what it holds
> May not be dwelt on by the common day.
>
> (ll. 264–66)

In these poems there are the specifics of everyday home life, the carpets, the furniture, the window blinds, etc. Some of the imagery evoking them is very inventive of course, as in the game pie in 'Audley Court', 'where quail and pigeon, lark and leveret lay,/Like fossils of the rock'. But one's impression when reviewing them as a whole is that they are set in a natural rather than an artificial world. The homes are rural, surrounded by large gardens and the countryside. It is the world captured by Francis Kilvert in his diaries: at times close to paradise, but also vulnerable to traumatic experience. In Tennyson's 'English Idyls' the quality of natural observation is amazing, and the phrasing employed to evoke some of the phenomena endlessly economical and adroit. In 'The Brook' he coins the suggestive phrase 'serpent-rooted beech', and expresses most evocatively that time in very early spring 'before the leaf,/When all the wood stands in a mist of green'. He also presents, with Pre-Raphaelite sharpness, a picture of an 'old bridge which, half in ruins then,/Still makes a hoary eyebrow for the gleam/Beyond it' (ll. 79–81), and it is difficult to imagine the phenomenon of the sunbeam shining through the ripples of a stream, and appearing reticulated on the stream's bed, better expressed:

> I make the netted sunbeam dance
> Against my sandy shallows.
>
> (ll. 176–77)

A line or so later he is not content to tell us that a girl merely has chestnut hair; it has to be the colour of a freshly opened chestnut, moreover from a shell which 'divides threefold to show the fruit within'. Verlaine thought that a serious objection to Tennyson was that when he should have been showing suffering he was cultivating memories;[11] perhaps a more serious objection would have been that he threw flower catalogues at us. Many of us criticize this feature of the poetry, but all that Tennyson was doing was presenting to us what he knew: the natural world irradiating human experience, and human experience irradiating the natural world.

It came very easily to the Victorians, but somewhere there has been a break in sensibility, and it does not come easily to most moderns. On the one hand the domestic poems seem to tie in to a kind of realism, and to be only a step away from the prosaic world of the ultra-realistic novel, but on the other hand the principal themes – of court-ship, love, marriage, loss, separation, and death, all unfolding in a world of hearth, garden and field – are timeless, and put the partici-pants in touch with Theocritus (who is a prominent presence behind the poems). There are emphatic resonations in the poetry, so that Rose in 'The Gardener's Daughter' lives in a kind of paradise, 'Not wholly in the busy world, not quite/Beyond it'; it is perfectly appropriate that another text should be shadowily present:

> but she, a Rose
> In roses, mingled with her fragrant toil,

> Nor heard us come, nor from her tendance turned
> Into the world without;
>
> (ll. 141–44)

'Tendance' is a word that immediately evokes another paradise (Bk VIII, l. 47 of *Paradise Lost*), and Milton is strongly present in 'Edwin Morris' too:

> she moved,
> Like Proserpine in Enna, gathering flowers:
> Then low and sweet I whistled thrice; and she,
> She turned, we closed, we kissed, swore faith, I
> breathed
> In some new planet:
>
> (ll. 111–15)

Paradise Lost, IV. 269 is remembered here, and with it the preceding mythological background, and Homeric myth is recalled, via Keats's 'On First Looking into Chapman's Homer', in the final phrase. Theocritus's seventh *Idyll* is in the background of 'Audley Court' and 'Sea Dreams' is closely modelled on the twenty-first *Idyll*. Even a very light occasional poem turns out to have literary precedents: when Tennyson invited F. D. Maurice to escape 'from noise and smoke of town' and come down to Farringford to see 'crocus, anemone, violet', he doubtless expected that his appeal would be the more effective not only by being in verse, but by recalling Milton's invitatory sonnet to Edward Lawrence (no. 17), and beyond that Horace's *Ode* (I. iv).

These idyllic settings are reminiscent of Eden, but like Eden are very easily lost and in many cases not even attained. The ideal of the small country vicarage is middle class, but opposed to it are the more strenuous ideals of the aristocracy – the class harking back to the other concepts of heroism and the hierarchic life. Tennyson himself had encountered the immovable mass of this section of society when he wooed Rosa Baring, and the humiliation and disappointment of his failure either to conquer it, or to infiltrate it, left its mark on many poems – *Maud*, 'Aylmer's Field', 'Locksley Hall', and 'Edward Gray' being the principal ones.[12] As far back as the late Middle Ages there had been a section of the English aristocracy that had wedded itself to the new commercial and industrial forces, sometimes to improve its position, sometimes just to survive. The old heroism of feudal values became incorporated in the new heroism and giganticism of industry and progress. The Barings were typical examples of this formidable alliance, and like the mining family in *Maud* some of their wealth was in coal. Between the upper and the lower millstones of progress and conservatism the delicate plant of the middle-class domestic idyll had little chance of survival, and this vulnerability, built into most of them, gives them much of their poignancy. It is in 'Aylmer's Field' that one of the most powerful phrases in Victorian poetry occurs: 'filthy marriage-hindering Mammon'. Much of Tennyson's anger is vented against these old families that oppose the course of true love; in 'Aylmer's Field' he speaks of

> These old pheasant-lords
> These partridge-breeders of a thousand years,
> Who had mildewed in their thousands, doing nothing
> Since Egbert.
> (ll. 381–84)

Tennyson makes the complaint that middle-class commentators have justifiably made for centuries, that noblemen are not *really* noble in most cases. So in the domestic idyll is glimpsed, when Edith is 'nursing a child, and turning to the warmth/The tender pink five-beaded baby-soles', but it is thwarted by the exclusive parents. Still, poetic justice overtakes the wicked family in the end, as it does in *Locksley Hall* too. In these poems the aristocratic girls are sacrificed for the sake of family name, and in both 'Aylmer's Field' and 'The Flight' the biblical figure of Jephthah is invoked by way of parallel 'The Lord of Burleigh' is a sort of fairy-story with a bitter-sweet ending, since when the aristocratic Lord woos the 'village maiden' in the disguise of a poor landscape-painter he promises her a 'cottage pleasant', as typically ideal, one imagines, as 'the cottage in the vale' in *The Palace of Art*. But then he turns out to be an aristocrat after all, and she is burdened with 'an honour/Unto which she was not born'. Especially in the light of the other poems one has a keen sense of the fraud that has been perpetrated on her.

Patmore's poetry of domestic life is like Tennyson's in many respects, although the unofficial war between the aristocracy and the middle class is not a preoccupation for him. But like Tennyson the home life is conceived of as in a rural setting or in a half-rural small town such as Salisbury. Natural description is prevalent, and as with Tennyson it completes the whole sense of life. In Patmore this is entirely appropriate, since the interconnectedness of man and nature is closely related to the metaphysical relation between God and his creation and the married man and woman. Patmore has many affinities with seventeenth-century poets, not merely his world picture, but his sense of rhythm and diction, and sometimes even detailed aspects of his taste. His sensitivity to women's clothes (or his clothes fetishism if one wants to be cruel about it) is reminiscent of Herrick's:

> Her ball-dress seemed as breathing mist,
> From the fair form exhaled and shed.
>
> (*The Angel*, II. iii. 65–66)

Homely details are present, for instance the perennial picture of the tamed man holding up a skein of yarn to be wound (II. i. 10). Patmore, like Tennyson, has a predilection for venerable homes, and the hero of *The Angel* derives from one, as does his wife to be, Honoria, who lives in Salisbury Close:

> Red-brick and ashlar, long and low,
> With dormers and with oriels lit,
> Geranium, lychnis, rose arrayed
> The windows, all wide open thrown;
> And some one in the Study played
> The Wedding-March of Mendelssohn.
> And there it was I last took leave:
> 'Twas Christmas: I remembered now
> The cruel girls, who feigned to grieve,
> Took down the evergreens; and how
> The holly into blazes woke
> The fire, lighting the large, low room
> A dim, rich lustre of old oak
> And crimson velvet's glowing gloom.
>
> (I. i. 15–28)

However, the homes envisaged by Patmore are not merely utilitarian places in which to eat and sleep. In our language the word 'house' and even more emphatically the word 'home' have already had deep associations, in some contexts even of a religious and mystical kind. Where the Victorians differ from us is their readiness to extend the connotations of holiness into the everyday home, so that for original readers the phrase 'sanctity of home' in 'Aylmer's Field' had an import which it simply does not have for the modern reader. Patmore uses and extends these associations more than any other poet. One has the impression that the home is the chief, perhaps the *only* repository of civilized values in society. Time and time again the home is presented as shrine or temple:

> For something that abode endued
> With temple-like repose, an air
> Of life's kind purposes pursued
> With ordered freedom sweet and fair.
>
> (*The Angel*, I. i. 97–100)

To Felix the laws of the house 'seemed to be/The fair sum of six thousand years'/Traditions of civility'. It is scarcely surprising that Ruskin said of Patmore, 'you cannot read him too often or too carefully; as far as I know, he is the only living poet who always strengthens and purifies'.[13] In our century Yeats has been praised for rehabilitating the outmoded concepts of order and ceremoniousness, but actually Patmore beat him to it. In Book II, Canto iii he regards the 'undressed, familiar style' as something 'for strangers', something for the idle who wear 'sloth's unceremonious rags'; home, on the other hand, is supposed to be more like 'a gracious Court' where the behaviour should befit 'immortal life'. Later the house is a 'joyful shrine'. Heady claims, yet coexisting with precise and up-to-date details of everyday Victorian life – a combination which, as Mario Praz claims, reminds us of Donne.[14] As with Tennyson, some of the poetry veers dangerously close to bathos, but elsewhere there is startling beauty, as in the beautiful image where he characterizes 'ardent desires': 'Pure as the permeating fires/That smoulder in the opal's veins' (II. iii. 120). Patmore and Rossetti are not usually compared, yet lines such as these are not so far from *The House of Life*:

> And lovers, on the love-lit globe,
>   For love's sweet sake, walk yet aloof,
> And hear Time weave the marriage-robe,
>   Attraction warp and reverence woof!
>
> (II. v. 45–48)

There is another parallel to be made with Donne in these domestic poems, that they rely a good deal on the effective reproduction of conversations in good idiomatic English. The works treated in the chapter are a good place to pursue what I have called elsewhere 'the colloquial tradition'. There is plenty of direct speech in these poems (indeed, a poem such as 'Walking to the Mail' is entirely made up of it), and it blends in well with the narrative voice. Some of it is as casual and natural as the direct speech of novels, and perhaps novels were an influence on them (just as, in reverse, the poems may have influenced the poetic presentation of nature which is one of the distinctive features of the Victorian novel). As befits an anti-heroic poem the first conversation the wedded pair have in *The Angel* is not on an impossibly exalted level; it is actually able to embrace the inconsequential and the contingent:

> 'Look, is not this a pretty shawl,
>   Aunt's parting gift.' 'She's always kind.'

> 'The new wing spoils Sir John's old Hall:
>   You'll see it, if you pull the blind.'
>
> (II. xi. 135–38).

There is something that adumbrates John Betjeman in these lines, not merely the protest at a lapse of architectual taste, but the record of a visual detail that will not be edged out even by serious emotional experiences. Certainly the relaxed and realistic movement of the speech in these poems makes a significant contribution to the creation of versimilitude. It does not usually resonate as much as the other parts of the poetry, but it does represent the diurnal texture of life.

I have concentrated in this chapter on Tennyson and Patmore, since they are the principal poets in this line, but other poets are often equally effective at dealing with the casual and relaxed atmosphere of home life; one thinks especially of Clough and Browning. Many of the features indicated in this chapter are also prominent in *The Bothie* and *Amours de Voyage*. Poetry should never be automatically treated as authoritative and reliable documentary evidence, but the body of Victorian poetry dealing with domestic life should make one question whether the myth of the stiff and claustrophobically unpleasant Victorian home, typified by Samuel Butler's *The Way of All Flesh* (1903), is the complete story.

As I have already suggested, death and separation was an ever-present threat hanging over the domestic idyll, not merely because that is a traditional literary topos, but because in the real life of that century the fact of death could not be blinked. In response to it, as if by a species of over-compensation, there was even a cult of death (see below pp. 161–63).

In Tennyson the forces of destruction, which are directly opposed to the comfort, the security, and the apparent stability of home, are rarely at bay. In 'The Brook' human life does not have the brook's inexorability, and generational renewal is only a partial answer. The domestic idylls are often most poignant because they are contemplated from a distance, either of time or of place (rather as all those exiles in remote parts of the globe had a particular kaleidoscope of images that they clung to of the English home). The classic example is Enoch Arden, dreaming of home when marooned on his savagely beautiful tropical island:

> There often as he watched or seemed to watch,
> So still, the golden lizard on him paused,
> A Phantom made of many phantoms moved
> Before him haunting him, or he himself
> Moved haunting people, things and places, known

Far in a darker isle beyond the line;
The babes, their babble, Annie, the small house,
The climbing street, the mill, the leafy lanes,
The peacock-yewtree and the lonely Hall,
The horse he drove, the boat he sold, the chill
November dawns and dewy-glooming downs,
The gentle shower, the smell of dying leaves,
And the low moan of leaden-coloured seas.

(ll. 596–608)

Those exiles who had to endure what are called in 'The Brook' 'the
branding summers of Bengal' (and there were many more sufferers of
this kind then than now) were easily able to identify with these lines
– which goes some way towards explaining why *Enoch Arden* was such
a popular poem in the days of empire. The exiles' dream of domestic
peace is a very familiar theme. In 'He Fell Among Thieves' Henry
Newbolt imagines the thoughts of a soldier about to die:

He saw the gray little church across the park,
The mounds that hide the loved and honoured dead;
The Norman arch, the chancel softly dark,
The brasses black and red.

(ll. 21–24)

However, the overwhelmingly poignant moment in Tennyson's
poem comes when Enoch returns, and is able to see his wife, now
married to Philip, who is a sort of male 'angel in the house' (l. 420);
but he feels as isolated from his family as a ghostly revenant might be:
there is 'the genial hearth', but separated from him by a pane of glass.
It is basically the experience of the dead in *The Coach of Death*, who
see 'the light of their blest firesides', but it is more poignant when
registered by one who is a 'dead man come to life'. Death then was
the great threat, what Patmore called 'The heartless and
intolerable/Indignity of "earth to earth"'. When the clergyman chooses
a text for Edith's funeral sermon in 'Aylmer's Field' it is fraught with
religious meaning: 'Behold, your house is left unto ye desolate' and
he offers the survivors little hope or comfort. But there was consolation for those in the right spiritual states; the prospect existed of
home in the after-life, an immortal extension of the domestic idyll.
This is the prospect of the girl in Tennyson's 'The May Queen' about
to leave her colourful and exuberant life:

For ever and for ever, all in a blessed home –
And there to wait a little while till you and
                    Effie come –

To lie within the light of God, as I lie upon your
            breast –
And the wicked cease from troubling, and the weary
            are at rest.
                        (Conclusion, ll. 57–60)

Notes

1. L. Stone, *The Family, Sex and Marriage in England, 1500–1800* (1977).

2. See for instance K. Thomas's review of Stone, in *TLS* (21 October 1977), pp. 1226–27.

3. J. Ruskin, *Works*, xviii, 122

4. Ibid., xxxv, 36.

5. Pater, *Works*, viii, 178.

6. M. Arnold, quoting Goethe, 'was uns alle bandigt, DAS GEMEINE!', Preface to *Essays in Criticism* (1865), in *The Complete Works of Matthew Arnold*, edited by R. H. Super, 11 vols (Ann Arbor, 1960–77), iii, 290.

7. J. Buckley, *The Growth of a Poet* (1960), p. 83.

8. C. Ryals, *Theme and Symbols in Tennyson's Poems to 1850* (Philadelphia, 1964).

9. P. Drew, '"Aylmer's Field": a Problem for Critics', *The Listener*, 71 (2 April 1964), 553, 556–57.

10. W. E. Fredeman, '"The Sphere of Common Duties": The Domestic Solution in Tennyson's Poetry', *BJRL*, 54 (Spring 1972), 357–383.

11. In his Introduction to *The Oxford Book of Modern Verse: 1892–1935* (Oxford, 1936), W. B. Yeats quotes Verlaine on Tennyson: 'When he should have been broken-hearted he had many reminiscences' (p. ix).

12. For the importance of Rosa Baring see R. W. Rader, *Tennyson's 'Maud': The Biographical Genesis* (Berkeley and Los Angeles, 1963).

13. Ruskin, *Sesame and Lilies*, ii, *Works*, xviii, 120.

14. M. Praz, *The Hero in Eclipse* (1956), pp. 438–39.

Chapter 9
The Elegiac

Victorian poets had a tendency to be serious, reflective, and melancholic. Their thoughts often turned towards death, loss, regret for the vanished past, lament for the transience of life. Collectively these states of mind constitute the elegiac, and a number of distinguished and effective elegies were produced in the period. The elegiac often extends its boundaries beyond the usual objects of lament, friends, members of the family, lovers, to express more general regret. In these lines of Emily Brontë one hears the pure and unadulterated note of elegiac feeling, in this case imagined rather than based on any specific event:

> Cold in the earth, and the deep snow piled above
>   thee!
>   Far, far removed, cold in the dreary grave!
> Have I forgot, my only love, to love thee,
>   Severed at last by time's all-wearing wave?
>   'R. Alcona to J. Brenzaida',
>   (ll. 1–4)

The poem concludes with a plangent outcry:

> And even yet, I dare not let it languish,
>   Dare not indulge in memory's rapturous pain;
> Once drinking deep of that divinest anguish,
>   How could I seek the empty world again?
>   (ll. 29–32)

These lines capture the pure essence of elegiac feeling, and one often encounters it in Victorian poetry, but in many of the poems studied in this chapter the feeling is less pure and concentrated, and other considerations come into play. To some extent these wider aspects have already been considered in Chapter 6 so that I shall be restricting myself here to the poetic celebration of dead people and other forms of personal loss. J. R. Watson notes the prevalence of the elegiac and says that 'we may find it unhelpful or even unhealthy',[1] but it is ubiquitous. He cites with approval Margaret Hale's impatience at any kind of self-indulgent brooding over loss in Elizabeth Gaskell's *North and South (1854)*. Most Victorians, however, were more prone to encourage such feelings than to suppress them. We should not castigate the Victorians too severely, since there is a sense in which the elegiac is very central to the inherent genius of poetry; that is because epitaphs, of their very nature, are wistfully separated from original experience and original loves, rather as all celebratory and reflective poetry is. Absence may ambitiously aspire to the state of presence, but will never finally attain it.

There were a number of serious elegies in earlier English poetry, including Chaucer's *Book of the Duchess*, Milton's *Lycidas*, Donne's *Anniversaries*, Pope's 'Elegy on the Death of an Unfortunate Lady', Gray's 'Elegy Written in a Country Churchyard', Wordsworth's *Elegiac Stanzas*, and Shelley's *Adonais*. Victorian poets often continue the moods and cadences of these works, and often continue to explore similar attitudes. One might have thought that the significant decline in orthodox religious faith, indicated elsewhere as a central aspect of the period, would have altered the nexus of emotions and attitudes in the face of death, but actually there was not a great difference, since although earlier poets enjoyed the consolations of belief in the after-life it did not always take the edge off the felt sharpness of death.

In one important sense the Victorian elegies continue the tendency exhibited in previous examples to pay as much attention to the mourner as to the mourned. Given the fact that the experiences belong to the celebrant rather than to the dead person this is inevitable, and since the experience belongs to poets the elegies will naturally concern themselves very self-consciously with theories of poetry.

In Memoriam is by far the most important elegy in the period. In the past it was not necessary for poets to know the object of their lament very well: Donne had never met Elizabeth Drury, Milton was merely a slight acquaintance of Edward King, Gray's 'rude forefathers' could only be distantly imagined, and Shelley had only the briefest acquaintance with Keats. The presence of death always guaranteed seriousness and earnestness, but in Tennyson's case Arthur Hallam was a close and loved friend whose death was a shattering personal experience, calling into doubt the whole stability and reliability of human existence. It was the central event in Tennyson's life, and left its mark on many other poems. The immediate response to the news of the death was a moving and direct outcry: 'Hark! the dogs howl!' The poem was not printed in Tennyson's lifetime:

Hark! the dogs howl! the sleetwinds blow,
The church-clocks knoll: the hours haste,
I leave the dreaming world below.
Blown o'er frore heads of hills I go,
Long narrowing friths and stripes of snow –
Time bears my soul into the waste.
I seek the voice I love – ah where
Is that dear hand that I should press,
Those honoured brows that I would kiss?
Lo! the broad Heavens cold and bare,
The stars that know not my distress.

(ll. 1–11)

The poem continues, portraying Hallam as larger than life, and in his ghostly form somehow reproachful, so that the mourner is impelled to feel guilt. Aspects of this spontaneous outflow continue in *In Memoriam*, but augmented with many other emotional currents and speculative considerations. There was a gap of seventeen years between the death and the publication of *In Memoriam*, and the poem grew cumulatively, without any forethought on Tennyson's part. The central event, the death of Hallam, was the light that made all other events and states of mind gather round it like multiple arcs forming myriads of concentric circles. The poem was given a plot organization by a rudimentary narrative – the celebration of three Christmases and the culmination achieved by a wedding in which life goes optimistically on. Individual episodes retain the freshness of discrete and spontaneous units of experience.

Faced with a long poem like this, the reader will inevitably ask what it is about. And he will be forced to conclude that it is not principally about Arthur Hallam. Its central concern is the manner in which the survivor comes to terms with grief, not by forgetting it, not by getting used to it, but by seizing on it as a central source of power in the imaginative life. It becomes the dark skein running through all experience, providing it with an interest and a colour it might not otherwise have had. The poet seeks consolation not in comforting orthodox assertions of immortality (although these are sometimes made) but in the operations of memory, perception, creativity, and speculation. Often in the poem the speculations are sceptical and agnostic; these should not be registered as inferior stages on the route to higher and more enlightened knowledge, but part of the final scheme of things. In the Epilogue the marriage is partly offered as an answer to time's depredations, and a guarantee of human survival. But even as Tennyson enjoys it he is haunted by images of nature surviving after human life has gone:

Dumb is that tower which spake so loud,
And high in heaven the streaming cloud,
And on the downs a rising fire:

And rise, O moon, from yonder down,
   Till over down and over dale
   All night the shining vapour sail
And pass the silent-lighted town,

The white-faced halls, the glancing rills,
   And catch at every mountain head,
   And o'er the friths that branch and spread
Their sleeping silver thro' the hills.

(Epilogue, ll. 106–16)

The dumb tower is the church tower, which earlier had rung its
celebratory peal of bells, but it might be an emblem of the speaking
poet, whose death will not be noticed by nature. In a sense Tennyson
has not advanced beyond the first impassioned outcry of 'Hark! the
dogs howl!' where the 'friths and stripes of snow' are the central
features in a waste-land which does not recognize man's distress. If *In
Memoriam* has made an advance on the earlier poem it is in the recognition that the 'friths' are beautiful, and that they require man's
consciousness for that beauty to be registered. Even though man might
not be there any longer he is able to imagine the beauty that has
outlived him, and that power of mind helps to give man an essential
definition, an 'undisputed sovereignty' as Emily Brontë puts it in 'To
Imagination'. On the whole in *In Memoriam* the search for self-definition
is successful, and provides some cause for optimism. Tennyson realized
that a long poem emphasizing the consciousness of an individual might
run the danger of being egotistical (a danger from which Wordsworth's
The Prelude, published, like *In Memoriam*, in 1850, is not entirely free),
but his work is partly saved from this by being dominated by love for
another being and by a vein of humility.

Because the operation of the liberated mind is so dominant in the
poem, our response to *In Memoriam*, like the sufferer's response to
grief, is not necessarily linear and time bound. As Eliot realized, 'time
is no healer, the patient is no longer here'. Tennyson wanted the
patient to be here, which involved a less emphatic emphasis on the
passage of time than one might expect in so long a poem. A comprehensive series of perspectives on life and death is provided, and the
sheer length of the work gives scope for a wider spectrum of moods
than most elegies, from despair,

> So find I every pleasant spot
>> In which we two were wont to meet,
>> The field, the chamber, and the street,
> For all is dark where thou art not.
>>> (VIII. 9–12)

to guilt:

> Behold me, for I cannot sleep,
> And like a guilty thing I creep
> At earliest morning to the door.
>>> (VII. 6–8)

to dead calmness:

> Calm is the morn without a sound,
>> Calm as to suit a calmer grief,
>> And only through the faded leaf
> The chestnut pattering to the ground
>>> (XII. 1–4)

to anger:

> Be near me when my faith is dry,
>> And men the flies of latter spring,
>> That lay their eggs, and sting and sing
> And weave their petty cells and die.
>>> (L. 9–12)

There are more positive states – particularly when Tennyson has recovered from the initial shock and begins to have fond (though distanced) memories of his friend and tries to pierce the veil of death. Previous elegies had often tried to offer consolation by investing nature with positive attributes – so that Shelley finds solace in Keats's becoming 'one with nature'. Nature for Tennyson, however, is a more enigmatic being. On the one hand she is allied to the destructive forces of time and decay, so that the powerful metaphysical image of the 'fibres' of the yew tree netting 'the dreamless head', and the dizzying prospects of geological time are hardly reassuring. But on the other hand she is concerned with offering distractions and anodynes in her beautiful appearances, and of providing the main type for beliefs of cyclical renewal.

In Memoriam is very scenic – there are many instances of where the units of composition correspond to events occurring at specific times and places, and this gives it an immediate and personal feel. It goes over ground familiar to elegiac poetry, yet without seeming derivative; for instance there is a good deal about the guilt a poet might harbour as he feels in danger of exploiting his grief and about the merely thera-peutic value of its expression:

> But, for the unquiet heart and brain
> A use in measured language lies;
> The sad mechanic exercise,
> Like dull narcotics numbing pain.
>   (v. 5–8)

Renaissance poets were wont to harbour such scruples, in writing poetry about love and death.

There is, then, specificity in the poem, but it exists alongside quite different generic features, so that Tennyson seems to be speaking not only about his own grief but that of others. *In Memoriam* was first published anonymously, and one reader thought it told the story of a grieving widow for her sailor husband. To James Knowles Tennyson said: 'It is rather the cry of the whole human race than mine. In the poem altogether private grief swells into thought of, and hope for, the whole world.'[2] Section VI uses a number of comparisons to indicate the force of grief – the son toasted by his father even as he dies, the mother praying for her drowned son, the bride preparing herself for her wedding even though 'her future lord/Was drowned in passing through the ford' (ll. 38–9). These are illustrative examples, but so vivid that at the time they seem like the prime matter of the poem. This explains why *In Memoriam* was so popular with everyone from Queen Victoria downwards: it seemed to be speaking not merely *to* them but *for* them.

One outcome of this tendency towards the universal in *In Memoriam* is that Arthur Hallam is not very particularized and vivid to us in the poem. The street where he used to live, Wimpole Street, is much more observed and imagined. This is partly in accord with elegiac tradition: Edward King and John Keats are not strongly presented to us as inter-esting individuals in the Milton and Shelley poems celebrating them. We know that Hallam had a facetious wit, for instance, but one would never guess it from the poem. In this sense *In Memoriam* is very unlike *The Book of the Duchess*, which does give a vivid picture of John of Gaunt's wife. Tennyson presents us with a figure, but the predominant impression of Hallam is that he is dead, and haunts the imagination like a shadowy ghost. The initial response to the death, 'Hark! the dogs howl!', dwells on this image, and it is carried forward into *In Memoriam*:

> The vapour labours up the sky,
>   Uncertain forms are darkly moved,
> Larger than human passes by
>   The shadow of the man I loved.
>   (ll. 18–21)

In *In Memoriam* Hallam achieves high and sublime stature:

> So, dearest, now thy brows are cold,
>   I see thee what thou art, and know
>   Thy likeness to the wise below,
> Thy kindred with the great of old.
>   (LXXIV. 5–8)

It would be rash to claim that *In Memoriam* is as great a poem as the *Divina Commedia*, but like that earlier work it does make an imaginative grasp of the universe by way of the opposed yet related forces of love and death. And finally by way of the mediation of the loved and lost person the poets catch a glimpse of God:

> Whereof the man, that with me trod
>   This planet, was a noble type
>   Appearing ere the times were ripe,
> That friend of mine who lives in God,
>
> That God, which ever lives and loves,
>   One God, one law, one element,
>   And one far-off divine event,
> To which the whole creation moves.
>   (Epilogue, ll. 137–44)

In Memoriam is in a class by itself in the period; no other elegy has its stature or universality. The other elegies, good as they may be, are placed on a lower rung. The most famous of these is Arnold's *Thyrsis*, which, as it happens, is also a man's lament for a male friend. Aligned with the fact that the loved person was a poet he was also in a sense a rival and a competitor, and this makes the comparison between *Thyrsis* and the classical pastoral models very close – indeed reminiscences of these pastorals are woven into the poem itself. Arnold and Clough had been classical scholars together at Oxford, and it had always been almost as natural as breathing to imbue the surrounding countryside with pastoral attributes; thus it was natural for Arnold, in mourning Clough, to use this idiom – possibly for the last time in English poetry with much conviction:

> But Thyrsis never more we swains shall see;
>   See him come back, and cut a smoother reed,
>   And blow a strain the world at last shall
>   heed –
> For Time, not Corydon, hath conquered thee!
>
> (ll. 77–80)

The flower catalogues in the poem, listing homely English wild flowers, are reminiscent of the floral tributes brought to the dead in Theocritan and Virgilian elegy. As in much traditional elegy the poet feels the presence of his own mortality, not in a panic-stricken way, but melancholic and regretful:

> Yes, thou art gone! and round me too the night
> In ever-nearing circle weaves her shade.
>   I see her veil draw soft across the day,
>   I feel her slowly chilling breath invade
>   The cheek grown thin, the brown hair sprent
>   with grey;
>   I feel her finger light
> Laid pausefully upon life's headlong train.
>
> (ll. 131–37)

As with *In Memoriam*, where the figure of Hallam is vague, we do not get an especially clear picture of Clough from *Thyrsis*, and the pastoral obliqueness is not always easy to translate or decode:

> He loved his mates; but yet he could not
>   keep,
> For that a shadow loured on the fields.
>
> (ll. 43–44)

Does this refer to the difficulties he had swearing to the Thirty-nine Articles of the Church of England in order to qualify for a Fellowship at Oriel College? And do the following lines refer to his resignation?

> He went; his piping took a troubled sound
> Of storms that rage outside our happy ground;
> He could not wait their passing, he is dead.
>
> (ll. 48–50)

Clough's poetry does depict some of the contemporary 'storms' – the Risorgimento in Italy for instance – but although it is sometimes troubled and there are signs that on occasions he may have been a 'too quick despairer' the phrasing does not do full justice to all aspects of Clough. Sometimes his response to trouble was to adopt a quizzical and urbane wit. Arnold knows all about the forces that can impede a poet in the modern age, and his regret that Clough succumbed to them is partly the expression of self-pity and self-doubt. The hopeful sign in the poem is akin to the positive aspects of *Lycidas* – that there is hope for the continuation of poetic genius, and the focus of that optimism is the Scholar Gipsy's tree which 'yet crowns the hill'. The strength of this poem lies partly in the fact that it is a lament for Arnold's own lost, romantic youth.

A very different elegy is Arnold's *Rugby Chapel*, published in 1867, but perhaps begun in the mid 1850s when Thomas Arnold (who died in 1842) was beginning to be subjected to some hostile criticism. The work has all the trappings of elegiac poetry in its melodramatic guise – gloom, austerity, coldness, and solemnity – yet it celebrates a man who was a radiant beacon for his son and many others. Arnold imagines him in the past, blessed with 'radiant vigour' and he imagines him in the after-life similarly endowed 'in some far-shining sphere'. There is a graphic depiction of the journey of life, much rougher than the average urbanite might expect, 'through sunk/Gorges, o'er mountains in snow'. On this trek Thomas Arnold is the encouraging leader. It is an interesting journey, since although it is figurative and allegorical it is closely based on the Lake District rambles which the Arnold children enjoyed and which are evoked in the very beautiful poem 'Resignation'. Since Thomas Arnold was a public figure the poem celebrating him is at once private and public, but with more awareness of the public image than is provided in *Thyrsis*. In addition Arnold produced elegies on celebrities unknown to him personally – 'Heine's Grave' and 'Haworth Churchyard.' Since the Brontës were belated Romantics it is appropriate that they should be celebrated in terms directly reminiscent of *Adonais*:

> Unquiet souls!
> – In the dark fermentation of earth,
> In the never idle workshop of nature,
> In the eternal movement,
> Ye shall find yourselves again!
>
> (ll. 134–38)

Another variation is what might be called the 'lyrical elegy', and 'Requiescat' is an example of this; the last two stanzas are:

> Her life was turning, turning,
>   In mazes of heat and sound;

> But for peace her soul was yearning,
>   And now peace laps her round.
>
> Her cabined, ample spirit,
>   It fluttered and failed for breath.
> Tonight it doth inherit
>   The vasty hall of death.
>   (ll. 9–16)

The anapaestic foot in line 11 is rather disruptive and disconcerting incidentally.

Like Arnold, Swinburne often makes use of his extensive classical education, and typical of this is the close echo of Catullus in the poem celebrating Baudelaire: 'Ave Atque Vale'. This is the same genre as Arnold's public elegies, since Swinburne only knew Baudelaire through his works. Like Tennyson he reaches out to touch something, and what he touches is surviving verse:

> These I salute, these touch, these clasp and fold
> As though a hand were in my hand to hold.
>   (ll. 107–8)

Appropriately, the flower catalogue in this poem is bizarre and decadent, since Baudelaire was a 'gardener of strange flower'.

So far, since most of the elegies have been for fellow poets and male friends, they have approximated quite closely to classical models, but there is a large body of Victorian elegies for wives and lovers. It is probably the case that there was, in the nineteenth century, something approaching a cult of death; it impinged on the average consciousness much more and disease was less under control than it is now. The elaborate culture surrounding it possibly had morbid sources, but it was also a way of making a virtue out of necessity, of acknowledging the overwhelming fact rather them shying away from it. The growth of the 'cult' aspects might be directly related to the decline in deep and consolatory belief. Poetry was marshalled to make its contribution to the cult, and there is a mass of very minor and very bad elegiac poetry, especially in the context of domestic mourning. Death and its accoutrements absorbed much of the psychic energy which in our century is concentrated on sexuality.

Inevitably the most prominent work in which death and domesticity meet is Patmore's 'The Unknown Eros.' His first wife, Emily Andrews, died after fifteen years of marriage, and his second wife after sixteen years, so that he was acquainted with bereavement. 'Departure' sounds the domestic note:

And it was like your great and gracious ways
To turn your talk on daily things, my Dear,
Lifting the luminous, pathetic lash
To let the laughter flash.

(ll. 21–24)

but there is recognition of the harsh inexorability of death when, at the end, the woman is bereft of the power to maintain grace and demonstrate love:

And go your journey of all days
With not one kiss, or a good-bye,
And the only loveless look the look with which
    you passed.

(ll. 31–33)

'Tired Memory' is a poem in which Patmore tried to find religious faith, though deprived of the wife who seemed to encourage and validate it. Another poet worth mentioning who celebrated the virtues of the dead wife is William Barnes. After his wife died in 1852 he composed two elegies, one in 'National English' the other in dialect. The dialect version is the more powerful, with its measured and sonorous tones:

Since I noo mwore do zee yuour feace,
    Up steairs or down below,
I'll zit me in the lwonesome pleace,
    Where flat-boughed beech do grow:
Below the beeches' bough, my love,
    Where you did never come,
An' I don't look to meet ye now,
    As I do look at hwome.

(ll. 1–8)

'The Wind at the Door' is another poem of loss, with the imagined presence of the wife so near – and yet so far.

Patmore and Barnes are sometimes haunted by death, but Rossetti is perhaps the most consistently death-haunted poet of the period, and his whole work is pervaded with death or death-like states of loss, separation, and dreaming. *The House of Life* sonnet cycle is pervaded by death and metaphorical versions of death, and the poet is often dubious about distinctions between life and death – as in 'The Monochord' (LXXIX): 'Nay, is it Life or Death, thus thunder-crowned?' In the strange poem 'Death-in-Love' (XLVIII) the winged figure of Love is actually not breathing, and equated with the personification of Death. In 'through Death to Love' (XLI) 'wild images of Death' flood into the relationship, and in 'Winged Hours' (XXV) there are premonitions of death – of 'bloodied feathers scattered in the brake.' 'Memorial Thresholds' (LXXXI), like *The Blessed Damozel* imagines the possibility of sense of loss beyond the grave, where 'mocking winds whirl round a chaff-strown floor'. 'Lost Days' (LXXXVI) anticipates scenes of Dantesque torture in the after-life, with a bitterness that takes them beyond the elegiac mood. The final poem in the collection, 'The One Hope' (CI), is a longing desire for peace and hope beyond the grave. The whole sequence is shot through with actual or imagined loss, and intense desire (which is often nurtured on absence and transience) becomes very closely associated with the elegiac. The death of Rossetti's wife Lizzie in curious circumstances in 1862 could only have intensified his natural poetic predilection for his particular brand of wan morbidity.

The final major love elegist to consider is Hardy, but the poems he wrote mourning the death of his first wife in 1912 belong to the modern period. Like their Victorian predecessors they exploit the congruence of emotion and geographical place, but in a curious way, because of their starkness and avoidance of sentimentality, they are very moving. There is, however, a Hardy poem from our period that is elegiac, probably written near the time of the death of an early love, Tryphena Sparks, in 1890: 'Thoughts of Phena'. He regrets that he has no relics,

> Not a line of her writing have I,
> > Not a thread of her hair.
>
> (ll. 1–2)

Here there is a bleakness by comparison with *In Memoriam* where Tennyson does enjoy the consolation of reading through Hallam's letters (XCV):

> So word by word, and line by line,
> > The dead man touched me from the past,
> > And all at once it seemed at last
> The living soul was flashed on mine.
>
> (ll. 33–36)

Like many of the other great Victorians – like Tennyson, Arnold, and Rossetti – Hardy was time-haunted, and many of his central motives are very similar, but the style and character of his poetry feels very different, suggesting that principal motives will not always explain the individual character of a poet.

Finally there is an elegy worth considering that is not quite like the others in this chapter, which celebrate friends, mistresses, wives, and poets. Hopkins's 'Felix Randal' deals with a blacksmith who was one of the parishioners in a Lancashire town.[3] It is a touching poem about a man broken by sickness, and Hopkins's attitude to him is influenced not by a poetic fancy but by the common metaphors which typify the relationship of priest to parishioner: father to child. So that in its pitying solicitude it is like the great elegies which mourn the deaths of children – Ben Jonson's on his son for instance. But finally we see that this poem, like *Thyrsis*, is a lament for a maker, for that is what Felix Randal was, and poets are always particularly touched by the deaths of makers:

> When thou at the random grim forge, powerful
> amidst peers,
> Didst fettle for the great grey drayhorse his
> bright and battering sandal!
>
> (ll. 13–14)

Notes

1. J. R. Watson, *Everyman's Book of Victorian Verse* (1982), p. xvi.

2. Tennyson to James Knowles, *Nineteenth Century*, 33 (1893), 182.

3. A. Thomas, SJ, 'Hopkins's *Felix Randal*: The Man and the Poem', *TLS* (19 March 1971), 331–32.

Chapter 10
Victorian Satire

The general impression is that there was not very much Victorian
satire, since the predominant picture is of a poetic tradition that was
serious, often elegiac, and sensitive to the beautiful. There were satirical poems, such as Bulwer Lytton's *The New Timon* (1846) and Alfred
Austin's *The Season* (1861, revised 1869), but these were mediocre
works, and in a worn-out eighteenth-century poetic tradition; they are
not regarded as part of any main stream. Houghton and Stange go so
far as to state specifically that there is an 'almost total absence of
successful satire in Victorian poetry'.[1] However, it will be seen that
there is a good deal of satirical poetry, but much of it occurring incidentally in poetry not exclusively satirical.

The absence of critical interest in Victorian verse satire may be due
to the Victorians themselves. One often takes the cue, in writing a
literary history, from the age itself. The Victorian poets were ashamed
of satire, doubted whether it was real poetry, and tried to preserve
pride of place for life-enhancing, grandiloquent, positive, and beautiful
poetry. Most of them were wedded to the notion of the bardic and
an exalted image of poetry. Time and time again one finds the status
of satire called into question. Patmore, in an essay called 'The Decay
of Modern Satire'[2], thought there had been no significant satire since
the Anti-Jacobin poetry of the 1790s, and he even ruled Byron out of
court. Most of the major poets were cautious and distrustful of satire,
and were alarmed at its destructive tendencies. Experience had taught
them to regard societies as more fragile than they had previously
appeared, and they thought that a poet such as Heine was too negative
to be of any use in rebuilding or recasting society. They took their lead
from the Romantics (other than Byron that is), who were anxious to
promote the poet as a dignified priest devoid of instinctive satirical
tendencies. Wordsworth had referred to the 'scorn and condemnation
personal/That would profane the sanctity of verse'.[3] Naturally enough,
the feeling that poetry should be concerned with beauty withdrew it
from satire, which was traditionally more hospitable to the ugly and
the grotesque. Satire required uncouth sounds for its expression, and

there was a fear that the most honey-tongued genius could have his voice made bitter once he courted the vituperative muse. Perhaps there was a remembrance of how Milton's mellifluous poetry had been spoilt when it had to make room for names like Colkitto, Macdonnel, and Galasp.[4] There was anxiety that the poetic quality of lines could be damaged if the poet had to mention a less than euphonious modern name – as Tennyson did in 'The Wise, the Pure, the lights of our dull clime', in referring to O'Connell.

In Arnold especially we find explicit statements on the status of satire. In his prose he is able to exhibit a strongly satiric instinct, but the tone that came most naturally to him in his poetry was the elegiac rather than the critical or spiteful: he does not resort, for instance, to the satirical voice when he visits the Grande Chartreuse, where the medieval way of life had prolonged itself into modern times with the oddity of Rip Van Winkle. In his famous inaugural lecture as Professor of Poetry at Oxford (14 November 1857), he spoke up for tolerance and the adequate view of life. He preferred the vital freshness, charm, and geniality of Aristophanes to the 'sceptical, frivolous and dissolute' tone of the key Roman satirist Menander.[5] Arnold's ideal was to 'see life steadily and see it whole', as he envisaged Sophocles had done:

> But be his
> My special thanks, whose even-balanced soul,
> From first youth tested up to extreme old age,
> Business could not make dull, nor passion wild;
> Who saw life steadily, and saw it whole.
>
> ('To a Friend', ll. 8–12)

This may be a limited view of poetry, since many theorists have thought that passion is a necessary ingredient in poetry. In Arnold's opinion the adequate view of life was 'the most invincible tendency to live', whereas the satiric, however much it was concerned indirectly with the prolongation of life, was more associated with the force of death. Menander, in Arnold's view, contained 'the seed of death'.[6]

Of almost equal significance was Arnold's onslaught on Horace: 'If human life were complete without faith, without enthusiasm, without energy, Horace, like Menander, would be the perfect interpreter of human life.'[7] But it is not, Arnold is anxious to say. Arnold, coming nearer to his own time, was critical of the eighteenth-century frame of mind. He wrote: 'it proceeds by ratiocination, antithesis, ingenious turns and conceits. The poetry is often eloquent, and always, in the hands of such masters as Dryden and Pope, clever; but it does not take us much below the surface of things, it does not give us the emotion of seeing things in their truth and beauty'.[8] Arnold was, in fact, out of tune with the century whose most significant poetic achievement was satire. And he saw in the example of Heine the danger of inflicting wounds on others:

> Therefore a secret unrest
> Tortured thee, brilliant and bold!
> Therefore triumph itself
> Tasted amiss to thy soul.
> Therefore, with blood of thy foes,
> Trickled in silence thine own.
> Therefore the victor's heart
> Broke on the field of his fame.
>
> ('Heine's Grave', ll. 121–28)

Perhaps at the back of Arnold's mind, all during his life, was the belief expressed by his father Thomas Arnold in 'The Poetry of Common Life' (1831) that poetry 'exalts and ennobles us, and puts us into a higher state of mind than that which we are commonly living in'.[9] Given beliefs of this kind, it was only natural that the poets and readers should eschew poetry that they considered degrading. The civilization was too committed to the idea of progress and the ultimate perfectibility of man to contemplate a harsh view of itself with equanimity. It was too committed to ideas of reform and organization to harbour much toleration for the necessarily destructive and anarchic images that satire presents. Tennyson's sketch of the poet in 'The Poet' does not leave much room for hate:

> The poet in a golden clime was born,
>   With golden stars above;
> Dowered with the hate of hate, the scorn of scorn,
>   The love of love.
>
> He saw through life and death, through good and
>   ill,
>   He saw through his own soul
> The marvel of the everlasting will,
>   An open scroll.
>   (ll. 1–8)

There was no room on the scroll for rude words. These then were the prevailing attitudes, and they had a degree of force. Nevertheless there was a satiric tradition in Victorian poetry, and it is worthy of attention.

Satire is an identification of and a protest against those adverse conditions of human life which are regulable or eradicable by acts of will. It has command of a wide range of tone, from the disarming

Chaucerian smile to the animal savagery of Swift. It attacks follies and vices embodied in both invented figures and actual historical personages (although by the time the real personages appear in poetry they are alchemized into something not quite real). It tends to deal with man in his social contexts and in circumstances where his values and behaviour impinge on others. It is on the fringe of other modes: of the comic, of the elegiac (when it bewails a decline from primitive virtue); and of the tragic (when it laments the macrocosmically foolish situation of man). When satire draws close to the tragic, as it does with Swift and Goya for instance, it is on the point of ceasing to be satire, since it deals with endemic elements in the human condition that are not reformable. As Macneice puts it, 'Goya had the laugh–/But can what is corrupt be cured by laughter?' (*Autumn Journal*, VI. 43–44). At its best it remains art because it is creative. Good satire is not crude invective or name-calling. If there is a specific living victim for satire to attack, the poet creates a vivid rival image of that victim in art, whose palpability and potency is superior to the living person's. The satirist creates a vacuum, and his own substitutions rush in to fill the place. The creative drive in the satirical poet is usually more powerful than the reformative, and in most cases the wish to create a fully realized ridiculous world is a stronger motive than a sense of indignation. Chaucer would have been the first to be sorry if he thought his satire might reduce the incidence of effete prioresses (always supposing it could); Praed and Clough would have been the first to be sorry if they thought their verse had any impact on the incidence of empty-headed girls. Satire often looks like a radical literary mode, but there are distinctions to be made between the satire that is genuinely radical and criticizes the very bases of a society, and the satire that criticizes behaviour not conforming to the theoretical bases. In some societies – such as Chaucer's for instance – the deviance from theoretical standards of godliness was so prevalent, and the observance of goodness so rare, that one wonders whether the standards can in any sense be called 'norms'. Even so, until the Romantic Movement it was assumed that most societies had enough moral presence of mind to be able to make some formulation of good standards. After the Romantic Movement, there tended to be less faith in the social and collective mind, and it was more common to believe that the highest levels of awareness could only be achieved by individuals. These individuals were never anxious to attribute any moral conscience to a consensus.

Satire that takes its stand on the righteousness of the individual and the wickedness of the majority is most radical; this was the kind of satire that Byron wrote, and in so far as Victorian poets were heirs to the Romantic Movement, this is the kind of poetry that they wrote.

However, many of them remained conservative enough (by standards of some modern radical thinkers) to believe that there was a prospect for the good life in some kind of social context – if the social fabric could be made anew. In this they were the heirs of Blake, Shelley, and Byron. The latter especially is not famous for his explicit views on what good the society can do for the individual, but he states implicitly that the best forms of life are impossible without a sophisticated social structure. Victorian satire is a mixture of the individualism that was naturally suspicious of social contracts and the progressivism that placed faith in the power of social discipline to achieve worthy humanitarian ends. Like most of the men of letters, the Victorian poets shared, at some time or other, in the general air of confidence. There was hope in the air, a notion that the present was going to bring better things, and that future centuries would be able to recognize the improved development of man as a species. But some of that confidence looked like arrogance and presumption, and there was a facile belief in the effectiveness of technology to make radical improvements in the human lot that was only shattered in our century by critics of H. G. Wells.

Poets are congenitally suspicious of mechanical philosophies, living as closely as they do to organic concepts of life. The Victorian poets speak with dissident voices against excessive faith in tight social organization. *Locksley Hall* (1842) strikes an early note:

> Cursed be the social wants that sin against the
> strength of youth!
> Cursed be the social lies that warp us from the
> living truth!
> Cursed be the sickly forms that err from honest
> Nature's rule!
> Cursed be the gold that gilds the straitened
> forehead of the fool!
>
> (ll. 59–62)

One cannot imagine an early-eighteenth-century poet writing that – he would have conceived of society as an instrument to redeem man from the ill effects of the Fall and original sin.

The anti-progress tone gets shriller in *Locksley Hall Sixty Years After* (1886):

> 'Forward' rang the voices then, and of the many
> mine was one.
> Let us hush this cry of 'Forward' till ten
> thousand years have gone.
>
> (ll. 77–78)

And the speaker reminds himself that to talk of progress is often to
do no more than talk:

> Is it well that while we range with Science,
>   glorying in the Time,
> City children soak and blacken soul and sense in
>   city slime?
> There among the glooming alleys Progress halts on
>   palsied feet,
> Crime and hunger cast our maidens by the thousand
>   on the street.
> There the Master scrimps his haggard sempstress of
>   her daily bread,
> There a single sordid attic holds the living and
>   the dead.
>   (ll. 217–22)

Here was something more radical than eighteenth-century satire –
though admittedly oblique in its narrative frame. The poem poses the
notion that there is something basically wrong with the way capitalist
society is constructed, not just the way it is managed. William Morris
held such attitudes with even more vigour. *The Pilgrims of Hope*
(1885–86) is his only long poem to deal with contemporary life, and
it portrays modern London as a living hell, run by bourgeois capitalists
for their own profit. Clough likewise shows us the cost of things in
human terms, and discomforting ones they are too. In *The Bothie*
Philip writes to Adam about the beauty of Lady Maria, and says, in
a tone of heavy irony:

> Perish the poor and the weary! what can they
>   better than perish,
> Perish in labour for her, who is worth the
>   destruction of empires?
>   (v. 52–53)

And he imagines a miner:

> While thou art eating black bread in the poisonous
>   air of thy cavern,
> Far away glitter[s] the gem on the peerless neck
>   of a Princess.
> Dig, and starve, and be thankful.
>   (v. 66–68)

The same question is posed in *Maud*, whose faultlessly beautiful heroine lives at the expense of labour. In *Maud* the social conditions are so bad that something resembling civil war is being waged:

> Is it peace or war? Civil war, as I think, and
>   that of a kind
> The viler, as underhand, not openly bearing the
>   sword.
>
>   (I. i. 27–28)

Morris finds the situation unchanged thirty years later in *The Pilgrims of Hope*:

> Peace at home – what peace, while the rich man's
>   mill is strife,
> And the poor is the grist that he grindeth, and
>   life devoureth life?
>
>   (ll. 235–36)

But there is a difference: the hero of *Maud* is unhinged, and his shrill rhetoric could be taken as the indication of a mind diseased; but Morris's hero is in deadly earnest and he is in full possession of his wits.

Poetry dealing with the condition of society can succeed without naming names and being too ephemeral. The Victorians never quite had the knack we recognize in Augustan poets, who were able to introduce specific politics into poetry simply because their powers of imaginative transformation were higher. Also, the political issues of the Victorians are closer to ours, so that our political opinions cannot be suspended in the kinds of ways possible when we read eighteenth-century poetry. This explains why some of Tennyson's cruder and more vociferous poems have not survived very well, such as the anti-Celt 'Hail Briton'. His conservatism is not always appealing, especially when he imagines political liberties slowly broadening down, 'from precedent to precedent'. Some of the poems urged on by personal invective are less than attractive parts of the *oeuvre*.

The social satire is more effective, but a less coherent view was possible for the Victorian poet than for his predecessors. The 'use of riches' continued to be a theme, but faced with the widespread despoliation of the countryside the possibility that 'laughing Ceres' would 'reassume the land' was becoming increasingly remote, and a good deal of the response was closer to melancholy than satiric anger. Although there was an available rhetoric attributing prophetic powers to the poet, there was in fact a lack of faith in the kind of prophetic poet's

voice that Marvell had described in 'Tom May's Death', and lines in
the trial edition of *Maud* express it:

> What use for a single mouth to rage
> At the rotten creak of the old machine;
> Though it makes friends weep and enemies smile,
> That here in the face of a watchful age,
> The sons of a gray-beard-ridden isle
> Should dance in a round of an old routine,
> And a few great families lead the reels,
> While pauper manhood lies in the dirt,
> And Favour and Wealth with gilded heels
> Trample service and tried desert.[10]

It was increasingly difficult to find standpoints; certainly religion did
not offer one, since it was so hedged about with questioning, and likely
to find itself the object of satire rather than a secure resting-place. One
thinks of Tennyson's 'St. Simeon Stylites', described by Leigh Hunt
as 'a powerfully graphic, and in some respects appalling satire on the
pseudo-aspirations of egotistical asceticism and supersitition',[11] and
Browning's 'Caliban upon Setebos', though no one has ever quite
agreed what this is about.[12]

There are points where the continuation of the eighteenth-century
satirical impulse is very strong. For instance, the tradition of the pen-
portrait is vigorously alive; there are vivid examples in *Maud*. One
finds the dandy:

> That jewelled mass of millinery,
> That oiled and curled Assyrian Bull
> Smelling of musk and of insolence;
>
> (I. 232–4)

A nice syllepsis there. There is the *nouveau* who has bought himself
a commission:

> a padded shape,
> A bought commission, a waxen face,
> A rabbit mouth that is ever agape;
>
> (I. 358–60)

There is the modish clergyman:

> The snowy-banded dilettante,
> Delicate-handed priest;
>
> (I. 310–11)

then the peace-at-any-price man:

> This broad-brimmed hawker of holy things,
> Whose ear is crammed with his cotton, and rings
> Even in dreams to the chink of his pence.
>
> (I. 370–72)

These strong portraits derive their strength from the fact that Tennyson was not fighting with shadows, but with people vividly before him, and closely related to his obsessions. Feeling is important in satire as a motive force, as Johnson realized in his life of Pope,[13] and Rader has confirmed what many had suspected, that *Maud* was fuelled by private anger and strong feeling (see above p. 145). In the trial edition there was even more anger, as in these lines about the *nouveau*:

> Captain! he to hold a command
> He can hold a cue, he can pocket a ball;
> And sure not a bantam cockerel lives
> With a weaker crow upon English land,
> Whether he boast of a horse that gains,
> Or cackle his own applause, when he gives
> A filthy story at second-hand,
> Where the point is missed, and the filth
> remains.[14]

Tennyson probably dropped these lines because he felt that private vindictiveness was beginning to run away with him; almost certainly he incorporated into this portrait some features of the rich and vacuous grandson of the Bobby Shafto of the nursery rhyme, the husband of Rosa Baring. Rosa left her mark on a host of poems, and one of the bitterest, 'How thought you that this thing could captivate', was never published in his lifetime. Related to the anger and disappointment which flourished in the relationship as vigorously as the love were feelings about class, status, privilege, and authority in society, and these left their mark on poems such as 'Aylmer's Field', which has a strong vein of anti-aristocratic satire, since it expresses all the frustration felt by ambitious young men with talent but not much status who find themselves 'thwarted by one of these old father-fools'. The state of mind infects the poem, and throws light on other aspects of life, not immediately related to the love-relationship, such as the law, which the hero Leolin pursues in order to make his fortune and win Edith: it is a 'codeless myriad of precedent' and a 'wilderness of single instances' which can only be mastered by a kind of 'lawless science'.

It is interesting to note that one of the other poems that has been compared here to Tennyson's satirical work, Morris's *The Pilgrims of Hope*, is also fuelled by strong personal feeling; it does not run merely on political passion. The hero slips reluctantly into a *ménage-à-trois* with his wife and the political activist Arthur (modelled on Ruskin and Rossetti), and the trio goes to Paris to fight for the Commune, where the public betrayal mirrors the private betrayal. Morris cannot exclude from this political poem, which was, after all, published in *Commonweal* (the organ of the Socialist League), his intense private anguish over the relationship between Rossetti and Jane. Neither can he exclude the strong vein of anger that runs through his political thinking. Members of the upper classes form a gallery of grotesques, from 'the squire's thick-lipped son', to the 'sleek-faced' society women, to 'the white-haired fool on the bench' and the 'well-dressed reptile' who breaks up a socialist meeting. As with Tennyson, strong feeling, much of it not at all altruistic and disinterested, drives the satire along.

The only Victorian poem that comes at all close to *Maud* for sheer power in expressing a negative and almost deranged view of life is Swinburne's *Triumph of Time*, which also taps the negative resources of anger and despair as well as the positive ones of love and enthusiasm. The poem grew, most likely, from an unsatisfactory encounter (so brief that it could not really be called an affair) with a Miss Faulkner in the summer of 1862. Most of the poem is wild, wilful self-pity of a lyrical intensity, but we should remember that Swinburne was not only a beautiful songster; he was also a satirical writer and an incisive thinker. This sudden flash of anger in a love poem reminds us of the abrupt transitions in *Maud*:

> 'What should such fellows as I do?' Nay,
> My part were worse if I chose to play;
> For the worst is this after all; if they knew me,
> Not a soul upon earth would pity me.
> And I play not for pity of these; but you,
> If you saw with your soul what man am I,
> You would praise me at least that my soul all
>   thro'
> Clove to you, loathing the lives that lie;
> The souls and lips that are bought and sold,
> The smiles of silver and kisses of gold,
> The lapdog loves that whine as they chew,
> The little lovers that curse and cry.
>   (ll. 237–48)

As with Shakespeare, to bring a whining dog on to the scene when one is piqued is for Swinburne almost a Pavlovian reaction. *Maud* is under the aegis of *Hamlet* and so is this poem, since the first line of the quotation is an allusion to the play.

Satire of individuals, either real or imaginary, is a curious business, since it often highlights elements that cannot be reformed. Some of the grotesques we encounter in satire remind us that there is, in art at least, a correlation between physical and mental states so complete that reform is out of the question. If Chaucer's Pardoner, for instance, were to reform he would still be left with a body indicative of past moral degeneracy, and it is probably the case that his bodily state inhibits reform. To look at a person satirically may mean depriving him of some of the features which constitute varied and flexible humanity, in order to convert him into a limited allegorical machine conveying a certain point of view. One sees this happening in an early poem of Tennyson's, describing a Cambridge acquaintance, Thomas Sunderland. Here are the last two stanzas:

> Most delicately hour by hour
> He canvassed human mysteries,
> And trod on silk, as if the winds
> Blew his own praises in his eyes,
> And stood aloof from other minds
> In impotence of fancied power.
>
> With lips depressed as he were meek,
> Himself unto himself he sold:
> Upon himself himself did feed:
> Quiet, dispassionate, and cold,
> And other than his form of creed,
> With chiselled features clear and sleek.
>
> ('A Character' ll. 19–30)

Tennyson did not write much more of this kind of thing, perhaps, as Ricks suggests,[15] because Sunderland subsequently went mad. There are, however, two important dialect poems that are, in a gentle sense, satirical: the Northern Farmer poems (see above pp. 56–7). Though critical, these are portraits *con amore* in a Chaucerian tradition, and in neither does Tennyson have any serious intention of reforming. He is content to delineate.

I have been suggesting that in many respects, Victorian satire does not continue the eighteenth-century traditions, but there is one important field in which there certainly is continuity: artistic controversy. It is vast in area, comprising on the one hand high-flown aesthetic debate, and on the other puny, vicious, personal literary squabbles.

There were a number of important literary squabbles during the century. As in previous eras there were important moral and aesthetic issues at stake, but most of the real energy and interest was concerned with aggression between personalities. It is interesting that Clough, who is generally thought of as the major Victorian verse satirist, did not get himself involved in such quarrels, but Tennyson, whom one regards as the aloof bardic figure, did. One of the most famous literary quarrels of the century was between Tennyson and Bulwer Lytton. Lytton's poem *The New Timon* attacked Tennyson when he was awarded a pension in 1845; Tennyson replied with 'The New Timon, and the Poets', published anonymously (signed 'Alcibiades') in *Punch* for 28 February 1846. Shakespeare's Timon died with a noble hatred:

> So died the Old: here comes the New.
>   Regard him; a familiar face:
> I *thought* we knew him: What, it's you,
>   The padded man – that wears the stays –
>
> (ll. 5–8)

The ninth and tenth stanzas come close to the imagery of Pope's Sporus portrait in the 'Epistle to Arbuthnot':

> What profits now to understand
>   The merits of a spotless shirt –
> A dapper boot – a little hand –
>   If half the little soul is dirt?
>
> *You* talk of tinsel! why we see
>   The old mark of rouge upon your cheeks.
> *You* prate of Nature! you are he
>   That spilt his life about the cliques.
>
> (ll. 33–40)

However, Tennyson did not warm to literary quarrels in the way that Pope did, and on 7 March 1846 he published a retraction in *Punch* called 'Afterthought'. This is a good example of the almost instinctive distrust of satire felt by the major Victorian poets. When Tennyson saw that personal bile had entered into the quarrel he drew back, deciding that antagonism was an unworthy element in the bardic career. Pope had more self-protective devices at hand to hide from himself the fact that there were personal reasons for his hatred; one of them was the ability to cast himself in the role of the dispassionate protector of the public good. But given the status and reputation of poetry in Pope's time it was more possible to make a correlation between literary crimes and social ones. Because so much Victorian poetry was administering to private needs and individual perceptions outside the scope of social utility it was harder to make connections of that kind explicit. Tennyson and Browning followed the lead of Pope in their quarrel with Alfred Austin: they looked with Olympian disdain on the pinpricks of a Grub Street insect – who, as it happened, was only about five feet high. Austin wrote a carping series of criticisms collected together in *The Poetry of the Period* (1870). Tennyson responded in a poem not printed until 1931:

> Somebody being a nobody,
> Thinking to look like a somebody,
> Said that he thought me a nobody:
> Good little somebody-nobody,
> Had you not known me a somebody,
> Would you have called me a nobody?
>
> (ll. 1–6)

Swinburne was incensed by Austin, and attacked him in *Under the Microscope* (1872) and a vicious poem (in manuscript in the Ashley Library) concluding:

> Let that Muse her breath exhaust in
> Sickly, broken winded Austin . .[16]

Improbable rhymes with Austin were also a feature of Browning's attacks, which were so involved that it is necessary to attribute a degree of obsession to Browning. N. B. Crowell has suggested, plausibly, that it is not merely the last 500 lines of *Pacchiarotto* that are are about Austin, but the whole work.[17] Browning called Austin 'Quilp-Hop-o'-my thumb' and 'banjo Byron'. Austin became Poet Laureate in his respectable middle age, and he repented at leisure some of the hasty indiscretions of his youth.

A quarrel that occasioned even more personal spite and passion was the so-called 'Fleshly School of Poetry' controversy. Robert Buchanan attacked Pre-Raphaelite poetry, especially as exemplified by Rossetti and Swinburne (see above p. 132). The victims replied, Rossetti writing an article and a cutting limerick:

> As a critic, the Poet Buchanan
> Thinks Pseudo much safer than Anon;
>   Into Maitland he shrunk,
>   But the smell of the skunk
> Guides the shuddering nose to Buchanan.

He was among the other low forms of life put under Swinburne's powerful lens in *Under the Microscope*.

Satirists on the offensive in the Victorian age – such as Austin and Buchanan – found their task more difficult than in the Augustan age, when it was easy to identify bad poetry by excessive enthusiasm, intolerant thought, exaggerated particularity, indulged passion, and rough numbers, since in *their* age a place had been found for all these abuses in the most approved poetry.

One area in which it was possible for the Victorian satirists to feel a unanimity with the public was French realism, which remained a minority taste. So Tennyson's hero in *Locksley Hall Sixty Years After* speaks with plenty of endorsement behind him, even if his tone is a little shrill:

> Authors – essayist, atheist, novelist, realist,
> rhymster, play your part,
> Paint the mortal shame of nature with the living
> hues of Art.
> Rip your brothers' vices open, strip your own foul
> passions bare;
> Down with Reticence, down with Reverence – forward
> – naked – let them stare.
> Feed the budding rose of boyhood with the drainage
> of your sewer;
> Send the drain into the fountain, lest the stream
> should issue pure.
> Set the maiden fancies wallowing in the troughs of
> Zolaism, –
> Do your best to charm the worst, to lower the
> rising race of men;
> Have we risen from out the beast, then back into
> the beast again?
> (ll. 139–48)

Here at least Tennyson was at one with Alfred Austin, who was anti-realist, and thought that poetry should be a 'Transfiguration of the Actual or Real into the Ideal at a lofty elevation'.[18]

A traditional theme of ancient satire was 'the use of riches', since the possession of wealth offered choices and responsibilities which very readily highlighted the nature of individuals and societies. Victorian England was collectively rich, and filled with rich individuals. On the whole, as we have already seen in the discussion of *Maud*, the way in which the riches were accumulated and used did not invite admiration. In some total and over-arching way the whole society stands condemned, but the poets did not quite have the energy or the means to make the telling indictment: that was left, in the main, to the prophetic prose writers like Carlyle, Ruskin, and Morris. Every so often, though, one finds poets angry and appalled at the end results of the mad pursuit of wealth; Tennyson and Morris have been mentioned earlier. A representative example of a minor poet is this extract from Arthur J. Munby's *Vestigia Retrorsum* (1891): 'The Vales of Medway' (in hexameters). It opens with the Edenic vision of Spring, and one might think at first that nothing had changed in England since Milton's 'L'Allegro.' But the patrimony is in the process of being squandered and recklessly ruined:

> Yes – what an Eden is here, if men were able to know it,
> Able to see with their eyes, willing and able to feel!
> But they are not: not a man, nor a child, nor even a
>   woman
> Cares that the land of their birth should be pure as of old.
> What? If they loved greensward, sweet air, and life-giving
>   waters,
> Would they stand mute, as they do, seeing all these
>   disappear?
> Seeing their mountain-lakes fast stolen and spoilt by the
>   stranger,
> Seeing the streams of the vale blackened and poisoned and
>   foul;
> Seeing the air they breathe, the needful breath of their
>   nostrils,
> Changed into filthiest gloom, acrid with sulphur and soot;
> Seeing their hideous towns, their mean and comfortless
>   dwellings,
> Sprawl o'er the innocent fields, ugly and aimless and bare:
> Yes! for Beauty is dead, and the excellent craft of the
>   builder
> Failed, when the builder himself ceased to be honest and
>   true.
>   (ll. 109–122)

The poem ends on a note of anger and despair. The satire here has affinities with elegiac lament, but tempered by hostility rather than wistfulness.

The last topic I turn to is architecture. This was an important theme in eighteenth-century satire, since buildings, by virtue of the cost and effort that goes into them, always make important cultural statements. Here too one encounters explorations of 'the use of riches' theme.

Perhaps more than any other art-form architecture is a barometer of the cultural weather of an era. In both the eighteenth and the nineteenth centuries there were 'battles of the styles' in which the issues went far beyond the stylistic differences between one tradition and another. The eighteenth-century battle was between baroque and Palladian – between the exuberant and the exotic and the restrained and the severe. Hence in his visit to Timon's villa Pope spells out the pretentiousness of structures like Blenheim, Canons, and possibly Sir Robert Walpole's Houghton. Ultimately in this battle neither side had an outright victory: English architecture retained, generally, a Palladian chastity, but the best of it assimilated from the baroque the ability to design in terms of imposing and picturesque masses. There was at last something like a spirit of reconciliation, which continued in the Grecian Revival at the end of the century. In the nineteenth century the battle lines were drawn further apart, not between rival branches of Classicism but between the Classic and the Gothic. As in the eighteenth century the battle of the styles was part of broader moral and political battles, but it would be true to say that it was its most vigorous not in poetry but in prose such as Ruskin's *The Seven Lamps of Architecture* (1849) and 'The Nature of Gothic' (1853). For most of the century the Gothic style was in the ascendancy. Some architects and patrons clung to the style with an almost religious fervour, but we should not forget that the nineteenth century was far more eclectic than the eighteenth, so that for every Pugin there were half a dozen architects building simultaneously in several styles, employed by clients whose political, social, and moral complexions were not necessarily betrayed in the styles they chose. There was an intelligent variety in Victorian taste that closed avenues, both straight and serpentine, previously open to Pope for satirical exploration.

The Gothic Revival was the dominant style (or rather, compendium of styles, since 'Gothic' covered a multitude of virtues and sins), but it occasioned mutterings of discontent. Tennyson helped to promote the cause, and yet he could be critical of the vogue, as in *Maud*, where the *nouveau* has a modern castle in a baronial style:

> New as his title, built last year,
> There amid perky larches and pine,
> And over the sullen-purple moor –
> Look at it – pricking a cockney ear.

> (I. 348–51)

Tennyson was more guilty of fake medievalism than just about any other Victorian poet, yet he is sensitive to its architectural manifestations. The answer lies partly in his life: the hated Tennyson

D'Eyncourts, who inherited the Tennyson fortune instead of Tennyson's father, used their newly acquired riches to rebuild Bayons in a pretentious neo-feudal style.[19] There is a point, but it is sharpened by personal feelings.

Another anti-medieval passage comes in Clough's *Dipsychus*, spoken by the Mephistophelean spirit:

> Come leave your Gothic, worn-out story,
> San Giorgio and the Redemptore;
> I from no building, gay or solemn,
> Can spare the shapely Grecian column.
> 'Tis not, these centuries four, for nought
> Our European world of thought
> Hath made familiar to its home
> The classic mind of Greece and Rome;
> In all new work that would look forth
> To more than antiquarian worth,
> Palladio's pediments and bases,
> Of something such, will find their places:
> Maturer optics don't delight
> In childish dim religious light,
> In evanescent vague effects
> That shirk, not face, one's intellects;
> They love not fancies fast betrayed,
> And artful tricks of light and shade,
> But pure form nakedly displayed,
> And all things absolutely made.
>
> (v. 204–23)

Clough was in Venice and composing this at the same time that Ruskin was writing *The Stones of Venice* and reviling Palladio, although the two visitors do not seem to have met during their stay. It is true that the Spirit provides only half the story, but Clough was sufficiently a respecter of certain eighteenth-century values to believe that they should be given their due. The classical rationalism of the Spirit is often devastatingly critical of the Romantic sentiment of Dipsychus. This classical undercurrent never entirely died out in the nineteenth century: we find it in Clough, Arnold, and Swinburne. A part of the classical inheritance was satirical awareness, which at its best draws on the collective wisdom of the tribe. The satirical voice was present as a tonic and a corrective against the kind of subjective and self-indulgent poetry that Arnold was anxious to avoid. Victorian Poets tended to keep in reserve various correctives which restricted Romantic excesses: one thinks of the taste for classical poetry, the taste for Dryden, the taste for Donne.[20] (the poet excluded from Palgrave's *Golden Treasury*). These never entirely died out; they remained as standards of vigour and precision which poets as diverse as Clough and Hopkins could reach out for.

In extreme forms the traditions of English rationalism could threaten to destroy the very grounds on which poetry is built, but in the form they are offered by Clough in this final quotation they represent an escape route from the morass of neo-Romantic poetry that at times threatened to overwhelm the entire age, and they offer a timeless recipe for effective satirical poetry:

> This austere love of truth; this righteous abhorrence of illusion; this rigorous uncompromising rejection of the vague, the untestified, the merely probable; this stern conscientious determination without paltering and prevarication to admit, *if* things are bad, that they are so; this resolute, upright purpose, as of some transcendental man of business, to go thoroughly into the accounts of the world and make out once for all how they stand: such a spirit as this, I may say, I think claims more than our attention – claims our reverence.[21]

Notes

1. *Victorian Poetry and Poetics*, edited by W. E. Houghton and G. R. Stange, second edition (Boston, 1968), p. xxii.

2. C. Patmore, *North British Review*, 29 (November 1858), 506–18.

3. W. Wordsworth, *The Prelude* (1850), XI, 60–61.

4. Milton uses these names in 'I did but bid the age to quit her clogs'.

5. M. Arnold, Inaugural Lecture as Professor of Poetry (1857), in *The Complete Works of Matthew Arnold*, edited by R. H. Super, 11 vols (Ann Arbor, 1960–77), I, 30.

6. Ibid., I, 30.

7. Ibid., I, 36.

8. Ibid., IX, 202.

9. T. Arnold, *Miscellaneous Works* (1845), p. 253.

10. *The Poems of Tennyson*, edited by C. Ricks (1969), p. 1059.

11. L. Hunt, *Church of England Quarterly Review*, 12 (October 1842), 371.

12. *Caliban* has been described as both an attack on orthodox theology, and an attack on anthropomorphic theology. See M. Timko, *Criticism*, 7 (1965), 141–50.

13. See especially Richardson's story of Pope's face contorted by passion when reading an adverse review; cited in S. Johnson's *Lives of the Poets*, edited by L. H. Hind (1925), II, 198.

14. *Poems of Tennyson*, p. 1058.

15. C. Ricks, *Tennyson: A Biographical and Critical Study* (1972), p. 52.

16. Quoted by N. B. Crowell in *Alfred Austin: Victorian* (Albuquerque, 1953), pp. 123–24

17. Ibid., pp. 111–20.

18. Ibid., p. 132.

19. For details of Bayons in its heyday see *The Tennyson Album: a Biography in Original Photographs*, edited by A. Wheatcroft (1980), and for a study of its decline see M. Girouard, 'Picturesque Gothic in Decay: Bayons Manor, Lincolnshire', *Country Life*, 127 (1960), 430–33.

20. For the taste for Donne see K. Tillotson, 'Donne's Poetry in the Nineteenth Century', in *Elizabethan and Jacobean Studies Presented to Frank Percy Wilson* edited by H. Davis and H. Gardner (Oxford, 1959), pp. 307–26.

21. 'Lecture on the Development of English Literature from Chaucer to Wordsworth', in *Prose Remains of Arthur Hugh Clough*, edited by B. Clough (1888), pp. 347–48.

Chapter 11
Nature and Science

The study of nature in Victorian poetry is inextricably bound up with the study of religion and science, since the revolution that took place in religious and scientific thought inevitably had a direct effect on attitudes to nature. Nature must always loom large in any study of Victorian poetry, since it was one of the three or four most important poetic themes. Reviewing *In Memoriam* Charles Kingsley thought that the idea of the 'dignity of Nature in all her manifestations' was 'the root idea of the whole poetry of this generation'.[1]

During the Romantic Movement nature was regarded as a phenomenon to which one could turn for guidance, spiritual sustenance, and psychic restoration – particularly when the power of orthodox Christianity to supply these things was waning or questionable. In the Middle Ages nature usually occupied an equivocal position, since it was fallen, and, though shadowing spiritual reality in an inscrutable way, actually separated from the transcendental world. But from the Renaissance onwards efforts were needed if not to close the gap between the spiritual and the natural world, at least to narrow it. Natural religion developed apace; from the study of nature deductions could be made not merely about the character of God but about his very existence. Two important texts were Joseph Butler's *Analogy of Religion, Natural and Revealed* (1736) and William Paley's *A View of the Evidences of Christianity* (1794). The love of nature was emphasized by various surviving elements of the eighteenth-century cult of sensibility, and augmented by the Romantic Movement beliefs became so ingrained that it was able to outlast the decline of orthodoxy, and remain almost as an article of faith. Henry James recognized the pre-eminence of the interest in nature as one of the salient features of English culture:

> If the history of that movement toward a passionate
> scrutiny of Nature, which has culminated in England, in
> our day, with Tennyson and Browning, could be scientifi-
> cally written, we imagine it would be found to

throw a great deal of light on the processes of the human
mind. It has at least drawn into its services an incalculable
amount of ingenuity, of imagination, of intellectual force.
There are descriptive phrases and touches in Tennyson and
Browning which represent, on this subject, an extra-
ordinary accumulation of sentiment, a perfect entangle-
ment of emotion, which give the key, as it were,
to a civilization.[2]

Seen in certain lights nature was an ordered, purposive, benign, and
unified force, indicative of some kind of good and intelligent deity –
though not necessarily one that dogmatic Christianity would recognize. Nature offered prospects of sublime terror to Wordsworth on
occasions, but for the most part its influence on him was wholesome
and salutary, and symptomatic of spiritual unity in the universe.
Shelley and Coleridge nurtured similar beliefs, yet faced with the
sublimity of Mont Blanc Shelley recognized a power far removed from
man's consciousness:

> Power dwells apart in its tranquillity,
> Remote, serene, and inaccessible.
>
> (ll. 134–35)

But, as I have frequently pointed out so far in this study, the
Victorians were not able to maintain the confidence and optimism
possible for the Romantics. And the destructive force was science and
its sceptical and inquiring turn of mind. On the one hand, as we shall
see, science nurtured a love of nature in some ways as intense as
anything that one can recognize in previous centuries, but on the other
hand, by stressing the mechanical and chemical aspects of natural
processes, it took away the magic and left no room for spiritual direction. The fear expressed in Keats's *Lamia* proved justified: philosophy
did indeed 'unweave the rainbow'. J. W. Beach is right when he asserts
that animism has not survived among cultivated people.[3]

Eventually poets such as Tennyson, Browning, and Arnold lost an
all-embracing enthusiasm for nature, especially as an ethical and moral
force. Swinburne and Meredith, in Beach's words, 'managed to divest
the concept of nature of most of its supernatural and transcendental
character'[4]; but at the same time they retained an intense interest in
nature as a force surcharged with poetical possibilities, many of them
amenable to man. Hardy found nature hostile to man, and offering
very little of a systematic kind as guide to human laws and societies.
It should be remembered that it was in the Victorian age that the
famous phrase 'the pathetic fallacy' was coined by Ruskin.[5] In certain

directions Ruskin had as intense a love of nature as any man who has ever lived; he continued to believe (at least in print) that it offered certain grim and inexorable laws and lessons, but he saw the poetic bond between psychological states and natural conditions, for so long the stock-in-trade of poetry, as one, regretfully, to be broken in the modern sceptical age: 'So far as it *is* a fallacy, it is always the sign of a morbid state of mind, and comparatively of a weak one. Even in the most inspired prophet it is a sign of the incapacity of his human sight or thought to bear what has been revealed to it.'[6]

The critical forces just described would seem to be sufficiently strong to relegate interest in nature to a very minor place in the Victorian scheme of things. However, this was not the case. The scientific advances actually encouraged enthusiasm for natural observation, and new scientific knowledge was widely disseminated by literature and lectures. The microscopic and telescopic survey of the universe revealed an alarming and disconcerting place to man (particularly since anthropocentricity no longer seemed tenable to most observers), but it also revealed a rich and varied series of prospects. The ages of piety had been impressed by how the variety of the world praised God, but it was in the sceptical Victorian age that the burgeoning multiplicity of nature was startlingly revealed. The Victorian patrons of art loved finish and detail in their paintings, and it was with excitement and appreciation that they discovered that nature could more than satisfy that taste. George Eliot, wandering along lanes near Ilfracombe in Devon, found intricacy that could outlive William Henry Hunt's work, 'a delicious crowding of mosses and delicate trefoil, and wild strawberries, and ferns great and small'. Faced with this riotous and proliferating abundance she wanted to know the names of everything and recognized this desire 'as part of the tendency that is now constantly growing in me to escape from all vagueness and inaccuracy into the daylight of distinct, vivid ideas'.[7] The quest for factual accuracy is mainly associated with the Victorian novelists, but the poets engaged in it too. Even before questions of meaning and relevance arose the Victorians found this taste a perpetual delight, and two critical studies have explored the development of it: Patricia Ball's *The Science of Aspects* (1971) and Carol Christ's *The Finer Optic* (1975). Ultimately something had to be done with all the multitudinous detail, but in the meantime the surface appeals and the immediate pleasures were endlessly fascinating. Coleridge seems to inaugurate the taste for minute observation of particulars, although he was perhaps guided by Wordsworth's highly perceptive sister Dorothy. The minute study on the one hand encouraged objective knowledge to types and species, but on the other hand it intensified the impression of the fleeting and the evanescent in the world. The Paterian statement that 'our physical life is a perpetual motion' of elements, and that 'all melts under our feet'[8] is anticipated over and over again in Coleridge's *Notebooks*. As Carlyle said, 'by an unconscious power the poet perceives unity in nature; indeed the poet's powers work analogously with those of nature itself', but increasingly in the Victorian period the opposite was found to be true – that the poet explored diversity and multiplicity.

This sense of diversity was emphasized by detailed, studied, scientific attention to nature. Tennyson is famous as a myopic, yet his eyesight was sharp enough to register 'the reflection of moonlight in the eye of a nightingale in a hedgerow',[9] and if anything his shortsightedness intensified his perception of the minute particulars. In Switzerland on one occasion he was seen on his hands and knees looking at the colour of an Alpine rose through a dragon-fly's wings.[10] When in *Maud* he speaks of the 'million emeralds' which 'break from the ruby-budded lime' (I. iv. 102) he is giving an entirely accurate account of the red flecks on the buds of lime trees. We feel he has looked at the tree with the kind of care which the temporarily lame Coleridge of necessity devoted to his lime-tree bower when he watched 'Some broad and sunny leaf, and loved to see/The shadow of the leaf and stem above/Dappling its sunshine' ('Lime-Tree Bower', ll. 49–51). When in 'The Gardener's Daughter' he describes 'hair/More black than ashbuds in the front of March' (ll. 27–28) he has looked at ash trees as carefully as Coleridge looked at his ash in the 'roaring dell'. In his quest for the Holy Grail Percivale finds time to give to the play of water in a brook the kind of intense attention that we associate with Hopkins's drawings and notes on nature:

> and then a brook
> with one sharp rapid, where the crisping white
> Played ever back upon the sloping wave,
> And took both ear and eye.
>
> (*The Holy Grail*, ll. 380–83)

The Pre-Raphaelite painters followed Ruskin's advice in going to nature in a state of humility and receptivity, 'rejecting nothing, selecting nothing'[11] and produced intense representation of detail that no previous paintings can rival. The lizards in *Ferdinand Lured by Ariel* of Millais, though tiny, are scrupulously done, and stand any amount of magnification. Rossetti was in the Pre-Raphaelite circle, but he was not assiduous enough as a painter to pursue such detail (and in any case he had misgivings about its aesthetic validity), but as a poet he often shows highly developed awareness of natural forms. His lines about the principles of growth of sycamore buds send the reader to check up on the facts of the natural world, and discover that his perception is sharpened and tutored by Rossetti:

> The thronged boughs of the shadowy sycamore
>> Still fledge young leaflets half the summer
>>> through;
> From when the robin 'gainst the unhidden blue
> Perched dark, till now, deep in the leafy core.
>> The embowered throstles' urgent clangours gore
>> The Summer silence. Still the leaves come new
>> Yet never rose-sheathed as those which drew
> Their spiral tongues from spring-buds heretofore.
>
> ('The Day Dream', ll. 1–8)

And if he never knew it before Rossetti's 'The Woodspurge' (1870) would inform the reader that 'the woodspurge flowered, three cups in one'. In this powerful short poem the grieving mind concentrates on a narrow circuit of nature, and the 'ten weeds' do not offer consolation, insights into the workings of the universe, or even salutary distraction: they are merely present as bald facts of the universe which impinge with stark pristineness on the receptive consciousness:

> From perfect grief there need not be
>> Wisdom or even memory:
> One thing then learnt remains to me, –
> The woodspurge has a cup of three.
>
> (ll. 13–16)

In 'True Woman' Rossetti's botanical accuracy is employed to provide an emblematical reading of the snowdrop's 'heart-shaped seal of green'.[12]

The poet most open to the world's multitudinousness was Browning; indeed, he exhibits 'negative capability' even more completely than the original coiner of the phrase, Keats. Arnold though that poets 'must begin with an Idea of the world in order not to be prevailed over by the world's multitudinousness',[13] but Browning seems to have been unconcerned to have such simple unifying ideas, and did not want to relinquish the delights of multiplicity. 'The Englishman in Italy' is a sensuous, rich, and to some degree pointless revel in the pleasure of the seashore:

> – Our fisher arrive
> And pitch down his basket before us,
>> All trembling alive

With pink and grey jellies, your sea-fruit;
    You touch the strange lumps,
And mouths gape there, eyes open, all manner
    Of horns and of humps
Which only the fisher looks grave at,
    While round him like imps
Cling screaming the children as naked
    And brown as his shrimps;
                (ll. 54–64)

In 'Sibrandus Schafnaburgensis' Browning describes the effects a disgusting sub-life has on a book he dropped into a hole in a tree. There are obviously other ways in which nature can be aggressive than with Tennysonian teeth and claws:

Here you have it, dry in the sun,
    With all the binding all of a blister,
And great blue spots where the ink has run,
    And reddish streaks that wink and glister
O'er the page so beautifully yellow:
    Oh, well have the droppings played their
                tricks!
Did he guess how the toadstools grow, this
                fellow?
Here's one stuck in his chapter six!
                (ll. 41–48)

In 'By the Fire-Side' not only is the love relationship remembered but the details by the pathway:

By boulder-stones where lichens mock
    The marks on a moth, and small ferns fit
Their teeth to the polished block.
                (ll. 48–50)

This anticipated Seamus Heaney's ivy with 'its milk-tooth frills' in 'In the Beech' (1984) by about one hundred and thirty years. In 'Two in the Campagna' the psychological state is recorded, and the wide 'champaign with its endless fleece/Of feathery grasses everywhere', but the speaker also notices 'Five beetles, – blind and green as they grope/Among the honey-meal (ll. 17–18). And Browning's characters exhibit this sharp perception. The 'Person of Quality' in 'Up at a Villa – Down in the City' lives a life of sensations rather than thoughts:

> The wild tulip, at end of its tube, blows out
>   its great red bell
> Like a thin clear bubble of blood, for the
>   children to pick and sell.
>
>   (ll. 24–25)

One expects that Caliban, living close to the ground, will be able to notice such detailed things:

>   and the pie with the long tongue
> That pricks deep into oakwarts for a worm,
> And says a plain word when she finds her
>   prize,
> But will not eat the ants; the ants themselves
> That build a wall of seeds and settled stalks
> About their hole.
>
>   (ll. 50–55)

There are hundreds and hundreds of examples of this vigorous and lively perception in Browning; very often it threatens to crowd out the ostensible subjects of the poems. The kind of attention to the facts of the visible universe we have been considering produced an interesting result: the relentless and disinterested vision had a tendency to eliminate the distinctions between beauty and ugliness. One was left with bare fact, absolute and significant and demanding attention no matter what one's feelings might be. A new kind of terrible beauty is born; one sees it in *Childe Roland*:

> As for the grass, it grew as scant as hair
>   In leprosy; thin dry blades pricked the mud
>   Which underneath looked kneaded up with blood.
> One stiff blind horse, his every bone a-stare,
> Stood stupefied, however he came there:
>   Thrust our past service from the devil's stud!
>
>   (ll. 73–78)

The grotesque fascinated the Victorians (it is a dominating theme in Dickens, Ruskin, and Hardy), and they registered it not merely as an artificial phenomenon but as a natural one, as Browning does in some of the passages just quoted. Hardy was aware, in a famous journal entry of January 1887, 'that Nature is played out as a Beauty',[14] but it continued to maintain its fascination as a mysterious, significant, and grotesque entity; like other later Victorians he was more interested in strangeness than conventional beauty. So long as spectators of nature

were constrained to find indications of their conventional and limited
God in natural forms the spectrum of their vision was limited; but once
free from such inhibitions they were able to register it in a more
enquiring fashion and recognize its disturbing elements.

In the case of Hopkins, however, far from acting as a constraint,
his religious views supported and were supported by a particularly
intense view of nature in which distinctions between beauty and ugliness scarcely existed. God was present in all created things; all created
things spoke distinctly of God. This view was not necessarily one
which Roman Catholics held; Browning's Blougram, for instance,
takes a quite opposite view:

> Some think, Creation's meant to show him forth:
> I say it's meant to hide him all it can,
> And that's what all the blessed evil's for.
>
> (ll.652–54)

Hopkins's senses were ever alert, and just as Coleridge had found
something arresting in urine in a chamber-pot[15] so Hopkins found frost
shapes in urinals fascinating.[16] Like Browning has was excited by the
richness of the world. As C. Devlin puts it: 'all the multitudinous
degrees of perfection in created things combine like some mathematical
formula to express the intrinsic degree of Christ's created perfection'.[17]

Hopkins revived interest in the slightly unfashionable Catholic
theologian Duns Scotus, who preached a philosophy of individuality:
that the universe is filled with special and individual objects whose
identity celebrates God. Hopkins felt the need to find a theology that
would support his long-indulged taste for close and loving observation;
it was not that a system of belief compelled particular habits of vision.
Like Coleridge, Hopkins kept extensive journals recording natural
phenomenon in great detail. It would be no exaggeration to say that
not even the most assiduous scientists of previous centuries had looked
at certain aspects of nature with the care of Hopkins, and indeed on
many occasions he out-Ruskins Ruskin. And in addition he forged a
new prose language to keep track of his visual experiences. The visual
awareness shows up in his poetry. Conventional beauty is there
(although seen in an unconventional manner):

> sweetest, freshest, shadowiest;
> Fairyland; silk-beech, scrolled ash, packed sycamore,
> wild wychelm, hornbeam fretty overstood
> By. Rafts and rafts of flake-leaves light, dealt so,
> painted on the air,

> Hang as still as hawk or hawkmoth, as the stars
> or as the angels there,
> Like the things that never knew the earth, never off
> roots
> Rose.
> ('Epithalamion', ll. 23–28)

Frightening and majestic nature is there:

> And the sea flint-flake, black-backed in the regular
> blow,
> Sitting Eastnortheast, in cursed quarter, the wind;
> Wiry and white-fiery and whirlwind-swivelled
> snow
> Spins to the widow-making unchilding unfathering deeps.
> (*The Wreck of the Deutschland*, ll. 101–04)

It is seen in such a way that Hopkins renders its precise kinetic movement. And elemental, base nature is represented:

> in pool and rut peel parches
> Squandering ooze to squeezed dough, crust,
> dust; stanches, starches
> Squadroned masks and manmarks treadmire toil
> there
> Footfretted in it.
> ('That Nature is a Heraclitean Fire', ll. 6–9)

Such destructive and depressing images are only bearable to Hopkins
because there is the eternal possibility of resurrection. For Hopkins the
fascinating and miraculous paradox was that a teeming and variegated
nature was fathered forth by a God 'whose beauty is past change'.

The scientific approach to nature meant that it could be appreciated
without a restless search for meaning; a sort of scientific aestheticism
was possible. One might call it 'science for science's sake', and it
should not be forgotten that even Hopkins wrote articles for *Nature*.[18]
He did not espouse interest in natural appearances for their own sake;
he was more concerned to see in them indications of the nature of God.
Yet even this approach did not allay residual guilt felt in the enjoyment
of studying the visible world, and on a number of occasions he
renounced the pleasures of perception as a form of penance.[19] John
Clare has been heralded as a naturalist in his own right.[20] Many poets
were content to be fascinated with the independent appearances of
nature, and there is a certain amount of purely descriptive poetry. The

Victorian poets are usually at their most interesting, however, when their record of natural phenomena is related to the thematic and psychologically expressive parts of their works, in a manner that could be described as incidental, symbolic, or illustrative. It is inevitable that nature should figure so largely in this way, since so much of our experience and thinking takes its sustenance from our surroundings, as Wordsworth eloquently puts it in the Prospectus to *The Excursion*:

> . . . my voice proclaims
> How exquisitely the individual Mind
> . . . to the external World
> Is fitted: – and how exquisitely, too –
> Theme this but little heard of among men –
> The external World is fitted to the Mind.
>
> (ll. 62–68)

Coleridge too attests to the importance of the interrelation of inner and outer worlds; in 'Frost at Midnight' he speaks of

> a companionable form,
> Whose puny flaps and freaks the idling Spirit
> By its own moods interprets, everywhere
> Echo or mirror seeking of itself.
>
> (ll. 19–22).

It was because feelings and thoughts so easily found correlatives in the natural world that the pathetic fallacy developed, since it was tempting to assume that there was a reciprocal relationship between man and nature. In *In Memoriam* natural phenomena are often used illustratively, yet we seem to be just a step away from the animate:

> Calm is the morn without a sound,
> Calm as to suit a calmer grief,
> And only through the faded leaf
> The chestnut pattering to the ground:
>
> Calm and deep peace on this high wold,
> And on these dews that drench the furze,
> And all the silvery gossamers
> That twinkle into green and gold.
>
> (XI. 1–8).

And even when Tennyson is being sceptical he seems to be drawing close to a situation where there are actual rather than assumed connections between man's inner and outer weather:

And but for fear it is not so,
The wild unrest that lives in woe
Would dote and pore on yonder cloud

That rises upward always higher,
And onward drags a labouring breast,
And topples round the dreary west,
A looming bastion fringed with fire.

(xv. 14–20).

In 'Tennyson and Musset', Swinburne noted how vivid Tennyson's perception was – he was particularly struck by the description of a wave 'green-glimmering toward the summit' with 'all/Its stormy crests that smoke against the skies' (*Launcelot and Elaine*, ll. 481–82). What Swinburne called 'the subtle and sure fidelity of that happy and studious hand' has meant that readers have often tended to think of Tennyson as a descriptive poet, but more often than not his images are functional.[21]

Poetry in general heightens ordinary experiences, or finds an appropriate language for intense experiences. So that intense and vivid perception, which to a large extent was nurtured by the scientific movements, was naturally at home in poetry, Victorian poetry was more concerned than previous poetry had been with powerful feelings that bring the participants to the edge of hallucination, madness, and visions of pyschedelic intensity. Tennyson derives much of his inspiration from dream-like states, and there was a good deal in his psychological make-up that for normal purposes would have to be regarded as disordered, neurotic, and even paranoiac. But poetically he was able to use these traits to advantage. Many of Tennyson's characters share the disposition of their creator. Mentally disordered states can, on the one hand, present extremely disordered views of the outside world, but on the other hand they can present intensely accurate and heightened impressions. This is particularly evident in the case of Broadmoor's most illustrious painter Richard Dadd (1817–87). Of course accuracy of this kind is often abnormal, since normal vision is a pragmatic compromise for the sake of convenience. Pre-Raphaelite paintings, for instance, often seem to have surreal intensity, resulting not from disordered mental states (Hunt and Millais seem to have been relatively sane men) but from the abnormal and prolonged degree of attention necessary to record the objects. Intense, sustained attention will tend to produce something like hallucination. For the average person intensity of that order only occurs under the impulse of powerful associated feelings or hallucinogenic drugs. The hero of *Maud* was perhaps normal once, but psychological stress has forced attention on to the microscopic; and the microscopic, like the macroscopic, diverges from the kind of vision that has been traditionally regarded as normal:

> See what a lovely shell,
> Small and pure as a pearl,
> Lying close to my foot,
> Frail, but a work divine,
> Made so fairly well
> With delicate spire and whorl,
> How exquisitely minute,
> A miracle of design!
>   (II. 49–56)

Of course the opening lines of *Maud* show a more conventional state of paranoia, in which colour is at once heightened and given a fresh association:

> I hate the dreadful hollow behind the
>   little wood,
> Its lips in the field above are dabbled
>   with blood-red heath.
>   (I. i. 1–2)

Often in Tennyson and other poets the minute details are not specifically registered by the characters, but their presence in the environments *could*, one feels, be taken note of, and gives the reader some sense of what it is like to live in a highly charged state of mind. Something of this kind is true of Pre-Raphaelite paintings, as Ruskin noted apropos of Hunt's *The Awakening Conscience*: 'Nothing is more notable than the way in which even the most trivial objects force themselves upon the attention of a mind which has been fevered by violent and distressful excitement. They thrust themselves forward with a ghastly and unendurable distinctness, as if they would compel the sufferer to count, of measure, or learn them by heart.'[22] In Tennyson's 'Mariana' we are not told that the setting impinges on the sufferer as she utters her repetitive refrains, but doubtless the details have struck Mariana at some time or other, and underline the emotional state she is in:

> With blackest moss the flower-plots
>   Were thickly crusted, one and all:
> The rusted nails fell from the knots
>   That held the pear to the gable-wall.

> The broken sheds looked sad and strange:
>> Unlifted was the clinking latch;
>> Weeded and worn the ancient thatch
> Upon the lonely moated grange.
>
> (ll. 1–8)

'"Looked" to whom' one might be tempted to ask; to anyone registering the scene with a consciousness like Mariana's? Millais captures something of the intensity in his painting based on the poem, and in both painting and poem we seem to be caught in an over-determined world, to be close, in fact, to something like the pathetic fallacy; but as Ruskin observed, rendering of this kind 'is based on a truer principle of the pathetic than any of the common artistical expedients of the schools'.[23] In Browning's 'Two in the Campagna' the lover notices the thistle-ball floating on the wind because all his senses are alert during the vivid minute, and having noticed it he also gives it a function as an analogue for his passive consciousness.

As Coleridge observed, in 'Frost at Midnight', the spirit seeks everywhere for 'echo or mirror . . . of itself'. In 'By the Fire-Side' the speaker remembers the burgeoning growth of nature on the Alpine walks he took years before, as he was about to enter into a sexual relationship with the woman he eventually married. The natural details have a sexual exuberance, and we feel, as we often feel in the novels of Hardy and Meredith, that the thinnest partition divides man's existence (including his mental existence) from the rest of nature:

> For the drop of the woodland fruit's begun
> These early November hours,
>
> That crimson the creeper's leaf across
>> Like a splash of blood, intense, abrupt,
>> O'er a shield else gold from rim to boss,
> And lay it for show on the fairy-cupped
>> Elf-needled mat of moss,
>
> By the rose-flesh mushrooms, undivulged
>> Last evening – nay, in to-day's first dew
> Yon sudden coral nipple bulged,
>> Where a freaked fawn-coloured flaky crew
> Of toadstools peep indulged.
>
> (ll. 59–65)

Browning felt less embarrassed depicting tumescence in nature than in man. Interestingly, he was the first English poet to use the word 'tumescent' in poetry.

Since Rossetti was a member of the Pre-Raphaelite Brotherhood one would expect him to provide accurate details of nature. It is true that in comparison with Hunt and Millais he was idle and lacking in rigour, and was the despair of Ruskin,[24] but evidence has already been produced for his ability to perceive carefully when required, and in both his painting and his poetry he rivals most of his contemporaries in the intensity with which emotion and setting are intertwined. He was too sceptical to entertain the kinds of transcendental ideas about the universe one finds in the great Romantics, and as David Riede has demonstrated in a recent study he adopted a stance of retrenchment in the face of his predecessors,[25] but nevertheless he often writes as if he believed in the possibility of a magical, mystically charged order of creation. 'Silent Noon' (Sonnet XIX of *The House of Life*) is a typical poem. The naturalistic details can all be accounted for: the meadow sounds like one in the Upper Thames Valley at Kelmscott Manor, where Rossetti conducted an intense relationship with Janey Morris:

> Deep in the sun-searched growths the dragon-fly
> Hangs like a blue thread loosened from the sky: –
> So this winged hour is dropped to us from above.
>
> (ll. 9–11)

The closely observed relationship of insect to sky is in effect emblematized and indicative of a providential scheme of things. The final image of 'A New Year's Burden' seems to have a natural valency, not merely an invented one:

> The branches cross above our eyes,
>   The skies are in a net:
> And what's the thing beneath the skies
>   We two would most forget?
>   Not birth, my love, no, no, –
>   Not death, my love, no, no, –
>   The love once ours, but ours long hours ago.
>
> (ll. 15–21)

The most extended treatment of love and nature as an inextricable whole in Rossetti is the long poem *The Portrait*; this needs to be savoured in full, since selected quotations cannot do justice to it. Rossetti's poetry provides a kind of response to the *Angst* of a universe from which God is absent, since for his although the settings may not have a firm objective magic, there is no question that they are haunted by something – as if they have absorbed traces of the emotional events that have been transacted there. Most Victorian landscape that has any power at all will have such associationism at heart. Arnold's Oxford landscapes in *The Scholar Gipsy* and *Thyrsis* cast their spell because they suggest that an attenuated pastoral is possible even in the nineteenth century, and because they remind Arnold of his youth.

The earlier part of the chapter mentioned Darwinism and the change it necessitated in man's attitude to nature. The new science has been a constant leitmotif in our discussion; it is never very far from the surface of the poetry. But on many occasions evolutionary theory has actually formed part of the subject-matter of the poetry, and I should like to close by considering it.

From the very first there had been a connection between evolutionary theory and poetry. Charles Darwin's grandfather, Erasmus Darwin, expressed his beliefs, in heroic couplets, that all warm-blooded animals may have descended from a single ancestral filament endowed by the First Causes. The evolutionary theory is developed in his *Zoonomia* (1794–96) and *Phytologia* (1799). Goethe also expressed evolutionary ideas in poetry: *The Metamorphosis of Animal* (1806). In the Romantic Movement, far from science and poetry being at war there were often alliances between them, as when Wordsworth claimed that 'Poetry is the breath and finer spirit of all knowledge; it is the impassioned expression which is in the countenance of all science.'[26] It is difficult for a modern person to read that quotation in its original spirit, since we are so used to thinking of science as a branch of activity utterly divorced from the arts, but semantically that separation seems not to have occurred until some time around 1840, when William Whewell coined the word 'scientist'.

Evolutionary theory often did not seem a threat to orthodox religion because it dealt with processes and not first causes, and did not eliminate the place of spiritual principles in the universe. Sir Charles Lyell's *Principles of Geology* (1830–33) embraced a certain number of evolutionary theories, but did not greatly perturb the religious establishment. Robert Chambers, in *Vestiges of the Natural History of Creation* (1844), believed in cosmic evolution rather than special creation, but he thought that the original impulse had been initiated by God. Tennyson's poetry shows knowledge of evolutionary theory well before Darwin's *Origin of Species* (1859), and he was obviously acquainted with the early scientific writing. His Cambridge tutor was William Whewell (the inventor of the word 'scientist') and he would have encouraged his pupil's interest in Laplace and Buffon. In *The Princess* there are frequent indications of interest in scientific thought, as in the mention, for instance, of 'huge Ammonites and the first bones of Time' (Prologue, l. 15).

It is in *In Memoriam* that we trace Tennyson's scientific attitudes most obviously, but he is reluctant to embrace the full nihilism of science. Extreme scepticism is given to the allegorical figure of Science, with a strong suggestion that this is not the last word:

> 'The stars,' she whispers, 'blindly run;
>   A web is woven across the sky;
>   From out waste places comes a cry
> And murmurs from the dying sun:
>
> And all the phantom, Nature, stands
>   With all the music in her tone
>   A hollow echo of my own, –
> A hollow form with empty hands.'
>
> (III. 5–12)

He recognizes the apparent purposelessness and instability of nature, but imagines that it is part of some divine plan of progress towards ultimate perfection. The survival of the fittest, of 'nature, red in tooth and claw' is a grim prospect, as is the thesis that man is but the fortuitous product of blind natural forces. He imagines evolution converted into a transcendental principle:

> Eternal process moving on,
>   From state to state the spirit walks
>   And these are but the shattered stalks,
> Or ruined chrysalis of one.
>
> (LXXXII. 5–8)

In later sections of *In Memoriam* Tennyson demonstrates that his optimistic philosophy is not at war with scientific theories, but somehow complementary to them. Evolutionary theory often spoke of 'links', and Tennyson sees new and improved souls as representatives of

> a closer link
> Between us and the crowning race
>
> Of those that, eye to eye, shall look
>   On knowledge; under whose command
>   Is Earth and Earth's and in their hand
> Is Nature like an open book.
>
> (CXXXI. 127–33)

A source of consolation for Tennyson was the view he came to, but which science confirmed and continued to confirm during his lifetime, that far from being chaotic Nature was ordered and exhibited a satisfying correlation between macrocosmic and microcosmic forms. He was not anxious to utilize science to promote scepticism and atheism, and when he met Darwin in 1869 he said, 'Your theory of Evolution does not make against Christianity.'[27] The scientist was perhaps unable to say anything other than, 'No, certainly not.' In the same year Tennyson helped to form the Metaphysical Society, and his poem 'The Higher Pantheism' was read at the inaugural meeting – interesting, perhaps, as an item in the history of ideas, but utterly worthless as poetry, and justifiably parodied by Swinburne in a wickedly funny burlesque, 'The Higher Pantheism in a Nutshell'. A very late poem, 'By an Evolutionist' (1888), preaches that knowledge of his kinship with lower life should not encourage man to surrender to sensual instincts, since he also has divided origins.

The relationship between Browning and evolutionary thought is more interesting than Tennyson's, since the central principles of it, concerning change and modification, are more completely connected to Browning's predominant interests as a poet rather than merely as a thinker. He had a fear of 'eternal petrification', of the freezing of matter or spirit into a final and central form. The 'pulsation of passion', the states where 'nought was fixed and firm' intrigued him and held his attention, and they are celebrated throughout his career. He was fascinated by primal chaos, in which everything was potentially everything else and by the power which shaped inchoate matter towards finished form. This power was diffused through the universe, and resemblance to it (an imperfect resemblance some hostile critics of Browning would claim) was found in the minds of poets. Hillis Miller writes of his enthusiasm for 'primal swamp and primeval mud',[28] which seems to be without the Tennysonian disgust, quite the opposite in fact. There is a sort of energetic glee in his *nostalgie de la boue*.

Evolutionary thought is explicitly referred to by Browning in *Paracelsus* (1835), at the climactic point when the sixteenth-century philosopher rises from his death-bed to speak about life's meaning. It is an eloquent 304-line lecture, given when Paracelsus has renounced his scientific ambitions. He sees God's presence in nature, even in the volcano:

> The centre-fire heaves underneath the earth,
> And the earth changes like a human face;
> The molten ore bursts up among the rocks,
> Winds into the stone's heart, outbranches bright
> In hidden mines, spots barren river-beds,
> Crumbles into fine sand where sunbeams bask –
> God joys therein.

(ll. 653–59)

Spring is a different, but equally forceful process, 'like a smile striving with a wrinkled face'. These images are of perennial processes in nature, and should not (*pace* Lionel Stevenson[29]) be interpreted as *primarily* references to extended evolutionary processes, although they are capable of bearing that reading. Since the various life-forms are referred to in the present tense it suggests that they continue to be available as a picture of evolutionary processes, rather as in Tennyson the growth of the child in the womb is a microcosmic image of such development. At the top of the pyramid is 'man – the consummation of this scheme/Of being' (we should not forget that Paracelsus is a Renaissance man):

> whose attributes had here and there
> Been scattered o'er the visible world before,
> Asking to be combined, dim fragments meant
> To be united in some wondrous whole,
> Imperfect qualities throughout creation,
> Suggesting some one creature yet to make,
> Some point where all those scattered rays
> should meet
> Convergent in the faculties of man
> (ll. 685–92)

The final product enables the philosopher to infer the prior stages:

> from the grand result
> A supplementary reflux of light,
> Illustrates all the interior grades, explains
> Each back step in the circle.
> (ll. 713–16)

As in Tennyson future development is possible: 'progress is/The law of life, man is not Man as yet' (ll. 742–43), and 'in completed man begins anew/A tendency to God' (ll. 772–73). Poetry of this kind administered very conveniently to the spheres of optimism and self-confidence in Victorian thought, the 'upward tending' impulse. And the strengthening force in the process in love, 'blind, oft-failing, yet believing'. As with Lucretius the poetic and the scientific views of the universe cannot be separated.

The Victorian poets were more prepared than their Romantic predecessors had been to face up to the violence and indifference of nature, the apparently prodigal waste of it all, and in many poems it is presented as a far from cosy place. Among the most important poems in the period on nature must be counted Meredith's 'The

Woods of Westermain'. It exhibits in a vivid form many of the preoccupations of the time – although the particular combination of features
could only emanate from Meredith. At the entrance of the poem there
is a challenge:

> Enter these enchanted woods
>> You who dare.
>>> (ll. 1–2)

Like other Victorians, Meredith responds fully to the burgeoning and
irrepressible richness of nature, the light and shade, the quickness and
the slowness. The slow-chewing oxen suggest what creation may have
been like before the human intelligence came on the scene, 'when mind
was mud' (l. 77) and Earth 'a slimy spine' and 'Heaven a space for
winging tons' (ll. 80–81). A slightly ponderous periphrasis for ptero-
dactyls here. However, Meredith does not wish merely to versify an
evolutionary scheme on exclusively scientific grounds; there is room
for mythology and the old gods too, although the inversion in these
lines suggests at first that there is not:

> Banished is the white Foam-born
> Not from here, nor under ban
> Phoebus lyrist, Phoebe's horn,
> Pipings of the reedy Pan.
> Loved of Earth of old they were,
> Loving did interpret her;
> And the sterner worship bars
> None whom Song has made her stars.
>> (ll. 92–99)

'The white Foam-born' is of course Aphrodite. As in the De Rerum
Natura of Lucretius, love presides over the universe:

> Love, the great volcano, flings
> Fires of lower Earth to sky;
>> (ll. 166–67)

But the love has to avoid self-seeking, since egoism is the 'scaly
Dragon-fowl' that can destroy the harmony. As the poem draws to
a close we see that the reason the woods are so dangerous is that they
provide contradictory messages: on the one hand of 'luminousness',
on the other hand, if one approaches them in a negative frame of mind,
of death. The poem ends with a horrible image of a macrocosmic
dance of death:

Earthward swoops a vulture sun,
Nighted upon carrion:
Straightway venom winecups shout
Toasts to One whose eyes are out:

(ll. 454–57)

The 'One' is none other than the figure of death.

Notes

1. Charles Kingsley, *Fraser's Magazine*, 42 (September 1850), p. 246.

2. Henry James, 'Review of Stopford Brooke's *Theology in the English Poets*' (1875), *The Nation*, 20 (21 January 1875), 41–42; reprinted in *Literary Reviews and Essays by Henry James*, edited by A. Mordell. (New Haven, 1957), p. 316.

3. J. W. Beach, *The Concept of Nature in Nineteenth-Century Poetry* (New York, 1936), p. 8.

4. *Ibid.*, p. 15

5. Ruskin's 'Of The Pathetic Fallacy' is Chapter 12 of *Modern Painters*, III, in *Works*, V, 201–20.

6. Ruskin, *Works*, V, 218.

7. *The George Eliot Letters* edited by G. Haight (New Haven, 1954), II, 250–51. Haight thinks that Holman Hunt is intended here, but Hugh Witemeyer in *George Eliot and the Visual Arts* (New Haven, 1979) suggests that it may be Barbara Bodichon's friend William Henry Hunt ('Bird's Nest Hunt' as he was called), p. 135.

8. Pater, 'Conclusion' to *The Renaissance*, in *Works*, I, 237.

9. *Alfred Lord Tennyson: A Memoir*, edited by H. Tennyson, 2 vols (1897), I, 79.

10. Cited in C. Christ, *The Finer Optic* (New Haven 1975), p. 17.

11. Ruskin, *Works*, III, 624.

12. See my article on this image in *The Explicator*, 43 (1985), 19–20, in which I correct a misreading, based on ignorance of the appearance of the flower, by David Riede.

13. *The Letters of Matthew Arnold to Arthur Hugh Clough*, edited by H. F. Lowry (1932), p. 97.

14. *The Life of Thomas Hardy*, edited by F. E. Hardy (1962), p. 185.

15. *The Notebooks of S. T. Coleridge*, edited by K. Coburn (1957–62), I, 1766; cited P. Ball, *The Science of Aspects* (1971) p. 27.

16. *The Journals and Papers of General Manley Hopkins*, edited by H. House and G. Storey (1959), p. 196.

17. *The Sermons and Devotional Writings of Gerard Manley Hopkins*, edited by C. Devlin (1959, reprinted 1967), p. 351.

18. Hopkins contributed the following articles to *Nature*: 'A Curious Halo', 'Shadow-beams in the East at Sunset', 'The Remarkable Sunsets' [on the volcanic eruptions of Krakatoa] and 'The Red Light Round the Sun – the Sun Blue or Green at Setting' (1882–84).

19. Hopkins records his renunciations in the *Hopkins Journals*: November 1865, 'on this day by God's grace I resolved to give up all beauty until I had leave for it' (p. 71); 1869, 'a penance I was doing from Jan. 25 to July 25 prevented my seeing much that half-year' (p. 190); 23 July 1874 he denied himself the pleasure of looking at a beautiful scene because he 'talked too freely and unkindly' (p. 249).

20. J. Fisher, 'Clare: Naturalist and Poet', *The Listener*, 66 (19 October 1961), 614–15.

21. A. C. Swinburne, *The Complete Works of Algernon Charles Swinburne* (1925–27) XIV, 341.

22. Ruskin, Letter to *The Times*, 25 May 1854, *Works*, XIII, 334.

23. Ibid., XIII, 334.

24. See Ruskin's letter to D. G. Rossetti in *Ruskin: Rossetti: Pre-Raphaelitism Papers, 1854–1862*, edited by W. M. Rossetti, (1899), pp. 103–4.

25. D. Riede, *Dante Gabriel Rossetti and the Limits of Victorian Vision* (Ithaca, New York, 1983), pp. 201–2.

26. W. Wordsworth, Preface to *Lyrical Ballads* (1802 edition), edited by R. L. Brett and A. R. Jones (1963), p. 253.

27. Cited in *Alfred Lord Tennyson: A Memoir*, edited by H. Tennyson (1897), II, 57.

28. J. H. Miller, *The Disappearance of God* (Cambridge, Mass., 1964), p. 84.

29. L. Stevenson, *Darwin Among the Poets* (Chicago, 1932), p. 219.

Chapter 12
Art and Artists

Throughout the history of English poetry, art and artists have been key themes: poets have described objects of art and explored the creativity of artists. As I have said elsewhere in this study, poets have always made a ready response to other makers. The Renaissance revived interest in notions of the sister arts, especially *ut pictura poesis*, and indeed there was a special term for paintings and other artefacts described in verse: *ecphrasis*. Central principles and values have often informed a number of arts simultaneously, and there are scores of critical works exploring the grounds of parallelism. Some of them are extremely ambitious, and try to uncover the pervasive *Zeitgeists* of periods which are so prominent that they make their impact felt on arts in all media.[1] This critical activity can be at once exciting and risky, and it is not the main purpose of this chapter to pursue such criticism, since in our period it requires a full-length monograph. There may be a psychic state in Victorian England so insidiously powerful that it makes its influence felt on all artistic products in analogous ways, but there is not going to be time to try and identify it here, and in any case I am rather sceptical as to the existence of this mysterious entity. In the end it is safer to accept that each art develops in its own way and in terms of its own disciplines, with an occasional peripheral stimulus from another art. To diminish the particular qualities of individual media lessens the forceful impact they are likely to make on their own terms and reduces the intensity of aesthetic pleasure. Baudelaire, who might have been expected to pursue the most self-indulgent forms of parallelistic criticism, was in fact rather sceptical about the unlicensed crossing of frontiers: 'Doubt has led certain artists to beg the aid of all the other arts. Experiment with contradictory means, the encroachment of one art upon another, the importation of poetry, wit and sentiment into painting – all these modern miseries are vices peculiar to the eclectics.'[2] The main aim of this chapter, then, is not to lay bare the central sources that will explain the operations of the whole of Victorian culture, but to consider some representative poems that take art and artists as their topic. In the course of doing this some *apercus* of an interdisciplinary kind might be glimpsed.

Many Victorian poets were slightly wary of art, since nature was so central in their consciousnesses. Their suspicion of artifice, at least in its more obvious forms, made them less naturally prone to describe paintings, tapestries, and statues than their Renaissance predecessors. Many of them were also reluctant to acknowledge the debt they owed to the visual arts in forming their own visual habits of mind – at least as a subject of poetry. This reluctance was already beginning in the Romantic Movement, when Wordsworth, for instance, was anxious to underplay the contribution made by the Picturesque taste to the development of his perceptions.[3] For final effectiveness as a visionary and a poet he thought one had to go beyond mere taste and learnt habits of vision. Sometimes acknowledgement of the influence of painting and the other visual arts on modes of perception is suppressed; at other times it has been so insidious a process that it scarcely surfaces in consciousness, and this is why historians are so anxious to track down the unacknowledged influences. It has been shown by a number of critics that the contribution made by art in the formation of Hopkins's particular habits of perception was very considerable, but it does not explicitly show up in his poetry.[4]

The trouble with describing paintings in poetry is that it tends to create a static tableau-like effect, allied to the genres of emblem and allegory; this may have been attractive to Renaissance poets, but for the most part the Victorians wanted more dynamism and movement, more spontaneous life, more drama. However, there are some Victorian poems in which the tableau effect is obviously required, and here *ecphrasis* is the naturally appropriate mode. Chief of the early poems is Tennyson's *Palace of Art*. It is a lengthy description of a series of galleries built for the soul's delectation on a cliff top high above a valley floor. In modern literature it is the *locus classicus* of aesthetic escapism; it is the sort of place a person might build who was rich in the sense defined in James's *Portrait of a Lady*: able to realize the dreams of his imagination. There is a group of cloisters with fountains, and a suite of rooms decorated to suit varied moods. There are grim tapestries:

> One seemed all dark and red – a tract of sand,
>   And some one pacing there alone,
> Who paced for ever in a glimmering land,
>   Lit with a low large moon.
>
>   (ll. 65–68)

And there are pleasant ones:

And one, the reapers at their sultry toil.
  In front they bound the sheaves. Behind
Were realms of upland, prodigal in oil
  And hoary to the wind.
                              (ll. 77–80)

The arts seems trapped in a ceaselessly revolving cycle, since literature inspired the pictures of 'mythic Uther's deeply-wounded son',
then these pictures have inspired the poem, then the poem inspired the
four vividly intense illustrations produced by Rossetti for the Moxon
edition of Tennyson's *Poems* (1855). Christian art jostles with pagan:
in close proximity one finds Christ and his mother, Saint Cecelia,
Europa, and Ganymede; there is something corrupt in this widely
eclectic taste which is reminiscent of Browning's Bishop at St Praxed's.
Some of the works glorify the English poets Shakespeare and Milton
– rather as the Pre-Raphaelite Ford Madox Brown did in his painting
The Seeds and Fruits of English Poetry (1853). There is a very Victorian
eclecticism about it all: the past is there to be rifled and appropriated
for self-indulgent delectation, and it is like many a Victorian treasure-
house assembled in this country and the United States (one thinks of
Isabella Stewart Gardner's palace of art in Boston, where Titian's *Rape
of Europa* is cheek by jowl with primitive Christian art). Indeed the
poem, despite its admonitory moral, may have fostered the taste for
the exotic treasure-house. Looking at Randolph Hearst's castle at San
Simeon (the monstrosity that is partly the model for Citizen Kane's
Xanadu) it occurs to one that Tennyson might have had a lot to answer
for. Tennyson's palace offers the opportunity, by virtue of its detach-
ment, for an uncommitted relationship with artistic and intellectual
culture, so that the soul sits 'as God holding no form of creed,/But
contemplating all'. (ll. 211–12) The Renaissance regarded painting as
'silent poetry', and finally the soul finds the quiet maddening:

  'No voice,' she shrieked in that lone hall,
    'No voice breaks through the stillness of this world;
      One deep, deep silence all!'
                              (ll. 258–60)

There is something stagnant about the life dominated by static art,
it is like being left behind in 'a still salt pool' while the sea's waters
plunge with vital energy. Art is absolute and associated with 'dreadful
eternity'; when one speaks to it 'there comes no murmur of reply'. The
soul, close to some form of psychic death, has to leave and retire to
'a cottage in the vale'. In an arch finale the palace is not destroyed; no
intemperate Guyon comes along to lay waste to the artificial paradise,

and there is a remote possibility of return: 'Perchance I may return with others there/When I have purged my guilt' (ll. 295–96). *The Palace of Art* shows how limited the possibilities are for descriptive poetry dealing with art; it does not offer sufficient opportunities for surprise and dynamism, and modern poets essaying the genre have discovered these limitations – there is the case of R. S. Thomas's slightly inert commentaries on French Impressionist paintings.[5] Tennyson did not write many more poems like this one (although there are instances of *ecphrasis* in *The Princess* and *The Idylls*). Nevertheless, quite a few of his works treat life in the spirit of mesmerized inanition; 'The Lotos-Eaters', 'Mariana', 'The Lady of Shalott', and 'Tithonus,' for instance.

After Tennyson the Victorian poet responding most enthusiastically to the pictorial as a poetic subject was Rossetti, and since he was a practising artist this is hardly to be wondered at. He had fewer guilt feelings than Tennyson about the attractiveness of art, and he occupies a central place in the development of the aesthetic movement. I do not suppose anyone ever said to him, 'Rossetti, we cannot live in art', not even William Morris. Psychologically he was drawn very easily into the static, enclosed, mysterious dream-like world of art, especially of the past. He produced some of the most effective poetic evocations of paintings since the Renaissance. The fourteen 'Sonnets on Pictures' are beautiful examples of their kind: subtle and imaginative responses to works by Giorgione, Mantegna, Ingres, Memling, Michelangelo, Botticelli, and Leonardo da Vinci. The only modern painter he celebrates, other than himself, is Edward Burne-Jones, whose work is saturated with the spirit of the past. These works adumbrate Walter Pater's famous prose reveries in the presence of works of art and catch an elusive mood which less sensitive spectators might miss. This is the study of Giorgione's *A Venetian Pastoral* in the Louvre:

> Hush! beyond all depth away
> The heat lies silent at the brink of day:
>   Now the hand trails upon the viol string
>   That sobs, and the brown faces cease to sing,
> Sad with the whole of pleasure.
>
> (ll. 4–8)

Without poetry of this kind as an inspiration Pater might never have been able to write his vivid prose evocation of the same painting in *The Renaissance: Studies in Art and Poetry* (third edition 1888) The silent paintings that are the subjects of Rossetti's poems seem to require explication, but they are enigmatic; they pose more questions than they can answer, and their mysterious depths attract Rossetti by virtue of their strangeness. The sestet of the sonnet dealing with Leonardo's *Our Lady of the Rocks* is representative of Rossetti's treatment:

> Mother of grace, the pass is difficult,
> Keen as these rocks, and the bewildered souls
>   Throng it like echoes, blindly shuddering
>   through.
> Thy name, O lord, each spirit's choice extols,
>   Whose peace abides in the dark avenue
> Amid the bitterness of things occult.
>   (ll. 9–14)

A large body of Rossetti's poetry is closely related to his own painting. This offers an interesting test case for parallelistic criticism, as do Blake's works in various media. Are these poems commentaries and reveries on paintings which predate the poems rather as Mantegna's and Botticelli's paintings predate the poems on them, or is Rossetti going back to some prior state in his mind, where, in Yeats's words, 'the arts play like children about the one Chimney.'[6] If one takes the view that there are original experiences which are the precursors of works of art re-creating them then it may be possible, with artists like Blake and Rossetti, who are masters of more than one art, to go back to these original mental states which exist irrespective of the various media which subsequently represent them. Obviously there is some common ground between Rossetti's own poetry and painting, but finally not as much as one might expect, since each art has its own traditions and its own disciplines, and I feel, as Pater felt in his essay on Giorgione, rather sceptical about these ur-states, of which arts in different media are mere 'translations into different languages of one and the same fixed quantity of imaginative thought'.[7] Some of Rossetti's poems on his own paintings describe them; others articulate ideas and emotions to which the paintings are only able to bear silent witness. Some of the paintings have poems painted on to them as commentaries. *Astarte Syriaca* is an example. Rossetti was an early enthusiast for Blake's work, and owned one of his notebooks; like Blake he was interested in the possibilities of amalgamating different arts to produce a unified impression. One of the pages of *The House of Life* was engraved in 1880 as a pastiche of Blake, with the soul hovering over 'A Sonnet is a Moment's Monument' and the text surrounded with sprays of wild rose. The sestet regards the sonnet as a coin, with one face depicting the soul, the other 'to what Power 'tis due'. An accompanying emblem depicts the meaning with the traditional motifs of butterfly and serpent biting its tail. This composite art owes something to Blake and something to Renaissance traditions. The enigma tradition of the Renaissance emblem obviously appealed to Rossetti, though he was temperamentally reluctant to solve all the enigmas absolutely. He liked to retain some air of mystery, some sense of the occult.

Rossetti, as a practising artist, was able to provide a very authoritative account of the psychology of the artist and his methods of work. There are a number of interesting poems in this vein. 'St. Luke the Painter' is a thumbnail sketch of the history of art, from its early application of 'devious symbols', to the academic traditions of the High Renaissance, when practitioners 'turned in vain/To soulless self-reflection of man's skill', to the modern era, when some revival of holiness was possible. 'The Portrait' is a fascinating study of a painting as memorial, and Rossetti's artistic training accentuated his readiness to conceive in terms of visual images. 'The Soul's Sphere' (*House of Life*, LXII) speaks of 'the soul's sphere of infinite images'. We have seen elsewhere evidence for a sense of vision nurtured on the painter's eye for detail and colour (see above pp. 187–88). It is sometimes said that Rossetti failed to secure a major place in the history of both painting and poetry because his talents were too widely dispersed. This is a questionable view, since each art supplemented the other. Perhaps his painting could have been improved with more time spent on it, but the poetic spirit augmented it admirably – as one sees when one looks at the pedestrian work of other members of the Pre-Raphaelite Brotherhood not similarly blessed with the poetic faculty. However, William Michael Rossetti thought that the regretful poem 'Lost on Both Sides' (*House of Life*, XCI) charted the divided allegiances that an artist must feel when pursuing different arts:

> So separate hopes, which in a soul had woed
>> The one same Peace, strove with each other
>>> long,
> And Peace before their faces perished since.
>
> (ll. 9–11)

The most that can be said is that the poem might just about sustain such a reading, but does not naturally invite it – if only because the pursuit of different arts did not produce that level of discord.

Rossetti is a delicate and fascinating painter-poet, but the man who must take pride of place in this chapter is Browning. It is quite possible that he contributed as much as Ruskin to the propagation of taste for Italian Renaissance art in Victorian England, and that 'Fra Lippo Lippi' and 'Andrea del Sarto' were as influential as *Mornings in Florence* in preparing generations of tourists for a sensitive and informed appreciation of Florentine art. Ruskin himself was prepared to credit

Browning with a level of expertise rivalling his own, in a generous passage in *Modern Painters*,[8] Browning knew his Italy; even Henry James, whose knowledge of the country and its art was wide and expert, realized that the poet surpassed him easily.[9] The story of Browning's long love-affair with Italy has recently been told by Jacob Korg.[10] Browning spent fifteen years of married life there, a certain amount of it grubbing around in antique shops looking for lost masterpieces. Rare and recondite masters especially appealed to him. The delight in pursuit and discovery is recorded in 'Old Pictures in Florence':

> Wherever a fresco peels and drops,
>   Wherever an outline weakens and wanes
> Till the latest life in the painting stops,
>   Stands One whom each fainter pulse-tick
>   pains:
> One, wishful each scrap should clutch the brick,
>   Each tinge not wholly escape the plaster,
> – A lion who dies of an ass's kick,
>   The wronged great soul of an ancient Master.
>
>   (ll. 41–48)

The poems brings to life the freshness of discovery captured so touchingly in Edith Wharton's short story 'False Dawn' (1924). Many of the painters were at that time obscure and unknown – Taddeo Gaddi, Lorenzo Monaco, Ghirlandaio – but generations of English and American tourists were impelled to find out more about them simply by having read the poem. Browning helped to propagate the myth of the Renaissance:

> But at any rate I have loved the season
>   Of Art's spring-birth so dim and dewy;
>   (ll. 177–78)

The poem has a political message, since these old painters embody and enshrine the consciousness of Italy, in Browning's time unrealized still as a nation. At that time Giotto's Campanile was still unfinished, and Browning dreamt of the time when Italy might be reunited and the 'long-pent fire' of its beauty 'spring from its sleep'. Both of these dreams came to pass.[11]

As Browning saw it the Renaissance was a time of liberation for the arts, the time when creators were able to face life directly and record physical and emotional fact, when the picture replaced the ideogram, when spontaneity replaced academic timidity, when secularity replaced religiosity: in short when proto-Brownings started to appear. The key work celebrating this release is 'Fra Lippo Lippi'. This poem, like many of Browning's poems about art, does not so much describe specific paintings as go behind them to find out what kind of creative character was responsible for them. Browning did this by reading Vasari's *Lives of the Italian Artists* and other studies and by supplementing the impressions derived from research by knowledge of the paintings themselves. Browning accords Lippo Lippi more importance than he deserves if he is trying to offer him as a key figure in the growth of a certain kind of pictorial realism; that pride of place should go to Masaccio, but by slightly careless reading Browning misplaced him (he is the painter who appears as 'Hulking Tom' in the poem). The conservative view of art is voiced by the Prior, who believes in an iconic, non representational art:

> Your business is not to catch men with show,
> With homage to the perishable clay,
> But lift them over it, ignore it all,
> Make them forget there's such a thing as flesh.
>
> (ll. 179–82)

Lippo takes the view, on the other hand, that

> If you get simple beauty and nought else,
> You get about the best thing God invents;
>
> (ll. 216–17)

He is a *risqué* artist, sexually licentious, but his lubricity simply makes him responsive to the beauty of the world, and in his terms a better exponent of religious themes. Browning does not particularly want to glamorize the life of a roué monk and 'sportive ladies',[12] it is just that he thinks Lippo Lippi's proclivities are an important constituent part of a lively response to life around him. Browning could sympathize with Lippo Lippi because he was similarly open and impressionable, and regarded such faculties as essential for artists working in any media. It seems that Browning had a roving eye and a closer understanding of erotic adventures than one might imagine especially erotic adventures in the mind of the type Hardy was so adept at cultivating.[13] A piece of evidence crops up in one of those rare moments when a fragment of *Sordello* comes into uncharacteristically clear focus:

> Ah, beneath
> That cool arch stoops she, brownest cheek! Her
> wreath

> Endures a month – a half-month – if I make
> A queen of her, continue for her sake
> Sordello's story? Nay, that Paduan girl
> Splashes with barer legs where a live whirl
> In the dead black Giudecca proves sea-weed
> Drifting has sucked down three, four, all indeed
> Save one pale-red striped, pale-blue turbaned post
> For gondolas.
>   (III. 687–96)

That was in Venice. Italy did something to the repressed northern consciousness, giving it images of a stranger sexuality than northern climes could provide. A startling and disconcerting episode occurred during Ruskin's visit to Turin in 1858, when he saw a girl of about ten, lying on the sand like a snake. He described her at length in *The Cestus of Aglaia* (1865), 'Like a lizard . . . a few black rags about her loins, but her limbs nearly bare, and her little breasts, scarce dimpled yet, – white, – marble-like'.[14] She continued to haunt him, 'her figure mingling, against my will, with other images', and as late as November 1884 he was bringing the lizard girl to the attention of his Oxford audiences.

Browning's eye was also alert in Florence. The poor orphan Lippo Lippi in the streets attentively 'watching folk's faces' is, curiously, quite close to the Victorian poet who paced the streets of Florence looking for suggestive odds ands end and ultimately found a scrap that contained the kernel of *The Ring and the Book*. 'Fra Lippo-Lippi' had immediate relevance when it was first published in 1855, since this was the year before the Pre-Raphaelite *annus mirabilis* and debates about realism in painting were under way. Ruskin's *Modern Painters* was half published, but George Eliot said that she would rather have the poem 'than an essay on Realism in Art'.[15] Like Pre-Raphaelitism Lippo's realism is not the uncompromising photographic kind; it is a realism irradiated by warm, human personality, the kind of realism the English tradition tended to cherish in preference to the tougher Continental variety.

It is a tribute to Browning's capacity to see issues from a variety of angles that he was able to give a sympathetic portrait of an artist who had no wish to join in the headlong rush to secularity represented by the new movements in art. Barrie Bullen convincingly suggests that Browning probably had Fra Bartolommeo in mind when he wrote 'Pictor Ignotus',[16] but the figure has become a generic representative of all those artists who must have found themselves out of key with progress. Browning has no wish to recommend an artist of this kind, but he can sympathize with him. The artist has a vision of the ideal conditions for his art – that the finished work should be carried through the streets like Cimabue's Madanna, and remain an object of public esteem, so that when the painter dies he will 'not go to heaven, but linger here,/Here on my earth, earth's every man my friend'. He does not like the new traditions of secular easel painting, in which the works are more like 'garniture and household-stuff', and he continues to paint in fresco an endless series of 'Virgin, Babe and Saint,/With the same cold calm beautiful regard'.

There is a reflective melancholy about this poem 'Pictor Ignotus' and it would be a vulgar reading to attribute feelings of 'sour grapes' to the artist. The 'youth' who represents advances in painting is Raphael, and the poem is not explained simply by saying that this monotonous artist is jealous of the brilliant *ingénu*. Raphael, in company with Michelangelo, is also the cynosure of the much more famous poem 'Andrea del Sarto', and it would be equally inadequate to regard this poem as merely a study in jealousy. It is more complicated and subtle than that.

Andrea is an artist endowed with great technical facility, but somehow he does not have the genius of the giants who preceded him: Raphael and Michelangelo. Like the Mannerists of the sixteenth century, and he is a kind of Mannerist, he has the *maniera* but not the spirit to go with it. He has received recognition and even royal patronage, but he feels a sense of deficiency. And it affects his production: 'All is silver-grey/Placid and perfect with my art.' He recognizes that 'incentives come from the soul's self', but fears his art emanates from other sources, one of them the trammelling necessity to earn sufficient money to exercise a degree of control over his errant wife. His wife is his Muse, and her face appears in painting after painting (Browning is true to history here); it is a beautiful face, but perhaps the beauty is too accessible to the artist. And besides, perhaps beauty is not enough; Michelangelo was famed for his *terribilita*, his significance and his gawky awkwardness, and when Andrea dreams of painting a great picture, 'the Virgin's face' will not be his wife's. To succeed he has to break free, but it is evident from the poem that he is unable to, and he is trapped in the inert twilight world. He has even come to accept his prison:

> I am grown peaceful as old age to-night.
> I regret little, I would change still less.
>
> (ll. 244–45)

It is not difficult to follow through the implications of this poem to creativity generally, and Browning is doubtless trying to say something about his own art–though there has been disagreement as to what it is. Browning could never be regarded as a 'faultless poet', but he experienced irritation and frustration in having his Muse, Elizabeth, closeted with him, so that the poem probably has elements of oblique self-portraiture in it, which give the poem some of its urgency and memorability. Andrea and Lippo Lippi are such powerful creations that they are a constant impediment to a true understanding of the real historical originals, and this is a testimony to Browning's creative power – however much one may have doubts concerning his utility as an art historian.

Elsewhere Browning's 'negative capability' has been mentioned. Was it such that he could look at the world through the eyes of different artists and adopt a varied range of modes of perception? I think it was. Lippo Lippi seizes on the immediate:

> Have you noticed, now,
> Your cullion's hanging face? A bit of chalk,
> And trust me but you should, though!
>
> (ll. 306–08)

He is sufficiently late medieval to like a crowded panel:

> God in the midst, Madonna and her babe
> Ringed by a bowery flowery angel-brood,
> Lilies and vestments and white faces.
>
> (ll. 348–50)

Andrea, deficient perhaps as a colourist, is more aware of outlines and forms: 'Morello's outline', a misplaced line in Raphael's work, the 'serpenting beauty, rounds on rounds' of his own work.

As a post-Romantic writer Browning espoused the expressive aesthetic of creation, and he knew that artists reveal a great deal through their chosen media, but in 'One Word More', the epilogue to his collection *Men and Women*, he develops the interesting thesis that artists actually reveal more about themselves when working in an unfamiliar medium, so that Raphael's sonnets and Dante's drawings are more personal than their professional work. This is not far from the 'Andrea del Sarto' thesis. Incomplete mastery of a medium is more likely to lead to interesting results than the complete control of a virtuoso. Browning writes (though it might not find wide endorsement today):

> You and I would rather see that angel,
> Painted by the tenderness of Dante,
> Would we not? than read a fresh Inferno.
>
> (ll. 50–53)

He tries to imagine the unseen side of the moon, 'the novel/silent silver lights and darks undreamed of'. And there he will do a most un-Browning-like thing: he will hush and bless himself with silence!

Notes

1. One of the most ambitious studies is M. Praz's *Mnemosyne: The Parallel Between Literature and the Visual Arts* (1970).

2. Baudelaire, 'On Eclecticism and Doubt' (1846), in *Art in Paris, 1845–1862* translated and edited by J. Mayne (1965), p. 97. For the interest in parallelism in the period see R. Park, '"Ut Pictura Poesis": The Nineteenth-century Aftermath', *JAAC*, 28 (1969), 155–64.

3. See J. R. Watson, *Picturesque Landscape and English Romantic Poetry* (1970), especially pp. 97–105.

4. F. Fike, 'Gerard Manley Hopkins's Interest in Painting after 1868: Two Notes', *VP*, 8 (1970), 315–33. See also J. Bump, 'Manual Photography: Hopkins, Ruskin, and Victorian Drawing', *Texas Quarterly*, 16 (1973), 90–116, and *All My Eyes See: The Visual World of Gerard Manley Hopkins*, edited by P. K. P. Thornton (Sunderland, 1975). Hopkins was a proficient sketcher in a Ruskinian tradition, and many of his works are reproduced by Bump and by H. House in *The Journals of Gerard Manley Hopkins*, edited by H. House and G. Storey (1959), between pp. 456 and 457.

5. R. S. Thomas, *Between Here and Now* (1981).

6. W. B. Yeats, *Essays and Introductions* (1961), p. 355.

7. Pater, *The Renaissance*, in *Works*, I, 130.

8. Ruskin, *Works*, VI, 449.

9. H. James thought Browning superior to other writers in his presentation of Italy, both past and present: 'Shelley, let us say . . . is a light and Swinburne, let us say, a sound; Browning alone of them all is a temperature.' 'The Novel in *The Ring and the Book*' (1912), *Notes on Novelists* (1914), p. 318.

10. J. Korg, *Browning and Italy* (Athens, Ohio, 1983).

11. Giotto planned to add a spire about a hundred feet tall to the top of the Campanile, but it has never been built; Italy was united in 1861 under Victor Emmanuel II, although Venetia and Rome were not acquired until 1866 and 1870 respectively.

12. Browning's interest in bare limbs was inherited by his son Pen; see W. Irvine and P. Honan *The Book, The Ring and The Poet* (1974), p. 417.

13. See note 12 above.

14. Ruskin, *Works*, XIX, 82–83.

15. G. Eliot, *Westminster Review*, 65 (1856), 296.

16. J. B. Bullen, 'Browning's *Pictor Ignotus* and Vasari's *Life of Fra Bartolommeo Di San Marco*', *RES*, 23 (1972), 313–19.

Chapter 13
Religion

One of the major facets of the Victorian age was the loss of faith; it was inevitable that this should show up in the poetry. Loss of faith or dilution of faith had been possible in the eighteenth century, but not in so widespread a fashion, and not prompted by so many different directions of attack. In classes where any degree of education and contact with intellectual controversy was possible, crises in belief were almost inevitable. Not everyone was deconverted, but almost everyone who went through any crisis of faith was never quite the same again. The loss of faith became a major poetic subject, and much of the poetry it prompted was powerful and moving. Those who retained traditional piety also wrote poetry, but only very little of it is worth reading for its own sake. The main poetry of belief was written by Hopkins, and he was, as everyone knows, assailed by torturing doubts of a kind never experienced in previous centuries by believers, never, at least, in the precise form suffered by him. In previous centuries religious poetry was versified doctrine or versified conversation with God; only in exceptional circumstances, such as in Donne's poetry, was there much in the way of struggle or protest. Versified doctrine and versified prayer continued in the nineteenth century, but the poetry that catches our interest is concerned with struggle and loss of faith. In less accentuated forms 'loss of faith' could be loss of orthodox faith, and resulted in an attempt to redefine God in a more mystical fashion (as a force of nature for instance or as a vague pervasive spirit) or in a more gloomy and deterministic fashion. This redefinition was under way in the eighteenth century and during the Romantic Movement of course. At the best of times God might be invisible and inaccessible, the *deus absconditus* J. Hillis Miller writes about so tellingly in *The Disappearance of God* (Cambridge, Mass., 1975). In more extreme cases God was never there in the first place *to* disappear. The poetry in these circumstances is inevitably very human-centred and often very moving; it is, after all, more the stuff of poetry than versified doctrine. As I have shown in my chapter on nature poetry, the alteration in the religious environment had a colossal impact on man's attitude to the physical world.

The popular view of Victorian scepticism is that it was nurtured by Darwinism. It was indeed, but there were two other forces at work, which may in the end have been more effective; they were biblical criticism and philosophical positivism.

Modern fundamentalists go back to a time, which they imagine came to an end during the eighteenth century, when they suppose that everyone believed that every word in the Bible was literally true. In fact even then not every believer was so naive, and for centuries, as far back as the Church Fathers, the Bible had been treated not only as history but moral and spiritual allegory. Still, it was generally accepted that the Scriptures were divinely inspired. In the nineteenth century, however, the disciplines of classical scholarship were turned on the Bible, which ceased to be regarded, by many people, as a privileged text; it was, so they thought, like any other, and subject to the whims and vagaries of time. The text of the Bible could be examined in the same way that one examined the text of Homer or Virgil. This kind of study was mainly conducted in Germany, but in this country scholars such as Milman treated the Old Testament as a historical document. The most sensational work was D. F. Strauss's *Das Leben Jesu* (1835), translated as *Life of Jesus* (1846) by George Eliot. Ultimately, historical scepticism suggested that there could not have been a figure like Jesus, and his main value was symbolic or mythical.

Positivism was developed by the French philosopher Auguste Comte (1798–1857). He identified three stages of human thought: the anthropomorphic, the metaphysical (in which deities were seen as abstract powers), and the scientific. Comte replaced traditional religion with the new 'religion of humanity', which formed the basis for a good deal of George Eliot's thought.[1]

Evolutionary theory gave scientific support to the Comtean principles, since it outlined the process whereby one entity, whether in nature or society, was succeeded by another. Evolutionary theory was not first proposed by Darwin; it had been first thought of in the eighteenth century by Lamarck and Erasmus Darwin (Charles Darwin's grandfather). Darwin's *The Botanic Garden* (1789–91) and *Zoonomia* (1794–96) presented the theories in poetic form. Sir Charles Lyell's *Principles of Geology* (1830–33) and Robert Chambers's *Vestiges of the Natural History of Creation* (1844) questioned orthodox theology. As enormous perspectives of geological time opened up it became impossible to believe in the special and unique status of mankind. Darwin's *The Origin of Species* (1859) was important and controversial since it substantiated earlier theories with an enormous mass of detail and information. In proposing that evolution worked by chance rather than by design it seemed to banish an intelligent, organizing Deity from the universe. However, this did not prevent certain Christians, such as

Charles Kingsley, from taking the sting out of the tail in Darwin by reconciling Darwinism with religion; we see a splendid parody of this procedure in Jenkinson's sermon in Mallock's *The New Republic* (1877). There were limits to what Darwinism could do – as a number of sceptics such as Mill, Morley, Huxley, Stephen, and Arnold realized. Nature, which behaved criminally, could not offer a system of ethics; that had to be constructed on some other basis, and often the finished system looked like religion without the transcendentalism.

Even as the forces of scepticism were getting under way a reactionary response occurred in the shape of the Oxford Movement, inaugurated in 1833 by John Keble's Assize Sermon. This was a protest against the Erastianism (secular dominance) and latitudinarianism of the age; it was an attempt to restore to the Church the power it had as an institution in the Middle Ages and the mysticism and piety which had been lost. Some of its impetus derives from Coleridge and the Romantic Movement; this is all the more curious because Coleridge's thought also underpinned the development of the very non-mystical Broad Church. Newman was generally regarded as the leading light in the Oxford Movement, and when he went over to Rome in 1845 this seemed to many an inevitable step: it was natural that authoritarian instincts should lead one to an institutionally strong organization like the Church of Rome. Hopkins followed Newman down this road twenty years later, but for many it was possible to remain in the Church of England and espouse seemingly Roman principles. The leader after Newman's defection was Pusey. The power of the Oxford Movement was very considerable, indeed its repercussions are felt to this day, and inevitably it had its influence on the poetry. Its basis was in the rediscovery of spirituality. It espoused romance, colourful ceremonial, an interest in the past traditions of the Church, and devotional intensity – all features that could very easily become the stuff of poetry. Indeed it might be claimed that the religious habit of mind, of seeing the invisible via the visible, the holy via the secular, the universal via the particular, the eternal via the historical, and the significant via the apparently contingent are directly analogous to poetic practices, so that it is natural for churchmen to be sympathetic to poetry (one thinks of Keble and Newman) and for agnostics to find their potential hostility to religion tempered by the recognition of its shared ground with poetry (Matthew Arnold's *Literature and Dogma* (1873) is a classic case of this). Even as he was in the process of privately losing his faith Ruskin could publicly affirm: 'Art has never shown, in any corner of the earth a condition of advancing strength but under this influence. I do not say observe, influence of "religion", but merely of a belief in some invisible power – god or goddess, fury or fate, saint or demon.'[2]

The lateral and quasi-poetic mode of thinking adopted by religious votaries comes broadly under the heading of typology. This has its roots in medieval theology, and it is often associated with High-Church Christianity, but, as George Landow has demonstrated in his work on Holman Hunt, it was also readily adopted by Low-Churchmen too.[3]

Two important figures in the High-Church camp are Christina Rossetti and Richard Watson Dixon. Their Pre-Raphaelite affiliations strengthened their tendency to introduce medieval elements into their religious lives and their poetry. D. G. Rossetti likewise has a distinctly medieval flavour in his religious poetry, but his religious instincts are not usually as deep or as committed as those of his sister. There is an aesthetic and sentimental impulse behind his religious and quasi-religious poetry and it does not finally have the earnestness or urgency of Christina's work. Dante was of course an influential father-figure for these poets. Keble stressed the importance of 'types' in his 'Tract 89', and Newman recognized that *The Christian Year* (1827) exemplified Keble's vision of a sacramental system, 'that is, the doctrine that material phenomena are both the types and instruments of real things unseen'.[4] In his lectures on poetry Keble states that

> poetry lends Religion her wealth of symbols and similes:
> Religion restores these again to Poetry, clothed with so
> splendid a radiance that they appear to be no longer
> merely symbols, but to partake . . . of the nature of
> sacraments[5]

The most famous lines on this theme are Keble's own:

> There is a Book, who runs may read,
>   Which heavenly Truth imparts
> And all the lore its scholars need,
>   Pure eyes and Christian hearts.
>
> ('Septuagesima Sunday', ll. 1–4)

Typology is principally a system for relating events in the Old Testament to those in the New Testament, and for revealing the transcendental significance of apparently insignificant events in the Bible, but in its extended sense it is a system for relating all historical events and all facets of nature to a meaningful interpretative scheme of things. Ultimately, as Jerome Bump has shown in his study of Hopkins, the natural details of the universe come under the aegis of a typological scheme, in which notions such as 'instress' and 'inscape' have their place.[6]

Also medieval in origin is a whole range of attitudes that one finds in the Pre-Raphaelite poets and Hopkins – concentration on the Virgin Mary, interest in the celibate, renunciatory, and ascetic life. It is but a step from Christina Rossetti's 'The Convent Threshold' to Hopkins's 'Heaven-Haven' and 'The Habit of Perfection'. *The Wreck of the Deutschland* has certain features that are Victorian, but what is not Victorian, for the most part, is the certainty that God exists (even though his nature and his purposes might be inscrutable and unpalatable) and is even capable miraculously of manifesting himself, in this instance as if to bring about the long-desired miracle of England returning to the Catholic fold. This is the doctrine of 'The Real Presence', towards which Hopkins was moving even in his pre-conversion days. In June 1864 he wrote to E. H. Coleridge: 'The great aid to belief and object of belief is the doctrine of the Real Presence in the Blessed Sacrament of the Altar. Religion without that is sombre, dangerous, illogical, with that it is – not to speak of its grand consistency and certainty – *loveable*. Hold that and you will gain all Catholic truth'.[7]

'Barnfloor and Winepress' (published in the *Union Review* in 1865) celebrates the importance of Christ's presence in the Eucharist:

> We scarcely call that banquet food,
> But even our Saviour's and our blood,
> We are so grafted on His wood.
>
> (ll. 31–33)

This is a sacramental mode of thought very close to Herbert's 'The Bunch of Grapes.'[8] In these religious poets one encounters states of mind which in some sense may be familiar to us, but seen in another way are like throw-backs to medieval experiences. *Acedia* was a state of mind akin to sloth, melancholy, and despair. None of the modern words quite translates it, but Jerome Bump is surely right to recognize its presence in a poem like Hopkin's 'See how Spring comes with disabling cold'. Kevin Morris has shown the persistence of certain medieval states of mind in figures who were interested in the revival of the spirit of medieval religion, who were interested in the spirit of medievalism, that is, as opposed to its colourful external trappings,[9] but this was a minority interest, and many people, apparently interested in medievalism and living and working in neo-medieval buildings, were incapable of understanding what the Middle Ages, especially in its religious aspects, were really like, and would certainly not have been interested in a whole-hearted revival had they been able to understand what that might involve. There are strands that have to be carefully disentangled: one might think that the Romantic Movement was somehow connected with a Catholic revival, since it sometimes flirted with medieval sentiment, but Hoxie Fairchild pointed out many years ago that the Romantic Movement, in its denial of 'the insufficiency of man and the transcendent objectivity of God', is not really compatible with Catholicism, and in so far as it is compatible with Christianity it is with Protestant extremism which tends towards irreligion.[10] Emerson's 'No law can be sacred to me but that of my own nature' is like a caricatured form of Romantic self-assertion, but it is some way off the self-surrender of Hopkins.

However, like some of the great seventeenth-century Anglican divines, Hopkins did not surrender gracefully and easily – no one with an intellect and an originality such as he possessed could be expected to – and his 'terrible sonnets' are some of the most moving and harrowing poems of religious struggle in the language. 'Carrion Comfort', 'No worst, there is none', 'I wake and feel the fell of dark' are records of searing experiences, making the acceptance of God in 'Patience, hard thing' and 'My own heart let me more have pity on' the more moving: 'Yet the rebellious wills/Of us we do bid God bend to him even so.' This is great poetry, but as Hoxie Fairchild admits much of the other poetry from the Catholic and High Anglican School, though interesting and historically important, is not really much good as poetry. The principal works are Keble's *The Christian Year* and Newman's *Dream of Gerontius*, and although they have played a distinctive part in the religious lives of many Christians one hesitates to make great claims for them as works of art. The poetry of doubt is really much more interesting as poetry, and not merely because it happens to accord with modern attitudes. An adequate treatment requires a full-length book, and fortunately there is an excellent one, one of the very best books ever written on Victorian poetry, J. Hillis Miller's *The Disappearance of God* (Cambridge Mass., 1975). I shall try to glance at some of the issues Miller deals with so very effectively.

Miller is not concerned with out-and-out atheism, but with a God who is inaccessible and perhaps not even there. It is this withdrawn aspect of God that often makes Victorian religious poetry so poignant. Typical of the wistfulness and regret is Clough's 'That there are powers above us I admit', which ends:

> And when we lift up holy hands of prayer,
> I will not say they will not give us aid.

> (ll. 17–18)

In 'Epi-Strauss-ion' (1847) the new rationalism has banished mysterious stained-glass windows, to leave churches 'more sincerely bright; and sadly the aspostles are 'evanished all and gone'. Clough is starting to feel the chill of what Yeats called, in a telling phrase, 'the desolation of reality'.[11] Donne wanted revelation in 'Show me, dear Christ thy spouse' but Clough in 'Hymnos Ahymnos' ('a hymn, yet not a hymn'), decided that it might be best to believe in God as a dweller in the shrine of the human heart rather than in some 'upper air', but he realized that this would mean that in some important sense he did not exist; 'I will not ask to feel thou art.'

Clough, it will be remembered, resigned his Oriel Fellowship because he found difficulty in giving assent to the Thirty-nine Articles of the Church of England. Elsewhere in his poetry there is a much more emphatic negativity. 'Easter Day I' with its refrain 'Christ is not risen' is an assertion of the deadness of Christ – in that most superstitious of cities, Naples – and it seems to carry more weight than the positive poem 'Easter Day II' – for one thing it is 115 lines longer. The most cynical statement is '"There Is No God", the Wicked Saith', which ends:

> And almost every one when age
>   Disease, or sorrows strike him,
> Inclines to think there is a God,
>   Or something very like Him. (ll. 20–23)

But this poem is in the mouth of the Mephistophelean spirit in *Dipsychus*. Still, it shows that Clough was intellectually capable of envisaging such scepticism.

In Browning and Tennyson the loss of faith is never quite so much in the open as with Clough, and indeed they were not as sceptical. Like many Victorians they clung to a consoling sense that God might be there. It was part of a process that Walter Houghton identifies, in his masterly study *The Victorian Frame of Mind* (New Haven, 1957), as 'the will to believe'. It was possible for John A. Hutton to write *Guidance from Robert Browning in Matters of Faith* (1903), and promote him as 'the great Apologist of these last days, the man of God to our peculiar age'. Yet Hillis Miller says, justly, that we hear Browning speaking with something like his own voice in *Parleying with Gerard de Lairesse*:

> So, point me out which was it of the links
> Snapped first, from out the chain which used to
>   bind
> Our earth to heaven . . .
>   (6. 3–5)

Caponsacchi in *The Ring and the Book* has a 'feeling that there's God, he reigns and rules/Out of this low world', but that sounds more nineteenth-century than seventeenth, when priests did not have *feelings* about such things but rather more definite beliefs.

A problem that Browning felt acutely, and Tennyson felt it too, concerned natural religion. Formerly it had been possible for theologians to infer the existence of God from the wonders of creation, but this was a more plausible exercise in times when nature was mainly viewed as a bland and harmonious force. But for Browning, and this is mentioned in Chapter 11, the universe was the scene of a never-ending struggle between immense forces locked in elemental combat, perhaps never to be reconciled. The earth is 'a teeming crust – /Air, flame, earth, wave at conflict'. The principles of individuation are there, but always ready to collapse, and besides, Browning finds nothing attractive in the idea of 'eternal petrifaction'. His overriding image is rather like Hopkin's Heraclitean nightmare. A man of faith could posit a stable God in response to alarming states of flux, but unless he was capable of considerable mental agility this picture of a seething and unstable world would not naturally lead him to a concept of a firm and reliable maker. This was one of the principal disadvantages under which the concept of natural religion operated in the century.

'In light inaccessible hid from our eyes' goes the hymn, and God is hidden from Browning, so that man is like the asymptote – speeding towards God, but unable to reach him. In true Romantic and Protestant fashion Browning seems more responsive to the occult existence of the human soul, whose very inwardness is going to make self-revelatory and confessional poetry after the fashion of Donne and Herbert virtually impossible. He speaks of the 'inmost centre in us all', 'Where truth abides in fulness; and around,/Wall upon wall, the gross flesh hems it in'. Various masks and armour-cased deposits of personality are similarly isolating.

However, Browning was prepared to try and imagine other people whose religious lives (as well as their sexual and artistic lives) were more on display and available as poetic subject. It makes for an interesting religious poetry, but in it religion tends to appear more an issue or an earnest question than a fully lived experience. *Cleon*, *Karshish*, and *Bishop Blougram* are poems of this kind. Cleon has wind of Christian teaching, but his classical mind cannot take it in. Karshish, an Arab physician, puzzles over the implications raised by the resurrected Lazarus who has heard God speak directly to him with a human voice. Karshish is unable to come face to face with Christ since he 'perished in a tumult many years ago'. Blougram is a wily nineteenth-century churchman with a subtle and ingenious mind, difficult to pin down and fully capable of making a plausible defence of his very comfortable life. He is the kind of Roman Catholic cleric who throws plodding Protestant opponents into fits of anger and despair as he run rings round them – rather as Newman did when he defeated Charles Kingsley in that notorious ecclesiastical controversy.[12] Blougram makes out a good case for belief, to which unbelief is contrasted as a kind of nocturnal dream, but in doing so he gives the impression that faith can be embraced on rational and pragmatic grounds, and this certainly breaks with the tradition that sees faith as a gracious gift rather than a convenience. He seems to think that faith can be squared with conscience, but this does not accord with the way in which most theologians have defined faith. There is something very pragmatic about it all:

> Once own the use of faith, I'll find you faith,
> We're back on Christian ground. You call for
>   faith:
> I show you doubt, to prove that faith exists.
> The more of doubt, the stranger faith, I say,
> If faith o'ercomes doubt.
>   (ll. 600–4)

Blougram is condemned because he is a complacent opportunist, but actually detached from its context a good deal of what he says sounds more or less in line with much Victorian thought – those quoted lines are not far from the kind of thing Browning himself might believe. Unlike medieval mystics, who spent all their time trying to see God face to face, Blougram wants veils; he accepts the *deus absconditus* without being too perturbed:

> Some think, Creation's meant to show him forth:
> I say it's meant to hide him all it can.
>   (ll. 653–54)

This is not a view to which Hopkins would give assent. He continues:

> Under a vertical sun, the exposed brain
> And lidless eye and disemprisoned heart
> Less certainly would wither up at once
> Than mind, confronted with the truth of him.
>   (ll. 658–61)

Like a number of Catholic apologists in the nineteenth century Blougram has no nostalgia for the Middle Ages, in which people experienced belief, yet at the same time lied, killed, robbed, and fornicated 'full in belief's face'. At the same time he has retained, in the midst of the rational nineteenth century, a fear of scientific scepticism, so that he tells his listener he 'would rather die than avow' his fear that the liquefaction of Saint Januarius 'may be false'. Catholicism was an issue in the 1840s and 1850s, and R. A. Greenberg has shown that 'A Bishop

Orders His Tomb' says almost as much about contemporary attitudes to a supposedly corrupt Roman Church as about its ostensible period in the High Renaissance.[13] Other poems also fit into Victorian religious debates. 'Caliban Upon Setebos' was regarded at the time as a satire on anthropomorphic theology and on Calvinistic doctrines of predestination.[14]

The longest, and possibly most interesting Browning poems on the subject of religion are *Christmas-Eve and Easter-Day* (1850). They are a study of the different kinds of faith and the variety of evidences for Christianity. The first poem opens in the porch of a dissenting chapel on a rainy winter night. It is set in a squalid and disordered landscape, and the congregation is a collection of grotesques, and includes a 'fat weary woman' in 'a wreck of whalebones' and 'a tall yellow man, like the Penitent Thief'. The narrator is impatient with the revivalist, Low-Church fervour. Outside he is granted a vision of a moon-rainbow, and is swept away to Rome. (It is all a little like the visionary transport in *A Christmas Carol*.) Rome is guilty of 'errors and perversities', but truth still shines through. In section XIII the hero is snatched away again, to a German town – Göttingen perhaps. Here he listens to a theology professor giving a lecture on divinity and examining the evidence for Christianity with all the tools of the higher criticism at hand. The Papists and the Dissenters are in danger of poisoning the air, but the sceptical theologian runs no such risk, since he invites us to live in an airless bell-jar. In Section XXII we are back in the Chapel of Zion again. For the hero it is as if he had never left it; he thinks the preacher is like a vessel holding God's word, and he wishes it had fewer flaws, but concludes that 'the main thing is, does it hold good measure?' He hopes that the Pope and the German professor may ultimately see the light, and recognizes the 'God of Salvation'. In a broad sense, then, the conclusions this poem suggests are orthodox, and it is not hard to understand how many Victorian Christians found Browning on a wavelength not so remote from their own, even though his path to faith is questioning and erratic . *Easter-Day* asserts 'how very hard it is to be a Christian', and the movement of this poem is not unlike Clough's religious musings:

> – And certainly you name the point
> Whereon all turns: for could you joint
> This flexile finite life once tight
> Into the fixed and infinite,
> You, safe inside, would spurn what's out,
> With carelessness enough, no doubt –
> Would spurn mere life: but when time brings
> To their next stage your reasonings

Your eyes, late wide, begin to wink
Nor see the path so well, I think.

(ll. 49–58)

However, it is usually easier to see what Clough is driving at.

In the main poets that we have been considering doubt is the keynote. In its extreme form the pervasive doubt undermined faith not only in God, but in God's image reproduced in man. The enormous perspectives of geological time revealed that man as a species had come onto the scene comparatively recently, and was possibly but one of a long series of dominant beings in the world. This was a severe blow to the classical, medieval, and Renaissance conceptions of the centrality of man in creation, and of the fixity of other species. Hopkins, who in some circumstances might be registered as a survivor from some previous age of faith, was, in this respect, a child of his age, worried that species might have 'no absolute types' and that a sort of evolutionary chromatism threatened fixity.[15] He was sufficiently a traditionalist and sufficiently a romantic, however, to believe that man was 'more highly pitched, selved, and distinctive than anything [else] in the world',[16] although this did not guarantee the everlasting survival of the species. Tennyson recognized the mutability of species, and he was modern enough to be aware of the concepts of geological and astrological time. He refers to 'tracts of fluent heat' which constituted the earth at the dawn of creation (*In Memoriam*, cxviii, 9), but he was sufficiently optimistic to believe, as were some Victorian scientists, that nobler types were possible in the future. Man is possibly 'the herald of a higher race'. A bleaker prospect is entertained, however, by the secularist James Thomson in *City of Dreadful Night*, where the preacher prophesies extinction:

all our wretched race
Shall finish with its cycle, and give place
     To other beings, with their own time-doom
Infinite aeons ere our kind began;
Infinite aeons after the last man
     Has joined the mammoth in earth's tomb and womb.

(xiv. 55–60)

Similarly in the fragment 'Fame' (1874) Tennyson imagines a grim future, in the perspective of geological time:

This London once was middle sea,
     These hills were plains within the past,

> They will be plains again, and we,
> Poor devils, babble 'we shall last.'[17]

It was not even necessary to imagine remote times to see that nature was not easily reconcilable with comforting orthodoxies. Swinburne was aware of its destructive character, and in poems such as 'By the North Sea' and 'On the Cliffs' he celebrates the inexorable cruelty of the sea, which seems to leave little or no room for a benign creator.

There are times, however, when Victorian doubt seems to be less than alarming and disconcerting, and Browning often exhibits a cosy and unchallenging kind of doubt which is almost positive, but in *Easter Day* at least he creates a very telling image, suggesting the possibly extreme limitations of man's knowledge. In religious poetry this is a new note struck, and an indication that in this sphere the Victorians did have something startlingly new to say:

> See the enwrapping rocky niche,
> Sufficient for the sleep in which
> The lizard breathes for ages safe:
> Split the mould – and as light would chafe
> The creature's new world-widened sense,
> Dazzled to death at evidence
> Of all the sounds and sights that broke
> Innumerous at the chisel's stroke, –
> So, in God's eye, the earth's first stuff
> Was, neither more nor less, enough
> To house man's soul, man's need fulfil.
> Man reckoned it immeasurable?
> So thinks the lizard of his vault!
>
> (XXXVI. 53–65)

Notes

1. See U. C. Knoepflmacher, *Religious Humanity and the Victorian Novel* (Princeton, 1965, reprinted 1970) and T. Wright, *The Religion of Humanity: The Impact of Comtean Positivism on Victorian Britain* (Cambridge, 1986).

2. J. Ruskin, *Academy Notes* (1859), in *Works*, XIV, 243.

3. G. Landow, *Shadows and Types: Biblical Typology in Victorian Poetry* (1980).

4. J. H Newman, *Apologia Pro Vita Sua*, edited by A. D. Culler (Boston, 1956), p. 39. See H. Fraser, *Beauty and Belief: Aesthetics and Religion in Victorian Literature* (Cambridge, 1986).

5. J. Keble, *Lectures on Poetry*, translated by E. K. Francis (Oxford, 1912), II, 481.

6. J. Bump, *Gerard Manley Hopkins* (Boston, 1982), pp. 35–38. See also C. Brooks, *Signs for the Times: Symbolic Realism in the Mid-Victorian World* (1984).

7. *Further Letters of Gerard Manley Hopkins*, edited by C. C. Abbott, second edition (1956), p. 17.

8. For the typological reading of 'The Bunch of, Grapes' see J. H. Summers, *George Herbert, His Religion and Art* (1954), pp. 126–28.

9. K. L. Morris, *The Image of the Middle Ages in Romantic and Victorian Literature* (1984).

10. H. Fairchild. *Religious Trends in English Poetry* (New York, 1957), IV, 5.

11. W. B. Yeats, 'Meru' (1934), l. 7

12. C. Kingsley called Newman's intellectual integrity into question in an article in *Macmillan's Magazine* (January 1864). Newman responded in a series of seven articles, April to June 1864. These were republished in book form as *Apologia Pro Vita Sua* (1865), except that the first two, 'Mr. Kingsley's Method of Disputation' and 'The True Mode of Meeting Mr. Kingsley', were dropped.

13. R. A. Greenberg, 'Ruskin, Pugin, and the Contemporary Context of *The Bishop Orders his Tomb*', *PMLA*, 84 (1969), 1588–94.

14. See M. Timko, *Criticism* 7 (1965), 141–50.

15. *The Journals and Papers of Gerard Manley Hopkins*, edited by H. House and G. Storey (1959), p. 120.

16. *The Sermons and Devotional Writings of Gerard Manley Hopkins*, edited by C. Devlin (1959, reprinted 1967), p. 122

17. Not in *The Poems of Tennyson*, edited by C. Ricks (1969; Second Edition 1987), but printed in *Alfred Lord Tennyson: A Memoir*, edited by H. Tennyson (1897), II, 165.

Chapter 14
The City

The city has long been a key topic for poets – which is not to be wondered at since it is the focal point and principal manifestation of civilization and its arts. When man is in an extrovert and sociable mood, 'towered cities please us then/And the busy hum of men' – as Milton puts it in *Il Pensoroso*. The very word 'civilization' implies city, or *civis*. And in its perfected and transcendental form a city was envisioned as the home for heavenly societies, the Heavenly City or *Civitas Dei* of which Saint Augustine writes. The earthly city could often afford a glimpse of what the eternal city might be – especially when seen from a distance – but more usually it was a violent and depressing contrast, and in classical times pastoral poetry and poetry of retirement developed in response to the range of negative urban images. This turning of the poetic back on the city has been a pervasive feature of many poetic traditions, and it continues in the Victorian period – too emphatically according to one critic, G. Robert Stange.[1]

In classical times, however, the city did not always repel its poets; sometimes it attracted them to celebrate its diversity, its multitudinousness, its squalor, its vices, its rich and teeming life. We have seen in Chapter 10 how for some practitioners apparently repellent and unpoetic subjects are precisely what goads them into poetic expression, and the response of poets such as Horace and Juvenal exemplifies this. The city can provide astonishing juxtapositions, startling grotesques, and vivid evidences of the operation of the human will with a frequency and a density simply not possible in the country, and for many poets this richness has been a necessary source. *The Canterbury Tales* takes us on a journey from an earthly city to a heavenly one, and the reader feels that in the Middle Ages only the kind of focal point which cities could offer would bring so diverse a group of people into the company of each other, and it is the juxtaposition of varying types and the ensuing friction which is the life-force of the poem. To use terms which run through this study like a skein of coloured yarn, Chaucer is not in pursuit of beauty but significance, and something like this is true of many of our more interesting poets.

Poets of great fastidiousness and learning (one thinks of Donne, Jonson, and Pope) have been inexorably drawn by the magnetism of London, perhaps in part because of their classical learning: almost everything in the city was antipathetic to their learned and discriminating tastes, but there was the challenge of classical precedent and the recognition that the swarming and chaotic life demanded some sort of creative process and in any case was a healthy antidote to too much order and limitation.[2] Cleanliness and neatness may have been attributes much prized by these poets, yet there is a marked prevalence of *la nostalgie de le boue* in Jonson's 'On the Famous Voyage', Pope's *Dunciad*, and Swift's 'Description of a City Shower'. Pope recommended values of retirement, enlightened rural economy, and the life of the mind nurtured by learning, but as Maynard Mack shows in *The Garden and the City: Retirement and Politics in the Later Poetry of Pope 1713–1743* (Toronto, 1969) his distance from the city was carefully judged, so that at Twickenham (eight miles from Hyde Park Corner) he could be relatively close to his material. He also had to comply with laws relating to Catholics. For Renaissance poets the actual city could be the home for loose and dissolute behaviour and a whole range of offensive sense-impressions. When Satan arrives in Eden after leaving hell the experience is analogous to the man who has been long in populous City pent, 'Where Houses thick and Sewers annoy the Aire' and escapes 'to breathe/Among the pleasant Villages and Farmes' (*Paradise Lost*, IX. 445–48). But this was the image of the city in its fallen or unideal state; the other side of the coin was not forgotten, of the prospect of the heavenly city and the belief in human regeneration through the agency of the arts of civilization. Milton's London could obviously be very noxious and depraved, but escape was always readily at hand; at this time Lincoln's Inn Fields actually were fields.

Some time in the mid-eighteenth century there was a reorientation of the images. The negative images of the city (which of course had always been available) received a new accentuation by poets whose ideal environments were rural rather than urban and who placed more faith in the tuition of nature than of society. Principal of these was Cowper, originator of the famous tag 'God made the country and man made the town'. In *The Task*, Book III, he paints a lurid vision of the modern city as a sort of Sodom. As the Industrial Revolution got under way conditions worsened. In 'Clifton Grove' (1803) Henry Kirke White, like Paul Morel and Clara Dawes a century later, escapes from the grime of Nottingham, where 'manufacture taints the ambient skies' (l. 20) to the pastoral seclusion of the 'murmuring Trent'. When in 'Frost at Midnight' Coleridge envisages an ideal habitat for his infant son it is to be different from his own:

For I was reared
In the great city, pent 'mid cloisters dim,
And saw nought lovely but the sky and stars.

(ll. 51–53)

In 'This Lime Tree Bower My Prison' he is sorry that his friend
Charles Lamb has 'pined,/And hungered after Nature, many a year,/In
the great City pent'. In both of these instances there is an echo of
Milton. Wordsworth considered himself more fortunate in the circumstances of his upbringing than Coleridge: 'I did not pine like one in
cities bred,/As was thy melancholy lot, dear friend!' (*The Prelude*
VIII. 433–34).

In *The Prelude* the city represents a monstrous wrong turning which
mankind has taken, and which Wordsworth could have taken had he
been less fortunate. Ben Jonson was able to surrender himself sufficiently to Bartholomew Fair to make something creative and vibrant
out of it; Wordsworth feels that he has to hold disturbing images of
the city at arm's length. However, he does know his London, and does
not go in for vague denunciation; there are in fact in Book VII of *The
Prelude* some powerful and concrete depictions of the teeming variety
of the city. The fair is the 'true epitome' of the city, without law,
meaning, and end. It fails to present him any prospect of a desirable
image of corporate life – for that he has to retreat to the Lakeland fair,
where all is ordered and everyone is known, where there are stalls, but
no booths (VIII. 25). In *Michael* the prodigal son loses himself in the
dissolute city and the effects of ruin radiate even into the remote countryside. French cities during the Revolution had summoned up images
of a kind of hell on earth, and had created a momentum of evil which
he did not believe possible in smaller communities. To survive as an
integrated human being Wordsworth has to rely on the ordering power
derived from Nature, its 'Composure, and ennobling Harmony'. The
city is more acceptable in early morning, viewed from Westminster
Bridge, when it has ceased to resemble a mill vomiting people, and
is now more reminiscent of a pastoral landscape. The problem with
this image (which Wordsworth's readers might worry about more than
he did himself) is that the sleeping state of the city could be regarded
as a sort of death-in-life, and to present the city in this somnolent state
is to evade the challenge of the city as an invigorating subject. Even
a sociable urbanite like Byron evinces the stock Romantic response;
where Milton found 'the busy hum of men' pleasant, for Byron 'the
hum/Of human cities torture' (*Childe Harold*, III, 72. 3–4).

It is no exaggeration to say that Wordsworth is frightened of the
city, and G. R. Stange follows this motif through the Victorian poets
in his essay 'The Frightened Poets in the Victorian City'. His thesis

is that the nineteenth-century poets took over the Romantic Movement attitudes too readily, perhaps because they were also frightened, perhaps because they inherited a set of attitudes which cultivated the private, the individual, the alienated, and the organic, thereby blinding themselves to the creative possibilities offered by the city. In short, they failed to make the kind of excited response to the city that we find in Baudelaire and, closer to home, Dickens. Stange considers that the particular kind of education and upbringing experienced by poets such as Tennyson, Clough, Arnold, Swinburne, and Morris, mainly in the countryside and the small towns of Oxford and Cambridge, predisposed them to hate or neglect the city. The one major poet with a city upbringing, Browning, unfortunately spent too much of his life in Florence, which, in comparison to metropolitan London, was like a cosy overgrown village. There is much to support Stange's view, but it is in many ways a partial article – witness the fact that it does not even mention the one poem that is in sight of a vision on a Baudelairean scale – Thomson's *The City of Dreadful Night*. (A fuller view of the treatment of the theme is given by William B. Thesing in *The London Muse: Victorian Responses to the City* (Athens, Georgia, 1982).)

Stange is particularly perturbed that Tennyson turned his back on the city as a possible poetic theme, and found almost nothing positive or lively to say about it. He seems more interested in the visionary city of Camelot – not built by human hand. The nadir of Tennyson's emotional life is set in a street characterized by visionary dreariness:

> Dark house, by which once more I stand
> Here in the long unlovely street,
> Doors, where my heart was used to beat
> So quickly, waiting for a hand
>
> (*In Memoriam*, VII. 1–4)

As his state of mind improves and the grief is changed into something else the street in which the Hallam family lived is strangely transformed:

> I come once more; the city sleeps;
> I smell the meadow in the street;
>
> I hear a chirp of birds; I see
> Betwixt the black fronts long-withdrawn
> A light-blue lane of early dawn,
> And think of early days and thee
>
> (CXIX. 3–8)

By a trick of light and a trick of the imagination the grim street is made pastoral in the early dawn; it is an experience like Wordsworth's 'Westminster Bridge' sonnet. It is not that the experience is invalid or unimportant, but one would not wish it to be the last word on Victorian London, and a contemporary of Tennyson's living in that same street, Wimpole Street, responded much more vigorously to the immediate environment. A powerful scene, for instance, is the nightmare meeting of the people from the slums of St Giles with the gentry from St James in Book IV of *Aurora Leigh*, and in Book III. 169–201 she presents a panoramic vision that seems to owe something to the John Martin sublime. But Tennyson is not able to be an observer or a connoisseur of what the city has to offer. A typically alarmed response is 'Beautiful City' (1889):

> Beautiful city, the centre and crater of European
> confusion,
> O you with your passionate shriek for the rights
> of an equal humanity,
> How often your Re-volution has proven but
> E-volution
> Rolled again back on itself in the tides of
> a civic insanity!
>
> (ll. 1–4)

Tennyson is thinking here of the French Revolution, of the Revolution of 1848, and the Paris Commune of 1871. There was an undercurrent of fear that revolution would break out in this country. Hopkins was worried by 'Loafers, Tramps, Cornerboys, Roughs, Socialists and other pests of society',[3] and in 'Tom's Garland' expresses his fear of the 'Man wolf' whose 'packs infest the age'. He saw the grim northern towns close at hand when he was a parish priest in Leigh, Lancashire, in 1879 and in Liverpool. In some of the most famous lines of the century Morris imagines London in its small, clean, fourteenth-century state rather than its large and dirty nineteenth-century manifestation (see above p. 105). Morris had a horror of the modern city, expressed most vividly in *The Pilgrims of Hope* (1885–86). London is a 'grim net', and its inhabitants do not live in homes but 'lairs' or 'dens'. Morris is known as a social reformer, and undoubtedly he loved individual men and woman, but urban humanity *en masse* appalled him:

> Dull and with hang-dog gait they stood or shuffled
> along,

While the stench from the lairs they had lain in last
    night went up in the wind.
And poisoned the sun-lit spring.
                      (ll. 176–70)

At times, with its heightened squalor and gloom, the city Morris
describes resembles Thomson's City of Dreadful Night. The hero of
the poem has imbibed from his mother the attitude that many men on
earth resemble the 'growth of creeping things' that quickens on 'the
fabled mud of the Nile'. Dreams of the future take place in the squalid
surroundings, and the ironies of the violent contrasts between present
reality and visionary hope are reminiscent of Henry James's exactly
contemporary work The Princess Casamassima (1886). However,
Morris's deepest hatred is reserved for the bourgeois capitalists who
fill 'the gaudy shops' with useless objects, and organize the war
machine. The positives in the poem are principally rural, and there are
intensely evocative pastoral idyllic scenes in a countryside that sounds
very like the Upper Thames Valley around Kelmscott.

And yet the poem embodies a dream that the city might be
redeemed. There is a prevision of it when the hero, his wife, and his
friend Arthur (who contains combined elements of Rossetti and
Ruskin) go to Paris in 1871 to participate in the revolution of the
communards:

And we stopped and turned to each other, and as each at
    each did we gaze,
The city's hope enwrapped us with joy and great amaze
                      (ll. 1016–17)

It resembles the optimistic moments in Orwell's Homage to Catalonia,
all too soon to be overturned and betrayed. Yet the memory of the
vision persists.

Faced with London and other large cities the poets seemed to suffer
something like a failure of nerve, but one should remember that
London had changed, even from the city the early Romantics had
known. It had expanded, largely without planning, and it had attracted
to itself thousands of people displaced from the land but possessing no
way of coping with chaotic city life. Conditions were unbelievably
squalid, and grim palls of smoke hung over it all for large parts of the
year. We should be cautious about accepting Gustave Doré's illustrations to Blanchard Jerrold's London: A Pilgrimage (1872) as literally true,
but his work indicates that London offered hints to visionary artists
who wanted to depict a city gripped by a gruesome and sublime
despair. Dickens likewise is not offering us a photographic represen-

tation, but his nightmarish city grows from something lodged in the mind of a sensitive observer, which finds an echo in the external world. Occasionally middle-class persons would make forays into the slums (sometimes like the journalist James Greenwood in Orwellian disguise)[4] and return with tales of unimaginable squalor. And often the grim outcast life was going on cheek-by-jowl with the life of privilege and ease – as the shocked Nathaniel Hawthorne and Henry James noted.[5] The city seemed to have a life of its own, a sort of gruesome potency; De Quincey writes in *Autobiography from 1785 to 1803* of the tremendous force of 'suction' – dragging people in, as if to the centre of some imprisoning web.[6]

Ruskin's horror was expressed many times, but here are two typical examples: first in 'The Study of Architecture in Our Schools' (1865):

> But our cities, built in black air which, by its
> accumulated foulness, first renders all ornament invisible in
> distance, and then chokes its interstices with soot; cities
> which are mere crowded masses of store, and warehouse,
> and counter, and are therefore to the rest of the world
> what the larder and cellar are to a private house; cities in
> which the object of men is not life, but labour; and in
> which all chief magnitude of edifice is to enclose
> machinery; cities in which the streets are not the avenues
> for the passing and procession of a happy people, but the
> drains for the discharge of a tormented mob, in which the
> only object in reaching any spot is to be transferred to
> another; in which existence become mere transition, and
> every creature is only one atom in a drift of human dust,
> and current of interchanging particles.[7]

And secondly his lecture to the British Institution, 'On the Present State of Modern Art, with Reference to the Advisable Arrangements of a National gallery . . .' (1867):

> our real wealth and progress in creative power are
> indicated only by Babylonian wildernesses of brickfield,
> white with slime, by a continually festering cancer of
> waste ground among skeletons of buildings, rotten before
> they are inhabited, and by the extending procession,
> wherever there was once cleanliness or dignity and peace,
> of the unclean paling, frescoed only by the bill-sticker
> with pictures of talking heads fallen from the guillotine,
> and advertisements of cheap clothes at the sign of the Bon
> Diable.[8]

Hopkins, who saw Victorian cities at close hand, working as a ministering priest, wrote:

> My Liverpool and Glasgow experience laid upon my mind
> a conviction, a truly crushing conviction, of the misery of
> town life to the poor and more than to the poor, of the
> misery of the poor in general, of the degradation even of
> our race, of the hollowness of this century's civilisation: it
> made even life a burden to me to have daily thrust upon
> me the things I saw.[9]

His horror of the impress of man is expressed in 'God's Grandeur':

> Generations have trod, have trod;
>   And all is seared with trade; bleared,
>   smeared with toil;
>   And wears man's smudge and shares man's
>   smell: the soil
> Is bare now, nor can foot feel, being shod.
>
>   (ll. 5–8)

The human prospect was of a piece with the urban scene. There were tens of thousands of prostitutes in London,[10] but few poets were able to depict them – although Rossetti (who was in fact very much an urban figure) does attempt to do justice to one of the women in 'Jenny'.

Fear of the city was directly related to fear of the mob, fear of mass violence. Occasionally there were eruptions, and although historians can produce cogent reasons for the absence of large-scale revolutionary movements in nineteenth-century Britain, it is difficult to explain why there was not more sporadic and spontaneous violence and hooliganism, as an instinctive response to intolerable living conditions, Somehow it was held in check, but Dickens's novels, *Barnaby Rudge*, *Oliver Twist*, and *A Tale of Two Cities* for instance, give voice to widespread fears. When Ruskin was in a theatre he marvelled that the fragile barriers segregating different sections of the audience did not suddenly give way:

> I never stand up to rest myself, and look round the
> house, without renewal of wonder how the crowd in the
> pit, and shilling gallery, allow us of the boxes and stalls to
> keep our places! Think of it; – those fellows behind there
> have housed us and fed us; their wives have washed our
> clothes, and kept us tidy; – they have bought us the best

places, – brought us through the cold to them; and there
they sit behind us, patiently, seeing and hearing what they
may. There they pack themselves, squeezed and distant,
behind our chairs; – we, their elect toys and pet puppets,
oiled and varnished, and incensed, lounge in front,
placidly, or for the greater part, wearily and sickly
contemplative.[11]

For poets like Tennyson and Arnold what *was* to be done with all
this but forget it? Arnold had expressed his fears of the unruliness of
the 'populace' in *Culture and Anarchy* (1869). Or perhaps the sensitive
poet could experience some intensely private upsurge of emotion when
everyone else was in bed, as Tennyson does in *In Memoriam* and
Arnold does in 'A Summer Night' (1852):

> In the deserted, moon-blanched street,
> How lonely rings the echo of my feet!
> Those windows, which I gaze at, frown,
> Silent and white, unopening down,
> Repellent as the world; – but see,
> A break between the housetops shows
> The moon! and, lost behind her, fading dim
> Into the dewy dark obscurity
> Down at the far horizon's rim,
> Doth a whole tract of heaven disclose!
>
> And to my mind the thought
> Is on a sudden brought
> Of a past night, and a far different scene.
> Headlands stood out into the moonlit deep
> As clearly as at noon;
> The spring-tide's brimming flow
> Heaved dazzlingly between;
>
> (ll. 1–17)

He is transported in the imagination from London, or some large
English city, to a beautiful Mediterranean city.

However, the inescapable presence of this great sprawling Babylon
haunted some poets and critics. Writing his article 'Modern Giants' in
the Pre-Raphaelite magazine *The Germ*, F. G. Stephens thought that
the modern city cried out for poetic and artistic treatment:

> there is the poetry of things about us; our railways,
> factories, mines, roaring cities, steam vessels, and the

endless novelties and wonders produced every day; which
if they were found only in the Thousand and One Nights,
or in any poem classical or romantic, would be gloried
over without end; for as the majority of us know not a bit
more about them, but merely their names, we keep up the
same mystery, the main thing required for the surprise of
the imagination.[12]

As if rising to the challenge William Michael Rossetti wrote 'Mrs.
Holmes Grey' according to a 'principle of strict accuracy', and Dante
Gabriel Rossetti produced some startlingly immediate depictions of
scenes from his French and Flemish trip of September 1849. Indeed, the
description of the morgue in 'The Paris Railway-Station' is one of the
most startlingly vivid pieces in the whole of Victorian literature:

> The face was black,
> And, like a negro's, swollen; all the flesh
> Had furred, and broken into a green mould.
>   Now, very likely, he who did the job
> Was standing among those who stood with us,
> To look upon the corpse. You fancy him –
> Smoking an early pipe, and watching, as
> An artist, the effect of his last work.
>
> (ll. 9–16)

One sees here at once an intense realism and the seeds of the extreme
decadence and detached aestheticism that was so dominant in the last
decade of the century: Rossetti imagines the murderer as an artist – but
working in the medium of human flesh. One recalls the decadent
theme of murder considered as one of the fine arts.[13] But the
unflinching observation recorded in this strange and vivid Rossetti
poem was fully in line with a part of the Pre-Raphaelite programme,
and in addition to being an other-worldly visionary Rossetti was an
intensely urban being, and a connoisseur of the latest slang. 'Did the
job' here has an urban raciness, and we should not forget that the Pre-
Raphaelite lovelies were not solely *princesses lointaines*; they were also,
to use a piece of up-to-date slang, 'stunners', whose portraits were
flogged off to any patron with the ready 'tin'.

Clough made similar recommendations that poets should turn to
the city for subject-matter in his famous review of Arnold's poetry and
Alexander Smith's *Life Drama:*

> There are moods when one is prone to believe that,
> in the last days, no longer by 'clear spring or shady

grove', no more upon any Pindus or Parnassus, or by the side of any Castaly, are the true and lawful haunts of the poetic powers; but, we could believe it, if anywhere, in the blank and desolate streets, and upon the solitary bridges of the midnight city, where Guilt is, and wild Temptation, and the dire Compulsion of what has once been done – there, with these tragic sisters around him, and with pity also, and pure compassion, and pale Hope, that looks like despair, and Faith in the garb of doubt, there walks the discrowned Apollo, with unstrung lyre; nay, and could he sound it, those mournful Muses would scarcely be able, as of old, to respond and 'sing in turn with their beautiful voices'.[14]

Even an ivory tower figure like Pater could write that, 'life in modern London . . . is stuff sufficient for the fresh imagination of a youth to build its "palace of art" of'.[15] To some extent Clough did try to rise to the challenge of the city, especially in *Dipsychus*, where prostitutes continually threaten to undermine the virtue of the hero, and in *Amours de Voyage*, where a violent political murder is acted out in the streets of Rome with a vividness and an immediacy that it would be hard to match in the rest of Victorian poetry. But Clough did not bring his urbane and intellectually sceptical style into collision with the enormities of outcast London, which is probably just as well. Curiously, when Clough came to describe the city he does not follow his own portentous programme, but produces something altogether more direct and closely observed; in *The Bothie* there is this extended epic simile:

> But as the light of day enters some populous city,
> Shaming away, ere it comes, by the chilly day-streak
>   signal,
> High and low, the misusers of night, shaming out the gas-
>   lamps –
> All the great empty streets are flooded with broadening
>   clearness,
> Which, withal, by inscrutable simultaneous access
>   Permeates far and pierces to the very cellars lying in
> Narrow high back-lane, and court, and alley of alleys: –
> He that goes forth to his walk, while speeding to the
>   suburb,
> Slowly to work, in their limbs the lingering sweetness of
>   slumber;
> Humble market-carts, coming-in, bring-in, not only

Flower, fruit, farm-store, but sounds and sights of the
country
Dwelling yet on the sense of the dreamy drivers; soon
after
Half-awake servant-maids unfastening drowsy shutters
Up at the windows, or down, letting-in the air by the
doorway;
School-boys, school-girls soon, with slate, portfolio,
satchel,
Hampered as they haste, those running, these others
maidenly tripping;
Early clerk anon turning out to stroll, or it may be
Meet his sweetheart – waiting behind the garden gate
there;
Merchant on his grass-plat haply, bare-headed; and now
by this time
Little child bring breakfast to 'father' that sits on the
timber
There by the scaffolding; see, she waits for the can beside
him;
Meanwhile above purer air untarnished of new-lit fires:
So that the whole great wicked artificial civilized fabric –
All its unfinished houses, lots for sale, and railway
outworks –
Seems reaccepted, resumed to Primal Nature and
Beauty: –
– Such – in me, and to me, and on me the love of
Elspie!
         (ix. 82–108)

This is a beautiful and effective piece of writing, but one can see how
it might fall foul of Stange, since it adopts some of the strategies of
Wordsworth's 'Westminister Bridge' sonnet: that is, the poem
responds positively to the city at those points where it is reminiscent
of the country, and where its ugliness is glazed over by a purer, transforming, irradiating light. The other attitude which might displease
Stange is that Clough (or rather, Clough's fictional character) cannot
bring himself to face the humanity of the city *en masse*, concentrating
instead on individuals. It is a device for keeping the enormity and
nightmare of the city at bay, and was adopted by other Victorian poets
of city life. Robert Buchanan's *London Poems* (1866) is not about the
pulsating anonymity of the mob, but about particular individuals.

  In fact the heady and over-written allegorical recommendations in
Clough's review are satisfied by at least one Victorian work: James

Thomson's *City of Dreadful Night*. Parts of the work had been published in 1867, but the completed version, with its various revisions, appeared in book form between 1870 and 1874. The city is nightmare-like and generalized, an exercise in the lugubrious sublime. Thomson knew this, and said that 'a penny steam boat will not carry one to a city where the people are all petrified'.[16] The book is influenced by a range of grim texts, from Job to the *Divina Commedia*, and the description of the River of Suicides is certainly Dantean in tone:

> The mighty river flowing dark and deep,
>   With ebb and flood from the remote sea-tides
> Vague-sounding through the City's sleepless sleep,
>   Is named the River of the Suicides;
> For night by night some lorn wretch overweary,
> And shuddering from the future yet more dreary,
>   Within its cold secure oblivion hides.
>
>   (XIX. 1–7)

In Section XII the poet imagines 'writing a great work with patient plan/To justify the ways of God to man' (a project reminiscent of Milton's), but then he wakes up from what has been a delusory daydream to find that he is in the stony city of real night. A sermon is preached in an irreligious 'mighty fane' and the 'Good tidings of great joy' delivered to those 'bent or recumbent in secluded stalls' is that 'There is no God'. Not unsurprisingly Thomson was published in the atheistical *National Reformer*.

Sometimes this work has a tart aphoristic touch that reminds one of Fitzgerald's *Rubáiyát*. Section XX is a splendid surrealistic episode in which the statue of an angel with a sword crashes down to fall between the paws of a sphinx – all by moonlight of course. One feels this was written for those whose tastes in painting would run to an artist like John Martin. However, it is all somewhat remote from the precision of Clough's London in the prose-poem 'A Sunday Morning Contemplation' (a piece whose rich texture of literary reminiscence adumbrates Eliot and Pound) where 'Goodge St. is still Goodge St. at right angles to Berners Street, that go where I will and how many times soever as I may, this angular positivity abides and is positive', so that he is driven to conclude, 'is it not a thing to drive a man to distraction?'.[17] By contrast, even in one of Thomson's more realistic poems, such as 'Sunday at Hampstead' or 'Sunday up the River', the transforming sense of dream or reverie is there:

> Was it truly a fact or a dream, my Love?
>   I think my brain still reels,

And my ears still throbbing seem, my Love,
   With the rush and the clang of wheels;
      Of a vast machinery roaring
      For ever in skyless gloom;
      Where the poor slaves peace imploring
      Found peace alone in the tomb.
                 ('Sunday at Hampstead', ll. 73–80)

In 'William Blake' he imagines his great predecessor wandering up and down 'in this desert of brick and stone', but unlike Blake he does not see the potential for *his* city to be transformed to a New Jerusalem by a strong imagination.

Other poets also registered the city as a kind of hell on earth, and in certain instances it did not perhaps need any great gifts of imagination to see it as such. The public hangings were a macabre spectacle, which drew Dickens back time and time again. Coventry Patmore has a powerful poem on this aspect of urban life:

The rabble's lips no longer cursed,
But stood agape with horrid thirst;
Thousands of breasts beat horrid hope:
Thousands of eyeballs, lit with hell,
Burnt one way all, to see the rope
Unslacken as the platform fell.
The rope flew tight; and then the roar
Burst forth afresh, less loud, but more
Confused and affrighting than before.
                 (ll. 21–29)

The 1853 version of this poem, 'A London Fête ', ends with the spectators who can afford it celebrating in those very Victorian institutions, gin-shops. Another striking poem that should be mentioned, responding as it does to the crime and sensationalism of the city, is Henry Cholmondeley Pennell's 'The Night Mail North (Euston Square, 1840)' (reprinted in J. R. Watson's anthology). This depicts the dramatic events and hair's-breadth timing which are daily events in the railway age, as a sportsman, a criminal, the father of an errant daughter, and a clerk carrying a reprieve are desperate to catch the train:

Through the mist and the dark and the driving
      sleet,
    As if life and death were in it,

> 'Tis a splendid race! a race against Time –
> And a thousand to one we win it.
>
> (ll. 52–55)

Human beings in the mass have a tendency to frighten and discon-
cert, and as I have already suggested the more sympathetic Victorian
city poems look at individuals, rather as Henry Mayhew sought out
representative individuals whose speech and other particularities could
be transcribed.[18] So in Arnold's 'East London' (1867) the poet meets
a preacher who is trying to bring 'everlasting light' to Bethnal Green,
and in 'West London' (1867) a beggar in Belgrave Square seeks alms
from working men rather than aristocrats, since she has an instinctive
sense that they are 'aliens'. Disraeli's 'two nations' have not drawn any
closer together. The Arnold poems are not much good, but they
almost certainly do grow from specifically observed incidents. Nothing
in Victorian poetry though has the haunting and typological authority
of the blind beggar Wordsworth encounters in the London of *The
Prelude*, Book VII.

In our period, up to 1890, it is almost certainly the case, in Stange's
words, that no poet made the city into 'a convincing milieu of spiritual
adventures',[19] in other words that no English poet did for English cities
what Baudelaire did for Paris and Whitman did for Manhattan. In the
1890s, however, the scene changed, and a whole string of collections
celebrated the newly discovered poetic possibilities of London: W. E.
Henley's *London Voluntaries* (1893) and *London Types* (1898), John
Davidson's *Fleet Street Eclogues* (1893), Ernest Rhys's *A London Rose*
(1894), Arthur Symons's *London Nights* (1895), and Laurence Binyon's
London Visions (1896). These poets recaptured some of the lyrical self-
confidence of urban and urbane eighteenth-century poets and found the
city a convenient reversal of everything that the previous generation
had found poetic. Symons's Prologue to *Days and Nights* (1889) is a
sort of anti-Tennysonian Palace of Art. These 1890s poets are the
immediate precursors of Pound and Eliot. Arthur Symons stated the
case very emphatically in his easay 'Modernity in Verse': 'And I think
that might be the test of poetry which professes to be modern: its
capacity for dealing with London, with what one sees or might see
there, indoors and out.'[20] This is not the place to assess those 1890s
collections, but one questions whether the devices, mannerisms, and
attitudinizing poses adopted to deal with the city were finally adequate
response to the enormity and sheer horror of the real thing. Perhaps
the Victorian poets were right to be frightened. In 1876, in *On London
Stones*, Austin Dobson wrote:

> Mine is an urban Muse, and bound
> By some strange law to paven ground;

> Abroad she pouts; – she is not shy
> > On London stones!
> > > (ll. 12–15)

In the later decades of the century many other poets assumed this posture, but the various strategies they employed for transforming the city into appropriate poetic material often continued the evasiveness which Stange regrets in the great Victorians.

Notes

1. G. R. Stange, 'The Frightened Poets', in *The Victorian City: Images and Realities*, edited by H. J. Dyos and M. Wolff, 2 vols (1973), II, 475–94.

2. B. Everett, 'Donne as a City Poet', *PBA*, 58 (1972), 245–73.

3. *The Letters of Gerard Manley Hopkins of Robert Bridges*, edited by C. C. Abbott (1955), p. 274.

4. For J. Greenwood's trip to the depths of London see 'A Night in a Workhouse', *Pall Mall Gazette*, III (12, 13, 15 January 1866), 137–38, 150, 161–62. The article has been reprinted in Peter Keating's anthology *Into Unknown England, 1866–1913; Selections from the Social Explorers* (Manchester, 1976).

5. See N. Hawthorne, 'Outside Glimpses at English Poverty', in *Our Old Home* (1863), pp. 232–58, and the H. James story 'A London Life' (1888).

6. De Quincey, *The Collected Writings of Thomas De Quincey*, edited by David Masson (1890), I, 178.

7. J. Ruskin, *Works*, XIX, 21.

8. Ruskin, *Works*, XIX, 210.

9. *The Correspondence of Gerard Manley Hopkins and Richard Watson Dixon*, edited by C. C. Abbott (1935, reprinted 1955, 1970), p. 97.

10. See S. Marcus, *The Other Victorians* (1964), for estimates of the numbers.

11. J. Ruskin, *Fors Clavigera*, 61 (January 1876), in *Works*, XXVIII, 490.

12. *The Germ*, [4 (May 1850)], edited by A. Rose (Oxford and Birmingham, 1979), pp. 170–71.

13. There is De Quincey's article 'On Murder Considered as One of the Fine Arts' (1827), in *Works* XIII, 9–124, and Oscar Wilde's 'Pen, Pencil and Poison: A Study in Green' (reviewing the life of Thomas Griffiths Wainewright) in *Complete Works of Oscar Wilde* (1966), 993–1008.

14. A. H. Clough, 'Recent English Poetry', *North American Review*, 77 (July 1853), in *Victorian Poetry and Poetics*, edited by W. E. Houghton and G. R. Stange, second edition (Boston, 1968), p. 397.

15. W. Pater, *Marius the Epicurean*, Ch. 16, in *Works*, III, 17.

16. J. Thomson apropos of his poem *The Voyage*.

17. The strangely Modernist piece is reprinted in K. Biswas, *Arthur Hugh Clough: Towards a Reconsideration* (Oxford, 1972), pp. 424–27.

18. See H. Mayhew, *London Labour and the London Poor* (1851, expanded 1861–62; 1864).

19. Stange, II, 491.

20. A. Symons, *Studies in Two Literatures* (1897), p. 188.

Chapter 15
Adumbrations of Modernism

New poetic movements demand that the immediate past be relegated
to the lumber-room, since the claim is that there has been a decisive
break with the values of the previous generation. Generations further
back pose less of a threat, and Modernism was not so extreme as to
wish to break with all traditions; it was the practices of the Victorians
that seemed to be particularly alarming. The usual explanation for this
alarm has been that the Victorians has established codes of poetic practice which were utterly antipathetic to Pound and Eliot, that they were
personal and subjective where the moderns wished to be impersonal
and objective, that they were concerned with expressing ideas and
opinions, and that poetic language was regarded by them as a functional tool rather than an entity with its own expressive possibilities.
The moderns could only flourish by ousting their fathers and re-
educating the literary audience. Recent history was a 'burden' as W. J.
Bate put it, and he argues that 'the remorseless deepening of self-
consciousness, before the rich and intimidating legacy of the past, has
become the great single problem that modern art . . . has had to face'.[1]
It was necessary for their survival and their sense of identity that the
recent history should be rewritten and the poets 'misread' – to use
Bloomean terminology.[2] But now that Modernism is increasingly
remote from us, and regarded as one more in a long line of historical
periods, we are able to see it in a more detached light, and to recognize
that the Modernists were to some degree alarmed by the Victorians
not because they were very different from themselves, but because they
were quite similar.

In the writing of Pound and Eliot one does in fact witness a piecemeal
recognition of this. Eliot, for instance, thought that criteria of objectivity could be promoted by invoking a classical rather than a romantic
aesthetic[3]; in this he resembled his fellow-countryman Irving Babbitt.[4]
So it was necessary for him to make serious qualifications about Blake:
'What his genius required, and what it sadly lacked, was a frame-work
of accepted and traditional ideas which would have prevented him
from indulging in a philosophy of his own, and concentrated his attention upon the problems of the poet.'[5]

But qualifications of that kind had been made in the Victorian period by Arnold (see above pp. 17–18) and there was a tradition of classicism then. Eliot knew this of course, and quotes Arnold on many occasions. Subjectivism was a *bête noire* of the Modernists, but then, the Victorians did not always cultivate it, and the employment of the dramatic monologue was an indication of their quest for something which would enable them to escape from the prison-house of self. Pound recognized the importance of the genre as a mode of liberation from disabling inwardness. He said, in his review of *Prufrock and Other Observations* (1917), that it was 'the most vital form of that period'.[6] The use of mask and persona and the creation of image and symbol to convey autonomous experience are well known as Modernist devices, but they were used by the Victorians, as this study has emphasized many times. The Modernists tended to see the Victorians as an extension of the Romantics, but without the verve and originality of their predecessors; whereas we are increasingly coming to see that although there is a continuity between the Romantics and the Victorians, the real dividing line between modern poetry and traditional poetry should not be drawn at 1910 but 1830–40. It was necessary for Pound to believe that, with the exception of George Crabbe, there had been no realism in the previous 150 years: 'Since the death of Laurence Sterne or thereabouts, there has been neither in England nor America any sufficient sense of the value of realism in literature, of the value of writing words that conform precisely with fact, of free speech without evasions and circumlocutions.'[7]

But Pound knew that this was not entirely the case, witness the influence Browning had on him.

It is possible that the early Modernists produced their Aunt Sally image of the Victorians not by thinking of the great Victorians, such as Tennyson and Browning, but by recalling their immediate 1890s predecessors, in whose hands the poetic traditions became threadbare and decadent. *Fin de siècle* poetry, thought Richard Aldington, had become 'turgid and boresome and sloppy and wordy'. Eliot and Pound are examples of extreme Modernists who found it necessary to disown the immediate past, but in the case of Yeats the process is less emphatic. He was, after all, pretty well in the swim of the late Victorian poetic tradition as a poetic tyro, and his qualified entry into the Modernist tradition was a matter of evolution, revision, and adaptation rather than out-and-out rejection of his predecessors. He wished to escape from the Parnassian tradition:

> I tried from then on to write out of my emotions exactly
> as they came to me in life, not changing them to make
> them more beautiful. 'If I can be sincere and make my

language natural, and without becoming discursive, like a
novelist, and so indiscreet and prosaic', I said to myself, 'I
shall, if good luck or bad luck make my life interesting,
be a great poet; for it will be no longer a matter of
literature at all.'[8]

This extract reveals how complicated literary categorization is, since
on the one hand it seems to recommend an expressive aesthetic, and
to invoke the old bogey of 'sincerity'[9] but on the other hand it takes
one into the realms of the 'anti-poetic' that have characterized
Modernism (with the proviso that not all Modernists would have
wished to draw on the support of the 'natural' in their search for the
arresting phrase). Hardy has constantly been regarded as an important
figure in this study – as a poet who in many senses connects Victorian
poetry with poetry since 1945, but almost bypassing Modernism altogether, especially in his espousal of a disconcerting sincerity and his
attachment to a poetic that does not break with the Victorians. At the
same time he has a starkness of outlook and an impatience with the
decorative and the self-indulgent that makes him seem not so very
different, sometimes, from the Modernists. Hopkins is a further
anomaly, treated virtually as a Modernist when his collected works
were first published, and yet seen increasingly by us as a great
Victorian.[10]

The general drift of this study has been to show that it does not
require very much effort of find adumbrations of twentieth-century
taste in Victorian poetry, even in parts of the main-line poetry. In the
poetic practice it is readily available for inspection. Victorian nonsense
poetry has not been dealt with in this study, mainly because it does
not readily fit into the line of realism and pyschological immediacy that
I have been following. However, it is of some importance for readers
of twentieth-century poetry, since in utilizing the potential autonomy
of language it helped to lay down some of the foundations on which
Modernist poetry is built, and it is not too difficult to trace connections
between the entertaining nonsense of Lear, Carroll, and the hundreds
of writers of parody, burlesque, and travesty and the inventive and
imaginative work of Pound and William Carlos Williams. Ultimately,
though, the inheritance has been indirect, since main-line twentieth-
century poets have not written entertaining nonsense (with the exception of works like Eliot's *Old Possum's Book of Practical Cats*), and the
stream has flowed into prose. *Finnegans Wake* is possibly the principal
heir of the nonsense tradition, it is generally acknowledged as a central
Modernist text, but its scale and scope makes it erudite nonsense rather
than entertaining nonsense. The Victorians themselves regarded the
nonsense tradition as diverting and amusing, and much of it remains

so for the modern reader, but the wisdom of hindsight has enabled us to recognize in the apparently pleasant whimsy and fantasy of the Victorians disturbing and unsettling images that speak of suppressed sexuality, sublimated violence, and the impulse towards lawlessness. There is a frontier land between nonsense poetry and serious literature in which one finds such surreal and Gothic works as *Goblin Market*

The vast body of Victorian poetry forms an important source of influence, but of almost equal significance is the field of Victorian poetic theory. As Carol Christ has shown in her excellent survey, *Victorian and Modern Poetics* (Chicago, 1984), many of the principles on which the Modernist aesthetic is constructed were thoroughly investigated by the Victorians, and in a terminology very similar to that employed by the Modernists, as poets such as Eliot and Pound were themselves often aware.[11] Yeats attached importance to Arthur Hallam's review 'On Some of the Characteristics of Modern Poetry' (1831), which discusses symbol and image in a way highly reminiscent of T. S. Eliot's,[12] and Marshall McLuhan has argued that this essay anticipates symbolist poetics.[13] It certainly anticipates Eliot's famous concept 'The Dissociation of Sensibility'.[14] After having been treated rather dismissively by Eliot and others Pater is increasingly taking his place as an important prefigurer of Modernism, especially in his theoretical statements.[15]

Yeats recalled that Wilde's 'very admiration for his predecessors in poetry, for Browning, for Swinburne and Rossetti, in their first vogue while he was a very young man, made any success seem impossible'.[16] and one can understand all too readily the curious mixture of admiration, envy, and depression that the contemplation of seemingly great works can induce, but now that we are sufficiently far from both the Victorian and the Modernist periods a fairer assessment is possible. We realize that the Victorians themselves were haunted by the fact of 'belatedness', and that the Modernists did, after all, find an independent and original voice, and it is no longer necessary to belittle the Victorians to emphasize that fact. It is surely now possible to recognize in Victorian poetry a magnificent and complex achievement.

Notes

1. W. J. Bate, *The Burden of the Past and the English Poet* (Cambridge, Mass. 1970), p. 4.

2. For the relations of poets to predecessors see H. Bloom, *The Anxiety of*

Influence, a Theory of Poetry (New York, 1973), and *A Map of Misreading* (New York, 1975).

3. For Eliot's recommendation of classicism and 'extinction of personality' see 'Tradition and Individual Talent' (1919), in *Selected Essays* (1932, reprinted 1934, 1951), pp. 17, 21–22.

4. I. Babbitt's anti-romantic stance is seen in *The New Laocoön* (Cambridge, Mass., 1910).

5. T. S. Eliot, *The Sacred Wood* (1920), pp. 157–58.

6. *Literary Essays of Ezra Pound*, edited by T. S. Eliot (1954), p. 419.

7. Ibid., p. 276.

8. W. B. Yeats, *Autobiographies* (1955), pp. 102–3.

9. For a history of the criterion of sincerity see P. Ball, 'Sincerity: The Rise and Fall of a Critical Term', *MLR*, 59 (1964), 1–11.

10. A. Sulloway, *Gerard Manley Hopkins and the Victorian Temper* (1972), discusses Hopkins as a Victorian.

11. Other studies of the relationship between Victorian and Modernist poetry are N. Friedman, 'From Victoria to Modern: A Sketch for a Critical Reappraisal', *VN*, 32 (1967), 20–28, and B. S. Flowers, *Browning and the Modern Tradition* (1976). A. C. Partridge, *The Language of Modern Poetry: Yeats, Eliot, Auden* (1976), includes the excellent chapter 'The Forebears of Modern Poetry', pp. 24–54. See also A. Robinson, *Poetry, Painting and Ideas, 1885–1914* (1985).

12. Reprinted in *Tennyson: The Critical Heritage*, edited by J. Jump (1967), pp. 34–49.

13. M. McLuhan, 'Tennyson and Picturesque Poetry', in *Critical Essays on the Poetry of Tennyson*, edited by J. Killham (New York, 1960), pp. 67–85.

14. 'The Dissociation of Sensibility' first used by Eliot in 'The Metaphysical Poets' (1921), in *Selected Essays*, p. 288. The phrase is discussed by F. Kermode in '"Dissociation of Sensibility"', *Kenyon Review*, 19 (1957), 169–94, and J. Smith 'Notes on the Criticism of T. S. Eliot', *Essays in Criticism*, 22 (1972), pp. 336–47.

15. See F. C. McGrath, *The Sensible Spirit: Walter Pater and the Modernist Paradigm* (Tampa, Florida, 1986).

16. Yeats, *Autobiographies*, p. 139.

Chronology

Note: Dates refer to first publication of works, whether in volume or in periodical form (with the exception of a few works appearing in 'trial editions' or remaining in manuscript). (D) for drama; (P) for painting.

DATE	POEMS	OTHER WORKS	HISTORICAL AND CULTURAL EVENTS AND LITERARY WORKS ABROAD
1830	Tennyson *Poems, Chiefly Lyrical*	Carlyle *On History* Lyell *Principles of Geology* (−1833)	Accession of William IV Grey PM (Whig) French 'Revolution of July' Opening of Liverpool and Manchester Railway. Huskisson killed by Stephenson's *Rocket*
1831	Ebenezer Elliott *Corn Law Rhymes*	Carlyle *Characteristics*	Poe: *Poems*
1832	Tennyson *Poems*	Carlyle *Biography*	Darwin's voyage on the *Beagle* (−1836)
1833	Browning *Pauline* E. Barrett *Prometheus Bound* (trans.)	Carlyle *Sartor Resartus* (−1834) Newman *et al.* *Tracts for the Times* (−1841)	Factory Act ('Children's Charter') Oxford Movement begins
1834	Taylor *Philip van Artevelde*	Bulwer *Last Days of Pompeii*	Melbourne PM (Whig), July; Peel PM (Cons.), Dec.

DATE	POEMS	OTHER WORKS	HISTORICAL AND CULTURAL EVENTS AND LITERARY WORKS ABROAD
1835	Browning *Paracelsus* Wordsworth *Yarrow Revisited, and Other Poems* Clare *The Rural Muse*	Bulwer *Rienzi*	Melbourne PM (Whig), April Fox Talbot's first photographs
1836	Browning *Porphyria's Lover* *Johannes Agricola* Newman *et al* *Lyra Apostolica*	Dickens *Sketches by Boz* *Pickwick Papers* (–1837)	Pugin: *Contrasts*
1837	Browning *Strafford* (D)	Carlyle *French Revolution* Dickens *Oliver Twist* (–1839)	Accession of Queen Victoria (20 June)
1838	E. Barrett *The Seraphim* Wordsworth *Sonnets*	Dickens *Nicholas Nickleby*	Anti-Corn Law League founded 'People's Charter' issued by Chartists
1839	Bailey *Festus*	Carlyle *Chartism*	Chartist Riots Stendhal: *Chartreuse de Parme*
1840	Barham *Ingoldsby Legends*, I Browning *Sordello*	Dickens *Master Humphrey's Clock* *Old Curiosity Shop* (–1841) Darwin *Voyage of the Beagle*	Marriage of Victoria and Prince Albert Houses of Parliament by Barry and Pugin (–1852)

DATE	POEMS	OTHER WORKS	HISTORICAL AND CULTURAL EVENTS AND LITERARY WORKS ABROAD
1841	Browing *Pippa Passes*	Carlyle *Heroes, Hero- Worship . . .* Dickens *Barnaby Rudge*	Peel PM (Cons.) Sept. Fenimore Cooper: *The Deerslayer* *Punch* founded
1842	Browning *King Victor and King Charles* Macaulay *Lays of Ancient Rome* Tennyson *Poems* Wordsworth *Poems, chiefly of Early and Late Years*	Dickens *American Notes*	Mines Act Chartist Riots
1843	Hood *Song of the Shirt* Horne *Orion*	Browning *Return of the Druses* Bulwer *Last of the Barons* Dickens *Christmas Carol Martin Chuzzlewit* Carlyle *Past and Present* Ruskin *Modern Painters*, I (–1860)	Wordsworth Poet Laureate

DATE	POEMS	OTHER WORKS	HISTORICAL AND CULTURAL EVENTS AND LITERARY WORKS ABROAD
1844	Barnes *Poems of Rural Life* E. Barrett *Poems* Patmore *Poems*	Dickens *The Chimes* Browning *Colombe's Birthday* (D) Chambers *Vestiges of Creation* Disraeli *Coningsby* Horne *New Spirit of the Age* Thackeray *The Luck of Barry Lyndon*	Factory Act (working hours restricted) Dumas: *Les Trois Mousquetaires*
1845	Browning *Dramatic Romances*	Dickens *The Cricket on the Hearth* Disraeli *Sybil*	Irish potato famine Newman's conversion to Roman Catholicism Merimée: *Carmen*
1846	C., E., and A. Brontë *Poems* Keble *Lyra Innocentium* Lear *Book of Nonsense*	Dickens *Dombey and Son* (–1848) G. Eliot trans. Strauss's *Life of Jesus* Thackeray *Snobs of England* (–1847)	Repeal of Corn Laws Russell PM (Whig), July Hawthorne: *Mosses from an Old Manse* Melville: *Typee*
1847	Barham *Ingoldsby Legends* Landor *Hellenics* Tennyson *The Princess*	A. Brontë *Agnes Grey* C. Brontë *Jane Eyre* E. Brontë *Wuthering Heights* Disraeli *Tancred* Thackeray *Vanity Fair* (–1848)	Foundation of Communist League Emerson: *Poems* Longfellow: *Evangeline* Melville: *Omoo*

DATE	POEMS	OTHER WORKS	HISTORICAL AND CULTURAL EVENTS AND LITERARY WORKS ABROAD
1848	Clough *Bothie of Toper-na-Fuosich*	A. Brontë *The Tenant of Wildfell Hall* Gaskell *Mary Barton* Kingsley *Yeast* Newman *Loss and Gain* Thackeray *Pendennis* (–1850)	Marx and Engels *Communist Manifesto* Chartist Petition Pre-Raphaelite Brotherhood founded Revolution in France Chateaubriand: *Memoires d'Outre-Tombe*
1849	Arnold *Strayed Reveller and Other Poems* Clough and Burbidge *Ambarvalia*	C. Brontë *Shirley* Dickens *David Copperfield* Froude *The Nemesis of Faith* Ruskin *Seven Lamps of Architecture*	Millais: *Lorenzo and Isabella* (P) Rossetti: *Girlhood of Mary* (P) Hunt: *Rienzi* (P) Melville: *Mardi*; *Redburn*
1850	Beddoes *Death's Jest Book* E. B. Browning *Poems* R. Browning *Christmas Eve and Easter Day* Tennyson *In Memoriam* Wordsworth *The Prelude*	Carlyle *Latter-Day Pamphlets* Kingsley *Alton Locke* *The Germ*, ed. W. M. Rossetti	Wordsworth d. Tennyson Poet Laureate Wiseman made cardinal Roman Catholic hierarchy restored in England Emerson: *Representative Men* Hawthorne: *Scarlet Letter* Melville: *White Jacket* Poe: *Works* Hunt: *Claudio and Isabella* (P); *Converted British Family . . .* (P) Millais: *Christ in the House of his Parents* (P)

DATE	POEMS	OTHER WORKS	HISTORICAL AND CULTURAL EVENTS AND LITERARY WORKS ABROAD
1851	Beddoes *Collected Poems* E. B. Browning *Casa Guidi Windows* Meredith *Poems*	Carlyle *The Life of John Sterling* Layard *Discoveries at Nineveh* Gaskell *Cranford* (–1853) Ruskin *Pre-Raphaelitism* *The Stones of Venice* I (–1853)	Rossetti: *Ecce Ancilla Domini* (P) Great Exhibition, Hyde Park J. M. W. Turner d. Hawthorne: *House of the Seven Gables* Melville: *Moby Dick* Hunt: *The Hireling Shepherd*; *Valentine Rescuing Sylvia from Proteus* (P)
1852	Arnold *Empedocles on Etna, and other Poems* Tennyson *Ode on Death of Wellington*	Browning *Essay on Shelley* Dickens *Bleak House* (–1853) Newman *Scope and Nature of University Education* (later *Idea of a University*) Thackeray *The History of Henry Esmond*	Derby PM (Cons.), February Wellington d. Aberdeen PM (Coalition), December Hawthorne: *Blithedale Romance* Melville: *Pierre* Stowe: *Uncle Tom's Cabin* Hunt: *Our English Coasts*; *Awakening Conscience* (P) Millais: *A Huguenot, Ophelia* (P) F. M. Brown: *Work*; *An English Autumn Afternoon*; *Pretty Baa-Lambs* (P)

DATE	POEMS	OTHER WORKS	HISTORICAL AND CULTURAL EVENTS AND LITERARY WORKS ABROAD
1853	Arnold *Poems*	C. Brontë *Villette*	Hawthorne: *Tanglewood Tales*
	Landor *Last Fruit off an Old Tree*	Bulwer *My Novel*	Gerard de Nerval: *Les Chimères*
		Gaskell *Ruth*	Millais: *The Order of Release, 1746* (P)
	Patmore *Tamerton Church Tower*	Kingsley *Hypatia*	Hunt: *The Light of the World* (P)
	Smith *Life Drama*		Rossetti began *Found* (P)
		Reade *Peg Woffington Christie Johnstone*	
		Thackeray *English Humourists of the Eighteenth Century The Newcomers* (–1855)	
		Yonge *The Heir of Redclyffe*	
1854	Aytoun *Firmilian*	Dickens *Hard Times*	Crimean War (–1856)
	Patmore *The Angel in the House*, I (–1862)	Gaskell *North and South*	Working Men's College, London, founded
		G. Eliot, trans. Feuerbach's *Essence of Christianity*	Thoreau: *Walden* Millais: *John Ruskin* (P)
	W. B. Scott *Poems*		Hunt: *The Scapegoat; The Finding of the Saviour in the Temple* (P)
	Dobell *Balder*		
	Tennyson *The Charge of the Light Brigade*		

DATE	POEMS	OTHER WORKS	HISTORICAL AND CULTURAL EVENTS AND LITERARY WORKS ABROAD
1855	Arnold *Poems*, second series Browning *Men and Women* Tennyson *Maud and Other Poems*	Dickens *Little Dorrit* (–1857) Kingsley *Westward Ho!* *Glaucus, or Wonders of the Shore* Meredith *The Shaving of Shagpat* Trollope *The Warden*	Palmerston PM (Lib.), February F. M. Brown: *The Last of England* (P) Millais: *The Rescue* (P) Whitman: *Leaves of Grass* Longfellow: *Hiawatha*
1856		Newman *Callista* Reade *It is Never Too Late to Mend* Rossetti, Morris *et al.* *Oxford and Cambridge Magazine*	Emerson: *English Traits* Flaubert: *Madame Bovary* Millais: *Autumn Leaves* (P) Wallis: *The Death of Chatterton* (P) Hughes *Eve of St. Agnes*; *April Love* (P)
1857	E. B. Browning *Aurora Leigh* Locker-Lampson *London Lyrics* Smith *City Poems*	C. Brontë *The Professor* G. Eliot *Scenes of Clerical Life* Hughes *Tom Brown's School Days* Kingsley *Two Years Ago* Meredith *Farina* Ruskin *The Political Economy of Art* Thackeray *The Virginians* (–1859) Trollope *Barchester Towers*	Indian Mutiny (–1859) Baudelaire: *Fleurs du Mal* Melville: *The Confidence Man* Rossetti *et al.*: Oxford Union Murals Brett: *Val d'Aosta* (P) Rossetti: *Tune of the Seven Towers* (P)

DATE	POEMS	OTHER WORKS	HISTORICAL AND CULTURAL EVENTS AND LITERARY WORKS ABROAD
1858	Clough *Amours de Voyage* Kingsley *Andromeda, and Other Poems* Landor *Dry Sticks Fagoted* Morris *Defence of Guenevere*	Arnold *Merope* (D) Trollope *Three Clerks* *Dr. Thorne*	Derby PM (Cons.), February W. L. Windus: *Too Late* (P) Brett: *The Stonebreaker* (P) Wallis: '*Thou wert our Conscript*' (P) Morris: *Queen Guinevere* (P)
1859	Fitzgerald *The Rubaiyát of Omar Khayyám* Tennyson *Idylls of the King* (−1885)	Collins *Woman in White* (−1860) Dickens *Tale of Two Cities* Darwin *Origin of Species* G. Eliot *Adam Bede* *The Lifted Veil* Meredith *Ordeal of Richard Feverel* Mill *On Liberty* Ruskin *The Two Paths* Smiles *Self-Help* Trollope *The Bertrams*	Palmerston PM (Whig-Lib.) Franco-Austrian War (−1861) Millais: *The Vale of Rest* (P)

DATE	POEMS	OTHER WORKS	HISTORICAL AND CULTURAL EVENTS AND LITERARY WORKS ABROAD
1860	E. B. Browning *Poems before Congress*	Dickens *Great Expectations* Eliot *The Mill on the Floss* Meredith *Evan Harrington* Peacock *Gryll Grange* Thackeray *Lovel the Widower* *The Four Georges* Trollope *Framley Parsonage* (−1861) Wilson *et al.* *Essays and Reviews*	Italian unification Emerson: *The Conduct of Life* Hawthorne: *Marble Faun* Wilberforce−Huxley debate at British Association meeting (at Oxford) Dyce: *Pegwell Bay* (P)
1861	Dixon *Christ's Company* Palgrave *Golden Treasury* Rossetti, trans. *Early Italian Poets*	G. Eliot *Silas Marner* Hughes *Tom Brown at Oxford* Mill *Utilitarianism* Reade *The Cloister and the Hearth* Thackeray *Adventures of Philip* (−1862) Trollope *Orley Farm* (−1862) Wood *East Lynne*	American Civil War (−1865) Prince Albert d.

DATE	POEMS	OTHER WORKS	HISTORICAL AND CULTURAL EVENTS AND LITERARY WORKS ABROAD
1862	E. B. Browning *Last Poems* Clough *Collected Poems* Meredith *Modern Love* C. Rossetti *Goblin Market and Other Poems*	Braddon *Lady Audley's Secret* Colenso *The Pentateuch Examined* Collins *No Name* G. Eliot *Romola* Ruskin *Unto this Last* Trollope *The Small House at Allington* (1864)	Hugo: *Les Misérables* Martineau: *Last Day in the Old Home* (P)
1863	Landor *Heroic Idylls* Woolner *My Beautiful Lady*	Gaskell *Sylvia's Lovers* *Cousin Phyllis* (–1864) Huxley *Man's Place in Nature* Kingsley *The Water-Babies* Lyell *The Antiquity of Man* Reade *Hard Cash*	Hawthorne: *Our Old Home* Longfellow: *Tales of a Wayside Inn* Rossetti began *Beata Beatrix* (P) Hughes: *Home from the Sea* (P)

DATE	POEMS	OTHER WORKS	HISTORICAL AND CULTURAL EVENTS AND LITERARY WORKS ABROAD
1864	Browning *Dramatis Personae* Dixon *Historical Odes* Hawker *Quest of the Sangraal* Tennyson *Idylls of the Hearth* (later called *Enoch Arden*)	Dickens *Our Mutual Friend* (–1865) Gaskell *Wives and Daughters* (–1866) Meredith *Emilia in England* (later called *Sandra Belloni*) Newman *Apologia pro Vita sua* Thackeray *Denis Duval* Trollope *Can you Forgive Her?* 1865	
1865	Clough *Letters and Remains* Newman *Dream of Gerontius*	Arnold *Essays in Criticism*, first series Carroll *Alice's Adventures in Wonderland* Meredith *Rhoda Fleming* Ruskin *Sesame and Lilies* Swinburne *Atalanta in Calydon* (D) *Chastelard* (D) Trollope *The Belton Estate* (–1866)	Russell PM (Whig-Lib.), October President Lincoln assassinated Whitman: *Drum-Taps*; *Sequel to Drum-Taps* Whittier: *Poems* Burne-Jones: *The Prioress's Tale* (P)

DATE	POEMS	OTHER WORKS	HISTORICAL AND CULTURAL EVENTS AND LITERARY WORKS ABROAD
1866	C. Rossetti *Prince's Progress and Other Poems* Swinburne *Poems and Ballads*	E. S. Dallas *The Gay Science* G. Eliot *Felix Holt* Ruskin *Ethics of the Dust* *Crown of Wild Olive* Trollope *The Claverings* (–1867) *The Last Chronicle of Barset* (–1867)	Derby PM (Cons.), June Hunt: *Isabella and the Pot of Basil*
1867	Arnold *New Poems* Morris *The Life and Death of Jason* Swinburne *Song of Italy* *Appeal to England*	Meredith *Vittoria* Trollope *Phineas Finn* (–1869) Ruskin *Time and Tide*	Second Reform Act Marx: *Das Kapital*, ı Twain: *Celebrated Jumping Frog*
1868	Browning *The Ring and the Book* G. Eliot *The Spanish Gipsy* Morris *Earthly Paradise*, ı (–1870) Swinburne *Siena*	Collins *The Moonstone* Trollope *He Knew he was Right*	Disraeli PM (Cons.), February Gladstone PM (Lib.), December Public executions abolished Louisa Alcott: *Little Women*
1869	Arnold *Collected Poems* Clough *Poems and Prose Remains* Hawker *Cornish Ballads* Tennyson *The Holy Grail and Other Poems*	Arnold *Culture and Anarchy* Blackmore *Lorna Doone* Mill *On the Subjection of Women* Ruskin *The Queen of the Air*	Suez Canal opened. Twain: *Innocents Abroad* Louisa Alcott: *Good Wives* Flaubert: *Education Sentimentale*

DATE	POEMS	OTHER WORKS	HISTORICAL AND CULTURAL EVENTS AND LITERARY WORKS ABROAD
1870	Rossetti *Poems* Swinburne *Ode on Proclamation of French Republic*	Dickens *Mystery of Edwin Drood* Disraeli *Lothair* Huxley *Lay Sermons* Meredith *Adventures of Harry Richmond* (–1871) Newman *Grammar of Assent*	Franco–Prussian War (–1871) Papal Infallibility declared Forster's Education Act Emerson: *Society and Solitude* Rossetti: *Dante's Dream*; *The Blessed Damozel* begun (P) Burne-Jones: *The Mill* (P)
1871	Browning *Balaustion's Adventure* *Prince Hohenstiel-Schwangau* Lear *Nonsense Songs and Stories* Swinburne *Songs before Sunrise*	Buchanan 'The Fleshly School of Poetry' Lewis Carroll *Through the Looking-Glass* G. Eliot *Middlemarch* (–1872) Darwin *The Descent of Man* Hardy *Desperate Remedies* Macdonald *At the Back of the North Wind* Ruskin *Fors Clavigera* (–1884) Trollope *The Eustace Diamonds* (–1873)	Trade unions legalized Religious tests abolished at Oxford and Cambridge Whitman: *Democratic Vistas*; *Passage to India* Zola: *Les Rougon-Macquart* (–1893)
1872	Browning *Fifine at the Fair* Morris *Love is Enough*	Butler *Erewhon* Hardy *Under the Greenwood Tree* *A Pair of Blue Eyes* (–1873)	Edison's telegraph Rossetti: *The Bower Meadow* (P) Burne-Jones: *Pan and Psyche* (P) Nietzsche: *Die Geburt der Tragödie*

DATE	POEMS	OTHER WORKS	HISTORICAL AND CULTURAL EVENTS AND LITERARY WORKS ABROAD
1873	Bridges *Poems* Browning *Red Cotton Nightcap Country* Dobson *Vignettes in Rhyme*	Arnold *Literature and Dogma* Mill *Autobiography* Pater *Studies in the Renaissance* Trollope *Phineas Redux* (−1874)	Rimbaud: *Une Saison en Enfer* Twain: *The Gilded Age*
1874	G. Eliot *Legend of Jubal* Thomson *The City of Dreadful Night*	Hardy *Far from the Madding Crowd* Meredith *Beauchamp's Career* (−1875) Trollope *The Way We Live Now* (−1875)	Disraeli PM (Cons.), February Factory Act Burne-Jones: *Perseus Slaying the Sea Serpent* (P)
1875	Browning *Aristophanes' Apology* *The Inn Album* Hopkins *The Wreck of the Deutschland* Meynell *Preludes* W. B. Scott *Poems: Ballads, Studies from Nature, Sonnets* Swinburne *Songs of Two Nations*	Hardy *The Hand of Ethelberta* (−1876) Trollope *The Prime Minister* (−1876) Ruskin *Mornings in Florence* (−1877) *Proserpina* (−1886) *Deucalion* (−1883) Symonds *Renaissance in Italy* (−1886) Tennyson *Queen Mary* (D)	Theosophical Society founded

DATE	POEMS	OTHER WORKS	HISTORICAL AND CULTURAL EVENTS AND LITERARY WORKS ABROAD
1876	Bridges *The Growth of Love* Browning *Pacchiarotto* Carroll *The Hunting of the Snark* Morris *Two Sides of the River* *Sigurd the Volsung* Swinburne *Erechtheus*	G. Eliot *Daniel Deronda* James *Roderick Hudson* Tennyson *Harold* (D)	Bulgarian atrocities Queen Victoria declared Empress of India Melville: *Clarel* Twain: *Tom Sawyer* Mallarmé: *L'Après-midi d'un faune* Impressionist exhibition in Paris
1877	Arnold *Collected Poems* Patmore *The Unknown Eros and Other Poems*	James *The American* W. H. Mallock *The New Republic* Meredith *The Idea of Comedy*	Russo–Turkish War Grosvenor Gallery opened Lanier: *Poems* Ibsen: *Pillars of Society* Zola: *L'Assommoir*
1878	Browning *La Saisiaz, Two Poets of Croisic* Swinburne *Poems and Ballads,* series II	Hardy *The Return of the Native* James *The Europeans* *Watch and Ward*	F. M. Brown began to decorate Manchester Town Hall *Whistler v. Ruskin* case
1879	Barnes *Poems of Rural Life in the Dorset Dialect* Bridges *Poems* Browning *Dramatic Idyls*, first series Tennyson *The Lover's Tale*	G. Eliot *Impressions of Theophrastus Such* James *Daisy Miller* Meredith *The Egoist* Trollope *The Duke's Children* (−1880)	Ibsen: *A Doll's House*

DATE	POEMS	OTHER WORKS	HISTORICAL AND CULTURAL EVENTS AND LITERARY WORKS ABROAD
1880	Bridges *Poems* Browning *Dramatic Idyls*, second series Swinburne *Studies in Song* *Songs of the Spring-tides* *Heptalogia* Tennyson *Ballads and Other Poems*	Disraeli *Endymion* Gissing *Workers in the Dawn* Hardy *The Trumpet-Major* *A Laodicean* (–1881) James *The Portrait of a Lady* (–1881) Meredith *The Tragic Comedians* Shorthouse *John Inglesant* Trollope *Dr. Wortle's School*	Gladstone PM (Lib.), April J. Harris: *Uncle Remus* Twain: *A Tramp Abroad* Maupassant: *Contes* Burne-Jones: *The Golden Stair*
1881	C. Rossetti *A Pageant, and Other Poems* Rossetti *Ballads and Sonnets* Wilde *Poems*	Mark Rutherford *The Autobiography of Mark Rutherford* Stevenson *Treasure Island* (–1882) Trollope *Ayala's Angel*	Browning Society founded Flaubert: *Bouvard et Pecuchet* Verlaine: *Sagesse* Ibsen: *Ghosts* Gilbert and Sullivan: *Patience* Frith: *Private View* (P)
1882	Scott *A Poet's Harvest* Swinburne *Tristram of Lyonesse, and Other Poems*	Hardy *Two on a Tower* Jefferies *Bevis*	Phoenix Park murder Society for Psychical Research founded Whitman: *Specimen Days in America*

DATE	POEMS	OTHER WORKS	HISTORICAL AND CULTURAL EVENTS AND LITERARY WORKS ABROAD
1883	Bridges *Prometheus the Fire-giver* Browning *Jocoseria* Dixon *Mano* Carroll *Rhyme? and Reason?* Meredith *Poems and Lyrics of the Joy of Earth* Swinburne *A Century of Roundels*	Jefferies *Story of my Heart* Moore *A Modern Lover* Trollope *Autobiography* Stevenson *The Black Arrow*	Schreiner: *The Story of an African Farm* Twain: *Life on the Mississippi* Hunt: *The Triumph of the Innocents* (P)
1884	Browning *Ferishtah's Fancies* De Vere *Poetical Works* Dixon *Odes and Eclogues* Symonds *Wine, Women, and Song* Thomson *Voice from the Nile and Other Poems* (posthumous)	Gissing *The Unclassed* Moore *A Mummer's Wife* Ruskin *The Art of England* *The Pleasures of England* *The Storm Cloud of the Nineteenth Century* Tennyson *Becket* (D) Meredith *Diana of the Crossways* (−1885)	Third Reform Act *Oxford English Dictionary* (ed. Murray) (−1928) Lanier: *Poems* (posthumous) Twain: *The Adventures of Huckleberry Finn* Burne-Jones: *King Cophetua and the Beggar Maid* (P)

DATE	POEMS	OTHER WORKS	HISTORICAL AND CULTURAL EVENTS AND LITERARY WORKS ABROAD
1885	Bridges *Eros and Psyche* Hopkins *Sonnets* ('terrible sonnets') Lang *Rhymes à la Mode* Morris *The Pilgrims of Hope* Stevenson *Child's Garden of Verses* Tennyson *Tiresias and Other Poems*	Haggard *King Solomon's Mines* Pater *Marius the Epicurean* Mark Rutherford *Mark Rutherford's Deliverance* Ruskin *Praeterita* (−1889) Stevenson *Prince Otto* Swinburne *Marino Faliero* (D)	*Dictionary of National Biography* begun, ed. Stephen Salisbury PM (Cons.), June Fall of Khartoum and death of Gordon Zola: *Germinal* Whistler's *Ten o'clock Lectures*
1886	Kipling *Departmental Ditties* Tennyson *Locksley Hall Sixty Years After* *Promise of May, and Other Poems*	Gissing *Demos* *Isabel Clarendon* Haggard *She* Hardy *The Mayor of Casterbridge* *The Woodlanders* (−1887) James *The Bostonians* *The Princess Casamassima* Moore *A Drama in Muslin* Stevenson *Dr Jekyll and Mr Hyde* *Kidnapped*	Gladstone PM (Lib.), February Salisbury PM (Cons.), August Trafalgar Square riots

DATE	POEMS	OTHER WORKS	HISTORICAL AND CULTURAL EVENTS AND LITERARY WORKS ABROAD
1887	Browning *Parleyings with Certain People* Dixon *Lyrical Poems* Meredith *Ballads and Poems of Tragic Life*	Gissing *Thyrza* Haggard *Allan Quartermain* Jefferies *Amaryllis at the Fair* Mark Rutherford *The Revolution in Tanner's Lane* Pater *Imaginary Portraits* Swinburne *Locrine* (D)	Queen Victoria's Golden Jubilee Independent Labour Party founded Zola: *La Terre* Burne-Jones: *The Depths of the Sea* (P)
1888	Allingham *Poetical Works* Henley *Book of Verses* Meredith *A Reading of Earth*	Arnold *Essays in Criticism, second series* Gissing *A Life's Morning* Hardy *Wessex Tales* Kipling *Plain Tales from the Hills* *Soldiers Three* Morris *A Dream of John Ball* Stevenson *The Master of Ballantrae* (–1889) *The Black Arrow* Ward *Robert Elsmere* Wilde *The Happy Prince and Other Tales*	Accession of Kaiser Wilhelm II Bellamy: *Looking Backward*

DATE	POEMS	OTHER WORKS	HISTORICAL AND CULTURAL EVENTS AND LITERARY WORKS ABROAD
1889	Browning *Asolando*	C. Booth *Life and Labour in London* (−1903)	Twain: *A Connecticut Yankee in King Arthur's Court*
	Lear *Nonsense Drolleries*	Gissing *The Nether World*	Tolstoy: *Kreutzer Sonata*
	Morris *The House of the Wolfings*	James *The Tragic Muse* (−1890)	Hunt: *Lady of Shalott* (P)
	Swinburne *Poems and Ballads*, third series	Jerome *Three Men in a Boat*	
	Tennyson *Demeter and Other Poems*	Pater *Appreciations*	
	Yeats *The Wanderings of Oisin*	Shaw *Fabian Essays*	
1890	Bridges *Shorter Poems*	Gissing *The Emancipated*	William Morris's Kelmscott Press founded
		Booth *In Darkest England*	W. James: *Principles of Psychology*
		Frazer *The Golden Bough* (−1915)	Ibsen: *Hedda Gabler*
		Mark Rutherford *Miriam's Schooling*	
		Morris *News from Nowhere*	
		Whistler *The Gentle Art of Making Enemies*	

General Bibliographies

Note: Each section is arranged alphabetically. Place of publication is London unless otherwise stated.

(i) Anthologies

Auden, W. H. and N. H Pearson,	*Tennyson to Yeats* (New York, 1950). (Vol. v of Poets of the English Language.)
Bloom, H. and L. Trilling,	*Victorian Prose and Poetry*, (1973). (Vol. v of The Oxford Anthology of English Literature.)
Brett, R. L.	*Poems of Faith and Doubt: The Victorian Age* (1965). (Good introduction and some annotation.)
Brown, E. K. and J. O. Bailey	*Victorian Poetry* (New York, 1942).
Buckler, W.	*The Major Victorian Poets: Tennyson, Browning and Arnold* (New York, 1973).
Evans, M. R.	*An Anthology of Victorian Verse* (1949).
Grigson, G.	*The Victorians* (1950).
Gray, D. J. and G. B. Tennyson	*Victorian Literature: Poetry* (New York, 1976). (Very generous selection.)
Hayward, J.	*The Oxford Book of Nineteenth-Century Verse* (1964). (85 poets, 600 poems.)
Heath-Stubbs, J. and D. Wright	*The Forsaken Garden: An Anthology of Poetry 1824–1909* (1950). (Some interesting and unusual choices, deliberately excluding poems in *The Oxford Book of Victorian Verse*.)
Houghton, W. E. and G. R. Stange	*Victorian Poetry and Poetics* (Boston, 1st edn 1959; 2nd edn 1968) (One of the most comprehensive assemblages of its kind: 915 pages of densely packed double columns, with good annotations and introductions. Eighteen poets covered in 2nd edn and generous selections from essays. Very much main-line taste.)

Lang, C. Y.   *The Pre-Raphaelites and Their Circle* (Chicago, 1968). (Good introduction, and sixteen plates, but disappointingly does not cover minor poets.)

Macbeth, G.   *The Penguin Book of Victorian Verse* (1969). (A quirky, off-beat, and hence interesting choice.)

Marshall, W. H.   *Victorian Poets* (1966).

Messenger, N. P. and J. R. Watson   *Victorian Poetry* (1974). (Selection from fourteen poets.)

Miles, A. H.   *Poets of the Century* 10 vols (1891–97); 12 vols (1905–7). (Samplings from about 190 poets, 42 of them women. Hopkins is included. Biographical introductions. A superb showcase.)

Peacock, W.   *Longfellow to Rupert Brooke*, English Verse, vol. v (1931).

Quiller-Couch, A. T.   *The Oxford Book of Victorian Verse* (Oxford, 1912).

Richards, B. A.   *English Verse 1830–1890*, in *Longman Annotated Anthologies of English Verse*, gen. ed. Alastair Fowler, (1980). (The most densely annotated anthology of Victorian Poetry ever; the companion volume to this book, since the view of the period presented here corresponds to the selection in the anthology.)

Sanford, D.   *Pre-Raphaelite Writing* (1973). (Selections from thirteen poets and a generous selection of related prose.)

Stephens, J., E. L. Beck, and R. H. Snow   *Victorian and Later English Poets* (New York, 1934). (Generous selections from thirty-three poets.)

Ward, T. H.   *The English Poets*, 5 vols (1880–1918). (Vol v: Browning, Tennyson, Arnold, etc. to John Davidson; no Hopkins. Essays by distinguished writers, including Gosse, Hardy, Mackail, and Drinkwater.)

Watson, J. R.   *Everyman's Book of Victorian Verse* (1982). (Selections from 105 poets, isolating, in the main, what the late-twentieth-century reader will find interesting rather than what the Victorians regarded as main line . A very finely woven net dredges up the plankton of the age.)

Williams, C.   *A Book of Victorian Narrative Verse* (Oxford, 1927).

(ii) Victorian background: historical, intellectual, cultural

Altholz, J. L., ed.   *The Mind and Art of Victorian England* (Minneapolis, 1976). (Eleven articles by American scholars.)

Altick, R. D.   *Victorian People and Ideas* (1974). (Broad sweep of Victorian life and thought.)

Batho, E. and B. Dobreé   *The Victorians and After, 1830–1914* (1938; rev. 1950 and 1962). (General survey; includes a chapter on the poetry and a forty-page bibliography of poets.)

Best, G.   *Mid-Victorian Britain, 1851–1857* (1971, repr. Frogmore, 1973). (Good social history; illustrated.)

Briggs, A.   *Victorian People: A Reassessment of Persons and Things, 1851–1867* (1954; repr. Harmondsworth, 1965). (Chapters on individual figures in relation to aspects of the period.)
Victorian Cities (1963; repr. Harmondsworth, 1968). (Chapters on individual cities.)

Brooks, C.   *Signs for the Times: Symbolic Realism in the Mid-Victorian World* (1984).

Buckley, J. H.   *The Victorian Temper: A study in Literary Culture* (1952). (Concentrates on rise and decline of the 'moral aesthetic'.)

Burn, W. L.   *The Age of Equipoise: A Study of the Mid-Victorian Generations* (1964).

Chadwick, O.   *The Victorian Church*, 2nd edn, 2 vols, Ecclesiastical History of England, ed. by J. D. Dickinson, vols VII–VIII (1970). (Magisterial study; much more than ecclesiastical history.)

Chandler, A.   *A Dream of Order: The Medieval Ideal in Nineteenth-Century English Literature* (1970, repr. 1971).

Chapman, R.   *The Victorian Debate: English Literature and Society, 1832–1901*. Literature and Society series, ed. by H. Tint (1968). (Covers many aspects of the age and its literature.)

Chapple, J. V.   *Science and Literature in the Nineteenth Century* (1986).

Chesterton, G. K.   *The Victorian Age in Literature* (1913).

Clark, G. K.   *The Making of Victorian England* (1962).

Cockshut, A. O. J.   *The Unbelievers: English Agnostic Thought, 1840–1890* (1964).

Conrad, P.   *The Victorian Treasure House* (1973)

Dale, P. A.   *The Victorian Critic and the Idea of History* (Cambridge, Mass., 1977).

DeLaura, D.	*Hebrew and Hellene in Victorian England: Newman, Arnold and Pater* (Austin, Tex., 1969).
Dyos, H. J. and M. Wolff, eds	*The Victorian City: Images and Realities*, 2 vols (1973). (Includes thirty-eight excellent essays on London and provincial cities and a collection of illustrations.)
Fraser, H.	*Beauty and Belief: Aesthetics and Religion in Victorian Literature* (Cambridge, 1986).
Gilbert, S. M. and S. Gubar	*The Madwoman in the Attic: The Woman Writer and the Nineteenth-Century Literary Imagination* (New Haven, 1979).
Girouard, M.	*The Return to Camelot: Chivalry and the English Gentleman* (New Haven, 1981).
Grisewood, H.	*Ideas and Beliefs of the Victorians* (1949).
Halevy, E.	*A History of the English People in the Nineteenth Century*, 2nd edn, 6 vols (1949–52).
Henkle, R. B.	*Comedy and Culture: England 1820–1900* (Princeton, 1980).
Holloway, J.	*The Victorian Sage: Studies in Argument* (1953). (On Carlyle, Disraeli, George Eliot, Newman, Matthew Arnold, Hardy.)
Houghton, W. E.	*The Victorian Frame of Mind, 1830–1870* (1957). (A masterly survey of the predominant attitudes.)
Jackson, H.	*Dreamers of Dreams: The Rise and Fall of Nineteenth-Century Idealism* (New York, 1948).
Jay, E.	*Faith and Doubt in Victorian Britain* (1986).
Jenkyns, R.	*The Victorians and Ancient Greece* (Oxford, 1980).
Knoepflmacher, U. C.	*Religious Humanism and the Victorian Novel: George Eliot, Walter Pater, and Samuel Butler* (Princeton, 1965; repr. 1970). (Useful generally for Comtean background.)
Knoepflmacher, U. C. and G. B. Tennyson, eds	*Nature and the Victorian Imagination* (Berkeley and Los Angeles, 1977). (Twenty-five excellent essays on a very wide range of topics.)
Lerner, L., ed.	*The Context of English Literature: The Victorians* (1978). (Eleven excellent introductory essays on literature, society, and art.)
Levine, G.	*The Emergence of Victorian Consciousness* (1978).
Marcus, S.	*The Other Victorians: A Study of Sexuality and Pornography in Mid-Nineteenth-Century England* (1964; repr. 1969). (Background to a side of life some way removed from Patmore's *Angel in the House*.)
Martin, R. B.	*The Triumph of Wit: A Study of Victorian Comic Theory* (Oxford, 1974).

Miyoshi, M.　　*The Divided Self: A Perspective on the Literature of the Victorians* (New York, 1969).

Morris, K. L.　　*The Image of the Middle Ages in Romantic and Victorian Literature* (1984).

Morton, P.　　*The Vital Science: Biology and the Literary Imagination, 1860–1900* (1984).

Pearsall, R.　　*The Worm in the Bud: The World of Victorian Sexuality* (1969).

Peckham, M.　　*Beyond the Tragic Vision: The Quest for Identity in the Nineteenth Century* (1962).
Victorian Revolutionaries: Speculations on Some Heroes of a Culture Crisis (New York, 1970). (Deals with figures, including Tennyson, Browning, and Swinburne, who 'managed to get outside of their culture, to escape its presuppositions'.)

Perkin, H.　　*The Origins of Modern English Society, 1780–1880* (1969).

Prickett, S.　　*Romanticism and Religion: The Tradition of Coleridge and Wordsworth in the Victorian Church* (Cambridge, 1976).

Reardon, B. M. G.　　*From Coleridge to Gore: A Century of Religious Thought in Britain* (1971).

Schulz, M.　　*Paradise Preserved: Recreations of Eden in Eighteenth- and Nineteenth-Century England* (1985).

Tillotson, G.　　*A View of Victorian Literature* (Oxford, 1978). (A posthumously published incomplete study, forming the first of two volumes planned to cover 1832–80 in the OHEL series. Contains chapters on 'Earnestness' and on Tennyson and Browning.)

Turner, F. M.　　*Between Science and Religion, the Reaction to Scientific Naturalism in Late Victorian England* (New Haven, 1974).
The Greek Heritage in Victorian Britain (New Haven, 1981).

Willey, B.　　*Nineteenth-Century Studies: Coleridge to Matthew Arnold* (1949; repr. Cambridge, 1980).
More Nineteenth-Century Studies: A Group of Honest Doubters (1956; repr. Cambridge, 1980).

Williams, R.　　*Culture and Society, 1780–1950* (1958, repr. Harmondsworth, 1961). (Influential study on history of the idea of culture.)

Wright, A.　　*Victorian Literature: Modern Essays in Criticism* (New York, 1961).

Wright, T. R.　　*The Religion of Humanity: the Impact of Comtean Positivism on Victorian Britain* (Cambridge, 1986).

(iii) Victorian poetry

A. Bibliographies and reference guides

Buckley, J.	*Victorian Poets and Prose Writers* (1966).
Cooke, J. D. and L. Stevenson	*English Literature of the Victorian Period* (1949).
Faverty, F. E., ed.	*The Victorian Poets: A Guide to Research* (Cambridge, Mass., 1969).
Fredeman, W. E.	*Pre-Raphaelitism: A Bibliocritical Study* (Cambridge, Mass., 1965).
Fredeman, W. E. and I. B. Nadel, eds	*Victorian Poets Before 1850; Victorian Poets After 1850* (vols XXXII and XXXV of *Dictionary of Literary Biography*; Detroit 1984 and 1985). (Full biographies and bibliographies of eighty-two poets, including some exceedingly obscure figures; also good critical assessments by important critics.)
Freeman, R.	*Bibliographies of Studies in Victorian Literature for the Ten Years 1965–1974* (New York, 1981).
Rosenbaum, B. and P. White	*Index of English Literary Manuscripts*, vol IV, 1800–1900; Part I, *Arnold to Gissing* (1982). (An indispensable work of reference, in the process of being completed.)
Slack, R. C.	*Bibliographies of Studies in Victorian Literature for the Ten Years 1955–1964* (Urbana, Ill., 1967).
Templeman, W. D., ed.	*Bibliographies of Studies in Victorian Literature, 1932–1944* (Urbana, Ill., 1945).
Vinson, J., ed.	*The Victorian Period* (1983). (Covers seventy authors; essays and bibliographical surveys by well-known critics. General introduction by A. Pollard.)
Watson, G., ed.	*The New Cambridge Bibliography of English Literature*, vol. III (1800–1900) (Cambridge, 1969). (The primary work of reference; revises *CBEL*, ed. F. W. Bateson, last updated in 1957.)
Wright, A.	*Bibliographies of Studies in Victorian Literature for the Ten Years 1945–1954* (Urbana, Ill., 1956).

B. Readership, publication, and reception

Altick, R. D.	*The English Common Reader: A Social History of the Mass Reading Public, 1800–1900* (Chicago, 1957). (A standard work.)
Armstrong, I., ed.	*Victorian Scrutinies: Reviews of Poetry, 1830–1870* (1972).

Cruse, A.   *The Victorians and their Reading* (Boston and New York, 1935).

Erickson, L.   *Robert Browning: His Poetry and His Audiences* (Ithaca, NY, 1984).

Jack, I.   *The Poet and his Audience* (1984).

Mermin, D.   *The Audience in the Poem: Five Victorian Poets* (New Brunswick, 1983).

C. History and criticism (general)

Armstrong, I., ed.   *The Major Victorian Poets: Reconsiderations* (1969). (Contributions by thirteen scholars.) *Victorian Scrutinies: Reviews of Poetry 1830–1870* (1972).

Bateson, F. W.   *English Poetry, A Critical Introduction* (1950).

Bayley, J.   *The Romantic Survival: A Study in Poetic Evolution* (1957).

Beach, J. W.   *English Literature of the Nineteenth and Early Twentieth Centuries, 1798 to the First World War* (New York, 1962). (Chapter 8 is on Victorian poetry.)

Chew, S. C. and R. D. Altick   *The Nineteenth Century and After (1789–1939)*, A Literary History of England, vol. IV; ed. by A. C. Baugh (2nd edn, 1967). (Chapters 26–35 on aspects of the period.)

Drinkwater, J.   *Victorian Poetry* (1923).

Evans, B. I.   *English Poetry in the later Nineteenth Century* (1933; repr. 1966).

Gaunt, W.   *The Aesthetic Adventure* (1945; repr. 1975). *The Pre-Raphaelite Tragedy* (1942). (Subsequently repr. as *The Pre-Raphaelite Dream*.)

Grierson, H. J. and J. C. Smith   *A Critical History of English Poetry* (1944). (Chapters 30–37 cover this period.)

Heath-Stubbs, J.   *The Darkling Plain: A Study of the Later Fortunes of Romanticism in English Poetry from George Darley to W. B. Yeats* (1950).

Hilton, T.   *The Pre-Raphaelites*. (1970; repr. 1979). (Mainly about the painters, but includes some information on poetry.)

Hough, G.   *The Last Romantics* (1949).

Hunt, J. D.   *The Pre-Raphaelite Imagination 1848–1900* (1977).

Johnson, E. D. H.   *The Alien Vision of Victorian Poetry* (Princeton, 1952). (One of the most important books on Victorian poetry since the war.)

Langbaum, R.   *The Modern Spirit: Essays on the Continuity of Nineteenth- and Twentieth-Century Literature* (New York, 1970).

Leavis, F. R.   *New Bearings in English Poetry* (1932; repr. 1950). (An important and influential work, which promoted Hopkins and the line of wit at the expense of Parnassianism. In broad terms fairly reliable, but specific judgements are often clumsy and insensitive.)

Le Roy, G. C.   *Perplexed Prophets: Six Nineteenth-Century British Authors* (Philadelphia, 1953). (Includes chapters on Arnold, James Thomson, and Rossetti.)

Levine, R. A., ed.   *The Victorian Experience: The Poets* (Athens, Ohio, 1982). (Ten essays on the main poets.)

Lucas, F. L.   *Ten Victorian Poets* (Cambridge, 1948).

Pollard, A., ed.   *The Victorians*, Sphere History of Literature in the English Language, vol. VI (1970). (Chapters 8–12 cover the period, with contributions by major scholars.)

Robinson, A.   *Poetry, Painting and Ideas, 1885–1914* (1985).

Saintsbury, G.   *A History of Nineteenth-Century Literature* (1896).

Stedman, E. C.   *Victorian Poets* (1876, rev. and extended 1887).

Stevenson, L.   *The Pre-Raphaelite Poets* (Chapel Hill, NC, 1972).

Symons, A.   *The Symbolist Movement in Literature* (1899). *Victorian Poetry, Stratford-upon-Avon Studies*, No. 15 (1972). (Eleven good essays on a wide variety of topics.)

Walker, H.   *Greater Victorian Poets* (1895). (Written at a time when Hopkins was unknown.)

Welland, D. S. R.   *The Pre-Raphaelites in Literature and Art* (1953).

Welby, T. E.   *The Victorian Romantics, 1850–1870: The Early Work of Dante Gabriel Rossetti, William Morris, Burne-Jones, Swinburne, Simeon Solomon and Their Associates* (1929).

D. Language, poetics, forms, and techniques

Armstrong, I.   *Language as Living Form in Nineteenth Century Poetry* (Totowa, NJ, 1982).

Attridge, D.   *The Rhythms of English Poetry* (1982). (By far the most challenging and interesting work on the subject.)

Bagehot, W.   *Wordsworth, Tennyson, and Browning or Pure, Ornate and Grotesque Art in English Poetry* (1864; repr. in

	The Collected Works of Walter Bagehot, ed. by N. St John Stevas, vol. II 15 vols, 1965–86.
Baker, W. E.	*Syntax in English Poetry: 1870–1930* (Berkeley and Los Angeles, 1967).
Bateson, F. W.	*English Poetry and the Language of English Poetry* (1934).
Christ, C.	*Victorian and Modern Poetics* (Chicago, 1984). (Excellent study of the unacknowledged debts of Modernist poetry.)
Foakes, R. A.	*The Romantic Assertion: A Study in the Language of Nineteenth Century Poetry* (New Haven, 1958).
Groom, B.	*The Diction of Poetry from Spenser to Bridges* (Toronto, 1955). 'On the Diction of Tennyson, Browning and Arnold', *SPE Tract*, 53 (Oxford, 1939).
Hair, D. S.	*Browning's Experiments with Genre* (Toronto, 1972).
Hood, T.	*The Rules of Rhyme: A Guide to English Versification* (1869; rev. 1877, when E. Bysshe's 'Rules for Making English Verse' added).
Langbaum, R.	*The Poetry of Experience: The Dramatic Monologue in Modern Literary Tradition* (New York, 1957).
Macauley, J. P.	*A Primer of English Versification* (Sydney, 1966). (Good elementary introduction.)
Patmore, C.	*Essay on English Metrical Law*, ed. by M. A. Roth (1961).
Potts, A.	*The Elegiac Mode: Poetic Form in Wordsworth and Other Elegists* (Ithaca, NY, 1967). (Chs. 9 and 10 on Victorian poetry; Ch. 11 on Hardy.)
Preminger, A., ed.	*Princeton Encyclopedia of Poetry and Poetics* (Princeton, 1965; enlarged 1974).
Saintsbury, G.	*A History of English Prosody* (1906–8). (A standard work, extremely detailed, but bogged down to some degree in theories of classical prosody.)
Sessions, I. B.	'The Dramatic Monologue', *PMLA*, 62 (1947), 503–16.
Schneider, E. W.	'Sprung rhythm: a chapter in the evolution of nineteenth-century verse', *PMLA*, 80 (1965), 237–53.
Shapiro, K. and R. Beum	*A Prosody Handbook* (New York, 1965). (A useful survey.)
Sinfield, A.	*Dramatic Monologue* (1977).
Strelka, J. P., ed.	*Theories of Literary Genre* (University Park, Pennsylvania, 1978).
Warren, A. H., Jr	*English Poetic Theory, 1825–1865* (Princeton, 1950).

E. Themes and motifs

Ball, P. M.   *The Central Self: A Study in Romantic and Victorian Imagination* (1968).
The Heart's Events: The Victorian Poetry of Relationship (1976).
The Science of Aspects: The Changing Role of Fact in the Works of Coleridge, Ruskin and Hopkins (1971).

Beach, J. W.   *The Concept of Nature in Nineteenth Century Poetry* (New York, 1936).

Bush, D.   *Mythology and the Romantic Tradition in English Poetry* (New York, 1957). (Chapters 5–12 cover the period.)
Science and English Poetry: A Historical Sketch, 1590–1950 (1950).

Charlesworth, B.   *Dark Passages: The Decadent Consciousness in Victorian Literature* (Madison, 1965).

Christ, C.   *The Finer Optic: The Aesthetic of Particularity in Victorian Poetry* (New Haven, 1975). (On detailed natural observation in poets from Coleridge to Hopkins.)

Colville, D.   *Victorian Poetry and the Romantic Religion* (Albany, NY 1970).

Cosslett, T.   *The Scientific Movement and Victorian Literature* (1983).

Ellis, S.   *Dante and English Poetry* (Cambridge, 1983).

Fairchild, H. N.   *Religious Trends in English Poetry, Christianity and Romanticism in the Victorian Era: 1830–1880*, vol. IV (New York, 1957). (Very comprehensive.)

Fletcher, P.   *Gardens and Grim Ravines: The Language of Landscape in Victorian Poetry* (Princeton, 1983). (On the importance of wild and tamed landscape in seven poets.)

Goldfarb, R.   *Sexual Repression in Victorian Literature* (Lewisburg, Pa., 1975).

Heath-Stubbs, J. F. A.   *The Darkling Plain, a Study of the Later Fortunes of Romanticism in English Poetry from George Darley to W. B. Yeats* (1950).

Johnson, W. S.   *Sex and Marriage in Victorian Poetry* (Ithaca, NY, 1975).

Johnston, J. H.   *The Poet and the City: A Study in Urban Perspectives.* (Athens, Ga., 1984).

Keith, W. J.   *The Poetry of Nature: Rural Perspectives in Poetry from Wordsworth to the Present* (Toronto, 1980).

Landow, G.   *Shadows and Types: Biblical Typology in Victorian Poetry* (1980).

Lucas, J., ed.   *Literature and Politics in the Nineteenth Century* (1971). (Includes essays on poetry.)

McGhee, R. D.   *Marriage, Duty and Desire in Victorian Poetry and Drama* (Lawrence, Kan., 1980).

Miles, J.   *The Pathetic Fallacy in the Nineteenth-Century* (Berkeley and Los Angeles, 1942).

Miller, J. H.   *The Disappearance of God: Five Nineteenth-Century Writers* (Cambridge, Mass., 1975). (A provocative and stimulating study.)

Praz, M.   *The Hero in Eclipse in Victorian Fiction* (1956). (Includes chapters on domesticity in the poetry.) *The Romantic Agony*, trans. by A. Davidson (1933; repr. 1951, 1956, 1960). (A classic study of deviant and exotic behaviour.)

Prickett, A. T. S.   *Victorian Fantasy* (Hassocks, 1979) (Studies in poetry and prose.)

Roppen, G.   *Evolution and Poetic Belief: A Study in Some Victorian and Modern Writers* (Oslo, 1956).

Sewell, E.   *The Field of Nonsense* (1952).

Stevenson, L.   *Darwin Among the Poets* (1932).

Sussman, H.   *Victorians and the Machine: Literary Responses to Technology* (Cambridge, Mass., 1968).

Tennyson, G. B.   *Victorian Devotional Poetry: The Tractarian Mode* (Cambridge, Mass., 1980). (Chapters on Keble, Newman, Isaac Williams, Christina Rossetti, and G. M. Hopkins.)

Thesing, W. B.   *The London Muse: Victorian Poetic Responses to the City* (Athens, Ga., 1982).

Vicinus, M.   *The Industrial Muse: A Study of Nineteenth-Century British Working Class Literature* (New York, 1974). (An excellent resurrection of marginal literature.)

Individual Authors

Notes on biography, major works and criticism

Each entry is divided into three sections:
(a) *Outline of author's life and literary career.* Dates of poems are those of the first published form.
(b) *Selected biographies.* Place of publication is London unless otherwise stated.
(c) *Selected critical works, etc.* Listed chronologically. Place of publication is London unless otherwise stated.

Modern editions of poems are not cited. Currently available scholarly editions include the Oxford Standard Authors series and the Longman Annotated English Poets series.

Series of collections of *Victorian reviews and modern critical essays* are not cited. Volumes on the principal poets are included in the excellent Critical Heritage series (Routledge and Kegan Paul), which reprint selected contemporary reviews and critical essays; the useful Casebook series (Macmillan), and the Twentieth-Century Views series (Prentice-Hall, Englewood Cliffs, New Jersey).

ARNOLD, Matthew (1822–88), son of the famous Thomas Arnold, Headmaster of Rugby and principal representative of Broad Church liberal Protestantism. Later (1841) Thomas was Professor of Modern History at Oxford. Matthew at once continued and reacted against the interests of his father. Much of his childhood happily spent at Fox How, near Ambleside, in the Lake District; Wordsworth lived in the vicinity Educated at Winchester College, 1836–37, and Rugby School, 1837–41 (where his father was securing his place in history as headmaster). Poetic career began at school with the printing of 'Alaric at Rome'. Balliol College, Oxford, 1841–44. Won Newdigate Prize with the poem 'Cromwell' (1843). Became friendly at university with the old Rugbeian, A. H. Clough. 1845 elected Fellow of Oriel College, Oxford. 1847 became private secretary to the Marquis of Lansdowne, who appointed him an inspector of schools in 1851. 1848 visited Switzerland, and very likely had a brief affair with 'Marguerite' which ended in 1849 (although P. Honan believes that the young woman is an imaginary creation, based on Arnold's friend Mary

Claude). First public collection of verse in 1849: *The Strayed Reveller, and Other Poems*. 1815 married Frances Lucy Wightman and visited the Grande Chartreuse on honeymoon (a Carthusian monastery, and the subject of a fine poem of his). 1852 *Empedocles on Etna, and Other Poems* and the following year *Poems*, with an important preface. *'Balder Dead'* was the most important new poem in the 1854 *Poems* (1855 on title-page). In 1857 he began his ten-year stint as Professor of Poetry at Oxford, and was the first holder of the office to lecture in English (previous incumbents had lectured in Latin). The lectures are now classics of English criticism. Gradually his ability to write poetry waned; his last major work being *Thyrsis* (1866). He had perhaps exhausted the workable vein of poetry, and found the urgency and immediacy of prose more appealing; certainly it grew more naturally out of a busy and often controversial public life. The most important prose work is *Culture and Anarchy* (1869), but there is a large output of material on a wide range of subjects, from education, to religion (*Literature and Dogma* of 1873 is the most important), to translations of Homer and social affairs. In 1870 he received the honorary DCL at Oxford and became the Senior Inspector of Schools, and the work involved fact-finding missions to the Continent. 1873 moved to Pains Hill Cottage, Cobham, Surrey. 1883–84 lectures in America; published as *Discourses in America* (1885). 1884 became Chief Inspector of Schools; retired 1886. 1886 the second visit to America. Died of sudden heart failure in Liverpool.

Trilling, L., *Arnold* (1939; rev. 1955).

Honan, P., *Matthew Arnold: a Life* (1981).

See: Tinker, C. B., and H. F. Lowry, *The Poetry of Arnold: A Commentary* (1940).
Jump, J. D., *Matthew Arnold* (1955).
Allott, K., *Matthew Arnold* (1955).
James, D. G., *Matthew Arnold and the Decline of English Romanticism* (1961).
Duffin, H. C., *Arnold the Poet* (1962).
Gottfried, L., *Matthew Arnold and the Romantics* (1963).
Culler, A. D., *Imaginative Reason: The Poetry of Arnold* (1966).
Madden, W. A., *Matthew Arnold: A Study of the Aesthetic Temperament in Victorian England* (1967).
Stange, G. R., *Arnold: The Poet as Humanist* (1967).
Roper, A. H., *Arnold's Poetic Landscapes* (1969).
Bush, J.N.D., *Matthew Arnold, a Survey of his Poetry and Prose* (1971).
Fulweiler, H. W., *Letters from the Darkling Plain, Language and the Grounds of Knowledge in the Poetry of Arnold and Hopkins* (1972).

BAILEY, Philip James (1816–1902). Born in Nottingham, son of Thomas Bailey, a jack-of-all-trades, which included hosiery manufacture, running the *Nottingham Mercury*, and producing volumes of poetry with titles like *What is Life?* and *The Carnival of Death* (1822). Philip received encouragement to pursue poetry from his father. He matriculated at Glasgow University, then went to London to study law, becoming a solicitor in 1840. *Festus* (1839), modelled on Goethe's *Faust* and the Byronic hero, preaches the doctrine of universal redemption (even Lucifer achieves salvation) and was one of the key products of the so-called 'Spasmodic School'. It was one of the most popular poems of the century, going through about one hundred editions. Its Romanticism and grandiloquence appealed in a decade dominated by rational and constricting Utilitarians, but in the 1850s (see the articles on Smith and Dobell) the vogue for this kind of work came to an end. *The Angel World* (1850) less successful. *The Mystic* (1855) and *The Age; A Colloquial Satire* (1858) also failures. First wife divorced; he was remarried in 1863 to Anne Sophia Carey. His later works disastrous. Lived mainly in Nottingham towards the end of his life.

See: Gosse, E., 'P.J.B.', in *Portraits and Sketches* (1912), 59–93
       McKillop, A. D., 'A Victorian Faust', *PMLA*, 40 (1925), 743–46.
       Weinstein, M. A., *W. E. Aytoun and the Spasmodic Controversy* (1968).

BARNES, William (1801–86), educated in Dorchester, married Julia Miles, the central motive of his poetry. Became schoolteacher at Mere (Wiltshire), then in Dorchester. In 1844 produced *Poems of Rural Life, in the Dorset Dialect*, and thereafter three more collections of dialect poetry, as well as poems in 'National English'. He cultivated a very wide range of interests, and was one of the best informed of all English poets on matters of language. Took the view that the Anglo–Saxon element should be much more prominent in English than the Latinate. He should not be mistaken for a backward provincial. He was ordained in 1847. His wife died 1852. In 1861 presented with the living of Winterbourne Came. A fine poem by Hardy, 'The Last Signal', celebrates his funeral.

       Baxter, L. B., *The Life of Barnes* (1887).
       Dugdale, G., *William Barnes of Dorset* (1953).
       Badham-Thornhill, D.G.B., *William Barnes of Dorset* (Beaminster, 1964).
       Hearle, T. W., *William Barnes the Schoolmaster* (Dorset, 1966).
       Hinchy, F. S., *The Dorset William Barnes* (Blandford, 1966).

See: Jacobs, W. D., *Barnes, Linguist* (Albuquerque, New Mexico, 1952).
       Levy, W. T., *Barnes, The Man and His Poems* (Dorchester, 1960).

BRONTË, Charlotte (1816–55), Emily Jane (1818–48), and Anne (1820–49), daughters of Rev. Patrick Brontë. Brought up in Haworth Parsonage on the edge of Yorkshire moors with elder sisters Maria and Elizabeth and mentally unstable brother Branwell (1817–48). After less than a year of misery at Cowan Bridge School, later depicted in *Jane Eyre* as Lowood, Charlotte and Emily withdrawn following death by typhoid of elder sisters. Charlotte studied and later taught at Roe Head School, followed briefly by Emily and Anne. As children they collaborated on fantastic tales of the mythical Glass town and Angria, some of which survive as Gondal poems. All three sisters governesses, 1837–39. Rev. William Weightman became Patrick Brontë's curate, 1839, but died of cholera three years later; Anne's secret love for him revealed in poetry and *Agnes Grey*. Charlotte and Emily travelled to Brussels to study at M. Heger's school, 1842; later Charlotte taught there (until 1844) and fell in love with Heger. Experiences fictionalized in *Villette* (1853). All three sisters published their *Poems* (1846) under pseudonyms Currer, Ellis, and Acton Bell. Charlotte's first novel, *The Professor*, refused by several publishers. *Jane Eyre*, *Wuthering Heights*, and *Agnes Grey*, by Charlotte, Emily, and Anne respectively, published 1847, and Anne's *Tenant of Wildfell Hall* 1848. Charlotte's *Shirley* (1849). In

her last years Charlotte moved out of restricted literary sphere and became
friendly with Thackeray, Harriet Martineau, and Elizabeth Gaskell.
Married Patrick Brontë's curate, Rev. A. B. Nicholls, 1854. Died in
pregnancy, 1855, leaving fragment of a novel entitled 'Emma', published
in *Cornhill Magazine*, April 1860. *The Professor* published posthumously,
1857.

> Gaskell, E. C., *The Life of Charlotte Brontë*. 2 vols (1857)
> Gerin, W., *Anne Brontë* (1959); *Charlotte Brontë: The Evolution of
>   Genius* (Oxford, 1967); *Emily Brontë: A Biography* (Oxford, 1971).
> Hewish, J., *Emily Brontë, A Critical and Biographical Study* (1969).
> Peters, M., *Unquiet Soul: A Biography of Charlotte Brontë* (1975).
> Blom, M. H., *Charlotte Brontë* (1978).

> See: Ratchford, F. E., *The Brontës' Web of Childhood* (New York, 1941).
>   Winnifrith, T., *The Brontës and their Background: Romance and Reality*.
>   (1973).
>   Dingle, H., *The Mind of Emily Brontë* (1974).
>   Eagleton, T. F., *Myths of Power, a Marxist Study of the Brontës*
>   (1975).
>   Moglen, H., *Charlotte Brontë: the Self Conceived* (1976).
>   Davies, S., *Emily Brontë the Artist as a Free Woman* (1983).

BROWNING, Elizabeth Barrett (1806–61) born Coxhoe Hall, near Durham.
Spent childhood at Hope End, a large country house near Ledbury,
Herefordshire. Injured her spine in 1821 and spent rest of her life as an
invalid or semi-invalid. Family moved to Sidmouth, Devon, 1826.
Suffered loss of her favourite brother Bro, who drowned in 1840 at
Torquay. A recluse in Wimpole St, London, until courtship and marriage
with Robert Browning in 1846. A prolific writer. Spent most of her
married life in Florence, where she died. One son, Pen. The poems most
remembered are *The Cry of the Children, Sonnets from the Portuguese*, and
the blank verse poem in nine books *Aurora Leigh*. The poems celebrating
her interest in liberal politics in Italy, *Casa Guidi Windows* and *Poems before
Congress* now command little attention. Feminist criticism tries to
rehabilitate her, but she is not a ubiquitous presence in this study, simply
because so much of the poetry is turgid.

> Hewlett, D., *Elizabeth Barrett Browning* (1953).
> Taplin, G B., *The Life of Elizabeth Barrett Browning* (1957).
> Hayter, A., *Elizabeth Barrett Browning* (1965).
> McAleer, E. C., *The Brownings of Casa Guidi* (1979).
> Mander, Lady M.R.G., *Mrs. Browning, the Story of Elizabeth Barrett*
>   (1980).
> Karlin, D., *The Courtship of Robert Browning and Elizabeth Barrett*
>   (Oxford, 1985).

> See: Hayter, A., *Mrs. Browning: A Poet's Work and its Setting* (1962).

BROWNING, Robert (1812–89) brought up in Camberwell, a suburb of
London. His father had rebelled against the system of exploitation on the
family estates in St Kitts, and supported himself by working as a clerk in
the Bank of England. He was an enthusiastic book collector, and his
library of 6,000 volumes was the basis of Browning's wayward and erudite
knowledge – much of which found its way into the poetry. His mother,
Sarah Anna née Wiedemann, of Scottish and German background was

musical and devout. Most of Browning's education private (he could not stay the course at London University), but he imbibed the culture of thoughtful middle-class circles – including the Flower sisters. Very influenced by Shelley in the early years. The plan (not executed) for *Pauline* (1833) was to reproduce a series of poems emanating from a group of invented characters, and the 'world was never to guess that [they] . . . were not other than one and the same individual'. The presentation of poetic material through personae was thus laid down as a method at an early stage in his career. In the spring of 1834 he accompanied the Russian Consul-General on a mission to Russia. His most formative journeys abroad were to Italy in 1838 and 1844. Two important early works are *Paracelsus* (1835) and *Sordello* (1840), the latter largely responsible for promoting the idea that Browning was obscure and contemptuous of a public. The decade from 1837 to 1847 mainly taken up with playwriting, but the relationship with the actor Macready cooled when the plays proved obscure and unclear. *Colombe's Birthday* was submitted to Kean in 1844, but not acted until 1853. The dramatic ventures came to almost nothing in establishing Browning's fame, but they did help him to develop his most characteristic feature: the dramatic monologue. Many of the poems that appeared in the Bells and Pomegranates series (1841–46) took this form.

In January 1845 Browning began a correspondence with Elizabeth Barrett that led to a meeting, several hundred letters, marriage, and elopement in that order. The letters exchanged form a classic collection of English love epistles. Mrs Browning's ill health made residence in Italy imperative, and Browning only returned to England to live after her death in 1861. The collection largely responsible for establishing his reputation was *Men and Women* (1855), but so long as his wife was alive an embargo was placed on the creation of his main claim to fame: *The Ring and the Book* (1868). The Brownings had one son, Pen, who became a painter. After Elizabeth's death Browning became emotionally entangled with Frances Julia Wedgwood and Lady Ashburton, but the affairs led nowhere – except to guilt and embarrassment. In the 1860s the process whereby Browning became something of a public institution was under-way; the bluff exterior as a carapace for a sensitive and creative soul explored most revealingly in Henry James's *The Private Life* (1892). His didactic presence was recognized in the foundation of the Browning Society even in his lifetime. 1868, Honorary Fellow of Balliol College, Oxford; 1884 LLD. at University of Edinburgh. His later work has usually been regarded as difficult and unrewarding, but recent attempts have been made to present a case for it. He spent the last autumn of his life revisiting the small Italian town of Asolo, associated with his early work *Sordello* and *Pippa Passes*, and *Asolando* was published on the same day that he died in Venice, 12 December 1889. For the Modernists he was one of the few Victorian poets who had redeeming features, and his reputation has never dipped quite as low as Tennyson's.

Miller, B., *Robert Browning: A Portrait* (1952).
Irvine, W. and P. Honan, *The Book, The Ring, and the Poet: A Biography of Robert Browning* (1974).
Maynard, J., *Browning's Youth* (Cambridge, Mass., 1977).
Thomas, D., *Robert Browing, a Life Within Life* (1982).
Karlin, D., *The Courtship of Robert Browning and Elizabeth Barrett* (Oxford, 1985).

See: DeVane, W. C., *A Browning Handbook* (1935; rev. 1955).
Raymond, W. O., *The Infinite Moment . . .* (1950; repr. 1965).
Honan, P., *Browning's Characters: A Study in Poetic Technique* (1961).
Crowell, N. B., *The Triple Soul: Browning's Theory of Knowledge* (Albuquerque, New Mexico, 1963).
Martin, H., *The Faith of Browning* (1963).
King, R. A., *The Bow and the Lyre: The Art of Browning* (1964).
Litzinger, B., *Time's Revenges: Browning's Reputation as a Thinker, 1889–1962* (1964).
Ward, M., *Browning and His World*, 2 vols (1967–69).
Shaw, W. D., *The Dialectical Temper: The Rhetorical Art of Robert Browning* (1968).
Drew, P., *The Poetry of Browning, a Critical Introduction* (1970).
Crowell, N. B., *A Reader's Guide to Browning* (1972).
Gridley, R. E., *Robert Browning* (1972).
Hair, D., *Browning's Experiments with Genre* (1972).
Jack, I., *Browning's Major Poetry* (1973).
Ryals, C. de L., *Browning's Later Poetry 1871–1889* (Ithaca, Ny, 1975).
Flowers, B. S., *Browning and the Modern Tradition* (1976).
Tucker, H. Jr, *Browning's Beginnings* (1980).
Gridley, R. E., *The Brownings and France* (1982).
Korg, J., *Browning and Italy* (Athens, Ohio, 1983).

BUCHANAN, Robert (1841–1901), born in London, son of proprietor and editor of socialist newspapers. Expelled from private school at Rothesay; two years at University of Glasgow, where he was close friend of David Gray. Determined to have a literary career, and made his way into the company of Lewes, George Eliot, Browning, Dinah Mulock, and Peacock. *Poems and Love Lyrics* (1858) his first volume of poetry. *Undertones* (1863) composed under the 'watchful eye' of Peacock; a series of dramatic monologues spoken by classical and mythological figures. *Idyls and Legends of Inverburn* (1865) is a series of dramatic monologues of ordinary Scottish folk. *London Poems* (1866) ventures into harsh realism, with treatment of slum-dwellers. Buchanan aimed to be a general man of letters, and reported Bismarck's invasion of Schleswig-Holstein. He also wrote numerous novels, reviews, and critical essays. His main claim to fame now is his attack on the aesthetes, beginning with a scandalous portrait of Swinburne in *The Session of the Poets* (1866) and culminating in the notorious *Contemporary Review* (October 1871) article disparaging Rossetti, enlarged in the pamphlet 'The Fleshly School of Poetry and other Phenomena of the Day' (May 1872). This seriously disturbed Rossetti's balance, but the tougher Swinburne replied in the savage *Under the Microscope* (1872) and an article 'The Devil's Due' (the latter leading to a lawsuit in which Buchanan was awarded £150 damages). Yet curiously his *White Rose and Red: A Love Story* (1873) anticipates D. H. Lawrence's sexual philosophy. He was also an enthusiastic advocate of Walt Whitman, who he met in 1885. In the 1880s he wrote many dramas, and *The City of Dream* (1888), which is a wide-sweeping review of man's creeds. *The Outcast* (1891) is a Byronic satire on the times. In *The Wandering Jew* (1893) Christ is blamed for all the evils committed in his name. He became bankrupt in 1894 and his final years were a struggle. One of the mainstays of his life was Harriet Jay. He was very much a picturesque continuation of the earlier traditions of Grub Street. He is permanently set in the amber of Pound's *Hugh Selwyn Mauberley* as 'foetid Buchanan'.

Jay, H., *Robert Buchanan: Some Account of his Life, his Life's Work and Literary Friendships* (1903).

Cassidy, J., *Robert W. Buchanan* (New York, 1973).

See: Walker, A. S., *Buchanan, the Poet of Modern Revolt: an Introduction to his Poetry* (1901).

Cassidy, J., 'Buchanan and the Fleshly Controversy', *PMLA*, 67 (1952), 65–93.

Murray, C., *D. G. Rossetti, A. C. Swinburne and R. W. Buchanan: the Fleshly School Revisited* (1983).

CLARE, John (1793–1864), brought up as an agricultural labourer in Helpston, Northamptonshire, at a time when enclosure was altering the open and picturesque nature of the countryside. Had access to books in a country-house library, and much influenced by seventeenth- and early-eighteenth-century poetry when he came to write himself. His early collections were *Poems Descriptive of Rural Life and Scenery* (1821), *The Village Minstrel* (1821), and *The Shepherd's Calender* (1827). Clare was a primitive and an oddity, but his texts were tidied up by his editor, John Taylor, to make them acceptable. Recent editorial practice has tended to reverse this trend, to produce something close to Clare's unpunctuated manuscripts. His early poetry was a very direct, well-informed, and unsentimental view of the countryside. Then in the 1830s and 1840s a change came over his poetic character; his work began to represent more of the inner man; it gave signs of a greater forthrightness and purposeful commitment. Alas, some of the impetus for this new direction had its sources in growing madness. He spent the last two decades of his life in asylums: at Matthew Allen's establishment in High Beech. Epping Forest, and in Northampton Asylum. The authorities encouraged him to write, but the late poems were not published until after his death, and the last collection during his lifetime was *The Rural Muse* (1853). Sexual fantasy is an important component in his later poetry, but not much of it celebrates his wife Martha Turner (Patty). There was also an obsession with Byron, and his own attempt at a *Childe Harold*. He is an unusual poet, with precise and detailed perception at one end of the creative spectrum and Blakean vision at the other.

Martin, F., *The Life of John Clare* (1865).

Cherry, J. L., *Life and Remains of John Clare* (1873).

Storey, E., *A Right to Song, the Life of John Clare* (1982).

See: Barrell, J., *The Idea of Landscape and the Sense of Place 1730–1840* (Cambridge, 1972).

Storey, G. M., *The Poetry of John Clare* (1974).

Brownlow, T., *John Clare and Picturesque Landscape* (Oxford, 1983).

Chilcott, T. J., *A Real World and Doubting Mind: A Study of the Poetry of John Clare* (1985).

Deacon, G., *John Clare and the Folk Tradition* (1985).

CLOUGH, Arthur Hugh (1819–61) born in Liverpool to a prosperous landed family moving into trade. His father emigrated to Charleston, North

Carolina, to run an export business. His mother was a cultivated religious woman, with stern ideas on duty. Clough came back to England in 1828 to be educated first at Chester then at Rugby School, where he came under the spell of Thomas Arnold. As with Matthew Arnold the ethos of the school provided him with attitudes and ideas both to follow and to react against for the rest of his life. In 1837 he went up to Balliol College, Oxford, and came under the spell of his mathematical tutor, W. G. Ward, whose High Anglicanism was so indistinguishable from Romanism that it was condemned by the Convocation of the University in 1845. Clough himself ended up in a middle position of agonized agnosticism, and his tortured scrupulosity often hindered his capacity to act decisively. The contradictory pressures placed on him probably led to his second-class degree in 1841 and his failure to be elected to a Balliol Fellowship. In 1842 he was elected a Fellow of Oriel, where he stayed until 1848, resigning, in the end, on the principle that he could not continue to subscribe to the Thirty-nine Articles of the Church of England. *The Bothie . . .* is a loving evocation of university life. He spent much of 1849 in Italy, witnessing the country's struggles for independence and composing *Amours de Voyage*. Unlike Tennyson, he did not regard himself principally as a 'career poet', and his work had to be forced out of him sometimes. *The Bothie . . .* (1848) and *Ambarvalia* (1849) were the only collections published in England in his lifetime (although *Amours de Voyage* did appear in *The Atlantic Monthly* in 1858), and the masterpiece *Dipsychus* remained unfinished. He was Principal of University Hall, London, from 1849 to 1852, and Professor of English Literature from 1851 to 1852, but had to resign when he came into disagreement with the Dissenters running the institution. He lived in Cambridge, Massachusetts, among the Boston Brahmins, in 1852. In 1854 married Blanche Smith. The marriage was happy, but she is now remembered as votaress of grundyism, trying to limit the posthumously published *oeuvre* in the interests of propriety. He was an examiner in the Education Office, London, from 1853 to 1861. His latter years were taken up in translating Plutarch. He died in Florence.

Chorley, K., *Clough: The Uncommitted Mind* (1962).
Williams, D., *Too Quick Despairer: the Life and Work of A. H. Clough* (1969).

See: Levy, G., *Arthur Hugh Clough* (1938).
Armstrong, I., *Arthur Hugh Clough* (1962).
Houghton, W. E., *The Poetry of Clough: An Essay in Revaluation* (1963).
Veyriras, P., *Clough* (Paris, 1964).
Timko, M., *Innocent Victorian: The Satiric Poetry of Clough* (Athens, Ohio, 1966).
Greenberger, E. B., *Clough: The Growth of a Poet's Mind* (1970).
Biswas, R. K., *Clough: Towards a Reconsideration* (1972).

DE TABLEY, Lord (1835–95) was John Byrne Leicester Warren until he succeeded to the peerage in 1887. Born at Tabley House, near Knutsford, Cheshire, but spent most of his early life abroad with his mother. Entered Eton in 1848 and Christ Church in 1852, where he read history and classics. Spent time in the embassy in Constantinople then called to the Bar from Lincoln's Inn. Failed to win a seat in Parliament. Wrote monographs on numismatics and local flora. In 1883 became a Fellow of the Society of Antiquaries. He did not marry and lived a retired life. His first volume of *Poems* was 1859, the collected edition was 1903. In addition he wrote novels and metrical dramas. The poetry is often Browningesque, but his main inspiration was sought in classical learning. The mood of his work is often fatalistic. Interest in him was aroused by A. H. Miles's selection (1891), and he is a relatively forgotten poet well worth reviving.

See: Taplin, G. B., *The Life, Works and Literary Reputation of Lord de Tabley* (Cambridge, Mass., 1946).
Pitts, G., 'Lord de Tabley: Poet of Frustration', *West Virginia Universitv Philological Papers*, 14 (1963), 57–73.

DIXON, Richard Watson (1833–1900), born Islington. Educated at Methodist College, Richmond, Surrey, King Edward's School, Birmingham, and Pembroke College, Oxford, where he associated with the Pre-Raphaelites, Morris and Burne-Jones. Curate in Lambeth and Newington Butts. Taught at Highgate School, where he met the pupil G. M. Hopkins; a full and fascinating correspondence exists (ed. C. C. Abbott, 1935). Second master at Carlisle High School, 1862–68; minor canon at Carlisle Cathedral, 1868–75. Vicar of Hayton, 1875–83, and of Warkworth, 1883–1900. His first collection, *Christ's Company and Other Poems* (1861), is in the aesthetico-ritual tradition of late Tractarianism. *Mano* (1883) is a long poem in *terza-rima*. His last collections are *Odes and Eclogues* (1884) and *Lyrical Poems* (1887).

Sambrook, A. J., *A Poet Hidden: The Life of Richard Watson Dixon* (1962).

DOBELL, Sydney Thompson (1824–74) born Cranbrook, Kent. Educated privately. Spent most of his life in Cheltenham, but 1854–57 in Scotland. Associated with the 'Spasmodic School', and *Balder* (1853), dealing with the egotistic figure of the artist, is a key work in the movement. *The Roman* (1850) is about the liberation of Italy. His essays were posthumously published in 1876.

Jolly, E., *Life and Letters of Dobell*, 2 vols (1878).
Weinstein, M. A., *W. E. Aytoun and the Spasmodic Controversy* (1968).

DODGSON, Charles Lutwidge (1832–98) wrote under pseudonym 'Lewis Carroll'. He grew up in a family of eleven children, and from childhood was used to producing word games, squibs, parodies, and puzzles. Educated at Rugby and Christ Church, Oxford, where he became a don in 1855. His best-known work, *Alice in Wonderland* (1865), had its source in a boat trip on the Thames with three daughters of the Dean of Christ Church, H. G. Liddell. The sequel was *Through the Looking Glass, And What Alice Found There* (1871). Other works include *Phantasmagoria and other Poems* (1869) and *Sylvie and Bruno* (1889, 1893). He was also a keen amateur photographer. Carroll and Edward Lear are the two principal writers of nonsense literature in the period.

Reed, L., *The Life of Carroll* (1932).
Green, R. L., *The Story of Carroll* (1949).
Hudson, D., *Lewis Carroll* (1958).
Clark, A., *Lewis Carroll* (1979).

See: Empson, W., *Some Versions of Pastoral* (1935).
Sewell, E., *The Field of Nonsense* (1952).

EVANS, Sebastian (1830–1909) managed the art department of a glassworks near Birmingham and edited the *Birmingham Daily Gazette*. 1868 elected to Parliament; 1878 helped to found the Conservative weekly *The People*, which he edited until 1881. Exhibited at the Royal Academy and produced wood-carving and bookbinding. He was fascinated by the Grail legend, producing *In Quest of the Holy Grail* (1898). George Macbeth has described the title-poem of *Brother Fabian's Manuscript and Other Poems* (1865) 'the most important forgotten masterpiece of the Victorian period'.

FITZGERALD, Edward (1809–83), born at Bredfield House and lived with his parents at Boulge Hall (near Woodbridge, Suffolk) until 1838. Early education partly in France. Went up to Trinity College, Cambridge, 1826, where he was familiar with the Speddings and Thackeray. Later a close friend of Tennyson. A short-lived marriage. Most of his life spent near his birthplace. He is now exclusively remembered for one work: *The Rubáiyát of Omar Khayyám*. His self-indulgent and sceptical outlook completely out of line with the main current of Victorian culture.

> Terhune, A. K., *The Life of FitzGerald* (1947).
> Richardson, J., *FitzGerald* (1960).

> See: Arberry, A. J., *The Rubáiyát of Omar Khayyám* (1949).
> Arberry, A. J., *Omar Khayyám and FitzGerald* (1959).

HARDY, Thomas (1840–1928), son of builder and mason; his mother had been in service. Later in life he attempted to play down the humbleness of his background. Born in Higher Bockhampton. Educated at village school, then in Dorchester. Articled to Dorchester architect, John Hicks, 1856–62. Worked in London for neo-Gothic architect, Arthur Blomfield. Returned to Dorset, and became involved with a cousin, Tryphena Sparks. First novel, 'The Poor Man and the Lady' (now lost), not published. In the 1860s he began writing poetry, but no manuscripts have survived and it is not certain how much they were revised for *Wessex Poems* (1898) and other later collections. The only early poem to have survived for certain in original form is 'The Bride Night Fire', published in *The Gentleman's Magazine* (November 1875). His novel-publishing career begins with *Desperate Remedies* (1871) and ends with *Jude the Obscure* (1894–95). While on a church restoration project at St Juliot's in Cornwall he met and fell in love with Emma Lavinia Gifford. The courtship and memories of it prompted some of his best poetry. Married September 1874. Later the marriage marred by division and bitterness; the stages in the relationship are charted in the poems he wrote after her death in 1912. A remarkable and unusual work is the verse drama *The Dynasts*. His second wife Florence Dugdale, 1914. Order of Merit 1910. His ashes buried in Westminster Abbey, his heart in Stinsford, not far from his home, Max Gate. To a large extent the history of Hardy as a poet belongs to the next volume, but during this period he was moving towards a poetic aesthetic that in some ways resembles that of Hopkins.

> Hardy, F., *The Early Life of Thomas Hardy, 1840–1891* (1928).
> Hardy, F. *The Later Years of Thomas Hardy, 1892–1928* (1930).
> (Actually Hardy's carefully selected autobiography, except for the description of the funeral; M. Millgate's edition (1984) restores the text to the state in which Hardy left it.)
> Deacon, L. and T. Coleman, *Providence and Mr. Hardy* (1966). (A

controversial work, proposing sensational theories about Hardy's private life with Tryphena Sparks.)

Gittings, R., *Young Thomas Hardy* (1975).
Gittings, R. *The Older Hardy* (1978).
Millgate, M., *Thomas Hardy, a Biography* (Oxford, 1982).

See: Southworth, J. G., *The Poetry of Thomas Hardy* (New York, 1947).
Hynes, S., *The Pattern of Hardy's Poetry* (Chapel Hill, NC, 1961).
Marsden, K., *The Poems of Thomas Hardy: A Critical Introduction* (1969).
Bailey, J. O., *The Poetry of Thomas Hardy* (Chapel Hill, NC, 1970).
Davie, D., *Thomas Hardy and British Poetry* (1972).
Zietlow, P., *Moments of Vision The Poetry of Thomas Hardy* (Cambridge, Mass., 1974).
Paulin, T., *Thomas Hardy: The Poetry of Perception* (1975).
Pinion, F. B., *A Commentary on the Poems of Thomas Hardy* (1976).
Richardson, J. E., *Thomas Hardy, the Poetry of Necessity* (1977).
Taylor, D., *Hardy's Poetry* (1981).
Elliott, R. W., *Thomas Hardy's English* (1984).

HAWKER, Robert Stephen (1803–75), born Stoke Damerel, Devon. Educated Cheltenham School and Pembroke College, Oxford. At Magdalen Hall, Oxford 1824–28. Won the Newdigate Prize 1827. Married Charlotte Eliza Rawleigh in 1823 (d. 1863); (2) Pauline Anne Kuczynski in 1864. Curate in North Tamerton, Cornwall, 1831–34; Vicar of Morwenstow, Cornwall, 1834–75, with Wellcombe, Cornwall, 1851–1875. Embraced Roman Catholic faith just before his death. His *The Quest of the Sangraal* is a long blank verse poem, based on Arthurian legends. Tennyson admired it very much. He also wrote ballads celebrating old Cornish legends and traditions.

Byles, C. E., *Life and Letters of Hawker* (1905).
Brendon, P., *Hawker of Morwenstow* (1975).

See: Burrows, M. F., *Hawker: A Study of His Thought and Poetry* (1926).
Rowse, A. L., 'Robert Stephen Hawker of Morwenstow: a Belated Medieval', *Essays and Studies*, n.s. 12 (1959), 106–32.

HOPKINS, Gerard Manley (1844–89), son of Manley Hopkins, founder of a marine insurance firm and a minor poet; educated at Highgate School, London, and Balliol College, Oxford, 1863–66. The family was cultivated and artistic: his brothers Arthur and Everard became professional artists, and he produced accomplished sketches in a Pre-Raphaelite style. At Oxford he was the 'star' of his college, and surviving undergraduate essays are brilliant. He was influenced by Pater (for a time his tutor) and High Church figures such as Pusey and Liddon. In October 1866 he was received into the Roman Catholic Church by Newman, and in 1868 entered the Society of Jesus to begin training for the priesthood. His novitiate was at Manresa House, and in 1870 at Stonyhurst. In 1877 he was ordained as a priest and began his duties as subminster and teacher at Mount St Mary's College, Chesterfield. In July 1878 he became curate at the Jesuit Church in Mount St, London, and in October of the same year moved to St Aloysius's Church, Oxford, for a brief spell. This was followed by gruelling service in a series of industrial parishes in Bedford Leigh, near Manchester, Liverpool, and Glasgow. In 1884 he was appointed as Fellow in Classics at the Royal University of Ireland and Professor of Greek at University College, Dublin, the posts he held at the time of his death from typhoid fever. Buried in Glasnevin cemetery.

Very little published during his lifetime; *The Month* did not accept *The Wreck of the Deutschland* in 1876. A handful of poems in Miles, but the general public had to wait until the Bridges edition of 1918. He destroyed some of his own poems in 1868 – under the influence of the Florentine ascetic Savonarola. His *Journals* survive (up to 1875): mainly detailed observations of nature, often the source of poetic imagery. A full correspondence with Bridges, Patmore, and Dixon is now in print, a marvellous demonstration of a highly critical and creative intelligence in action. He is now widely regarded as one of the three or four greatest poets of the era.

> Lahey, G. F., *Gerard Manley Hopkins* (1930).
> Thomas, A., S. J., *Hopkins the Jesuit: The Years of Training* (1969).
> Bergonzi, B., *Gerard Manley Hopkins* (1976).

See: Pick, J., *Gerard Manley Hopkins, Priest and Poet* (1942).
> Gardner, W. H., *Gerard Manley Hopkins 1844–1889: A Study of Poetic Idiosyncrasy in Relation to Poetic Tradition* (1949).
> Weyand, N. ed., *Immortal Diamond: Studies in Gerard Manley Hopkins* (New York, 1949).
> Downes, D. A., *Hopkins: A Study of His Ignatian Spirit* (1959).
> Bender, T. K., *Gerard Manley Hopkins: The Classical Background and Critical Reception of His Work* (1966).
> Johnson, W. S., *Gerard Manley Hopkins, the Poet as Victorian* (Ithaca, NY, 1968).
> McChesney, D., *A Hopkins Commentary: An Explanatory Commentary on the Main Poems, 1876–89* (1968).
> Schneider, E. W., *The Dragon in the Gate: Studies in the Poetry of Gerard Manley Hopkins* (Berkeley and Los Angeles, 1968).
> Mariani, P. L., *A Commentary on the Complete Poems of Hopkins* (1969).
> Sulloway, A. G., *Gerard Manley Hopkins and the Victorian Temper* (1972).
> Heaney, S., *The Fire i' the Flint: Reflections on the Poetry of Gerard Manley Hopkins* (1974).
> Thornton, R .K. R., ed., *All My Eyes See: The Visual World of Gerard Manley Hopkins* (Sunderland, 1975).
> Milward, P., *Landscape and Inscape: Vision and Inspiration in Hopkins' Poetry* (1977).
> Milroy, J., *The Language of Hopkins* (1977).
> Robinson, J., *In Extremity: A Study of Hopkins* (1977).
> MacKenzie, N., *A Reader's Guide to Gerard Manley Hopkins* (Ithaca, NY, 1981).

See: Storey, G., *A Preface to Hopkins* (1981).
> Bump, J., *Gerard Manley Hopkins* (Boston, 1982).
> Downes, D. A., *The Great Sacrifice: Studies in Hopkins* (New York, 1983).

HORNE, Richard Hengist (1802–84), born Edmonston, educated at Enfield, failed to enter East India Service, accepted in 1825 a place as midshipman in the Mexican Navy, seeing service in Spanish–Mexican War.

Various adventures in Canada; returned to London 1825. Became passionately concerned with promoting the Shelleyan ideal of the visionary and useful Romantic artist. He wished to form a 'Society of English Literature' which would provide writers a pension for life. Wrote *Spirit of Peers and People: A National Tragi-Comedy* (1834). Moved in Browning circle, and studied historical villains, such as Cosimo de Medici, Gregory VII, and Judas Iscariot, to offer a critique of the idea that 'the end justifies the means'. Horne had a good knowledge of the Hegelian hero who would recognize when times were ripe for development, and such a character is central in *Orion* (1843), the book that sold for one farthing to reach the widest public. It shows the worker linking his strength to intellect to achieve dreams of freedom and equality. *A New Spirit of the Age* (1844) is an imitation of Hazlitt's *The Spirit of the Age* (1825), and presents a critical portrait of the main tendencies and characters of his time. Elizabeth Barrett helped in its production. 1845 helped Dickens to establish the *Daily News*. 1847 married. Worked on *Household Words*. Emigrated to the goldfields of Australia, but failed to make his fortune. 1869 returned to England a forgotten figure.

Pearl, C., *Always Morning* (Melbourne, Cheshire, 1960).
Blainey, A., *The Farthing Poet* (1968).

KEBLE, John (1792–1866), educated at Corpus Christi College, Oxford. Became Fellow and Tutor at Oriel College (where Newman and Pusey were also Fellows), and Professor of Poetry at Oxford 1831–41. His sermon on 'National Apostasy' in 1833 is generally regarded as having inaugurated the Oxford Movement. From 1836 until his death vicar of Hursley (five miles south-west of Winchester). His collection of sacred verse *The Christian Year* (1827) had enormous success, and the income from it enabled him to rebuild his parish church. *Lyra Innocentium* (1846) was rather less popular. Keble contributed forty-six poems (signed y) to the Tractarian anthology *Lyra Apostolica* (1836). Keble College, Oxford was founded as a memorial.

Lock, W., *Keble: a Biography* (1893).
Wood, E. F. L., *John Keble* (1909, 1932).
Battiscombe, G., *John Keble* (1963).

See: Yonge, C. M. *Musings over the Christian Year . . .* (1871).
Tennyson, G. B., *Victorian Devotional Poetry: The Tractarian Mode* (Cambridge, Mass., 1980).

LEAR, Edward (1812–88), born in London. Studied in Sass's Art School (immortalized as Gandish's in Thackeray's *The Newcomes*). Came under influence of Pre-Raphaelites, and his Middle Eastern landscape painting has some resemblance to that of J. F. Lewis (who Ruskin regarded as a kind of Pre-Raphaelite). Lived in San Remo, Italy, 1868–88. His painting is now much prized and collected, but his principal claim to fame is as a writer of nonsense poetry, beginning with the collection *A Book of Nonsense* (1846). Others included *Nonsense Songs, Stories, Botany, and Alphabets* (1871) and *Laughable Lyrics* (1877).

Davidson, A., *Lear: Landscape Painter and Nonsense Poet* (1938).
Richardson, J., *Lear* (1965).
Noakes, V., *Edward Lear: The Life of a Wanderer* (1968).
Lehmann, R. F. J., *Lear and His World* (1977).

See: Sewell, E., *The Field of Nonsense* (1952).
Byrom, T., *Nonsense and Wonder: The Poems and Cartoons of Lear* (1977).

MACAULAY, Thomas Babington (1800–59), born in Rothley Temple, Leicestershire; educated privately and at Aspenden Hall, Hertfordshire. Trinity College, Cambridge, 1818–22, where he won the Chancellor's Medal for English Verse in 1819 and 1821. Called to the Bar, 1826. Fellow of Trinity College, 1824–31. Contributor to *Edinburgh Review*, 1825–45. Elected Whig Member of Parliament for Calne, 1830; Legal Adviser to the Supreme Council of India, 1834–38. Member of Parliament for Edinburgh, 1839–47; 1852–56; Secretary of War, 1839–41; Paymaster-General, 1846–47. Lord Rector of University of Glasgow, 1849. Created Baron Macaulay of Rothley, 1857. He was a highly popular writer, as essayist, historian, and poet. *Lays of Ancient Rome* (1842) a best-seller, and remained in vogue for the rest of the century.

Trevelyan, G. O., *The Life and Letters*, 2 vols (1876).
Bryant, A., *Macaulay* (1932).
Potter, G. R., *Macaulay* (1959).
Clive, J., *Macaulay The Shaping of an Historian* (1973).
Millgate, J., *Macaulay* (1973).

MEREDITH, George (1828–1909), son of Portsmouth tailor; mother died when he was five. After his father's bankruptcy lived with relations near Petersfield. Little known about early years of education, but 1842–44 spent profitably at Neuwied on the Rhine, at the liberal and humane school of the Moravian Brothers. 1846–49 articled to the solicitor Richard Charnock, who had contact with literary circles. Early work printed in *The Monthly Observer*. Married Mary Ellen Nicholls, T. L. Peacock's widowed daughter, 1849; one son, Arthur. Some of happiness of early relationship perhaps expressed in strikingly beautiful 'Love in the Valley' (in *Poems* 1851, but very heavily revised in 1878), but bitterness of break-up of marriage motivates *Modern Love* (1862). His wife eloped with Pre-Raphaelite painter Henry Wallis in 1858 (in 1856 Meredith sat, or rather lay, as model for his famous *The Death of Chatterton*, now in Tate); she died 1861. The other works in the 1862 volume are 'Poems of the English Roadside', revealing his interest in varied modes of speech. His first successful (though at the time scandalous) novel *The Ordeal of Richard Feverel* (1859). In 1860s a columnist for the *Ipswich Journal* and chief reader for Chapman and Hall. Married Marie Vulliamy 1864; two children. Moved to Flint Cottage, near Box Hill, Surrey, 1868. Wrote a large number of difficult and elusive novels, ending in *Celt and Saxon* (1910). The use of language in them often borders on the poetic, and the same preoccupations that occur in the poetry (mainly with man and nature) are found in the fiction. Collections of poems include *Poems and Lyrics of the Joy of Earth* (1883), *Ballads and Poems of Tragic Life* (1887), *A Reading of Earth* (1888), *Poems . . .* (1892), *The Nature Poems* (1898) *A Reading of Life* (1901) and *Poems . . .* (1909). The only important critical work is *On the Idea of Comedy* (1877). Elected to Order of Merit (1905).

Stevenson L., *The Ordeal of George Meredith: A Biography* (New York, 1953).

Cline, C. L., ed., *The Letters of George Meredith*, 3 vols (Oxford, 1970).

Williams, D., *George Meredith: His Life and Lost Love* (1977).

See: Trevelyan, G. M., *The Poetry and Philosophy of George Meredith* (1906).

Sassoon, S. L., *Meredith* (1948).

Kelvin, N., *A Troubled Eden: Nature and Society in the Works of George Meredith* (Stanford, California, 1961).

Fletcher, I. ed., *Meredith Now* (1971).

Bernstein, C. L., *Precarious Enchantment: A Reading of Meredith's Poetry* (Washington, DC, 1979).

MORRIS, William (1834–96), son of wealthy stockbroker; childhood spent on edge of Epping Forest, where he rode his pony wearing toy suit of armour. Supposed to have read whole of Scott by the time he was seven. At Marlborough College (1848–51), where he pursued antiquarian interests. Family moved to Water House, Walthamstow (now the William Morris Gallery). 1853–55 at Exeter College, Oxford, where he met Edward Burne-Jones, Charles Faulkner, Richard Watson Dixon, Cormell Price, and William Fulford. When twenty-one had an income of £900 p.a., which he thought of using to establish a monastic 'Brotherhood'; all through his life he returned to notions of co-operative societies. Began composing poetry at university. After a trip to northern France in 1855 Morris decided to become an architect and entered articles with the Gothic Revivalist, George Edmund Street. In the office he met a lifelong friend, Philip Webb. Morris supported the *Oxford and Cambridge Magazine* in 1856, which included five of his poems and eight prose tales. Abandoned architecture for painting and shared a studio with Burne-Jones at 17 Red Lion Square, working under the influence of Rossetti. In 1857 joined with Rossetti, Burne-Jones, Arthur Hughes, and others on Pre-Raphaelite decorations of the Oxford Union; met and married Jane Burden. *The Defence of Guenevere and Other Poems* published at his expense (1858). Heavily inspired by Malory and Froissart. Moved into Red House, Bexleyheath, Kent, 1860, a thirteenth-century design by Webb. Furnishing it led to formation of the firm Morris, Marshall, Faulkner, & Co. in 1861, to produce neo-medieval furniture, fabrics, and glass. In 1865 took up residence over the firm's workshops in Queen Sq., Bloomsbury. Spent 1860s producing *The Earthly Paradise* (1868–70), the longest poem in the English language. Very eclectic influences, including the classics and the Icelandic sagas. In 1870s lived alternately in Kelmscott House, Hammersmith, and Kelmscott Manor, Oxfordshire, but the beauty of these surroundings marred by the intimate relationships between Rossetti and Jane. Unhappy love and unfaithful women a major theme in the poetry.

Looking for visions of ideal, simple societies Morris travelled to Iceland in 1871 and 1873. *Love is Enough* (1873) 'a sort of masque'. In 1875 published a translation of Virgil's *Aeneid*. His last major original poem *The Story of Sigurd and Volsung and the Fall of the Niblungs* published 1876. *News from Nowhere* (1890) is a Utopian romance. *Poems by the Way* (1891) his last volume of poems, and printed on the Kelmscott Press. Political involvement began in 1876 with a pamphlet on the Balkan atrocities. He was a founder member of the Society for the Protection of Ancient Buildings ('Anti-Scrape') 1877. January 1883 joined the Democratic

Federation (later the Social Democratic Federation), then in 1884 a
principal figure in the breakaway Socialist League, whose organ was the
Commonweal. When it moved in anarchist directions he set up (1890) the
independent Hammersmith Socialist Society. In the last years of his life he
concentrated on the Kelmscott Press, which issued fifty-three books, the
most famous being the edition of Chaucer, with illustrations by Burne-
Jones. A dominant influence on the Arts and Crafts Society and the Art
Worker's Guild. Died in Hammersmith, buried at Kelmscott.

> Mackail, J. W., *The Life of William Morris*, 2 vols (1899).
> Thompson, E. P., *William Morris: Romantic to Revolutionary* (1955;
> rev. 1977).
> Henderson, P., *William Morris: His Life, Work and Friends* (1967).
> Lindsay, J., *William Morris: His Life and Work* (1975).
> Faulkner, P., *Against the Age: An Introduction to William Morris*
> (1980).
> Stansky, P., *Redesigning the World: William Morris, the 1880s and the
> Arts and Crafts* (Princeton, NJ, 1985).

> See: Gardner, D. R., *An 'Idle Singer' and His Audience: A Study of
> William Morris' Poetic Reputation in England, 1858–1900* (The Hague,
> 1975).
> Oberg, C. H., *A Pagan Prophet, William Morris* (1978).

NEWMAN, John Henry (1801–90), educated at Trinity College, Oxford,
1817–22. Fellow of Oriel College, Oxford, 1822. Ordained 1824. As Vicar
of St Mary's, Oxford 1828–43 a leading figure in the Oxford Movement.
Contributed to *Tracts for the Times*, 1833–41. Converted to Roman
Catholicism in 1845 – for reasons fully stated in his *Apologia*. Established
the Oratory of St Philip Neri in Birmingham, 1848. Rector of the Catholic
University of Ireland, 1851–58. Created cardinal, 1879. Newman's early
poetry included in the Tractarian collection *Lyra Apostolica* (1836). *The
Dream of Gerontius* (1866) set to music by Elgar. His last collection is
Echoes from the Oratory (1884).

> Ward, W., *The Life of Newman* (1912).
> Harrold, C. F., *Newman* (1945).
> Trevor, M., *Newman*, 2 vols (1962).
> Dessain, C. S., *Newman* (1966).

> See: Tennyson, G. B., *Victorian Devotional Poetry: The Tractarian Mode*
> (Cambridge, Mass., 1980).

PATMORE, Coventry (1823–95), son of Peter and Eliza, born Woodford, Essex.
His father an editor, novelist, and critic, friend of Lamb, Hunt, Hazlitt,
and Milnes. Educated privately, but sent to Collège de France in Paris
when sixteen. Had an unhappy love-affair in France, recorded in two
poems in his first collection (1844). His father went bankrupt, and he
supported himself with hack writing until in 1846 he became assistant
librarian at the British Museum. Partly through reading Catholic
theologians he came to value the mystical significance of married love as
'the burning heart of the Universe'. He produced a larger body of literary
criticism than Tennyson and Browning. Married in 1847 to Emily Augusta
Andrews. The 1849 volume, *Tamerton Church Tower and Other Poems*
includes pieces later incorporated into *The Angel in the House* (completed in

1858). It charts the progress of a courtship, but with more emphasis on states of mind than incidents. His study of love continues in *Faithful for Ever* (1860) and *The Victories of Love* (1862), the latter composed while his wife was mortally ill (she died in 1862). In 1864 he resigned his job and went to Rome, where he met his second wife, Marianne Byles, and was received into the Catholic Church. Returned to England and lived at Heron's Ghyll, Sussex. His years here were of poetic uncertainty. Moved in 1874 to London and then to Hastings. *The Unknown Eros* (1877) a loose and flexible form. It moves to a contemplation of man's relationship to his Creator. It had less impact on Victorian readers than the popular *Angel in the House*. In the 1870s Patmore in correspondence on matters poetic with Hopkins. Second wife died 1880, his favourite daughter, Emily, in 1882, and his youngest son, Henry, in 1883. From this point, perhaps because of the family calamities, he ceased to write poetry. In 1881 he married Harriet Robson, governess to his daughters. She was an intelligent and lively woman. In his last decade he returned to prose writing, producing collections such as *Principle in Art* (1889) and *Religio Poetae* (1893). In 1891 moved to Lymington. Francis Thompson, W. E. Henley, and the Meynells were associates of the latter years.

Champneys, B., *Memoirs and Correspondence of Coventry Patmore* (1900).

Gosse, E., *Coventry Patmore* (1905).

Patmore, D., *The Life and Times of Coventry Patmore* (1949).

Oliver, E. J., *Coventry Patmore* (New York, 1956).

See: Page, F., *Patmore – A Study in Poetry* (1933).

Reid, J. C., *The Mind and Art of Coventry Patmore* (1957).

Ball, P. M., *The Heart's Events* (1976).

ROSSETTI, Christina (1830–94), sister of Dante Gabriel. Inherited strong religious convictions from her mother. *Verses* (1847) privately printed on press of maternal grandfather, Gaetano Polidori. Engaged in 1848 to a member of the Pre-Raphaelete Brotherhood, James Collinson, but broke it off in 1850 when he returned to Roman Catholic faith. Failed attempt in 1853 to run a school in Frome, Somerset. Seven poems printed in *The Germ*, but 'Uphill' the first to receive wide public attention, printed in *Macmillan's Magazine* (1861). Influenced by G. Herbert. *Goblin Market and Other Poems* published 1862, with decorated title-page by Dante Gabriel. He also designed the title-page and frontispiece for *The Prince's Progress and Other Poems* (1866). In the 1860s she had a relationship with Charles Cayley, a translator of Dante, but refused him in marriage because 'he was not a Christian'. Travelled to northern France in 1862 and Italy in 1865. *Sing-song: A Nursery Rhyme Book* (1872) illustrated by the Pre-Raphaelite artist Arthur Hughes is for children, Macmillan reprinted her early work in 1875, adding thirty-seven stray poems. *A Pageant and Other Poems* (1881) contains two sonnet cycles: *Monna Innominata* and *Later Life*. Her later years were haunted by loneliness and ill health. She produced devotional works for the Society for Promoting Christian Knowledge, but severed herself from the society when it refused to oppose vivisection. Died from cancer. In 1896 William Michael Rossetti edited *New Poems*, and in 1904 Macmillan published the standard edition. The poetry shows Pre-Raphaelite attention to detail, strong interest in emblematic and typological signification, and sensitivity to lyrical melody and cadence. Dante Gabriel tried to press her, not entirely successfully, to respond to 'real abundant Nature'.

Bell, M., *Christina Rossetti* (1898).
Sanders, M. F., *The Life of Christina Rossetti* (1930).
Stuart, D., *Christina Rossetti* (1930).
Shove, F., *Christina Rossetti, a Study* (Cambridge, 1931).
Thomas, E. W., *Christina Georgina Rossetti* (New York, 1932).
Waller, R. D., *The Rossetti Family, 1824–1854* (Manchester, 1932).
Zaturenska, M., *Christina Rossetti: A Portrait with a Background* (New York, 1949).
Sawtell, M., *Christina Rossetti, her Life and Religion* (1955).
Packer, L. M., *Christina Rossetti* (Berkeley, 1963).
Battiscombe, G., *Christina Rossetti: A Divided Life* (1981).

ROSSETTI, Dante Gabriel (1823–82), eldest son of the exiled Dante scholar Gabriele Rossetti, Professor of Italian at King's College, London, and Frances Polidori Rossetti. His immediate family circle nurtured genius; his sister Maria Rossetti became an author and an Anglican nun, his other sister Christina (q.v.) was the famous lyric poet, and his brother William Michael a man of letters and a minor poet. Educated at King's College School, 1837–42, then at Cary's Academy of Art until 1846, the latter a preparation for the Royal Academy which Rossetti entered in 1846. He left after a year to apprentice himself to Ford Madox Brown. Meanwhile his literary pursuits continued unabated and his range of interest was very wide, although there was always special attention to medieval works, such as Dante and the *Nibelungenleid*. In 1847 he began composing some of the poems by which he is known (although it is likely that he falsified evidence to support precocity). Even at this early age he felt divided aims as to whether to pursue a career in painting or poetry – expressed later in the sonnet 'Lost on Both Sides'. In 1848 Rossetti helped to form the Pre-Raphaelite Brotherhood with six other members: Millais, Holman Hunt, his brother William Michael, James Collinson, F. G. Stephens, and Thomas Woolner (q.v.). Associates of the group included W. H. Deverell, Ford Madox Brown, William Bell Scott (q.v.), Coventry Patmore (q.v.), and Dante Gabriel's sister Christina.

Most of the aims of the early Pre-Raphaelites are outlined in their periodical *The Germ* (1850). Unlike the German Nazarenes it was not strictly an archaizing movement (although nostalgia for the past was a feature never far from the surface, particularly with Rossetti); the label was meant to imply that painting had taken a wrong turn after Raphael (1483–1520) by becoming too influenced by mannered studio practices and doctrinaire schools of art, and the only way to correct this state of affairs was to paint in the spirit, but not necessarily the manner, of primitive painters such as Gozzoli (who the Pre-Raphaelites knew by way of Lasinio's engravings of the Campo Santo in Pisa). Ruskin eventually took up the cause of the Pre-Raphaelites, and it became the dominant movement of the 1850s, and caused many painters not in the original circle to paint in their manner. The theoretical doctrines of the movement, concerning direct vision and uncompromising authenticity, were easily transferable to poetry (although to some extent the battle had already been fought in the Romantic Movement), and Rossetti's 'My Sister's Sleep' and 'The Blessed Damozel', both exercises in the manner, were printed in *The Germ*. By 1853 members of the original group were drifting apart, but a second wave came in 1857 when Rossetti and young Oxford admirers decorated the Oxford Union. These included William Morris (q.v.) and Edward Burne-Jones. Jane Burden was snatched up into this circle, even as Lizzie Siddal had been removed from her environment in 1850. The Pre-Raphaelites cultivated a new style of feminine beauty, and in the real world it was randomly scattered, usually in the lower classes rather than the upper. The Pygmalion myth hovers over their approach to women.

The death of Lizzie in curious circumstances in February 1862 left Rossetti free to develop an intense relationship with Jane Burden – who by this time was Mrs Morris. As a painter Rossetti never became a public painter in the way that Millais and Hunt did; he preferred to work for private commissions, and sometimes sell the same painting one or two times over. He was not unastute financially. Similarly, as a poet he was not a public figure until the edition of his work in 1870. To produce it he found it necessary to exhume a manuscript of his work that had been buried in Lizzie's coffin. In both painting and poetry the image of woman as a mysterious, powerful, loved object is the dominant one, and he set himself against all the publicly promoted ideologies of the age. From 1870 onwards he became dependent on chloral, which accentuated his latent tendencies towards paranoia and depression. There was a period of heightened creativity in 1871 when Rossetti rented Kelmscott Manor with Morris, and was closeted alone for weeks; something like thirty poems for *The House of Life* date from this time. Rossetti's persecution mania was exacerbated when in 1871 Robert Buchanan attacked Rossetti as the principal exponent in a school of sensual poetry in 'The Fleshly School of Poetry'. Rossetti responded with an essay 'The Stealthy School of Criticism'. Buchanan's riposte was an expanded version of the original essay (1872). The last decade of his life was productive, in both spheres of art, culminating in the 1881 edition of his poems, but he was plagued by ill health, and attempted suicide in 1872. He continued to paint beautiful Pre-Raphaelite women, such as his mistress Fanny Cornforth, and Alexa Wilding. His most impressive painting, *Dante's Dream*, was sold to the Walker Art Gallery, Liverpool in 1881. Just before his death at Birchington in April 1882 he revised an early comic poem, *Jan Van Hunks*.

Rossetti, W. M., *Dante Gabriel Rossetti As Designer and Writer* (1895).
Waugh, E., *Rossetti: His Life and Works* (1928).
Angeli, H. R., *Rossetti: His Friends and Enemies* (1949).
Doughty, O., *A Victorian Romantic: Dante Gabriel Rossetti* (1949).
Fleming, G. H., *Rossetti and the Pre- Raphaelite Brotherhood* (1967).
Fleming, G. H., *That Ne'er Shall Meet Again* (1971).
Dobbs, B. and J. Dobbs, *Dante Gabriel Rossetti: An Alien Victorian* (1977).

See: Cooper, R. M., *Lost on Both Sides: Rossetti, Critic and Poet* (1970).
Soenstroem, D., *Rossetti and the Fair Lady* (Middleton, Conn., 1971).
Vogel, J., *Dante Gabriel Rossetti's Versecraft* (Gainesville, 1971).
Howard, R., *The Dark Glass: Vision and Technique in the Poetry of Dante Gabriel Rossetti* (Athens, Ohio, 1972).
Rees, J., *The Poetry of Dante Gabriel Rossetti: Modes of Self-Expression* (Cambridge, 1981).
Riede, D. G., *Dante Gabriel Rossetti and the Limits of Victorian Vision* (Ithaca, NY, 1983).

SCOTT, William Bell (1811–90), born in Edinburgh. Educated at Edinburgh High School; studied art at the Trustees' Academy, Edinburgh. Married Letitia Margery Norquoy. Worked with his father as an engraver. Moved to London in 1837, and pursued a career as a painter. Became a friend of Rossetti and Swinburne, and developed a Pre-Raphaelite style. 1843–64 in the Government School of Design in Newcastle upon Tyne, Painted murals at Wallington Hall, Northumberland, for the Trevelyans. Conducted a liaison with Alice Boyd at Penkill. Scott wrote neo-medieval poetry in *Poems* (1854), and a number of successful ballads in *Poems* (1875). The last collection was *A Poet's Harvest Home* (1882; rev. 1893). His *Autobiographical Notes* (1892) are an informative source for the Pre-Raphaelite movement.

> Horne, H. P., *Scott: Poet, Painter and Critic* (1891).
> Trevelyan, R., *Pre-Raphaelite Circle* (1978).

SMITH, Alexander (1830–67), born in Kilmarnock. Father a fabric designer; mother introduced him to Gaelic songs and Ossianic legends. Brought up mainly in Glasgow. Apprenticed at twelve to his father's trade. Self-taught in his spare time, and saturated in Romantic Movement poetry. Close friend of John Nichol, Hugh Macdonald, George Gilfillan, and James Hedderwick, editor of the Glasgow paper *Evening Citizen* – which first published his poems. *Life Drama* (1853): hero, Walter, hopes passionately to realize his ambition through poetry. A long poem, with digressions within digressions, rich in Keatsian imagery. It had a sudden success and went into four editions before 1856. Edited *Glasgow Miscellany*. 1854 appointed secretary to Edinburgh University. Smith was a 'Spasmodic' poet, and the style was ridiculed in William Edmondstoune Aytoun's *Firmilian; or, The Student of Badajoz. A Spasmodic Tragedy* (1854). The self-indulgence, extravagance, and gaudy imagery of the style were mocked, and Bailey and Dobell were pilloried alongside Smith. Smith spent the rest of his life trying to escape from the epithet 'spasmodic'.

> Weinstein, M. A., *W. E. Aytoun and the Spasmodic Controversy* (1968).

SWINBURNE, Algernon Charles (1837–1909), born into an aristocratic family and brought up in Bonchurch, Isle of Wight. His father Admiral Charles Henry Swinburne, his mother daughter of third Earl of Ashburnham. Principal element in early upbringing a submissive and erotic relationship to the sea. He was also a wide reader. Entered Eton 1849, and developed flagellation mania. Took considerable interest in Elizabethan dramatists. Matriculated at Balliol College, Oxford, in 1856. A member of the free-thinking Old Mortality Society. In 1857 associated with the Pre-Raphaelites, when they were decorating the Oxford Union. Left the university without a degree. Published the plays *The Queen-Mother* and *Rosamond* in 1860. Moved in high literary circles, meeting Tennyson, Meredith, Browning, Milnes (who introduced him to De Sade), Ruskin, and Whistler. 1864 visited Italy and wrote criticisms of Old Masters that influenced Pater. His love, Mary Gordon, married Colonel R. W. Disney-Leith, and plunged him into despair. Epoch-making works of the 1860s were *Atalanta in Calydon* (1865) and *Poems and Ballads* (1866), the latter causing a storm of protest so great that the publisher Moxon withdrew it. He was not exclusively an aesthete, since much of his poetry urged the cause of Italian republicanism. He met and revered Mazzini. Political lyrics collected in *Songs before Sunrise* (1871) and *Songs of Two Nations* (1875). *Erechtheus* (1876) was better received than earlier work. It deals in Aeschylean fashion with the sacrifice of Chthonia for the salvation of Athens. *Poems and Ballads, Second Series* (1878) is a quieter and more serene collection than the 1866 volume. He published a study of Blake in 1868, and like the great Romantic maintained a consistently anti-theistic attitude in his writings. He spent the last thirty years of his life at the Pines, Putney, in the custody of Theodore Watts-Dunton. The poetic decline was characterized by poems in praise of babies and imperialism. He produced a string of verse dramas in the 1880s. *Heptalogia* (1880) is a brilliant series of parodies – including a self-parody. His lyric gift remains undiminished in the late collection *A Channel Passage and Other Poems* (1904). Buried at Bonchurch.

Gosse, E., *The Life of Algernon Charles Swinburne* (1917).
Watts-Dunton, C., *The Home Life of Swinburne* (1922).
Lafourcade, G., *La Jeunesse de Swinburne, 1837–1867* (Paris, 1928).
Fletcher, I., *Swinburne* (1973).
Henderson, P., *Swinburne: Portrait of a Poet* (1974).
Thomas, D., *Swinburne: The Poet in His World* (1979).

See: Eliot, T. S., *The Sacred Wood* (1920).
Hearn, L., *Pre-Raphaelite and Other Poets* (New York, 1922).
Nicolson, H., *Swinburne* (1926).
Welby, T. E., *A Study of Swinburne* (New York, 1926).
Chew, S. C., *Swinburne* (Boston, Mass., 1929).
Symons, A., *Studies in Strange Souls* (1929).
Welby, T. E., *The Victorian Romantics: 1850–1870* (1929).
Rutland, W. R., *Swinburne: A Nineteenth-Century Hellene* (Oxford, 1931).
Praz, M., *The Romantic Agony* (1933).
Hyder, C. K., *Swinburne's Literary Career and Fame* (Durham, NC, 1933).
Lucas, F. L., *Ten Victorian Poets* (Cambridge, 1948).
Grierson, H. J. C., *Swinburne* (1953).
Peters, R. L., *The Crowns of Apollo: Swinburne's Principles of Literature and Art* (Detroit, 1965).
McGann, J. J., *Swinburne: An Experiment in Criticism* (Chicago, 1971).
Raymond, M. B., *Swinburne's Poetics: Theory and Practice* (The Hague, 1971).
Riede, D. G., *Swinburne: A Study of Romantic Myth-Making* (Charlottesville, 1978).
McSweeney, K., *Tennyson and Swinburne as Romantic Naturalists* (Toronto, 1980).

TAYLOR, Sir Henry (1800–86) born at Bishop Middleham, Durham. 1814 entered as a midshipman in the Royal Navy. Had a wayward education like Browning's in his father's large library. A friend from 1823 onwards of Southey. Began literary career as a writer for periodicals. An opponent of the Utilitarians. Familiar with most of the important literary figures of the day. 1839 married Theodosia Spring-Rice. A civil servant in the Colonial Office 1824–72, and the author of a sceptical essay *The Statesman*

(1836). Wrote a number of verse dramas, including *Isaac Comnenus* (1827), *Edwin the Fair* (1842), and *The Virgin Widow* (1850). The best one is *Philip van Artevelde* (1834), set in fourteenth-century Flanders, at the time of the struggle between Ghent and Bruges. Its preface (repr. in *Victorian Poetry and Poetics*) is important as a statement of a Classical aesthetic, working in reaction against the immediately preceding Romanticism. Byron, in particular, came in for hostile criticism and adverse comments were made about Shelley. He wished to restore reason and 'sound understanding' to poetry.

TENNYSON, Alfred (1809–92) (created a baronet in 1883), born Somersby, Lincolnshire, fourth son of Rev. George Clayton Tennyson the younger and of Elizabeth Tennyson (née Fytche). His father disinherited in favour of younger brother, and a family feud with this branch (later taking the name Tennyson D'Eyncourt). A good deal of madness and melancholia in the household. 1815–20 educated at Louth Grammar School; left to be privately educated. Saturated from an early age in poetry and other literature. 1823–24 wrote *The Devil and the Lady*, a pastiche of Jacobean drama. 1827 Alfred and his brother Charles published *Poems by Two Brothers*. In the same year went up to Trinity College, Cambridge, where he joined the 'Apostles' club (the importance of which is discussed in Peter Allen's *The Cambridge Apostles: The Early Years*, Cambridge, 1973). Met Arthur Henry Hallam, the most important friend in his life, and soon after his sister Emily, with whom he fell in love. In 1829 won the Chancellor's Gold Medal with the prize poem 'Timbuctoo'. 1830 *Poems, Chiefly Lyrical*, and a trip to the Pyrenees with Hallam, to bring military instructions to insurrectionists. In 1831 his father died and he left Cambridge without taking a degree. Hallam's review of the poems in *The Englishman's Magazine* (August 1831) makes an important contribution to Victorian poetics. July 1832 toured the Rhineland with Hallam, and in December *Poems* published (1833 on title page). In September 1833 Hallam died in Vienna, and his loss had a lasting effect on Tennyson's poetry, culminating in *In Memoriam* (1850). In about 1836, after an unsuccessful love-affair with Rosa Baring, he became engaged to Emily Sellwood, but marriage was delayed until 1850. The decade after *Poems* is known as 'the ten years' silence', but he was working away at his poetry, producing *Poems* (1842) and *The Princess* (1847). On Wordsworth's death in 1850 Tennyson became the Poet Laureate. In 1853 the family moved to Farringford on the Isle of Wight, and only moved in 1868 (to Aldworth, Hampshire) when invasion of privacy made peace and quiet impossible. *Maud* (1855) is probably Tennyson's most powerful poem. In 1859 publication of *Idylls of the King* began (virtually complete by 1872). Like Browning he ventured into play-writing, with *Queen Mary* (1875), *Harold* (1876), *The Cup* (1881), and *Becket* (1884), but although the works were produced on the stage they are not now regarded as an important part of the *œuvre*. He finally accepted the offer of a barony in 1884. Tennyson is buried in Westminster Abbey. He had two sons, Hallam and Lionel.

Tennyson, H., *Alfred Lord Tennyson: A Memoir*, 2 vols (1897).
Nicolson, H., *Tennyson: Aspects of His Life, Character and Poetry* (1923; repr. 1962).
Tennyson, C., *Alfred Tennyson* (1949).
Richardson, J., *The Pre-Eminent Victorian: A Study in Tennyson* (1962).

Henderson, P., *Tennyson, Poet and Prophet* (1978).
Colley, A. C., *Tennyson and Madness* (Athens, Georgia, 1983).
Martin, R. B., *Tennyson: The Unquiet Heart* (Oxford, 1983).

See: Tennyson, C., *Six Tennyson Essays* (1954).
Buckley, J. H., *Tennyson: The Growth of a Poet* (1960).
Rader, R. W., *Tennyson's 'Maud': the Biographical Genesis* (1963).
Ricks, C., *Tennyson: A Biographical and Critical Study* (1972).
Kincaid, J., *Tennyson's Major Poems* (1975).
Shaw, W. D., *Tennyson's Style* (Ithaca, NY, 1976).
Turner, P., *Tennyson* (1976).
Culler, A. D., *The Poetry of Tennyson* (1977).
Pinion, F. B., *A Tennyson Companion* (1984).
Peltason, T., *Reading 'In Memoriam'* (Princeton, NJ, 1985).
Thomson, A. W., *The Poetry of Tennyson* (1986).

THOMPSON, Francis (1859–1907), born into a Catholic family. Went to
London to follow his father's profession as a doctor, but soon became a
down-and-out. The efforts of a prostitute and his first publishers, Wilfred
and Alice Meynell, rescued him from total oblivion. His three volumes of
poetry were *Poems* (1893), *Sister Songs* (1895), and *New Poems* (1897).
Much of the poetry is in the nineteenth-century Parnassian tradition, but
he also drew sustenance from seventeenth-century religious poetry,
especially Crashaw and Cowley. His work is one of the last important
flourishings of poetic diction as a medium entirely separate from everyday
speech.

Danchin, P., *Thompson: La Vie et l'Œuvre d'un Poète* (Paris, 1959).
Reid, J. C., *Thompson, Man and Poet* (1959).
Butter, P. H., *Thompson* (1961).
Thomson, P. van K., *Thompson: A Critical Biography* (New York, 1961).
Walsh, J. E., *Strange Harp, Strange Symphony: The Life of Thompson* (1968).

THOMSON (B.V.), James (1834–82), born Port Glasgow. Father a merchant
sailor, who was disabled by a paralytic stroke which led to mental
deficiency and dipsomania. The family came to London in 1842, but by
1853 both parents were dead. James became a schoolmaster in the army,
teaching in Chelsea and Ballincollig, Ireland, where he met a life long
associate, Charles Bradlaugh (one of the most distinguished atheists of the
time). He fell in love with Matilda Weller and the profoundest experience
of his whole life was her sudden death in 1853. He began publishing in
Tait's Edinburgh Magazine in 1858. The same year he adopted the
pseudonym 'Bysshe Vanolis', which combined one of Shelley's names with
an anagram of the mystic German poet Novalis. Subsequently the name
was shortened to its initials: B. V. Shelley was James's favourite poet; he
wrote an essay on him for the *National Review* (1860). 1862 court-
martialled for swimming in a pool where bathing was prohibited. Became
a clerk, and in 1872 the secretary of a mining company, which gave him
the opportunity to travel in Colorado. 1873 reporter for the *New York
World*; witnessed struggle between Republicans and Carlists in Spain. *The
City of Dreadful Night* (1874) brought immediate fame. Other poems
published in collections of 1880 and 1881 (*Vane's Story . . . and Other
Poems*). The last years of his life marked by extreme alchoholism.

Salt, H. S., *The Life of James Thomson ('B.V.')* (1889)

Dobell, B., *The Laureate of Pessimism* (1910)

Meeker, J. E., *The Life and Poetry of James Thomson (B.V.)* (New Haven, 1917).

Walker, I. B., *James Thomson (B.V.)* (Ithaca, NY, 1950).

Vachot, C., *James Thomson (1834–1882)* (Paris, 1964).

See: Byron, K. H., *The Pessimism of James Thomson (B.V.) in Relation to His Times* (1965).

Schaefer, W. D., *James Thomson (B.V.): Beyond 'The City'* (Berkeley and Los Angeles, 1965).

Index